Highly Recommended

New Edition

OSWAAL BOOKS®

LEARNING MADE SIMPLE

AF731502

NCERT TEXTBOOK SOLUTIONS

CLASS 12

PHYSICS

Strictly based on the Latest NCERT Textbook

Powered by oswaal.ai LEARNING MADE SMARTER

Smart guidance that helps you learn, practise and improve.

Get the #OswaalEdge

1	2	3	4	5
100% Updated with the Latest NCERT Textbook	**Comprehensive Coverage** with all NCERT concepts	**Visual Learning Tools** with Concept Videos	**Extensive Revision Tools** with Crisp Revision Notes, Mind Maps & Mnemonics	**Complete Question Coverage** with all NCERT textbook questions

OSWAAL BOOKS®
LEARNING MADE SIMPLE

This Edition: 2026

ISBN: 9789359581361

Disclaimer

This publication has been prepared by qualified subject matter experts with rigorous editorial review. Despite our best efforts, errors may exist. Readers are encouraged to report any by scanning the QR code on the Table of Contents page so corrections can reach all users.

This book is a study aid. Examination results depend on multiple factors including individual preparation and the specific examination conducted. No particular outcome is guaranteed.

Links in this book provide access to supplementary content. Accessibility depends on internet connectivity and device compatibility. Third-party content linked herein was verified at the time of printing; however, the Publisher does not guarantee that such content will remain accurate, available, or appropriate over time.

Views expressed by individual contributors are their own and do not represent the Publisher's position. The Publisher does not endorse personal opinions or political statements contained herein.

All maps, boundaries, and diagrams are artistic representations for educational reference only and are not geographically or politically authoritative.

For details on personal data processing, see our Privacy Policy at www.oswaalbooks.com/privacy. This publication is governed by the laws of India. Disputes shall be subject to the exclusive jurisdiction of courts in Agra, Uttar Pradesh.

Published by: Oswaal Books and Learning Private Limited, Oswaal House, 1/11, Sahitya Kunj, M.G. Road, Agra-282002 (U.P.), India

contact@oswaalbooks.com

+91-562-2857671

Printed at: Shyamji Printers, Agra

Contents

❑❑

Stay Informed: NCERT Updates & Recent Improvements

NCERT Updates

Scan to get the latest syllabus updates & changes

Recent Improvements

Scan to stay updated with important changes in the book!

Learning is fun when you're always up to date! Keep scanning!

PREFACE

"*Education is the passport to the future, for tomorrow belongs to those who prepare for it today.*" – Malcolm X

In the pursuit of academic excellence, the journey often begins with curiosity. As students embark on the path to success in the exams, the Oswaal NCERT Textbook Solutions Book for the academic year 2026-27 stands as an invaluable companion, illuminating the way forward.

Success in any exam goes beyond memorization; it involves developing a deep understanding of every concept. The NCERT textbooks provide the essential foundation. Introducing the Oswaal NCERT Textbook Solutions Book, a vital tool to unlock the full potential of every student.

Let's uncover what this book covers for you:

1) **Updated for 2026-27** – The books are 100% updated for the academic year 2026-27, adhering strictly to the latest NCERT guidelines.

2) **Comprehensive Coverage -** We cover all concepts and topics outlined in the most recent NCERT textbooks.

3) **Visual Learning Aids -** Explore theoretical concepts and concept videos that offer a brief description of the topic and help visualize complex concepts.

4) **Effective Revision Tools -** Benefit from crisp Revision Notes, Mind Maps, and Mnemonics designed to facilitate efficient and effective review.

5) **Complete Question Coverage -** All questions from the NCERT textbooks are covered in our solutions, providing a thorough grasp of the subject matter.

What sets this book apart is the expertise behind its creation. The solutions within are the result of the meticulous efforts of expert faculty, individuals with a profound understanding of the curriculum, and the dedication to maintaining the highest quality standards.

May this book be your guide, encouraging you to not just study but to explore and understand.

Wishing you a fulfilling and successful academic journey.

Team,

Oswaal Books

Order Form

ONE FOR ALL OLYMPIADS (Multicolour)

Classes 1 to 8

Mathematics, English, Reasoning, General Knowledge, Science & Cyber

ONE FOR ALL OLYMPIADS Workbooks

Classes 1 to 8

Mathematics, English, Science

ONE FOR ALL WORKBOOKS (Multicolour)

Classes 1 to 5

Mathematics, English, General Knowledge, EVS, Hindi

NCERT WORKBOOKS (B&W)

Classes 1 to 5

English, Hindi, Mathematics & EVS

NCERT & CBSE One For All Workbooks

Classes 6 to 8

Mathematics, English, Science, Social Science, Hindi & Sanskrit

CBSE Work Books

Classes 9 & 10

English Lang. & Literature, Science, Social Science & Mathematics

CBSE & NCERT Laboratory Manual

Classes 6 to 12

Mathematics, Science, Physics, Chemistry & Biology

CBSE QUESTION BANKS (CHAPTER-WISE & TOPIC-WISE SOLVED PAPERS)

Classes 9 & 10

Hindi-A, Hindi-B, English Lang. & Lit. (With NCERT Workbook), Science, Mathematics, Social Science, Computer Applications, Sanskrit & English Communicative (based on CBSE Textbooks), Information Technology (Class-10th only), Artificial intelligence (Class-10th only)

Classes 11 & 12

Hindi Core (For Class-12 Only), English Core, Mathematics, Chemistry, Applied Mathematics (For Class-12 Only), Biology, Physics, Accountancy, Economics, Business Studies, Geography, History, Political Science, Computer Science, Entrepreneurship (For Class-12 Only), Informatics Practices, Physical Education, Sociology (For Class 12th Only), Psychology (For Class 12th Only)

CBSE Textbook Plus

Classes 10 & 12

English Lang. & Lit., Mathematics, Science, Social Science, English Core, Biology, Physics, Chemistry

CBSE Xcellence 95+

Classes 10 & 12

Sanskrit (शेमुषी), Sanskrit Communicative (मणिका), Physics, Chemistry, English Core

NCERT EXEMPLAR PROBLEMS-SOLUTIONS (Hindi & English Medium)

Classes 9 to 12

Science, Mathematics, Physics, Chemistry, Biology, Mathematics, गणित, विज्ञान, भौतिक विज्ञान, रसायन विज्ञान, जीव विज्ञान

NCERT Textbook Solutions

Classes 6 to 8

Mathematics, English, Hindi, Science, Social Science & Sanskrit

Classes 9 to 12

Science, Mathematics, Physics, Chemistry, Biology

CBSE 10 PREVIOUS YEARS' SOLVED PAPERS

Class 10

Combined: English Lang. & Lit, Science, Social Science,Mathematics Stan.

Class 12

Science (PCM)-(Chemistry, Physics, Mathematics & English Core), **Science (PCB)**-(Chemistry, Physics, English Core & Biology) **Commerce**-(Economics, Accountancy, Business Studies, English Core), **Humanities**-(Geography, History, Political Science & English Core)

CBSE Previous Years' Solved Papers Stand alone Series

Class 10

Hindi-A, Hindi-B, Mathematics Basic, Sanskrit, Computer Applications

Class 12

Applied Mathematics, Mathematics

CBSE RMT FLASH CARDS

Class 10

Mathematics, English Lang. & Lit., Social Science & Science

CBSE ONE FOR ALL

Classes 6 to 8

English, Hindi, Mathematics, Science, Social Science & Sanskrit

Class 10

English Lang. & Lit., Social Science, Science, Hindi-A, Hindi-B, Mathematics (Stand.) & Mathematics Basic

Class 12

English Core, Physics, Chemistry, Mathematics, Biology, Accountancy, Business Studies & Economics

FINAL HUSTLE FOR CBSE

Class 10

Science, Mathematics Standard & Social Science

Class 12

Science (Physics, Chemistry, Mathematics, Biology & English Core), **Commerce** (Accountancy, Business Studies, Economics, Mathematics & English Core), **Humanities** (History, Geography, Political Science & English Core)

CBSE SAMPLE QUESTION PAPERS

Class 9

Science, Mathematics

Class 10

Hindi-A, Hindi-B, English Lang. & Lit., Computer Applications, English Communicative, Mathematics Standard, Mathematics Basic, Science, Social Science, Sanskrit, Samajik Vigyan, Information- Technology, Artificial intelligence, Sanskrit Communicative

Class 12

Hindi Core, Hindi Elective, English Core, Mathematics, Applied Mathematics, Physics, Chemistry, Biology, Accountancy, Economics, Business Studies, Geography, History, Political Science, Computer Science, Informatics Practices, Physical Education, Entrepreneurship, Psychology & Sociology

CBSE 20 Combined Sample Question Papers

Classes 9 to 12

Class- 9 & 10: **Combined Book**

Class- 11 & 12: Science, Commerce & Humanities

CBSE Competency Focused Questions Chapter-wise

Classes 10 & 12

Class 10 :- (Combined Book) Science, Social Science & Mathematics Standard

Class 12 :- Science PCM, Science PCB & Commerce

How To Talk To AI

Crafting the Perfect Prompt

oswaal.ai
LEARNING MADE SMARTER

Think of AI as your super-smart study buddy — **the better you ask, the better it answers.** A **prompt** is simply the question or instruction you give to AI. Master this skill, and you'll unlock a powerful tool for learning.

The Basic Prompt Structure

[Role] + [Task] + [Context] + [Format]

Element	What It Means	Example
Role	Tell it who to be	*"Act as a Subject "........" teacher."*
Task	What you want it to do	*"...explain the concept of..."*
Context	Give background details	*"For Class ...., Chapter ...."*
Format	How you want the answer	*"...using bullet points and a diagram."*

Weak Prompt vs. Strong Prompt

☒ **Weak Prompt**
Tell me about this topic "..........".

☑ **Strong Prompt**
"Act as a subject "........" teacher. Explain the topic "........" clearly for school students. Use simple language, include key points, and give one example."

Pro Tips for Better Prompts

Be Specific
Say exactly what you need, not vague requests

Set the Level
Mention your class & board

Ask Examples
Add "with real-life examples" to remember better

Request Format
Ask for tables, flowcharts, or mnemonics

Iterate
Ask follow-ups to simplify or expand

Other Useful AI Tools for Students

ChatGPT
Explains concepts, solves questions, makes notes & projects
chatgpt.com

Google Gemini
Great for diagrams, visuals & numerical explanations
gemini.google.com

Perplexity AI
Research tool with verified info & sources
perplexity.ai

Photomath
Solves Maths problems with step-by-step solutions
photomath.com

Notion AI
Creates notes, organizes syllabus & project structure
notion.so

Quizlet AI
Makes flashcards & quizzes from any chapter
quizlet.com

Canva AI
Makes posters, charts, covers & PPTs easily
canva.com

Otter.ai
Records lectures & converts to written notes
otter.ai

Remember: AI doesn't read minds — it reads prompts. The clearer you are, the more it helps!

Exclusive School Books Suppliers

	KARNATAKA
BANGALORE	Pride Book World, 9448685507, Tanwer Books and Garments, 9916049273, Jipsy, 9620325985
MYSORE	Ragavendra Book Agency, 9591911489
	TELANGANA
HYDERABAD	Shri Sharada store Books & Stationers, 9700768789, Sri Balaji Book Depot, 9676996199, Vishal Book Distributors, 9246333166, Pranavi Publishers, 919948853126, Shri Sharada store Books & Stationers, 9700768789
	TAMIL NADU
CHENNAI	M.K. Stores, 9840030099, Sivaa Book Centre, 9952933315, Kamal Book House, 9841077369
ERODE	Selvam Book Centre, 919843199697
MADURAI	Selvi Book Shoppe, 9345037977, Madurai Book Shop, 9751937519
COIMBATORE CUDDALORE	Indian Book Centre, 9443093053
	MAHARASHTRA
PUNE	Madhusheela Books & Stationers, 7875899892, Pravin Sales, 8888038889
NANDED	Vijay Book Centre, 9822994436
JALNA	Anil Paper Mart, 919422722522
CHHATRAPATI SAMBHAJINAGAR	AARTI BOOK CENTRE, 919422203836
NAGPUR	Sandeep Book Depot, 9371078789
VASAI	Dinvin Books Excellence PVT. LTD. , 9867561128
MUMBAI	New Student Agencies LLP, 8355965098, Ravechi Book Stationery, 9769002371
	ANDHRA PRADESH
VISAKHAPATNAM	VKML Books, 8125168946
NANDYAL	Sathyam Book Store & Fancy, 9052439300
NELLORE	S V S Book Centre, 9347100774
VIJAYAWADA	VKML Books, 9966639957
	HARYANA
ROHTAK	Babu Ram Pradeep Kumar, 9813214692
VIZIANAGARAM	Himamsu Book Distributor, 9493434777
	MADHYA PRADESH
INDORE	Mahesh Book Depot, 9893855543
SHAHDOL	Anjali Book Centre, 917067572992

	JHARKHAND
DEOGHAR	Navyug Sahitya Mandir, 919031917035
BOKARO STEEL CITY	Bokaro Student Friends Pvt. Ltd, 919234628152
	MEGHALAYA
SHILLONG	New Book Centre, 9774088719
	WEST BENGAL
KOLKATA	Oriental Pub. Dist. Pvt. Ltd., 919903879153, United Book House, 9831344622
	UTTAR PRADESH
PRAYAGRAJ	Saraswati book depot, 7706855403
KANPUR	Raj Book, 9235616506
MATHURA	Sapra Traders, 9410076716, Agrawal Book House, 7906527213
GHAZIABAD	Vani Enterprises, 919891276834
	DELHI
DELHI	Mittal Books, 919810133323, Prakash Brothers, 919811179840, R.D. Chawla & Sons, 9810045752, Ameen Global Services, 919716028892, Need Prakashan Pvt Ltd, 9968383261
	GUJARAT
VADODARA	Career Skills Education and Research Foundation, 8469149288
BHARUCH	J.D. Agency, 9099944480
	KERALA
ERNAKULAM	Novel House School Supplies, 8792342807
	ASSAM
GUWAHATI	Central Book Agency, 9954707165
SILCHER	New Book Stall, 919435712617
JORHAT	Bajrang stationery, 9706978968
	RAJASTHAN
ANUPGARH	City Pride Departmental Store, 919414095677
BARMER	Dev Indra Enterprises, 7073282106
	MANIPUR
IMPHAL	Global Agencies, 917641814494
	PUNJAB
TARN TARAN	Sital Di Hatti, 919988206890
KHAMMAM	Sri Nivasa Book Stall, 919948247838
	CHHATTISGARH
RAIPUR	Central Book House, 9406016308

Our Distributors

	ANDHRA PRADESH
VISAKHAPATHAM	Sri Rajeshwari Book Link, 9848036014,
VIJAYAWADA	Sree Vidya Book Depot, 9491830839
	ANDAMAN & NICOBAR ISLAND
PORTBLAIR	Krishna Book Centre, 9474205570
	ARUNACHAL PRADESH
NAHARLAGUN	New Pothi Ghar, 8731832947
	ASSAM
SILCHAR	Book Emporium, 9675972993, 6000763186, New Book Stall, 9435712617
GUWAHATI	Kayaan Enterprises, (0361) 2630443,
	BIHAR
PATNA	Nova Publisher & Distributors, (0612) 2666404, Gyan Ganga Limited, 9304826651, Rishu Pustak Bhandar, 8294576789, Sri Durga Pustak Mandir, 9334477386, Vikas Book Depot, 919504780402, Bokaro Student Friends Pvt. Ltd, 7277931285
BIHAR SHARIF	Good Books , 8210685462
MUZAFFARPUR	Pustak Bhandar, 7870834225
	CHATTISGARH
AMBIKAPUR	M.P Department Stores, 9425254264
BOKARO	Bokaro Student Friends Pvt. Ltd, Bokaro, 7277931285
DURG	Bhagwati Bhawani Book Depot, 0788-2327620, 9827473100
RAIPUR	Gupta Pustak Mandir, 7974220323,
BILASPUR	Pustak Bhawan, 9300667909
	DELHI
DELHI	Mittal Books, (011) 23288887, 9899037390, A One Books, New Delhi, 8800497047, Batheja Super Store, 9871833924, 9811182352, Zombozone, 9871274082, LDS Marketing, 9811182352/9999353491, R.D. Chawla & Sons, 9810045752, Janta Book Depot, 9313046321 Bokaro Student Friends Pvt. Ltd, 7004074900

	GUJARAT
AHMEDABAD	Patel Book Agencies, 9898184248, 9824386112, 9825900335, Shalibhadra Stationers, 9904477855
VAPI	Goutam Book Sellers, 9081790813
VADODARA	Shree ji Book Depot, 9824649375, Nilesh Book Centre, 9924458748 Umakant Book Sellers & Stationer, 6359396370
AHMEDNAGAR	Hira Stationers, 9970150300
	HARYANA
ROHTAK	Swami Kitab Ghar, 9355611088, Babu Ram Pradeep Kumar, 9813214692
GURGAON	Book Care Centre Venture, 9654564783
REWARI	Repro Books Ltd, 8657315914, Annu book depot, 9053246268
	JHARKHAND
BOKARO	Bokaro Student Friends Pvt. Ltd. (0654) 2233094, 7360021503, Bharati Bhawan Agencies, 06542-265302, 9431740797
HAZARIBAGH	Khandelwal Book Depot, 9708607489
DEOGHAR	Navyug Sahitya Mandir, 9031917035
RANCHI	Pustak Mandir, 9431115138, Agarwal Book Depot, 9334869210, Jayshree Book House, 8434430311 Bokaro Student Friends Pvt. Ltd, 7360021508
DHANBAD	Bokaro Student Friends Pvt. Ltd, 6202834756
	KARNATAKA
HUBLI	Renuka Book Distributor, (0836) 2244124, Vidyamandir Book Distributors, 9980773976
BANGLORE	Krishna book house, 9739847334, Sapna Book House Pvt. Ltd., 9980513242, Sree Sai Ram Book Traders, 9738881088
	MADHYA PRADESH
INDORE	Pustak Bhawan, 8982150100, Bhaiya Store, 9425318103 S.P. & Publication, 7000025933
GWALIOR	Agarwal Book Depot, 9425116210
JABALPUR	Vinay Pustak Sadan, 8962362667, Anand Books and Stationers, 9425323508 Akash Book Distributor, 8989111444, Bharat Book House, 9826541542
KATNI	Shri Mahavir Agency, 9425363412

24/01/26

Our Distributors

	MAHARASHTRA
AMRAVATI	Delta Pen House, 9890350073
PUNE	Vikas Book House, 9921331187, Pravin Sales, 9890683475, New Saraswati Granth Bhandar, 9422323859 Sai Book Collection, 9623224343 Yash Agencies, 9850956542
MUMBAI	New Student Agencies, 7045065799, Shivam Books & Stationery, 8619805332
KOLHAPUR	Jai Book Co. 9404671543
NAGPUR	Laxmi Pustakalay and Stationers, (0712) 2727354, Vijay Book Depot, 9860122094 Renuka Book Distributor, 9765406133, Novelty Book Depot, 9657690220, Shree Mahalaxmi Pustakalaya, 7507099360
DHULE	Navjeevan Book Stall, 7020525561
YAVATMAL	Shri Ganesh Pustkalaya, 9423131275
NASHIK	Vishal Book Centre, Nashik - 8208249434
VASAI	Prime Book Centre, Vasai, 9890293662
	ODISHA
CUTTACK	A. K. Mishra Agencies, 9437025991, 9437081319
BHUBANESHWAR	M/s Pragnya, 8847888616, 9437943777, Padmalaya, 9437026922,
KEONJHAR	Students Corner, 7008435418
KORAPUT	Ambica Book Centre, 7008585008
	PUNJAB
AMBALA	Bharat Book Depot, 7988455354
PATIALA	Goel Sons, 9463619978, Adarsh Enterprises, 9814347613
JALANDHAR	Cheap Book Store, 9872223458, 9878258592, City Book Shop, 9417440753, Subhash Book Depot, 9876453625, Gaurav Book world, 9478821183
LUDHIANA	Amit Book Depot, 9815807871, Bhatia Book Centre, 9815277131, Gupta Brothers, 9888200206
CHANDIGARH	Mohindra Book Depot, 9814920226
BATHINDA	Goyal Sons , 9464478362, Bhagwati Book Depot, 9463120564
	RAJASTHAN
AJMER	Laxmi General Store, Ajmer, 0145- 2428942 9460652197
KOTA	Raj Traders, 9309232829
BHILWARA	Nakoda Book Depot, (01482) 243653, 9214983594,
JAIPUR	Saraswati Book House, (0141) 2610823, 9829811155, Goyal Book Distt., 9460983939, 9414782130
JODHPUR	Kitab Mahal, 9460957875
	TRIPURA
AGARTALA	Books Corner, 8794894165, 8984657146
	TAMIL NADU
COIMBATORE	Majestic Book House, 9791966665
CHENNAI	M.R. Book Store (044) 25364596, Kalaimagal Store, (044) 5544072, 9940619404, Vijaya Stores, 9381037417, Bookmark It-Books & Stat. Store, 7305151653, M.K. Stores, 9840030099, Tiger Books Pvt. Ltd., 9710447000,

MADURAI	Selvi Book Shoppe, 9843057435
	KERALA
ERNAKULAM	Academic Book House, (0484) 2376613, H & C Store, 9864196344
KOTTAYAM	Asad Book Centre, (0481) 2566992
CALICUT	Aman Book Stall, (0495) 2721282,
KOZHIKODE	T.B.S. Publishers Distributors, 7559822223
	TELANGANA
HYDERABAD	Sri Balaji Book Depot, (040) 27613300, 9866355473 Vishal Book Distributors, 9246333166
	UTTARAKHAND
DEHRADUN	Inder Book Agencies, 9634045280 Brothers Pustak Bhandar, 9897833882
	UTTAR PRADESH
AGRA	Sparsh Book Agency, 9412257817, Sanjay Publication, 8126699922 Arti book centre, 8630128856, Om Pustak Mandir, (0562) 2464014, 9319117771 Panchsheel Books, 9412257962, 9412257961 Manav Book World, 9760316933
MATHURA	Sapra Traders, 9410076716
PRAYAGRAJ	Mehrotra Book Agency, (0532) 2266865, 9415636890
AZAMGARH	Sasta Sahitya Bhandar, 9450029674
ALIGARH	K.B.C.L. Agarwal, 9897124960,
NAJIBABAD	Gupta News Agency, 8868932500
KANPUR	Radha News Agency, 8957247427, Raj Book Dist., 9235616506, H K Book Distributors, 9506033137/9935146730
GORAKHPUR	Vidyarthi Sahitya Bhandar, 6394026706
LUCKNOW	Om Book Depot, 7705871398, Azad Book Depot Pvt. Ltd., 7317000250, Ashirwad Book Depot, 9235501197, Book.com, 7458922755, Universal Books, 9450302161, Sheetla Book Agency, 9235832418, Vidyarthi Kendra Publisher & Distributor Pvt Ltd, 9554967415, Tripathi Book House, 9415425943, Navyug Book Agencies, 8073564410, Pustak Vatika, 7905317119
MEERUT	Ideal Book Depot, (0121) 4059252, 9837066307
NOIDA	Goyal Books Overseas Pvt.Ltd., 1204655555, 9873387003
PRAYAGRAJ	Kanhaiya Pustak Bhawan, 9415317109
RENUKOOT	Om Stationers, 7007326732
VARANASI	Bokaro Student Friends Pvt. Ltd , 9798050654
	WEST BENGAL
KOLKATA	Oriental Publishers & Distributor (033) 40628367, Katha 'O' Kahini, (033) 22196313, 22419071, Saha Book House, (033), 22193671, 9333416484, United Book House, 9831344622, Bijay Pustak Bhandar, 8961260603,
NORTH DINAJPUR	Sarkar Book Suppliers, 9830949359
COOCH BEHAR	S.B. Book Distributor, Cooch Behar, 9002670771
KHARAGPUR	Subhani Book Store, 9046891334
SINGRAULI	Ambedkar Book Depot, 9826115292
KANPUR	Lamba Book Stall, 9839024277
KARNAL	Chopra Book Store, 8950322681

24/01/26

ELECTRIC CHARGES AND FIELDS

CHAPTER 1

The charge is something possessed by material objects that makes it possible to exert electrical force and to respond electrical forces.

When a substance loses electrons it becomes positively charged. When a substance gains electrons, it becomes negatively charged.

When a glass rod is rubbed with silk, glass loses electrons and silk gains electrons. So, glass becomes positively charged and silk becomes negatively charged. But the total charge remains constant.

Classification of Charge

lassification of Charge based on the nature of Charges

Positive charge (vitreous)

Negative charge (Resinous)

Positive charge is constituted by positively charged particles called protons.

- Charge on proton: 1.6022×10^{-19} C
- Mass of proton: 1.0072766 a.m.u. or 1.6726×10^{-27} kg

Scan to know more about this topic

What is electric charge

Negative charge is constituted by negatively charged particles called electrons.

Charge on electron: 1.6022×10^{-19} C

Mass of electron: 9.1×10^{-31} kg

Opposite charges attract and similar charges repel each other.

lassification of charge based on their motion:

- **Static charge:** Static charge means fixed or stationary charge. This is due to imbalance of electric charge on the surface of a material.
- **Dynamic charge:** Dynamic charge means it can flow in a circuit and constitutes electric current.
- **Polarity of charge:** There are two kinds of polarity of electric charges:
  – Positive charge
  – Negative charge
- **Neutral system:** It is a system with no net charge as number of opposite charges cancel each other and as a result it is said to be neutral or non-conducting or an insulator.
- **Electrified system:** It is a system which has a net charge as number of opposite charges are not balanced and they do not cancel each other's magnitude and as a result it is said to be electrified or conducting or a conductor.

➢ **Depending on the flow of charges or flow of electricity:**

- **Conductor:** These are the substances in which electrons present in the outermost shell of atoms can easily come out and flow. These electrons are called free electrons.
  Example: Metals, human body, saline water etc.
- **Insulator:** These are the substances in which electrons from atoms cannot come out so easily and hence not available for free flow.
  Example: Wood, rubber etc.

➢ **Charging by Induction:** It is the transfer of charge from one body to another when they are just kept close to each other **without there being an actual contact.**

The charge that develops on uncharged body is opposite to the charge present on the charged body.

Process of Charging by Induction:

Diagram (i)

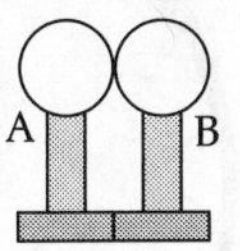

Two metal spheres are mounted on insulating stands.

Diagram (ii)

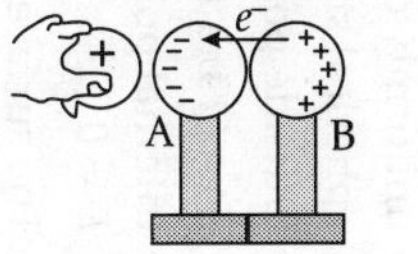

The presence of a +ve charge induces e^- to move from Sphere B to A. Both A and B get charged.

Diagram (iii)

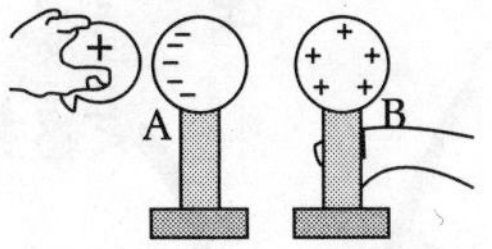

Sphere B is separated from sphere A using the insulating stand. The two spheres have opposite charges.

Diagram (iv)

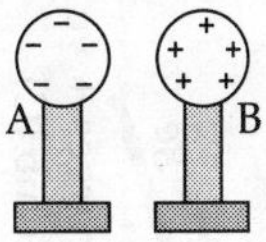

The charge get distributed uniformly over the surface of the spheres.

Scan to know more about this topic

Charging by Induction

Basic Properties of Electric Charge

- **Additivity of charge:** Charges are additive in nature. If a system contains n charges, q_1, q_2, q_3, ... q_n, then the total charge of the system is $q_1 + q_2 + q_2 + q_3 + ... q_n$.
- **Conservation of charge:** Total charge in an isolated system remains constant with time. Isolated system is one whose boundary cannot be crossed by any charge.
- **Quantisation of charge:** Charging takes place by exchange of electrons. Minimum charge on any body will be equal to the electronic charge $\pm e$ *i.e.*, $\pm 1.6 \times 10^{-19}$ C.

$\therefore$ Charge on any body will be integral multiple of electronic charge i.e.,

$$Q = \pm ne$$

this is called quantisation of charge.

Electric Charges and Fields

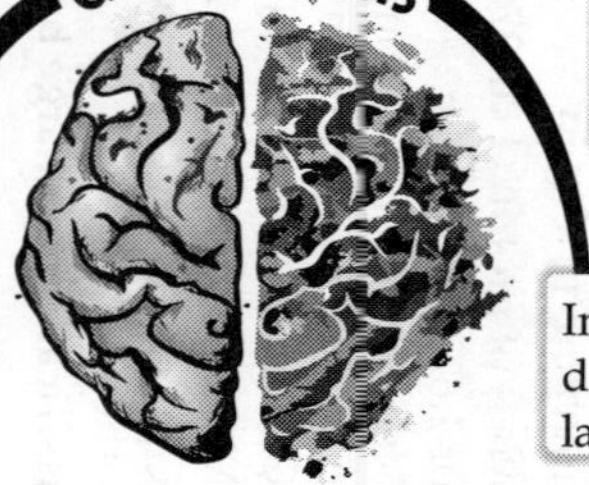

Electric charges

- Two kinds of charges + ve and – ve
- S.I. unit is Coulomb (C)
  1 C = charge flowing through a wire in 1s if current in it is 1A
- $e = 1.602 \times 10^{-19}$C.

Quantization of charge

All charges must be a multiple of charge (e)

$Q = ne$

Where n is an integer

Conservation of charge

It is not possible to create or destroy net charge of an isolated system.

Electric Field

$\vec{E} = \frac{\vec{F}}{q} \quad = k' \frac{Q}{r^2}$ (N/C)

∵ unit = N/C

- Due to discrete distribution of charges
  $\vec{E} = \sum_{i}^{n} \vec{E}_i$
- Due to continuous distribution of charge
  $\vec{E} = k' \int \frac{dQ}{r^3} \vec{r}$
  $|\vec{E}| = k' \int \frac{dQ}{r^2}$

Electric field lines

- Always normal to conducting surface
- Lines originating from +ve charge
- Terminating at –ve charge
- Never intersect each other
- Do not form closed loop
- Are imaginary lines.

Electric field due to point charge

Coulomb's Law

- Force between two charged particles

$\vec{F} = \frac{k\, q_1\, q_2 \vec{r}}{r^3} = \frac{k q_1\, q_2 \hat{r}}{r^2}$, force is attractive when q_1 and q_2 are of opposite sign, otherwise repulsive

$|\vec{F}| = \frac{k\, q_1\, q_2}{r^2}$

$k = \frac{1}{4\pi\varepsilon_0} \approx 9 \times 10^9 \text{Nm}^2\text{C}^{-2}$

- Force between multiple charges

$\vec{F}_1 = \vec{F}_{12} + \vec{F}_{13} + \vec{F}_{14} + \vec{F}_{15} + \ldots\ldots = \frac{q_1}{4\pi\varepsilon_0} \sum_{i=2}^{n} \frac{q_i}{r_{1i}^2} \hat{r}_{1i}$

where $\hat{r}$ is the unit vector along charge particle under consideration

$\hat{r}_{1i}$ = distance between Ist and i^{th} particle

"The electric force with which two charges attract or repel one another are not affected by the presence of other charges". It is known as Superposition Principle.

In 1985, Charles Augustin de Coulomb gave Coulomb's law

Electric Dipole moment, $\vec{p} = q\vec{d}$

- Electric field due to dipole at axial position,
  $\vec{E} = \frac{1}{4\pi\varepsilon_0}\left(\frac{2p}{r^3}\right)\hat{r}$
- Electric field due to dipole at an equatorial position,
  $|E| = \frac{1}{4\pi\varepsilon_0}\left(\frac{p}{r^3}\right)$
- Torque on an electric dipole placed in an electric field $(\vec{E})$
  $\vec{\tau} = \vec{p} \times \vec{E} = p\,E \sin\theta$

Gauss' Theorem

$\oint \vec{E}.\vec{ds} = q_{in}/\varepsilon_0 = \phi$

where, q_{in} = net charge enclosed

ϕ = flux through a closed surface

Applications of Gauss' Law

- Electric Field due to linear charge distribution
  $E = \lambda/2\pi\varepsilon_0 r$,
  λ = linear charge density
- Electric Field due to a plane sheet of charge
  $E = \sigma/2\varepsilon_0$,
  σ = charge per unit area
- Electric Field due to a charged conducting plate
  $E = \sigma/\varepsilon_0$,
  σ = charge per unit area
- Electric Field inside a conductor = 0

Electric field due to uniformly charged spherical shell at :

- Outside point,
  $E = Q/4\pi\varepsilon_0 r^2$
- Internal point,
  $E = 0$
- The surface,
  $E = Q/4\pi\varepsilon_0 R^2$

Electric flux

$\Delta\phi = \vec{E}.\Delta\vec{S}$, $\Delta\vec{S}$ = area vector

$\vec{E}$ = electric field

$\phi = \int \vec{E}.\vec{ds}$

Trace the Mind Map

- First Level
- Second Level
- Third Level

Coulomb's Law

Coulomb's law in scalar form: According to Coulomb's law, the force of interaction between any two-point charges is directly proportional to the product of the charges and inversely proportional to the square of the distance between them.

i.e.,
$$F \propto \frac{q_1 q_2}{r^2}$$

or
$$F = k\frac{q_1 q_2}{r^2}$$

Here k = constant of proportionality.

$k = 1$

(In cgs when it occurs in free space)

The value of k in S.I. is 9×10^9 Nm^{2}C^{-2}

It is derived from the defined expression where

$$k = \frac{1}{4\pi\varepsilon_0} = 9 \times 10^9 \text{ Nm}^2\text{C}^{-2}$$

In this ε_0 is permittivity of free space which is a constant

$$\varepsilon_0 = 8.85 \times 10^{-12} \text{ Nm}^{-2}\text{C}$$

When the charges are in a medium, then

$$F = \frac{q_1 q_2}{4\pi\varepsilon_0\varepsilon_r r^2}$$

where, ε_r is the relative permittivity of the medium.

Coulomb's law in vector form: The force between charges is a vector quantity and in vector form it is

$$\vec{F} = \frac{kq_1q_2\hat{r}}{r^2}$$

where, $\hat{r}$ is a unit vector defined as

$$\hat{r}_{12} = \frac{\vec{r}_{12}}{|\vec{r}_{12}|}$$

$$\hat{r}_{21} = \frac{\vec{r}_{21}}{|\vec{r}_{21}|}$$

Scan to know more about this topic

Coulomb's Law

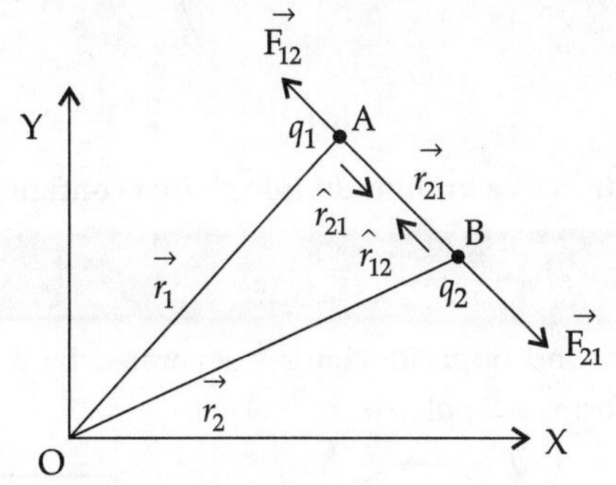

Force on 1st charge due to 2nd is

$$\vec{F}_{12} = \frac{kq_1q_2}{r^2}\hat{r}_{21}$$

Similarly, Force on 2nd charge due to 1st is

$$\vec{F}_{21} = \frac{kq_1q_2}{r^2}\hat{r}_{12}$$

Hence, it is mutual force in which Newton's 3rd law is valid.

As
$$\hat{r}_{12} = -\hat{r}_{21}$$

$$\therefore \quad \vec{F}_{12} = -\vec{F}_{21}$$

Therefore, Coulomb's law in vector form can also be written as:

$$\vec{F} = \frac{kq_1q_2 \times \vec{r}}{r^3} \quad \left(\because \hat{r} = \frac{\vec{r}}{r}\right)$$

- **Dielectric constant or relative electrical permittivity:** When the charges are situated in a medium other than the free space (air or vacuum), the force between them is given by

$$F_m = \frac{1}{4\pi\varepsilon_0} \times \frac{q_1q_2}{r^2}$$

where, ε is called the absolute electrical permittivity of the intervening medium.

The force between the same two charges held at same distance apart in vacuum is

$$F_0 = \frac{1}{4\pi\varepsilon_0} \times \frac{q_1q_2}{r^2}$$

dividing F_0 by F_m we get,

$$\frac{F_0}{F_m} = \frac{\varepsilon}{\varepsilon_0} = \varepsilon_r \text{ or } k$$

where, ε_r is called the electrical permittivity of the medium. It is also called **Dielectric constant** of the medium and is denoted by k.

Dielectric constant (k) of a medium is the ratio of absolute electrical permittivity of the medium to the absolute electrical permittivity of free space.

Electric Field

Every charge has an electric field around it over which, it exerts force on other charges. The region around it is called its electric field.

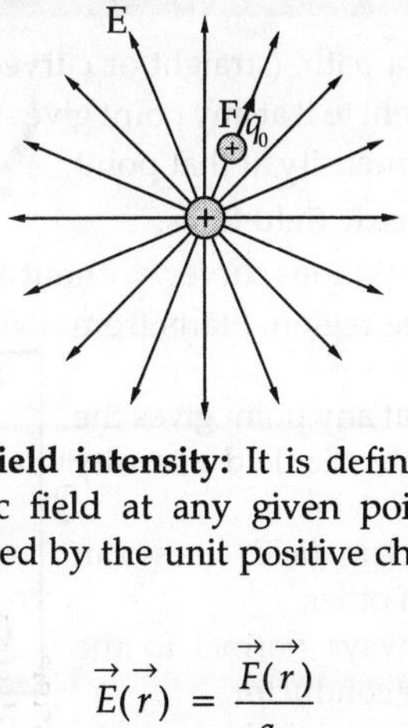

Scan to know more about this topic

Electric field

- **Electric field intensity:** It is defined as the strength of electric field at any given point. It is the force experienced by the unit positive charge placed at that point.

i.e.,
$$\vec{E}(\vec{r}) = \frac{\vec{F}(\vec{r})}{q_0}$$

where, $\vec{F}$ is the force acting on a small test charge $+q_0$ at any point $\vec{r}$, and $\vec{E}$ is the electric field intensity at this point.

- The SI unit of electric field intensity is Newton per Coulomb (N/C).

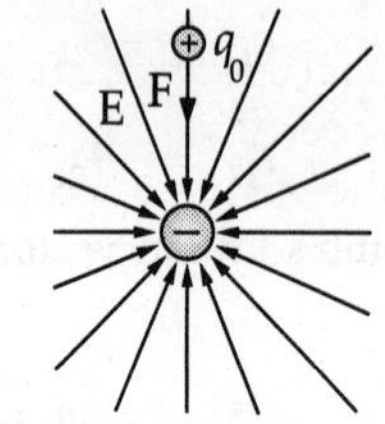

- **Electric field intensity due to a point charge Q** at any point O at a distance r is given as

$$\vec{E} = \frac{1}{4\pi\varepsilon_0}\frac{Q}{r_0^2}\hat{r}_0$$

The magnitude of electric field intensity in given as

$$E = \frac{1}{4\pi\varepsilon_0}\frac{Q}{r^2}$$

- **Electric field Intensity due to a system of charges** is given as the sum of the electric field intensities due to the individual charges at the same point.

$$\vec{E} = \vec{E}_1 + \vec{E}_2 + \vec{E}_3 + ... + \vec{E}_n$$

$$\vec{E} = \frac{1}{4\pi\varepsilon_0}\sum_{i=1}^{i=n}\frac{Q}{r_i^2}\hat{r}_l$$

Here, $\vec{r}_i$ is the distance of the point from the ith charge Q_i and $\hat{r}_i$ is unit vector directed from Q_i to the point.

In vector form:

$$\vec{E} = \frac{\vec{F}}{q_0}$$

$$= \frac{1}{4\pi\varepsilon_0}\sum_{i=1}^{i=n}\frac{Q_i}{|\vec{r}_0 - \vec{r}_1|^3}(\vec{r}_0 - \vec{r}_1)$$

Electric Field Lines

Electric field line is a path, (straight or curved) in electric field, such that tangent to it at any point gives the direction of the electric field intensity at that point.

➤ **Properties of electric field lines:**

(1) These are continuous curves, without any breakage in charge free region. Starts from +ve and end at –ve.

(2) Tangent to it at any point gives the direction of electric field intensity at that point.

(3) No two electric field lines can intersect each other.

(4) These are always normal to the surface of the conductor.

(5) Do not form any closed loops.

(6) Contract longitudinally on account of attraction between unlike charges.

(7) These exert a lateral pressure on account of repulsion between like charges.

Scan to know more about this topic

Electric field lines

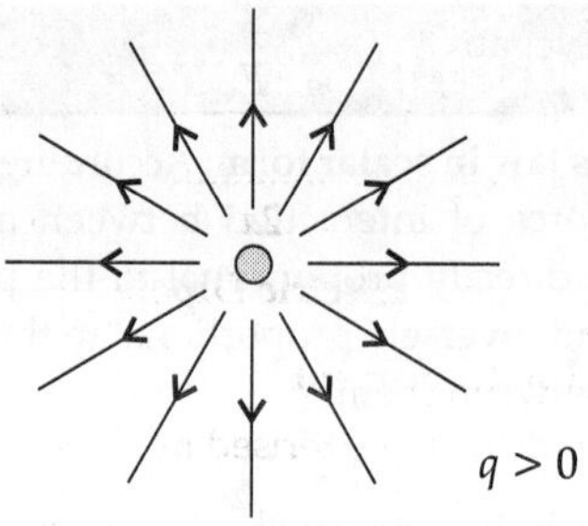

(a)

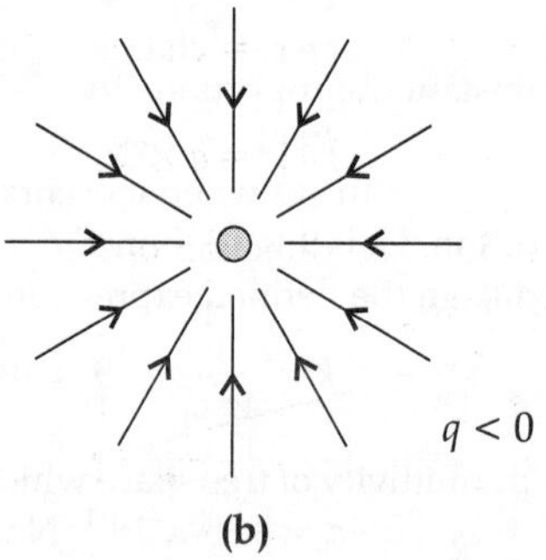

(b)

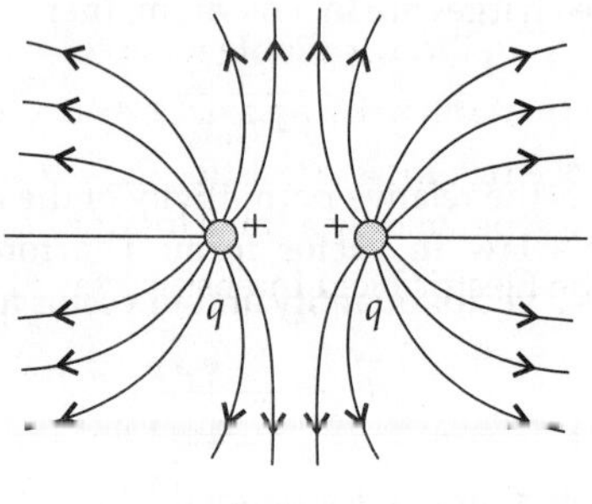

(c)

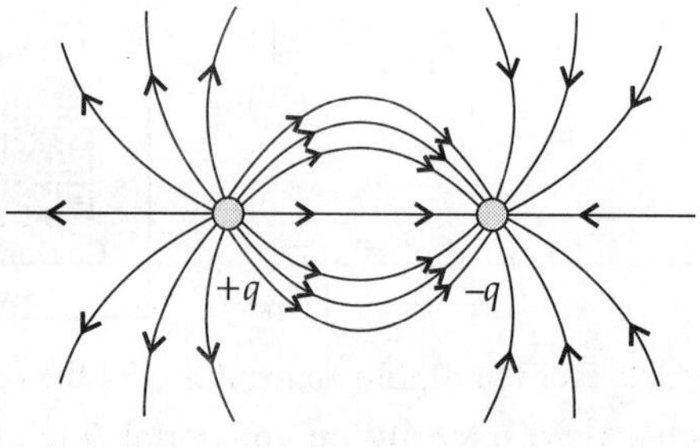

(d)

Field lines due to some simple charge configuration

Electric Dipole

Two equal and opposite charges separated by a certai distance forms a dipole.

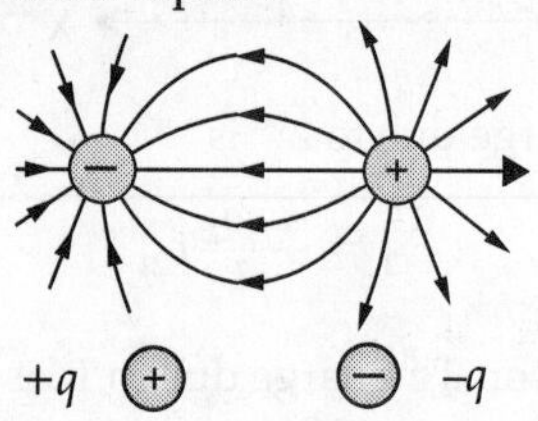

Scan to know more about this topic

Electric Dipol

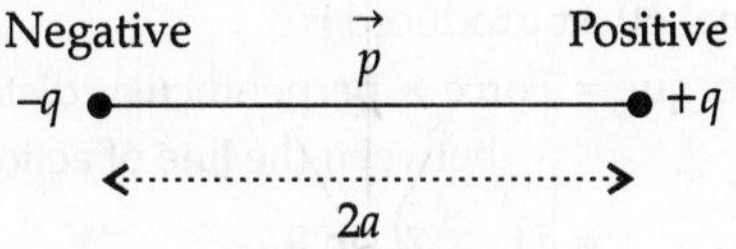

Electric Dipole

- **Electric dipole moment**

  Every dipole is characterised by electric dipole moment $(\vec{p})$ which is a measure of the strength of electric dipole.

$$|\vec{p}| = \text{charge} \times \text{length}$$

$$|\vec{p}| = q \times 2a$$

By convention, the direction of *p* is from negative to positive charge.

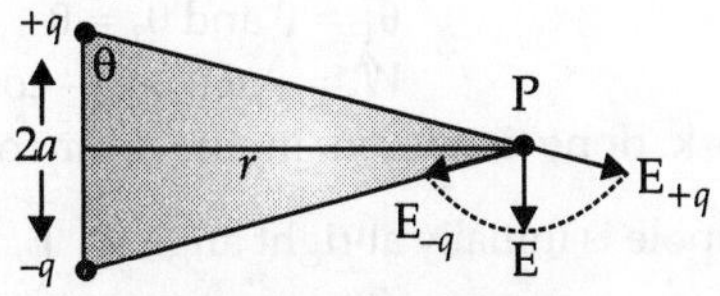

Electric dipole moment

- **Electric field intensity on axial line of electric dipole**

  For an electric dipole consisting of two point charges $-q$ and $+q$ separated by a small distance $2a$.

  Then, the Electric Field Intensity is given as

$$\vec{E} = \frac{|\vec{p}|}{4\pi\varepsilon_0} \cdot \frac{2r}{(r^2 - a^2)^2}$$

For shorter dipole, $2a \ll r$,

$$\vec{E} = \frac{|\vec{p}|\,2r}{4\pi\varepsilon_0\, r^4} = \frac{2|\vec{p}|}{4\pi\varepsilon_0 r^3}$$

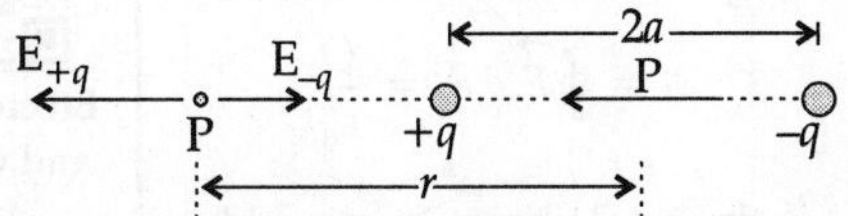

Electric Field of dipole on axial line of the dipole

- **Electric field intensity on equatorial line of electric dipole**

  For an electric dipole consisting of two point charges $-q$ and $+q$ separated by a small distance $2a$ with centre O and dipole moment $p = q(2a)$,

  The electric field intensity is given as

$$|\vec{E}| = \frac{|\vec{p}|}{4\pi\varepsilon_0(r^2 + a^2)^{3/2}}$$

In vector form, $$\vec{E} = \frac{-\vec{p}}{4\pi\varepsilon_0(r^2 + a^2)^{3/2}}$$

For shorter dipole, $2a \ll r$,

$$|\vec{E}| = \frac{|\vec{p}|}{4\pi\varepsilon_0 r^3}$$

Hence, $$|\vec{E}| \propto \frac{1}{r^3}$$

Thus, we find that electric field intensity due to an electric dipole varies inversely as cube of the distance of the point, whereas field intensity due to a single charge varies inversely as the square of the distance of the point from the charge, *p* is the dipole moment vector of magnitude $p = q \times 2a$ and directed from $-q$ to $+q$.

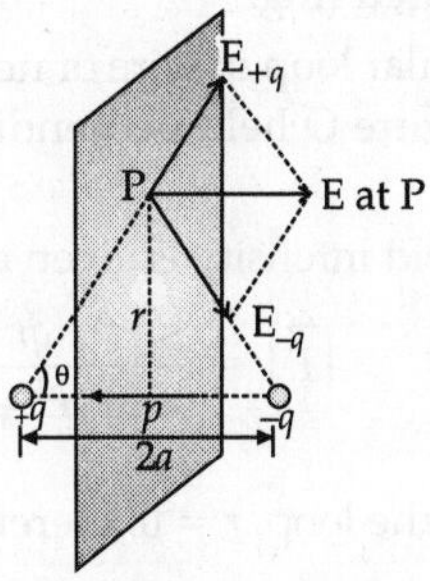

Electric field of dipole on a point on the equatorial plane of the dipole

➢ **Electric field due to continuous charge distribution:** The region in which charges are closely spaced is said to have continuous distribution of charge.

(1) Linear charge distribution: If charge is uniformly distributed over a wire, with λ = linear charge density = charge per unit length, then electric field at a distance *r* due to this wire is given as

$$\vec{E} = \int d\vec{E} = \int \frac{k\lambda dl}{r^2}\hat{r}$$

where, *dl* is the small length element.

(2) Surface charge distribution: If charge is uniformly distributed over a plate with σ = surface charge density = charge per unit area, Then total electric field at a distance *r* is given by:

$$\vec{E} = \iint \frac{k\sigma dS}{r^2}\hat{r}$$

(3) Volume charge distribution: If charge is uniformly distributed over a cubical surface with ρ = volume charge density = charge per unit volume, then total electric field at a distance *r* is given by:

$$\vec{E} = \iiint d\vec{E} = \iiint \frac{k\rho dv}{r^2}\hat{r}$$

Electric Flux (ϕ)

It represents the amount of electric field lines coming out or passing through any area.

Thus, electric flux Δϕ through an area element ΔS is defined by

$$\Delta\phi = \vec{E}.\Delta\vec{S} = E\,\Delta S \cos\theta$$

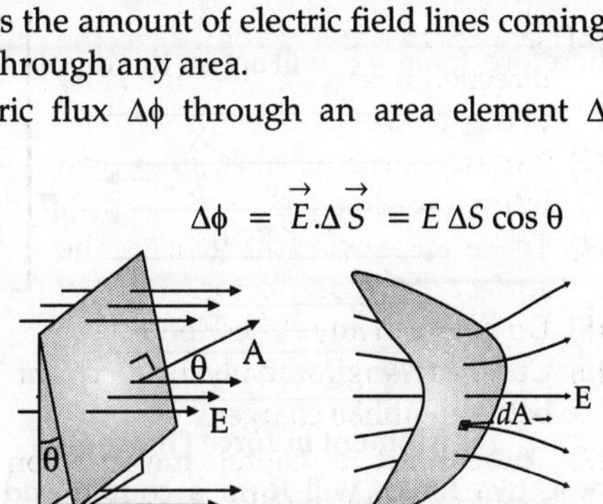

- Flux through an area depends not only on magnitude of electric field and area but also on the orientation of the area i.e., θ
- Unit of electric flux (ϕ) is Nm^2/C.
- Hence, total electric flux can be obtained by integrating.

$$\phi = \oint \vec{E}.d\vec{S}$$

➢ **Electric field intensity at any point on the axis of a uniformly charged ring:**

- Consider a circular loop of wire of negligible thickness, radius a and centre O held perpendicular to the plane of paper.

  Then electric field intensity is given as

$$|\vec{E}| = \frac{qr}{4\pi\varepsilon_0(r^2+a^2)^{3/2}}$$

at the centre of the loop, $r = 0$, therefore, $\vec{E} = 0$.

when $r >> a$, then, $\vec{E} = \dfrac{q}{4\pi\varepsilon_0 r^2}$

Hence, the circular loop of charge acts as point charge when r is at very large distance from the loop, as compared to the radius of the loop.

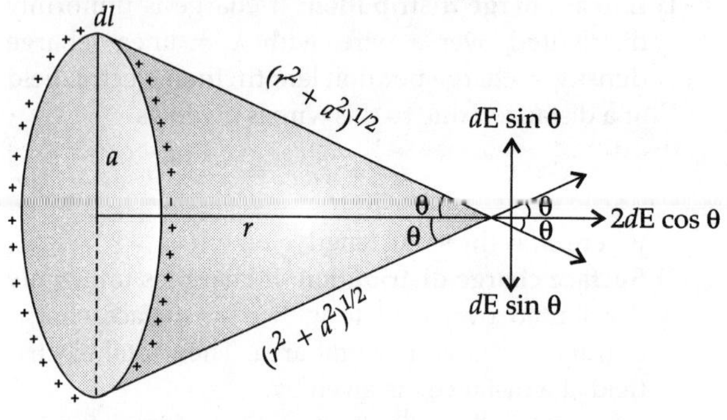

Electric field due to a uniformly charged ring

➢ **Torque acting on an electric dipole placed in an external electric field:**

An electric dipole of length $2l$ is placed at an angle θ with external electric field $|\vec{E}|$.

we know, $\vec{E} = \dfrac{\vec{F}}{q}$

$\Rightarrow \quad \vec{F} = q\vec{E}$

Therefore, force $q\vec{E}$ will act on the dipole as shown.

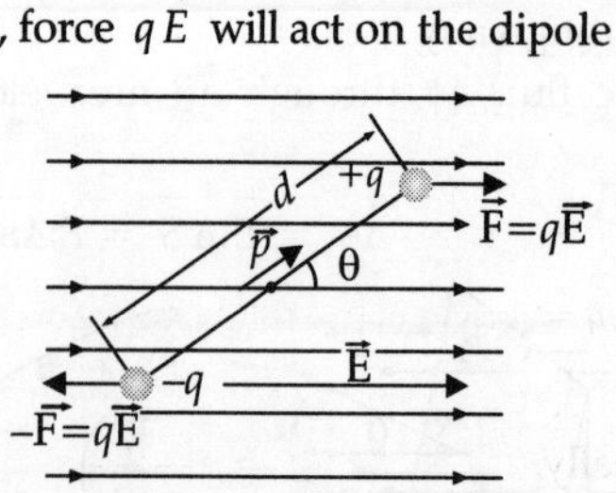

Moment of force (Torque)

These two forces will form a couple and rotate the dipole.

Rotational effect produced is

Torque = Force × perpendicular distance between the line of action of forces

$$\tau = q\vec{E} \times 2l \sin\theta$$

$$\tau = p\vec{E} \sin\theta$$

This is magnitude of torque which rotates the dipole and align it along the field.

➢ **Potential energy of dipole in an uniform electric field:**

When a dipole is placed in an external electric field it experiences a torque which try to align it in the direction of the electric field. The work done to oppose this is stored in form of potential energy.

$$U = W = -pE(\cos\theta_2 - \cos\theta_1)$$

where, U is the potential energy, p is the dipole moment

- When dipole is initially along the electric field,

  i.e., $\theta_1 = 0$ and $\theta_2 = \theta$

  then $W = -pE(\cos\theta - \cos 0)$

  This work done is stored in the form of potential energy.

- When dipole is initially at right angle to $\vec{E}$,

  i.e., $\theta_1 = 90°$ and $\theta_2 = \theta$.

  then, $W = -pE(\cos\theta - \cos 90°)$

  $= -pE\cos\theta$

  therefore, potential energy of dipole

  $= U = W = -pE\cos\theta$

  or $U = -\vec{p}.\vec{E}$

Gauss' Law

It states that the total electric flux coming out of the Gaussian surface is $\dfrac{1}{\varepsilon_0}$ times the total charge enclosed by the surface.

Scan to know more about this topic

Electric flux and Gauss' law

i.e., $$\phi = \oint \vec{E}.d\vec{S} = \frac{Q}{\varepsilon_0}$$

where, Q is the total charge enclosed by the surface and ε_0 is the permittivity of free space.

- In case, there is no charge inside the closed surface then net flux through it is zero. This means that the number of electric field lines entering the surface equals the number of electric field lines leaving the surface.
- If a closed surface encloses a number of charges, then net flux through it is

$$\oiint \vec{E}.d\vec{S} = \frac{Q_1 + Q_2 + Q_3 + ...}{\varepsilon_0}$$

$$= \sum_{i=1}^{i=n} \frac{Q_i}{\varepsilon_0}$$

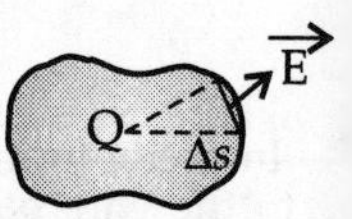

- In case, charge is uniformly distributed over the volume enclosed by the closed surface, then total charge enclosed will be

$$Q = \iiint \rho dv$$

where, ρ = charge per unit volume.

- Therefore, Gauss's law statement will be

$$\oint\!\!\oint \vec{E}.\vec{dS} = \frac{1}{\varepsilon_0}\iiint \rho dv$$

Applications of Gauss' Law

1) Electric field due to an infinitely long straight uniformly charged wire:

It is required to find electric field at a point P, at a distance r from the infinite wire.

To use the Gauss theorem, we choose a Gaussian surface in form of a cylinder of length 'L', radius 'r' such that point P lies on it symmetrically.

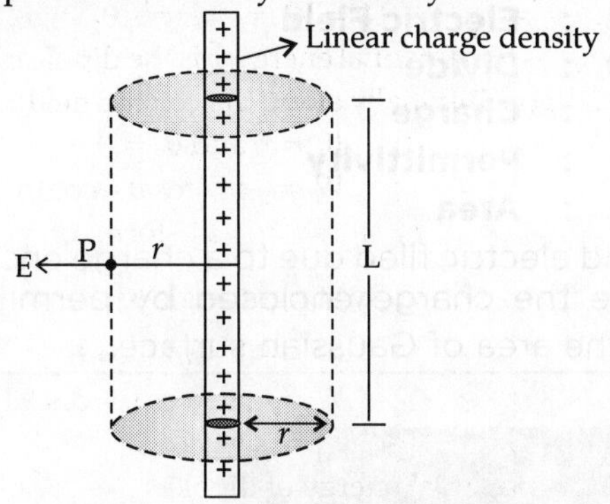

The Gaussian surface for a long thin wire of uniform linear charge density

- Electric field lines are normal to the wire and hence electric flux will be through the curved surface of the cylinder only.

Using Gauss theorem,

$$\oint\!\!\oint \vec{E}.\vec{dS} = \frac{\text{Charge enclosed}}{\varepsilon_0}$$

$$\iint \vec{E}.\vec{dS} + \iint \vec{E}.\vec{dS} = \iint \vec{E}.\vec{dS} + 0 = \frac{\lambda L}{\varepsilon_0}$$

$$\Rightarrow \quad E\oint dS = \frac{\lambda L}{\varepsilon_0}$$

$$\Rightarrow \quad E(2\pi rL) = \frac{\lambda L}{\varepsilon_0}$$

$$\Rightarrow \quad E = \frac{\lambda}{2\pi\varepsilon_0 r}$$

Vectorially, $\vec{E}$ at any point is given by

$$\Rightarrow \quad \vec{E} = \frac{\lambda}{2\pi\varepsilon_0 r}\hat{n}$$

where, $\hat{n}$ is the radial unit vector in the plane normal to the wire passing through the plane. $\vec{E}$ is directed outward if λ is positive and inward if λ is negative.

2) Electric Field due to uniformly charged infinite plane sheet:

For this we consider σ to be uniform surface charge density of an infinite plane sheet. We take here a rectangular parallelepiped of cross-sectional area A as a Gaussian Surface.

Here, the net flux through the Gaussian Surface is 2EA.

The charge enclosed by the closed surface is σA.

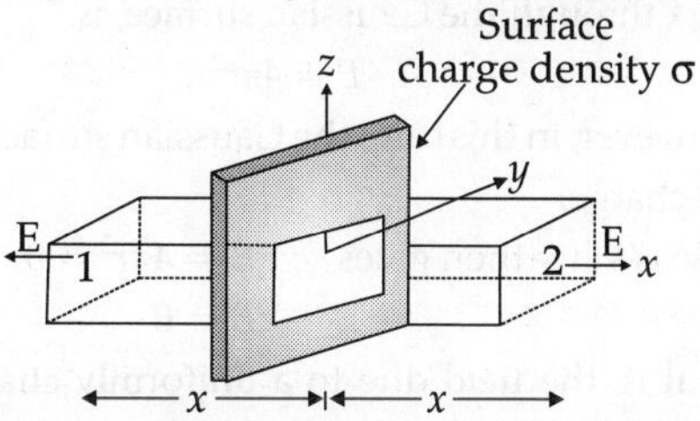

Gaussian surface for a uniformly charged infinite plane sheet

Therefore, By Gauss' law

$$2EA = \frac{\sigma A}{\varepsilon_0}$$

$$\text{or} \quad = \frac{\sigma}{2\varepsilon_0}.$$

$$\text{Vectorially,} \quad \vec{E} = \frac{\sigma}{2\varepsilon_0}\hat{n}$$

where, $\hat{n}$ is the unit vector normal to the plane.

(3) Electric field due to uniformly charged thin spherical shell:

For this we take, σ as the uniform charge density of thin spherical shell of radius R.

(a) Electric field outside the shell: For this we consider a point P outside the shell with radius vector r.

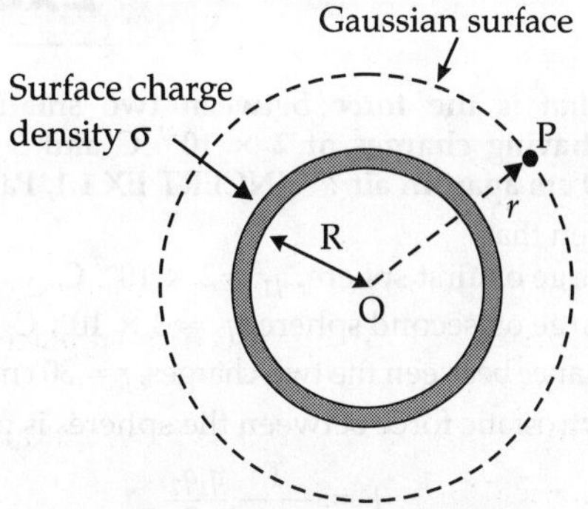

Gaussian surface for r > R

To calculate E, at P, we take the Gaussian surface to be a sphere of radius r and with centre O, passing through P. The flux through the Gaussian surface is $E \times 4\pi r^2$.

The charge enclosed is $\sigma \times 4\pi R^2$.

$$\text{By Gauss's law, } E \times 4\pi r^2 = \frac{\sigma}{\varepsilon_0}4\pi R^2$$

$$\text{or,} \quad E = \frac{\sigma R^2}{\varepsilon_0 r^2} = \frac{q}{4\pi\varepsilon_0 r^2}$$

where, $q = 4\pi R^2\sigma$ is the total charge on the spherical shell.

$$\text{Vectorially,} \quad \vec{E} = \frac{q}{4\pi\varepsilon_0 r^2}\hat{r}$$

The electric field is directed outward if $q > 0$ and inward if $q < 0$.

(b) Electric field inside the shell: For this we consider the point P is inside the shell. The Gaussian surface is again a sphere through P centred at O.

Flux through the Gaussian surface, is

$$E = 4\pi r^2$$

However, in this case, the Gaussian surface encloses no charge.

Gauss's law then gives $\quad E = 4\pi r^2 = 0$

i.e., $\quad E = 0 \quad (r < R)$

That is, the field due to a uniformly charged thin shell is zero at all points inside the shell.

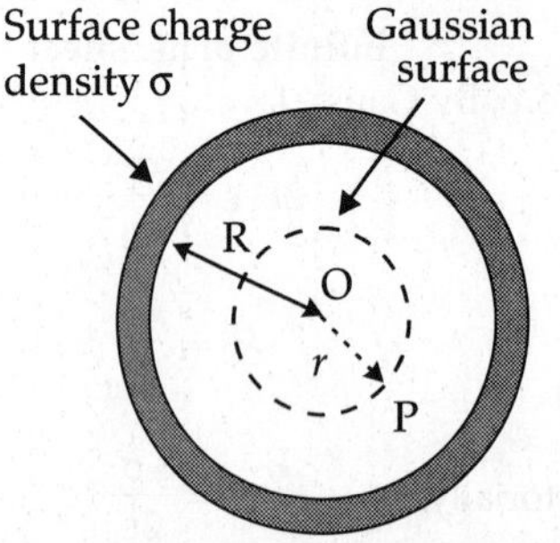

Gaussian surface for a point with r < R

(b) When P lies on the surface of the shell,

$$E = \frac{q}{4\pi\varepsilon_0 R^2}$$

MNEMONICS

Concept: Electric field due to charge enclosed

Equally Divide Cost Per Annum

Interpretation:

E : Electric Field
D : Divide
C : Charge
P : Permittivity
A : Area

To find electric filed due to a charge enclosed divide the charge enclosed by permittivity and the area of Gaussian surface.

NCERT CORNER

Exercise Questions

Q. 1. What is the force between two small charged spheres having charges of 2 × 10⁻⁷ C and 3 × 10⁻⁷ C placed 30 cm apart in air ? [NCERT EX 1.1, Page no. 42]

Ans. Given that,

Charge on first sphere, $q_1 = 2 \times 10^{-7}$ C

Charge on second sphere, $q_2 = 3 \times 10^{-7}$ C

Distance between the two charges, $r = 30$ cm $= 0.3$ m

Electrostatic force between the spheres is given by:

$$F = \frac{1}{4\pi\varepsilon_0} \cdot \frac{q_1 q_2}{r^2}$$

where, ε_0 = Permittivity of free space

and $\quad \frac{1}{4\pi\varepsilon_0} = 9 \times 10^9$ N

Then force, $\quad F = 6 \times 10^{-3}$ N

Since, the charges are of same nature; therefore, force between them will be repulsive.

Q. 2. The electrostatic force on a small sphere of charge 0.4 μC due to another small sphere of charge – 0.8 μC in air is 0.2 N.

(a) What is the distance between the two spheres?

(b) What is the force on the second sphere due to the first ? [NCERT EX 1.2, Page no. 42]

Ans. (a) Charge on first sphere, $q_1 = 0.4\ \mu C = 0.4 \times 10^{-6}$ C

Charge on second sphere, $q_2 = -0.8\ \mu C$

$= -0.8 \times 10^{-6}$ C

Electrostatic force on the first sphere, $F = 0.2$ N

Electrostatic force between the spheres is given by:

$$F = \frac{1}{4\pi\varepsilon_0} \cdot \frac{q_1 q_2}{r^2}$$

where,

ε_0 = Permittivity of free space

and $\quad \frac{1}{4\pi\varepsilon_0} = 9 \times 10^9\ \text{N m}^2\text{C}^{-2}$

$$r^2 = \frac{1}{4\pi\varepsilon_0} \cdot \frac{q_1 q_2}{F}$$

$$= \frac{0.4 \times 10^{-6} \times -0.8 \times 10^{-6} \times 9 \times 10^9}{0.2}$$

$$= 144 \times 10^{-4}\ \text{m}^2$$

$\therefore \quad r = \sqrt{144 \times 10^{-4}}$

$= 12 \times 10^{-2}$

Distance between the two spheres = 0.12 m.

(b) Both spheres attract each other with the same force. So, the force on the second sphere due to first sphere will be 0.2 N.

Q. 3. Check that the ratio $\frac{ke^2}{Gm_e m_p}$, is dimensionless. Look up a table of Physical Constants and determine the value of this ratio. What does the ratio signify ? [NCERT EX 1.3, Page no. 42]

Ans. The ratio is given as: $\dfrac{ke^2}{Gm_e m_p}$

where,

G = Gravitational constant in $Nm^2\,kg^{-2}$

m_e and m_p = Masses of electron and proton in kg

e = Electric charge in Coulomb, C

$k = \dfrac{1}{4\pi\varepsilon_0}$ in Nm^2C^{-2}

Therefore, dimension of the ratio

$$= \frac{[Nm^2C^{-2}][C^2]}{[Nm^2kg^{-2}][kg][kg]}$$

$$= M^0L^0T^0$$

From the table:

$e = 1.6 \times 10^{-19}$ C

$G = 6.67 \times 10^{-11}$ N m^2 kg^{-2}

$m_e = 9.1 \times 10^{-31}$ kg

$m_p = 1.66 \times 10^{-27}$ kg

So, the numerical value of the given ratio will be:

$$\frac{ke^2}{Gm_e m_p} = \frac{9\times10^9\times(1.6\times10^{-19})^2}{6.67\times10^{-11}\times9.1\times10^{-31}\times1.66\times10^{-27}}$$

$$\approx 2.3 \times 10^{39}$$

So, the value of this ratio is 2.3×10^{39}.

That means the above ratio is the ratio of the electric force to the gravitational force between a proton and an electron when the distance between them is constant.

Q. 4. (a) Explain the meaning of the statement 'electric charge of a body is quantised'.

(b) Why can one ignore quantisation of electric charge when dealing with macroscopic, i.e., large scale charges ? [NCERT EX 1.4, Page no.42]

Ans. (a) Electric charge of any body is quantised meaning only integral (1, 2, …*n*) number of electrons can be transferred from one body to another.

Charges do not get transferred in fractional form. So, the total charge possessed by a body is only an integral multiple of electric charge.

(b) In the case of large scale, the charges which are used over there are comparatively too huge to the magnitude of the electric charge. Hence, for the macroscopic level the quantisation of charge is of no use. Therefore, it is ignored and the electric charge is considered to be continuous.

Q. 5. When a glass rod is rubbed with a silk cloth, charges appear on both. A similar phenomenon is observed with many other pairs of bodies. Explain how this observation is consistent with the law of conservation of charge. [NCERT EX 1.5, Page no. 42]

Ans. When we rub two bodies together then a charge is developed on both of the bodies and the developed charge over the bodies are equal but opposite in nature. This phenomenon of getting a charge is called as charge by friction.

So, the net charge on both of the bodies will be zero because the negative charge developed in silk body will be exactly equal to the positive charge developed on the glass.

This phenomenon is in consistence and follows the law of conservation of charge. A similar phenomenon is observed with many other pairs of bodies.

Q. 6. Four point charges $q_A = 2\,\mu C, q_B = -5\,\mu C, q_C = 2\,\mu C$ and $q_D = -5\,\mu C$ are located at the corners of a square ABCD of side 10 cm. What is the force on a charge of 1 μC placed at the centre of the square ? [NCERT EX 1.6, Page no. 42]

Ans.

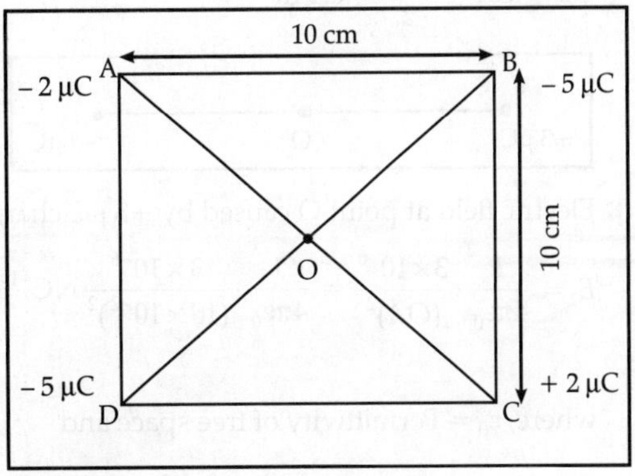

In given square,

Sides: $AB = BC = CD = DA = 10$ cm

Diagonals: $AC = BD = 10\sqrt{2}$ cm

$AO = OC = DO = OB = 5\sqrt{2}$ cm

At the centre point 'O', placed a charge of 1μC.

So, for the above cases:

The repulsive force between the corner A and the centre O is same in magnitude with the repulsive force by the corner C to the centre O, but these forces are opposite in direction. So, these forces will cancel each other and from A and C no forces are applied on the centre O.

Similarly, from the corner C the attractive force is applying on to the centre O and another force with the same magnitude is applying on the centre O, also these two forces are opposite in direction. So, it is also opposing each other.

Therefore, the net force applying at the centre is zero. Because all the forces are cancelled by each other.

Q. 7. (a) An electrostatic field line is a continuous curve. That is a field line cannot have sudden breaks. Why not ?

(b) Explain why two field lines never cross each other at any point. [NCERT EX 1.7, Page no. 42]

Ans. (a) An electrostatic field line is a continuous curve, because it represents the actual path of a unit positive charge, which experiences a continuous force. It cannot have sudden breaks because the moving test charge never jumps from one position to the other.

(b) This is because at the point of intersection, we can draw two tangents to the two lines of force. This would mean two directions of electric field intensity at the point of intersection, which is not possible.

Q. 8. Two point charges $q_A = 3\,\mu C$ and $q_B = -3\,\mu C$ are located 20 cm apart in vacuum.

(a) What is the electric field at the mid-point O of the line AB joining the two charges ?

(b) If a negative test charge of magnitude 1.5×10^{-9} C is placed at this point, what is the force experienced by the test charge ?

[NCERT EX 1.8, Page no. 42]

Ans. (a) Given that,

$q_A = 3\,\mu C = 3 \times 10^{-6}$ C

$q_B = -3\,\mu C = -3 \times 10^{-6}$ C

Distance $AB = 20 \text{ cm} = 0.2 \text{ m}$

In this situation, point, O is the mid-point of line AB.

So:

$$OB = OA = \frac{0.2}{2} = 0.1 \text{ m}$$

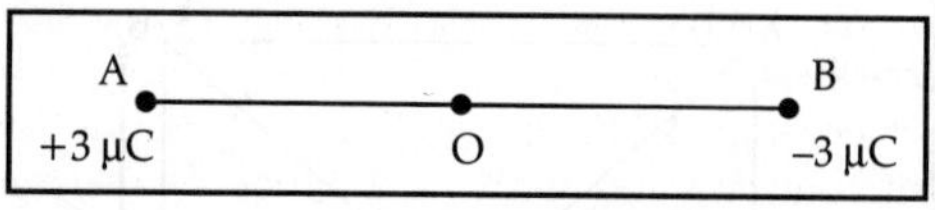

Electric field at point O caused by +3 μC charge,

$$E_1 = \frac{1}{4\pi\varepsilon_0} \cdot \frac{3\times10^{-6}}{(OA)^2} = \frac{1}{4\pi\varepsilon_0} \cdot \frac{3\times10^{-6}}{(10\times10^{-2})^2} \text{NC}^{-1} \text{ along}$$

OB

where, ε_0 = Permittivity of free space and

$$\frac{1}{4\pi\varepsilon_0} = 9 \times 10^9 \text{ N m}^2\text{C}^{-2}$$

Therefore,

Electric field at point O caused by –3 μC charge,

$$E_2 = \left| \frac{1}{4\pi\varepsilon_0} \cdot \frac{-3\times10^{-6}}{(OB)^2} \right|$$

$$= \frac{1}{4\pi\varepsilon_0} \cdot \frac{3\times10^{-6}}{(10\times10^{-2})^2} \text{NC}^{-1} \text{ along OB}$$

$$\therefore E_1 + E_2 = 2\times\frac{1}{4\pi\varepsilon_0} \cdot \frac{3\times10^{-6}}{(10\times10^{-2})^2} \text{NC}^{-1} \text{ along OB}$$

[Since the magnitude of E_1 and E_2 are equal and in the same direction.]

$$\therefore E = 2\times9\times10^9\times\frac{3\times10^{-6}}{(10\times10^{-2})^2} \text{NC}^{-1} \text{ along OB}$$

$$= 5.4 \times 10^6 \text{ NC}^{-1}$$

So, the electric field at mid-point O is $5.4 \times 10^6 \text{ NC}^{-1}$ along OB.

The direction of electric field is always positive to negative so that direction of electric field will in direction of OB.

(b) Now a test charge of magnitude 1.5×10^{-9} C is placed at mid point O.

Force experienced by test charge,

$$F = qE$$

$$= 1.5 \times 10^{-9} \times 5.4 \times 10^6$$

$$= 8.1 \times 10^{-3} \text{ N}$$

The force is directed along line OA.

Q. 9. A system has two charges $q_A = 2.5 \times 10^{-7}$ C and $q_B = -2.5 \times 10^{-7}$ C located at points A(0, 0, –15 cm) and B(0, 0, +15 cm) respectively. What are the total charge and electric dipole moment of the system ?

[NCERT EX 1.9, Page no. 42]

Ans. The charges are located at the given points as shown in the following co-ordinate system:

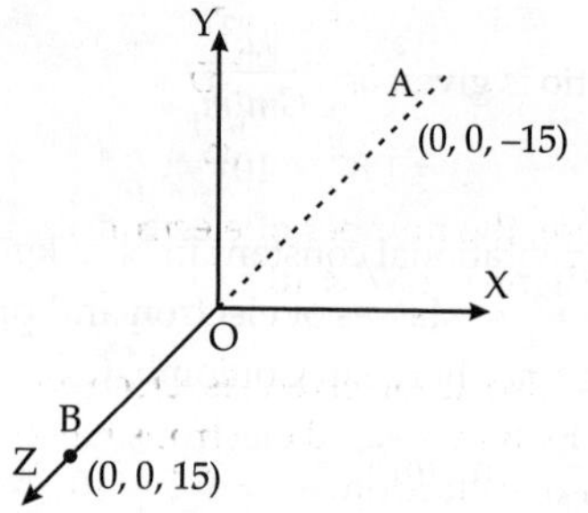

At point A, magnitude of charge, $q_A = 2.5 \times 10^{-7}$ C

At point B, magnitude of charge, $q_B = -2.5 \times 10^{-7}$ C

Total charge of the system,

$$q_A + q_A = 2.5 \times 10^{-7} \text{ C} - 2.5 \times 10^{-7} = 0$$

Distance between two charges at points A and B,

$$d = 15 + 15 = 30 \text{ cm} = 0.3 \text{ m}$$

Electric dipole moment of the system is given by,

$$p = q_A \times d = q_B \times d$$
$$= 2.5 \times 10^{-7} \times 0.3$$
$$= 7.5 \times 10^{-8} \text{ Cm}$$

So, the electric dipole moment of the system i = 7.5×10^{-8} Cm along negative Z-axis.

Q. 10. An electric dipole with dipole moment 4×10^{-9} Cm is aligned at 30° with the direction of a uniform electric field of magnitude $5 \times 10^4 \text{ NC}^{-1}$. Calculate the magnitude of the torque acting on the dipole.

[NCERT EX 1.10, Page no. 46

Ans. Given that,

Electric dipole moment, $p = 4 \times 10^{-9}$ Cm

Angle made by p with a uniform electric field, $\theta = 30°$

Electric field, $E = 5 \times 10^4 \text{ NC}^{-1}$

As we know that,

Torque acting on the dipole is given by the relation,

$$\tau = pE \sin\theta$$
$$= 4 \times 10^{-9} \times 5 \times 10^4 \times \sin 30°$$
$$= 20 \times 10^{-5} \times \frac{1}{2} = 10^{-4} \text{Nm}$$

So, the magnitude of the torque acting on the dipole is 10^{-4} Nm.

Q. 11. A polythene piece rubbed with wool is found to have a negative charge of 3×10^{-7} C.

(a) Estimate the number of electrons transferred (from which to which ?)

(b) Is there a transfer of mass from wool to polythene ?

[NCERT EX 1.11, Page no. 42]

Ans. (a) Given, the negative charge on polythene piece is 3×10^{-7} C.

Hence, electrons must be transferred from wool when polythene is rubbed against wool, electrons gets transferred from wool to polythene. Hence, wool becomes positively charged and polythene becomes negatively charged.

Amount of charge on polythene piece, $q = -3 \times 10^{-7}$ C.

Amount of charge on an electron, $e = -1.6 \times 10^{-19}$ C.

Number of electrons transferred from wool to polythene = n

n can be calculated using the relation

$$q = ne$$

$$n = \frac{q}{e}$$

$$= \frac{-3\times10^{-7}}{-1.6\times10^{-19}}$$

$= 1.87 \times 10^{12}$

Therefore, the number of electrons transferred from wool to polythene is 1.87×10^{12}.

(b) Yes,

Mass is also transferred as electron is transferred from wool to polythene and electrons have some mass.

Mass of one electron, $m_e = 9.1 \times 10^{-31}$ kg

Total mass transferred, $m = m_e \times n$

$= 9.1 \times 10^{-31} \times 1.87 \times 10^{12}$

$= 1.706 \times 10^{-18}$ kg

From above result, the mass transferred is too low that it can be neglected.

Q. 12. (a) Two insulated charged copper spheres A and B have their centres separated by a distance of 50 cm. What is the mutual force of electrostatic repulsion if the charge on each is 6.5×10^{-7} C. The radii of A and B are negligible compared to the distance of separation.

(b) What is the force of repulsion if each sphere is charged double the above amount, and the distance between them is halved? [NCERT EX 1.12, Page no. 42]

Ans. (a) Charge on sphere A, $q_A = 6.5 \times 10^{-7}$ C

Charge on sphere B, $q_B = 6.5 \times 10^{-7}$ C

Distance between the spheres, r = 50 cm = 0.5 m

Force of repulsion between the two spheres,

$$F = \frac{1}{4\pi\varepsilon_0}.\frac{q_A q_B}{r^2}$$

where, ε_0= Permittivity of free space

and $\frac{1}{4\pi\varepsilon_0} = 9\times 10^9$ N m^2 C^{-2}

So, $$F = \frac{9\times10^9 \times (6.5\times10^{-7})^2}{(0.5)^2}$$

$= 1.52 \times 10^{-2}$ N

Thus, the force between two spheres is 1.52×10^{-2} N.

(b) After doubling the charge,

Charge on sphere A, $q_A = 1.3 \times 10^{-6}$ C

Charge on sphere B, $q_B = 1.3 \times 10^{-6}$ C

The distance between the spheres is halved.

$\therefore$ $r = \frac{0.5}{2} = 0.25$ m

Force of repulsion between the two spheres,

$$F = \frac{1}{4\pi\varepsilon_0}.\frac{q_A q_B}{r^2}$$

$$= \frac{9\times10^9 \times 1.3\times10^{-6} \times 1.3\times10^{-6}}{(0.25)^2}$$

$= 16 \times 1.52 \times 10^{-2}$

$= 0.243$ N

So, the force between the two spheres is 0.243 N.

Q. 13. Figure ahead shows tracks of three charged particles in a uniform electrostatic field. Give the signs of the three charges. Which particle has the highest charge to mass ratio ?

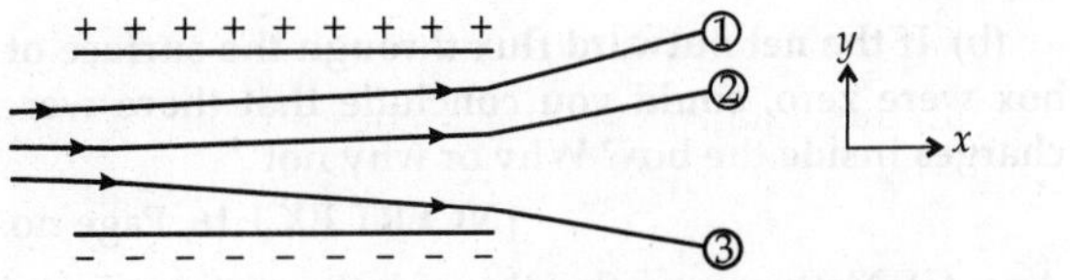

[NCERT EX 1.13, Page no. 43]

Ans. As we know that the opposite charges attract each other and same charges repel each other. So, it can be observed that particles 1 and 2 both move towards the positively charged plate and repel away from the negatively charged plate. It means these two particles are negatively charged. And for particle 3, it can also be observed that it moves towards the negatively charged plate and repels away from the positively charged plate. So, particle 3 is positively charged.

The charge to mass ratio (e/m) is directly proportional to the displacement or amount of deflection at a given velocity. Since the deflection of particle 3 is the maximum as compared to particles 1 and 2. Therefore, it will have higher charge to mass ratio.

Q. 14. Consider a uniform electric field $E = 3 \times 10^3 \hat{i}$ N/C.

(a) What is the flux of this field through a square of 10 cm on a side whose plane is parallel to the *yz* plane ?

(b) What is the flux through the same square if the normal to its plane makes a 60° angle with the *x*-axis ? [NCERT EX 1.14, Page no. 43]

Ans. (a) Electric field intensity, $= 3 \times 10^3 \hat{i}$ N/C

Magnitude of electric field intensity,

$|\vec{E}| = 3 \times 10^3$ N/C

Side of the square, s = 10 cm = 0.1 m

Area of the square, $A = s^2 = 0.01$ m^2

The plane of the square is parallel to the yz plane. Hence, angle between the unit vector normal to the plane and electric field, $\theta = 0$.

Flux (ϕ) through the plane is given by the relation,

$$\phi = |\vec{E}| A\cos\theta$$

$= 3 \times 10^3 \times 0.01 \times \cos 0°$

$= 30$ Nm^2/C

(b) Plane makes an angle of 60° with the x-axis. Hence, $\theta = 60°$

Flux, $$\phi = |\vec{E}| A\cos\theta$$

$= 3 \times 10^3 \times 0.01 \times \cos 60°$

$= 15$ Nm^2/C

Q. 15. What is the net flux of the uniform electric field of Question 15 through a cube of side 20 cm oriented so that its faces are parallel to the co-ordinate planes ?

[NCERT EX 1.15, Page no. 43]

Ans. All the faces of a cube are parallel to the coordinate axes. So, the number of field lines entering the cube is equal to the number of field lines emerging out of the cube. As a result, net flux through the cube is zero.

Q. 16. Careful measurement of the electric field at the surface of a black box indicates that the net outward flux through the surface of the box is 8.0×10^3 Nm^2/C.

(a) What is the net charge inside the box ?

(b) If the net outward flux through the surface of the box were zero, could you conclude that there were no charges inside the box? Why or why not ?

[NCERT EX 1.16, Page no. 43]

Ans. (a) Net outward flux through the surface of the box, $\phi = 8.0 \times 10^3$ Nm²/C

For a body containing net charge q, flux is given by the relation,

$$\phi = \frac{q}{\varepsilon_0}$$

Where, ε_0 = Permittivity of free space

$= 8.854 \times 10^{-12}\ N^{-1}C^2 m^{-2}$

$q = \varepsilon_0 \phi$

$= 8.854 \times 10^{-12} \times 8.0 \times 10^3$

$= 7.08 \times 10^{-8}$

$= 0.07\ \mu C$

So, the net charge inside the box is 0.07 μC.

(b) No, net flux emerging out through a body depends on the net charge contained in the body. If net flux is zero, then it can be inferred that net charge inside the body is zero. The body may have equal amount of positive and negative charges.

Q. 17. A point charge +10 μC is at a distance of 5 cm directly above the centre of a square of side 10 cm as shown in fig., what is the magnitude of the electric flux through the square? (Hint. Think of the square as one face of a cube with edge 10 cm.)

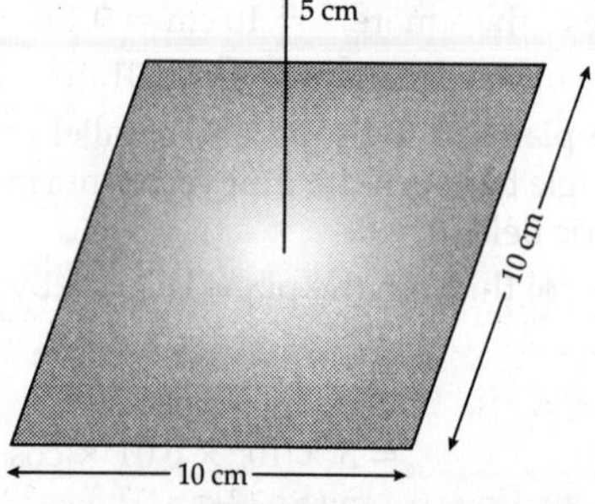

[NCERT Ex. Q. 1.17, Page 43]

Ans. The square can be considered as one face of a cube of edge 10 cm with a centre where charge 'q' is placed. According to Gauss's theorem for a cube, total electric flux is through all its six faces.

$$\phi_{Total} = \frac{q}{\varepsilon_0}$$

So, electric flux through one face of the cube, that is, through the square,

$$\phi = \frac{\phi_{Total}}{6}$$

$$= \frac{1}{6} \times \frac{q}{\varepsilon_0}$$

where, ε_0 = Permittivity of free space

$= 8.854 \times 10^{-12}\ N^{-1}C^2 m^{-2}$

$q = 10\ \mu C = 10 \times 10^{-6}$ C

$$\phi = \frac{1}{6} \times \frac{10 \times 10^{-6}}{8.854 \times 10^{-12}}$$

$= 1.88 \times 10^5\ Nm^2C^{-1}$

So, electric flux through the square is 1.88×10^5 Nm²C⁻¹.

Q. 18. A point charge of 2.0 μC is at the centre of a cubic Gaussian surface 90 cm on edge. What is the net electric flux through the surface ? [NCERT EX 1.18, Page no. 43]

Ans. As we know

Net electric flux (ϕ_{Net}) through the cubic surface is given by,

$$\phi_{Net} = \frac{q}{\varepsilon_0}$$

where, ε_0 = Permittivity of free space

$= 8.854 \times 10^{-12}\ N^{-1}C^2 m^{-2}$

q = Net charge contained inside the cube

$= 2.0\ \mu C = 2 \times 10^{-6}$ C

$$\phi_{Net} = \frac{2 \times 10^{-6}}{8.854 \times 10^{-12}}$$

$= 2.26 \times 10^5\ Nm^2C^{-1}$

The net electric flux through the surface is 2.26×10^5 Nm²C⁻¹.

Q. 19. A point charge causes an electric flux of -1.0×10^3 Nm²/C to pass through a spherical Gaussian surface of 10 cm radius centred on the charge.

(a) If the radius of the Gaussian surface were doubled, how much flux would pass through the surface?

(b) What is the value of the point charge?

[NCERT EX 1.19 Page no. 43]

Ans. (a) Given that,

Electric flux, $\phi = -1.0 \times 10\ Nm^2C^{-1}$

Radius of the Gaussian surface, r = 10.0 cm

Electric flux emerging out through a surface depends on the net charge enclosed inside the body and it does not depend on the size of the body. If the radius of the Gaussian surface is doubled, then the flux passing through the surface remains the same that is -1.0×10^3 Nm²C⁻¹.

(b) Electric flux is,

$$\phi = \frac{q}{\varepsilon_0}$$

where, q = Net charge enclosed by the spherical surface

ε_0 = Permittivity of free space

$= 8.854 \times 10^{-12}\ N^{-1}C^2 m^{-2}$

And we know that,

$q = \phi \varepsilon_0$

$= -1.0 \times 10^3 \times 8.854 \times 10^{-12}$

$= -8.854 \times 10^{-9}$ C

$= -8.854$ nC

So, the value of the point charge is −8.854 nC.

Q. 20. A conducting sphere of radius 10 cm has an unknown charge. If the electric field 20 cm from the centre of the sphere is 1.5×10^3 N/C and points radially inwards, what is the net charge on the sphere?

[NCERT EX 1.20, Page no. 43]

Ans. As we know,

Electric field intensity (E) at a distance (*d*) from the centre of a sphere containing net charge '*q*' is given by the relation,

$$E = \frac{q}{4\pi\varepsilon_0 d^2}$$

where, $E = 1.5 \times 10^3$ N/C

d = Distance from the centre = 20 cm = 0.2 m

ε_0 = Permittivity of free space

and $\frac{1}{4\pi\varepsilon_0} = 9 \times 10^9$ Nm²C⁻²

$$q = E(4\pi\varepsilon_0)d^2$$
$$= \frac{1.5\times10^3\times(0.2)^2}{9\times10^9}$$
$$= 6.67 \times 10^{-9}\text{ C}$$
$$= 6.67\text{ nC}$$

So, the net charge on the sphere will be – 6.67 nC.

Q. 21. A uniformly charged conducting sphere of 2.4 m diameter has a surface charge density of 80.0 μC/m².

(a) Find the charge on the sphere.

(b) What is the total electric flux leaving the surface E of the sphere? [NCERT EX 1.21, Page no. 44]

Ans. (a) Given that,

Diameter of the sphere, d = 2.4 m

Radius of the sphere, r = 1.2 m

Surface charge density, $\sigma = 80.0\ \mu C/m^2 = 80 \times 10^{-6}\ C/m^2$

Total charge on the surface of the sphere,

Q = Charge density × Surface area

$$= \sigma \times 4\pi r^2$$
$$= 80 \times 10^{-6} \times 4 \times 3.14 \times (1.2)^2$$
$$= 1.447 \times 10^{-3}\text{ C}$$

Therefore, the charge on the sphere is 1.447×10^{-3} C.

(b) Total electric flux (ϕ_{Total}) leaving out the surface of a sphere containing net charge Q is given by the relation,

$$\phi_{Total} = \frac{Q}{\varepsilon_0}$$

where, ε_0 = Permittivity of free space

$\varepsilon_0 = 8.854 \times 10^{-12}\ N^{-1}C^2m^{-2}$

$Q = 1.447 \times 10^{-3}$ C

$$\phi_{Total} = \frac{1.44\times10^{-3}}{8.854\times10^{-12}}$$
$$= 1.63 \times 10^8\ NC^{-1}m^2$$

So, the total electric flux leaving the surface of the sphere is $1.63 \times 10^8\ NC^{-1}m^2$.

Q. 22. An infinite line charge produces a field of 9×10^4 N/C at a distance of 2 cm. Calculate at the linear charge density. [NCERT EX 1.22, Page no. 44]

Ans. Electric field produced by the infinite line charges at a distance *d* having linear charge density λ,

$$E = \frac{\lambda}{2\pi\varepsilon_0 d}$$
$$\lambda = 2\pi\varepsilon_0 dE$$

where, d = 2 cm = 0.02 m

$E = 9 \times 10^4$ N/C

ε_0 = Permittivity of free space

$\frac{1}{4\pi\varepsilon_0} = 9 \times 10^9$ Nm²C⁻²

$$\lambda = \frac{0.02\times9\times10^4}{2\times9\times10^9}$$
$$= 10^{-7}\text{ C/m}$$

Thus, the linear charge density is 10^{-7} C/m.

Q. 23. Two large thin metal plates are parallel and close to each other. On their inner faces, the plates have surface charge densities of opposite signs and magnitude 17.0×10^{-22} C/m². What is E:

(a) in the outer region of the first plate.

(b) in the outer region of the second plate, and

(c) between the plates? [NCERT EX 1.23, Page no. 44]

Ans. From the above question the condition is represented by the figure below:

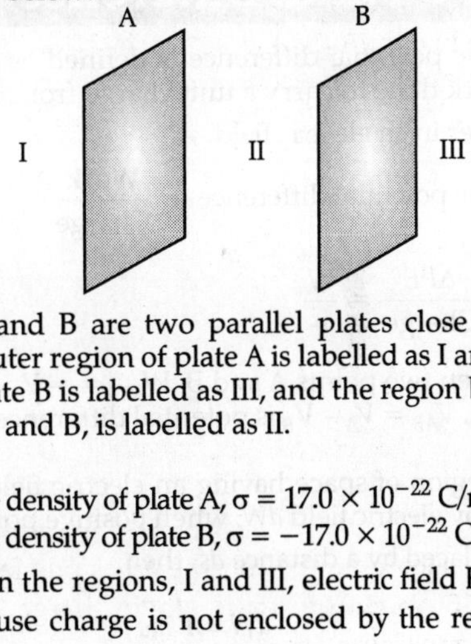

As, A and B are two parallel plates close to each other. The outer region of plate A is labelled as I and outer region of plate B is labelled as III, and the region between the plates, A and B, is labelled as II.

So,

Charge density of plate A, $\sigma = 17.0 \times 10^{-22}$ C/m²

Charge density of plate B, $\sigma = -17.0 \times 10^{-22}$ C/m²

(a) & (b) In the regions, I and III, electric field E is zero. This is because charge is not enclosed by the respective plates.

(c) Electric field E in region II is given by the relation,

$$E = \frac{\sigma}{\varepsilon_0}$$

where, ε_0 = Permittivity of free space $= 8.854 \times 10^{-12}\ N^{-1}C^2m^{-2}$

$$E = \frac{17.0\times10^{-22}}{8.854\times10^{-12}}$$
$$= 1.92 \times 10^{-10}\text{ N/C}$$

So, the electric field between the plates is 1.92×10^{-10} N/C.

CHAPTER 2

ELECTROSTATIC POTENTIAL AND CAPACITANCE

Electric Potential

Scan to know more about this topic

Electric potential

- Electric potential is the amount of work done by an external force in moving a unit positive charge from infinity to given point in electrostatic field without producing an acceleration.
- It is written as $V = \frac{W}{q}$

  where, W = Work done in moving charge q through the field,

  q = test charge
- The SI units of electric potential are $\frac{J}{C}$, Volt, $\frac{Nm}{C}$

Potential Difference

- Electric potential difference is defined as the amount of work done to carry a unit charge from one point to another in an electric field.

  $$\text{Electric potential difference} = \frac{\text{Work}}{\text{Charge}}$$

  $$= \frac{\Delta PE}{\text{Charge}} = \frac{W}{q}$$

  Between two points A and B, $W_{AB} = -V_{AB} \times q$

  where, $V_{AB} = V_A - V_B$ is potential difference between A and B.
- In a region of space having an electric field, the work done by electric field dW, when positive point charge q, is displaced by a distance ds, then,

  $$dW = \vec{F}.\vec{ds}$$

  $$\Delta V = V_{AB} = V_A - V_B = -\frac{W_{AB}}{q} = -\frac{\int_A^B q\vec{E}.\vec{ds}}{q} = -\int_A^B \vec{E}.\vec{ds}$$

Example 1. Calculate the electric potential at a point 3 cm away due to a charge of 3×10^{-7} C.

Sol. Here,

$$q = 3 \times 10^{-7}\text{ C}$$
$$r = 3\text{ cm} = 3 \times 10^{-2}\text{ m}$$

Using the expression for electric potential,

$$V = \frac{1}{4\pi\varepsilon_0}\frac{q}{r}$$

$$= \frac{9\times10^9 \times 3\times10^{-7}}{3\times10^{-2}}$$

$$= 9\times 10^9 \times 10^{-7+2}$$

$$V = 9 \times 10^4\text{ volts}$$

Electric Potential due to Point Charge

Scan to know more about this topic

Electric potential due to a point charge

- The electric potential by point charge q, at a distance r from the charge, can be written as

  $$V_E = \frac{1}{4\pi\varepsilon_0}.\frac{q}{r}$$

  where, ε_0 is permittivity of vacuum
- Electric potential is a scalar quantity.
- Dimension of Electric potential is $[ML^2T^{-3}A^{-1}]$
- For a single point charge q the potential difference between A and B is given by,

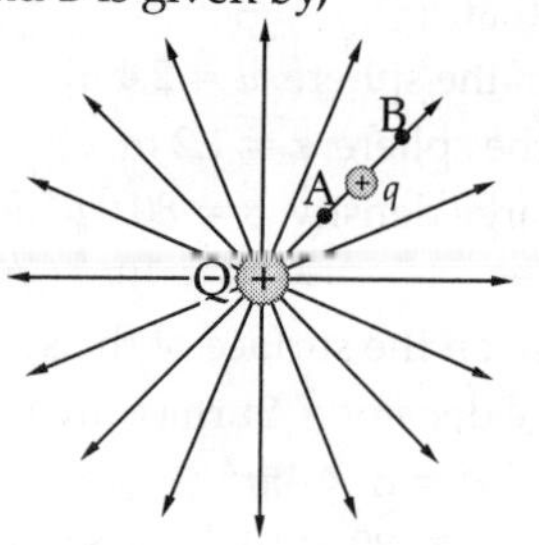

$$\Delta V = V_B - V_A = -\int_A^B \vec{E}.\vec{ds} = -\int_A^B Eds\cos 0° = -E\int_A^B ds$$

where, E is the field due to a point charge, $ds = dr$,

So,

$$V_B - V_A = -\int_{r_A}^{r_B} \frac{q}{4\pi\varepsilon_0}.\frac{dr}{r^2} = \frac{q}{4\pi\varepsilon_0}\left[\frac{1}{r}\right]_{r_A}^{r_B} = \frac{q}{4\pi\varepsilon_0}\left[\frac{1}{r_B} - \frac{1}{r_A}\right]$$

- If $r_B = \infty$, then $V_B = 0$

  So, $$V_A = \frac{1}{4\pi\varepsilon_0}.\frac{q}{r_A} = \frac{kq}{r_A}$$
- The electric potential is equal to the negative gradient of electric field since the potential gets weaker as we move away from the charge.

Dipole and System of Charges

- Electric dipole is two charged objects having equal but opposite electric charges which are separated by a distance.
- The net potential due to a dipole at any point on its equatorial line is always zero. So work done in moving a charge on equatorial line is always zero. So, a plane passing through the equitorial line is an equipotential surface.

Electrostatic Potential and Capacitance

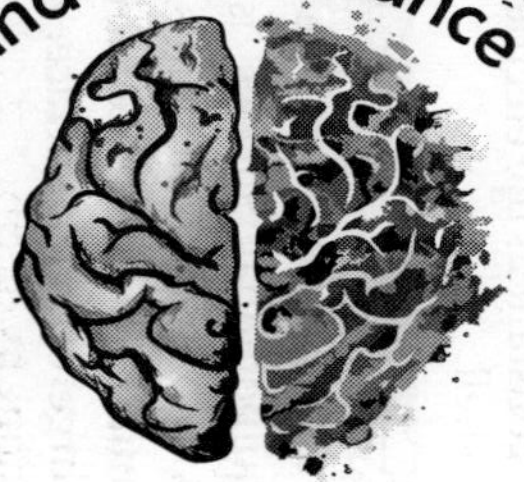

Electric potential

- Work done per unit test charge by an external agent in moving the test charge from reference point to the desired point. Its SI unit is J/C
  $V_0 = W/q_0$.

Electric potential due to a point charge

$V_P = Q/4\pi\varepsilon_0 r$

Potential due to a system of charges

$V = \frac{1}{4\pi\varepsilon_0}\sum\frac{Q_i}{r_i}$

Potential due to a dipole

$V = \frac{1}{4\pi\varepsilon_0}\frac{p\cos\theta}{r^2}$

where, $p = qd$

$\theta = \angle AON$

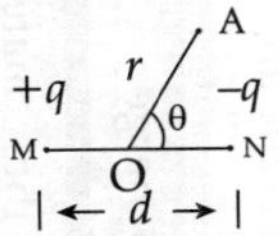

At $\theta = 0°, V = \frac{1}{4\pi\varepsilon_0}\frac{p}{r^2}$ [at axial position]

At $\theta = 90°, V = 0$ [at equitorial position]

Equipotential surface

- Potential is same at all the points of the surface.
- Component of electric field parallel to an equipotential surface is zero.

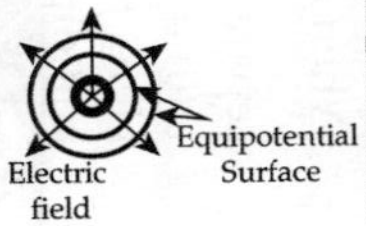

Electric potential energy

- It is negative count of work done by the electric force as the configuration of the system changes.
- $Ur_2 - Ur_1 = -W = \frac{q_1 \cdot q_2}{4\pi\varepsilon_0}\left(\frac{1}{r_2} - \frac{1}{r_1}\right)$
- If the separation between charges is 'r', then $U_{(r)} = \frac{q_1 \cdot q_2}{4\pi\varepsilon_0 r}$
- Potential Difference,
  $V_B - V_A = \frac{U_B - U_A}{q}$
  $U_B - U_A$ = Change in Potential energy
  q = Test charge

In 1774, Alessandro Volta wrote treatise "on the forces of attraction of electric field".

Capacitance, $C = \frac{Q}{V}$

Capacitance of a parallel plate capacitor,
$C = K\varepsilon_0 A/d$, K = dielectric constant

Parallel grouping of capacitors,
$C = C_1 + C_2 + C_3 + \cdots + C_n$
for two capacitors, $C = C_1 + C_2$

Energy stored in a capacitor,
$U = \frac{1}{2}CV^2 = \frac{Q^2}{2C} = \frac{1}{2}QV$

Series grouping of capacitors,
$\frac{1}{C} = \frac{1}{C_1} + \frac{1}{C_2} + \frac{1}{C_3} + \cdots + \frac{1}{C_n}$

For two capacitors, $C = \frac{C_1 C_2}{C_1 + C_2}$

Capacitance when dielectric slab is inserted between the plates
$C = K\varepsilon_0 A / [Kd - x(K-1)]$
where, x = thickness of the slab inserted

Capacitance for isolated sphere,
$C = 4\pi\varepsilon_0 R$

Dielectric

- Force $F = \frac{q_1 q_2}{4\pi K\varepsilon_0 r^2}$, K = dielectric constant of medium
- A dielectric is an electrical insulator that can be polarized by "application of" electric field.

Conductors & Insulators

Conductors	Insulators
A material which when placed in an electric field, the free electrons move in a direction opposite to the field.	A material in which electrons are tightly bound, and when exposed in an electric field, electrons do not move i.e., having no free electrons.

Properties of electric field

- Electric field inside a conductor is always zero.
- Electric field is always perpendicular to the charged surface.
- In static state, there will be no additional charge in a conductor.

Potential energy of a dipole

$dU = pE\sin\theta d\theta$

If we choose P.E. of dipole to be zero when $\theta = 90°$, then

$U_\theta - U_{90°} = \int_{90°}^{\theta} pE\sin\theta d\theta$

If it is rotated through angle θ against the torque,

$U_\theta = -pE\cos\theta = -\vec{p}\cdot\vec{E}$

Trace the Mind Map

- First Level
- Second Level
- Third Level

➢ Electric potential due to dipole at a point at distance r and making an angle θ with the dipole moment p is given by, $V = \frac{1}{4\pi\varepsilon_0}\frac{p\cos\theta}{r^2}$

➢ Potential at a point due to system of charges is the sum of electric potentials due to individual charges.

➢ In a system of charges $q_1, q_2, q_3, \ldots q_n$ having positive vectors $r_1, r_2, r_3, \ldots r_n$ relative to point P, the potential at point P due to total charge configuration is algebraic sum of potentials due to individual charges, so,

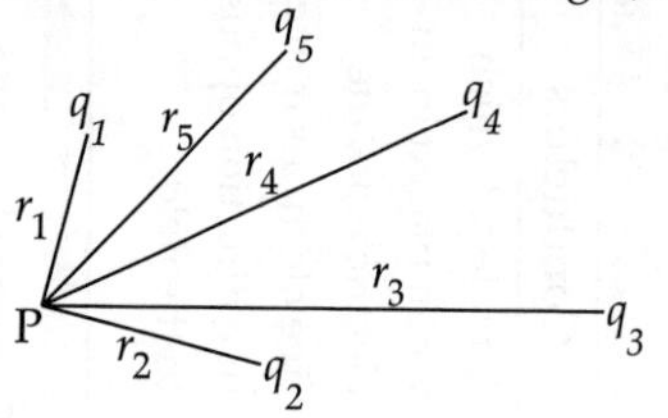

$$V = V_1 + V_2 + V_3 + \ldots + V_n$$

$$= \frac{1}{4\pi\varepsilon_0}\left(\frac{q_1}{r_1} + \frac{q_2}{r_2} + \frac{q_3}{r_3} + \ldots + \frac{q_n}{r_n}\right)$$

$$V = \frac{1}{4\pi\varepsilon_0}\sum_{i=1}^{n}\frac{q_i}{r_i}$$

➢ It is known that in a uniformly charged spherical shell, electric potential outside the shell is given as:

$$V = \frac{1}{4\pi\varepsilon_0}\cdot\frac{q}{r} \qquad [r \geq R]$$

where, q is total charge on shell and R is shell radius.

➢ The electric potential inside the spherical shell is constant as the electric field is zero inside a conducting shell.

Equipotential Surfaces

Equipotential Surface is a surface in space on which all points have same potential. No work is required to move the charge on such surface. Hence, the surface will have no $\vec{E}$ component, so $\vec{E}$ will be at right angle to the surface.

Scan to know more about this topic

Equipotential Surfaces

➢ Work done in moving a charge over equipotential surface is zero.

➢ Electric field is always perpendicular to equipotential surface.

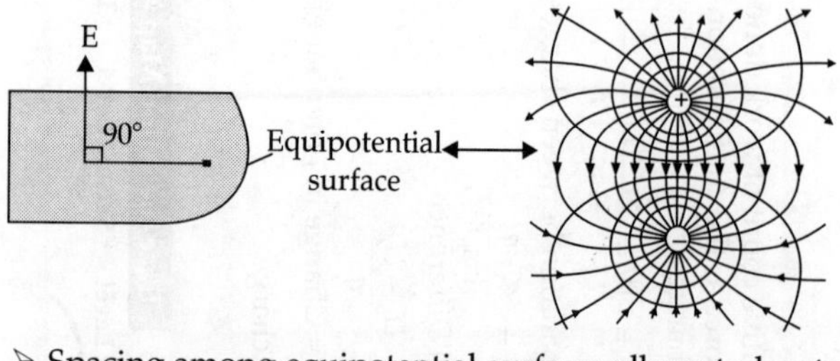

➢ Spacing among equipotential surfaces allows to locate regions of strong and weak fields.

➢ Equipotential surfaces never intersect each other. If they intersect then the intersecting point of two equipotential surfaces results in two values of electric potential at that point, which is impossible.

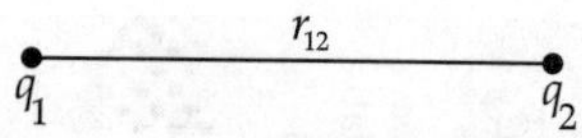

➢ **Potential energy of a system of two charges:**

$$U = \frac{1}{4\pi\varepsilon_0}\cdot\frac{q_1q_2}{r_{12}}$$

➢ **Potential energy of a system of three charges:**

$$U = \frac{1}{4\pi\varepsilon_0}\left(\frac{q_1q_2}{r_{12}} + \frac{q_1q_3}{r_{13}} + \frac{q_2q_3}{r_{23}}\right)$$

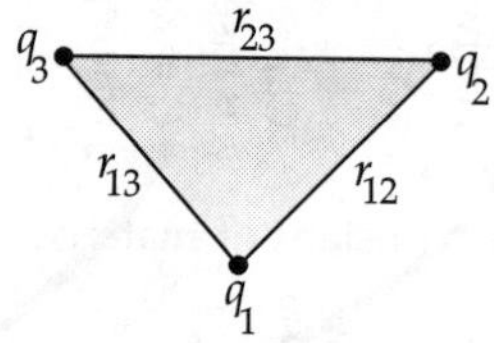

Example 2. Two point charge +10 μC and –10 μC are separated at a distance of 4 cm in air. Calculate the electrostatic potential energy of the system.

Sol. In this case:

$q_1 = +10\ \mu C, q_2 = -10\ \mu C, r = 9\text{ cm} = 9 \times 10^{-2}\text{ m}$

Using the expression of potential energy

$$U = \frac{1}{4\pi\varepsilon_0}\cdot\frac{q_1q_2}{r}$$

$$= \frac{9\times10^9\times10\times10^{-6}\times(-10\times10^{-6})}{9\times10^{-2}}$$

$$= -100 \times 10^{9-6-6+2}$$

$$= -100 \times 10^{-1}$$

$$= -10\text{ J}$$

This is the required value of electrostatic potential energy.

➢ **Potential energy due to single charge in an external field:** Potential energy of q at a distance r in an external field.

$$U = qV(\vec{r})$$

Here, $V(\vec{r})$ is the external potential at point r.

➢ Potential energy due to two charges in an external field

$$U = q_1V(\vec{r_1}) + q_2V(\vec{r_2}) + \frac{1}{4\pi\varepsilon_0}\cdot\frac{q_1q_2}{r_{12}}$$

➢ **Potential energy of a dipole in an external field:** When a dipole of charge $q_1 = +q$ and $q_2 = -q$ having separation '$2a$' is placed in an external field ($\vec{E}$).

$U(\theta) = -pE\cos\theta$

Here, $p = 2aq$ and θ is the angle between electric field and dipole.

Conductrors and Insulators

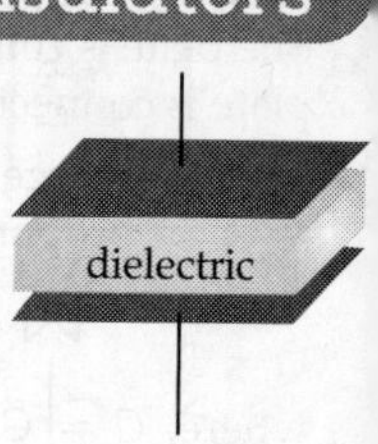

➢ Conductors are the materials through which charge can move freely. **Examples:** metals, semi-metals as carbon, graphite, antimony and arsenic.

➢ Insulators are materials in which the electrical current will not flow easily. Such materials cannot be grounded and do not easily transfer electrons. **Examples:** plastics and glass.

Dielectrics

- These are the material in which induced dipole moment is linearly proportional to applied electric field.
- Electrical displacement or electrical flux density $D = \varepsilon_r\varepsilon_0 E$.

where, ε_r= relative permittivity, ε_0 = permittivity of free space and E is electric field.

- If a dielectric is kept in between the plates of capacitor, capacitance increases by factor 'κ' (kappa) known as dielectric constant, so $C = \kappa\varepsilon_0 \frac{A}{d}$

where, A = area

κ = dielectric constant of material also called relative permittivity $\kappa = \varepsilon_r = \frac{\varepsilon}{\varepsilon_0}$

Material	Dielectric Constant (κ)	Dielectric strength (10^6 V/m)
Air	1.00059	3
Paper	3.7	16
Pyrex Glass	5.6	14
Water	80	-

- In dielectric, polarisation and production of induced charge takes place when dielectric is kept in an external electric field.

Electric Polarization

- Electric polarization P is the difference between electric fields D (induced) and E (imposed) in dielectric due to bound and free charges written as $P = \frac{D-E}{4\pi}$
- In terms of electric susceptibility: $P = \chi_e E$
- In MKS: $P = \varepsilon_0\chi_e E$,
- The dielectric constant κ is always greater than 1 as $\chi_e > 0$

Capacitor

- A capacitor is a device which is used to store charge.
- Amount of charge 'Q' stored by the capacitor depends on voltage applied and size of capacitor.
- Capacitor consists of two similar conducting plates placed at a certain distance from each other where one plate is connected to positive terminal while other plate is connected to negative terminal.
- Electric charge stored between plates of capacitor is directly proportional to potential difference between its plates, i.e.,

  $Q = CV$

  where, C = Capacitance of capacitor, V = potential difference between the plates
- In capacitor, energy is stored in the form of electrical energy, in the space between the plates.

Capacitance

- Capacitance of a capacitor is ratio of magnitude of charge stored on the plate to potential difference between the plates, written as $C = \frac{Q}{\Delta V}$

  where, C = capacitance in farads (F), Q = charge in Coulombs (C), ΔV = electric potential difference in Volts (V),

Example 2. A potential difference of 250 V is applied across the plates of a 25μF capacitor. Calculate the charge on the plates.

Sol. In this case;

$Q = ?$, $C = 25\mu F$ & $V = 250$ volts

Using the formula,

$$Q = CV$$
$$= 25 \times 10^{-6} \times 250$$
$$= 6250 \times 10^{-6}$$
$$Q = 6.25 \times 10^{-3}\ C$$

- SI unit of capacitance is farad (F)
- $$1\ F = \frac{1\ C}{1\ V} = 9\times10^{11} \text{ stat farad,}$$

  where, stat-farad is electrostatic unit of capacitance in C.G.S. system.
- Capacitance of a conductor depends on size, shape, medium and other conductors in surrounding.
- Parallel plate capacitor with dielectric between its plates has capacitance which is given as:

$$C = \kappa\varepsilon_0 \frac{A}{d},$$

where, $\varepsilon_0 = 8.85 \times 10^{-12}$ F/m

Example 4. The plates of two parallel plate capacitors have areas 50 cm² and 250 cm² with same charge. If the distance between the plates of first capacitor is 18 cm, what should be the distance between the plates of second capacitor so that potential difference is same ?

Sol. In this case,

$$A_1 = 50\text{ cm}^2 = 50 \times 10^{-4}\text{m}^2$$
$$A_2 = 250\text{ cm}^2 = 250 \times 10^{-4}\text{m}^2$$
$$d_1 = 18\text{ cm} = 18 \times 10^{-2}\text{m}$$
$$d_2 = ?$$

Equating the potentials of two capacitors; $V_1 = V_2$

$$\frac{Q_1}{C_1} = \frac{Q_2}{C_2}$$
$$C_1 = C_2 \quad (\because Q_1 = Q_2)$$
$$\frac{A_1\varepsilon_0}{d_1} = \frac{A_2\varepsilon_0}{d_2}$$
$$d_2 = \frac{A_2}{A_1}\times d_1$$
$$= \frac{250\times10^{-4}}{50\times10^{-4}}\times 18\times10^{-2}$$
$$= 90 \times 10^{-2}$$
$$d_2 = 90\text{ cm}$$

- Capacitor having capacitance of 1 Farad is too large

for electronics applications, so components with lesser values of capacitance such as μ (micro), n (nano) and p (pico) are applied such as:

PREFIX	MULTIPLIER	
μ	10^{-6} (millionth)	$1\ \mu F = 10^{-6} F$
n	10^{-9}(thousand millionth)	$1\ nF = 10^{-9} F$
p	10^{-12} (million-millionth)	$1\ pF = 10^{-12} F$

Combination of Capacitors in Series and Parallel

Capacitors in series

➤ If a number of capacitors of capacitances C_1, C_2, C_3, ... C_n are connected in series, then their equivalent capacitance is given by:

$$\frac{1}{C_s} = \frac{1}{C_1} + \frac{1}{C_2} + \frac{1}{C_3} + \dots\dots\dots\dots \frac{1}{C_n}$$

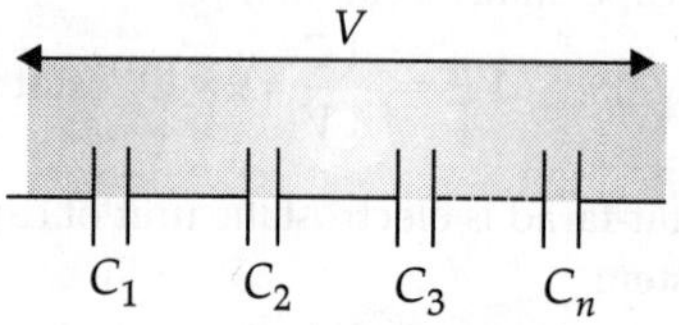

➤ In series combination, the charge on each capacitor is same, but the potential difference on each capacitor depends on their respective capacitance, i.e.,

$q_1 = q_2 = q_3 \dots\dots\dots\dots q_n = q$

➤ If V_1, V_2, V_3, ..., V_n be the potential differences across the capacitors and V be the emf of the charging battery, then

$V = V_1 + V_2 + V_3 + \dots\dots\dots + V_n$

➤ As charge on each capacitor is same, therefore

$q = V_1C_1 = V_2C_2 = V_3C_3 \dots\dots\dots$

the potential difference is inversely proportional to the capacitance, i.e.,

$$V \propto \frac{1}{C}$$

➤ In series, potential difference across largest capacitance is minimum.

➤ The equivalent capacitance in series combination is less than the smallest capacitance in combination.

Capacitors in parallel

➤ If a number of capacitors of capacitances C_1, C_2, C_3 .... C_n are connected in parallel, then their equivalent capacitance is given by,

$C_p = C_1 + C_2 + C_3 + \dots\dots\dots\dots + C_n$

➤ In parallel combination, the potential difference across each capacitor is same and equal to the emf of the charging battery, i.e.,

$V_1 = V_2 = V_3 = \dots\dots\dots\dots = V_n = V$

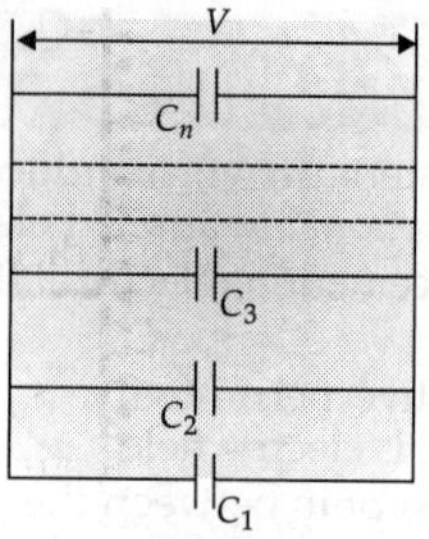

while the charge on different capacitors may be different.

➤ If q_1, q_2, q_3, ..., q_n be the charges on the different capacitors, then

$$q_1 + q_2 + q_3 + \dots\dots\dots\dots + q_n = VC_p$$

➤ As potential drop across each capacitor is same, so

$$\Rightarrow \quad V = \frac{q_1}{C_1} = \frac{q_2}{C_2} = \frac{q_3}{C_3} = \dots\dots = \frac{q_n}{C_n}$$

➤ The charges on capacitors are directly proportional to capacitances, i.e., $q \propto C$

➤ Parallel combination is useful when large capacitance with large charge gets accumulated on combination.

➤ Force of attraction between parallel plate capacitor will be $F = \frac{1}{2}\left[\frac{QV}{d}\right] = \frac{1}{2}QE$ where Q is charge on capacitor.

Capacitance of parallel plate capacitor with and without dielectric medium between the plates

➤ Parallel plate capacitor is a capacitor with two identical plane parallel plates separated by a small distance where space between them is filled by dielectric medium.

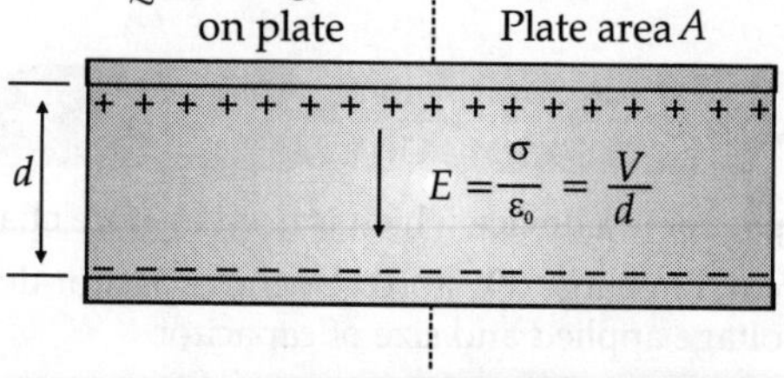

➤ The electric field between two large parallel plates is given as: $E = \frac{\sigma}{\varepsilon_0}$,

Where, σ = surface charge density and ε = permittivity

Surface charge density, $\sigma = \frac{Q}{A}$,

where, Q = charge on plate and A = plate area

➤ Capacitance of parallel-plate capacitor with area A separated by a distance d is written as $C = \varepsilon_r \varepsilon_0 \frac{A}{d}$

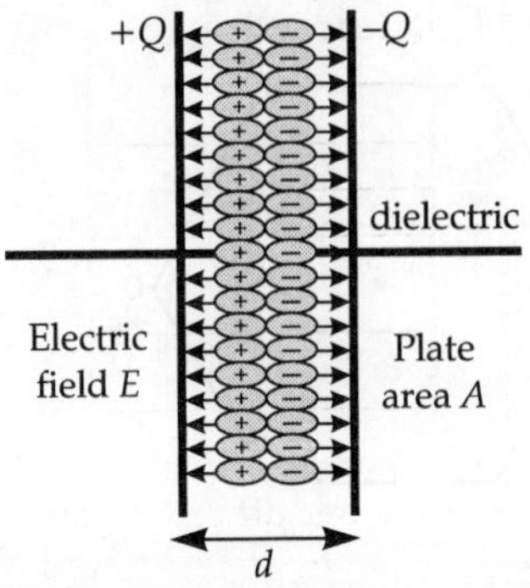

- If a dielectric slab is placed in between the plates of a capacitor, then its capacitance will increase by certain amount.
- Capacitance of parallel plate capacitor depends on plate area A, distance d between the plates, medium between the plates (κ) and not on charge on the plates or potential difference between the plates.
- If we have number of dielectric slabs of same area as the plates of the capacitor and thicknesses t_1, t_2, t_3,.... and dielectric constant κ_1, κ_2, κ_3...... between the plates, then the capacitance of the capacitor is given by

$$C = \frac{\varepsilon_0 A}{\frac{t_1}{\kappa_1} + \frac{t_2}{\kappa_2} + \frac{t_3}{\kappa_3} + ...},$$

Where, $d = t_1 + t_2 + t_3 + ...$

- If slab of conductor of thickness t is introduced between the plates, then

$$C = \frac{\varepsilon_0 A}{\frac{t}{\kappa} + \frac{(d-t)}{1}} = \frac{\varepsilon_0 A}{\frac{t}{\infty} + \frac{(d-t)}{1}}$$

$$C = \frac{\varepsilon_0 A}{d-t} \quad (\because \kappa = \infty \text{ for a conductor})$$

- When the medium between the plates consists of slabs of same thickness but areas A_1, A_2, A_3,... and dielectric constants κ_1, κ_2, κ_3..., then capacitance is given by

$$C = \frac{\varepsilon_0(\kappa_1 A_1 + \kappa_2 A_2 + \kappa_3 A_3 ....)}{d}$$

$$\therefore \kappa = \frac{C_m}{C_0} = \frac{\text{capacitance in medium}}{\text{capacitance in vacuum}}$$

- When space between the plates is partly filled with medium of thickness t and dielectric constant κ, then capacitance will be:

$$C = \frac{\varepsilon_0 A}{d - t + \frac{t}{\kappa}} = \frac{\varepsilon_0 A}{d - t\left(1 - \frac{1}{\kappa}\right)}$$

When there is no medium between the plates, then κ =1, so

$$C_{vacuum} = \frac{\varepsilon_0 A}{d}$$

- Capacitance of spherical conductor of radius R in a medium of dielectric constant κ is given by

$$C = 4\pi\varepsilon_0 \kappa R$$

Energy Stored in Capacitor

- In capacitor, energy gets stored when a work is done on moving a positive charge from negative conductor to positive conductor against the repulsive forces.

$$U = \frac{1}{2}\frac{Q^2}{C} = \frac{1}{2}QV = \frac{1}{2}CV^2$$

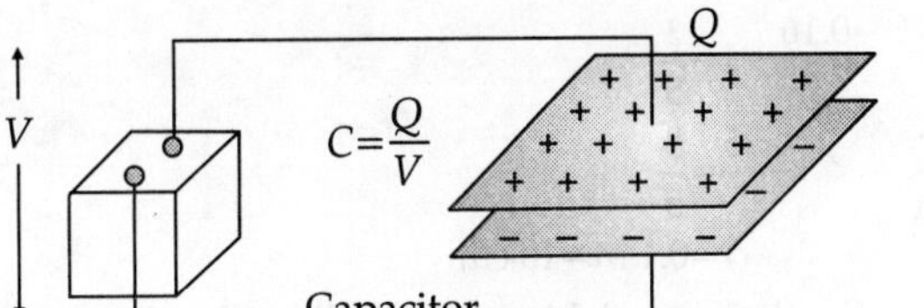

Capacitor

- **Polar atom:** Atom in which positive and negative charges possess asymmetric charge distribution about its centre.
- **Polarisation:** The stretching of atoms of a dielectric slab under an applied electric field.
- **Dielectric strength:** The maximum value of electric field that can be applied to dielectric without its electric breakdown.
- **Dielectric:** It is an electrically insulated or non-conducting material considered for its electric susceptibility.
- **Permittivity:** It is a property of a dielectric medium that shows the forces which electric charges placed in medium exerts on each other.

OR

It is the measure of resistance that is encountered when forming an electric field in a particular medium. More specifically, permittivity describes the amount of charge needed to generate one unit of electric flux in a particular medium.

NCERT CORNER

Exercise Questions

Q. 1. Two charges 5×10^{-8} C and -3×10^{-8} C are located 16 cm apart. At what point(s) on the line joining the two charges is the electric potential zero? Take the potential at infinity to be zero. [NCERT Ex. Q. 2.1, Page 79]

Ans. Given that,

$q_1 = 5 \times 10^{-8}$ C

$q_2 = -3 \times 10^{-8}$ C

$d = 16$ cm $= 0.16$ m

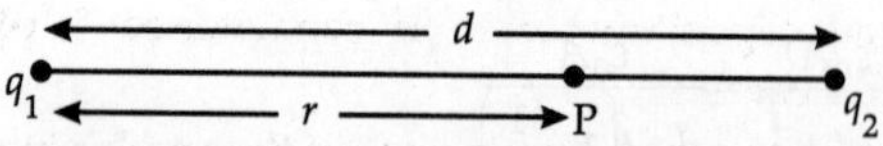

Now, let a point P on the line joining the two charges,

r = Distance of point P from charge q_1

Let the electric potential, V at point P be zero.

Potential at point P is the sum of potentials caused by charges q_1 and q_2 respectively.

$$\therefore V = \frac{q_1}{4\pi\varepsilon_0 r} + \frac{q_2}{4\pi\varepsilon_0 (d-r)} \quad \ldots\text{(i)}$$

Where,

ε_0 = Permittivity of free space

For $V = 0$, equation (i) becomes

$$\frac{q_1}{4\pi\varepsilon_0 r} = -\frac{q_2}{4\pi\varepsilon_0 (d-r)}$$

$$\frac{q_1}{r} = \frac{-q_2}{d-r}$$

$$\frac{5\times10^{-8}}{r} = -\frac{(-3\times10^{-8})}{(0.16-r)}$$

$$\frac{0.16}{r} - 1 = \frac{3}{5}$$

$$\frac{0.16}{r} = \frac{8}{5}$$

$$r = 0.1 \text{ m} = 10 \text{ cm}$$

So, the potential is zero at a distance of 10 cm from the positive charge between the charges.

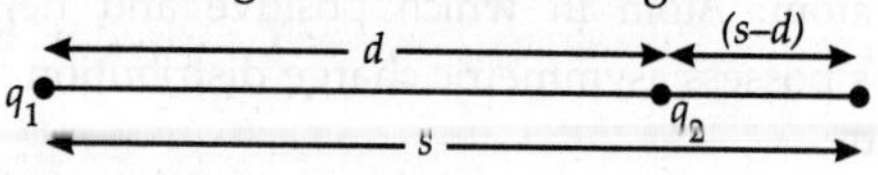

Let's assume a point P is outside the system of two charges at a distance s from the negative charge, where potential is zero, as shown in the figure shown above.

For above arrangement, potential is given by,

$$V = \frac{q_1}{4\pi\varepsilon_0 s} + \frac{q_2}{4\pi\varepsilon_0 (s-d)} \quad \ldots\text{(ii)}$$

For $V = 0$, equation (ii) reduces to

$$\frac{q_1}{4\pi\varepsilon_0 s} = -\frac{q_2}{4\pi\varepsilon_0 (s-d)}$$

$$\frac{q_1}{s} = \frac{-q_2}{s-d}$$

$$\frac{5\times10^{-8}}{s} = -\frac{(-3\times10^{-8})}{(s-0.16)}$$

$$1 - \frac{0.16}{s} = \frac{3}{5}$$

$$\therefore \frac{0.16}{s} = \frac{2}{5}$$

So that, $s = 0.4\ m = 40$ cm

That is, the required point is 40 cm away from q_1 and (40 – 16) = 24 cm from q_2 such that, potential is zero.

Q. 2. A regular hexagon of side 10 cm has a charge 5 μC at each of its vertices. Calculate the potential at the centre of the hexagon. [NCERT Ex. Q. 2.2, Page 79]

Ans. According to the above conditions, the figure shows six equal amounts of charges, q, at the vertices of a regular hexagon.

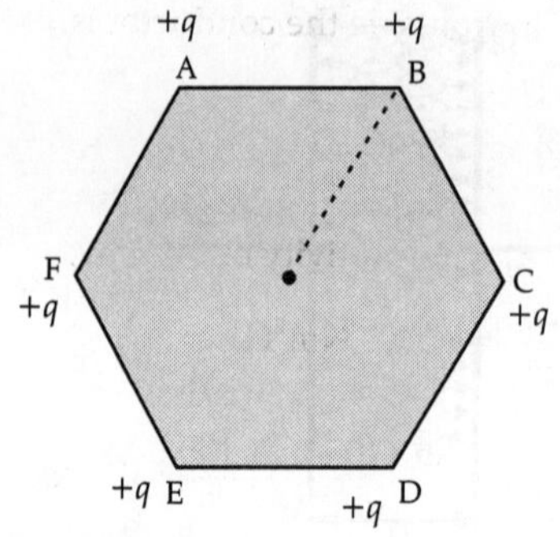

Given that,

$q = 5\ \mu C = 5 \times 10^{-6}$ C

Side of the hexagon, $l = AB = BC = CD = DE = EF = FA$ = 10 cm

Distance of each vertex from centre O, d = 10 cm

Electric potential at point O,

Where, $V = \frac{6\times q}{4\pi\varepsilon_0 d}$

ε_0 = Permittivity of free space

$$\frac{1}{4\pi\varepsilon_0} = 9\times10^9 \text{ NC}^{-2}\text{ m}^2$$

So that $V = \frac{6\times9\times10^9\times5\times10^{-6}}{0.1}$

$$= 2.7\times10^6 \text{ V}$$

So, the potential at the centre of the hexagon is 2.7×10^6 V.

Q. 3. Two charges 2 μC and –2 μC are placed at points *A* and *B*, 6 cm apart.

(a) Identify an equipotential surface of the system.

(b) What is the direction of the electric field at every point on this surface? [NCERT Ex. Q. 2.3, Page 79]

Ans. According to the condition of the question is represented in the shown figure.

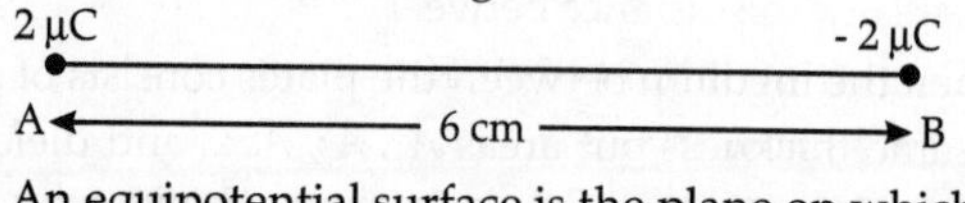

(a) An equipotential surface is the plane on which total potential is zero everywhere. This plane is normal to line *AB*. The plane is located at the mid-point of line *AB* because the magnitude of charges is the same.

(b) The direction of the electric field at every point on this surface is normal to the plane in the direction of AB.

Q. 4. A spherical conductor of radius 12 cm has a charge of 1.6×10^{-7}C distributed uniformly on its surface. What is the electric field

(a) inside the sphere.

(b) just outside the sphere

(c) at a point 18 cm from the centre of the sphere

[NCERT Ex. Q. 2.4, Page 79]

Ans. Given that,

Radius of the spherical conductor, r = 12 cm = 0.12 m

Charge is uniformly distributed over the conductor, $q = 1.6 \times 10^{-7}$ C

(a) As we know that,

An Electric field inside a spherical conductor is zero. This is because if there is field inside the conductor, then charges will move to neutralise it.

(b) Electric field E just outside the conductor is,

$$E=\frac{q}{4\pi\varepsilon_0 r^2}$$

Where,

ε_0 = Permittivity of free space

$$\frac{1}{4\pi\varepsilon_0}=9\times10^9\ Nm^2C^{-2}$$

So, $$E=\frac{1.6\times10^{-7}\times9\times10^9}{(0.12)^2}=10^5\ NC^{-1}$$

So, the electric field just outside the sphere is $10^5\ NC^{-1}$.

(c) Let the electric field at a point 18 m from the centre of the sphere = E_1

Distance of the point from the centre, d = 18 cm = 0.18 m

$$E_1=\frac{q}{4\pi\varepsilon_0 d^2}$$

$$=\frac{9\times10^9\times1.6\times10^{-7}}{(18\times10^{-2})^2}$$

$$=4.4\times10^4\ N/C$$

So, the electric field at a point 18 cm from the centre of the sphere is $4.4\times10^4\ NC^{-1}$.

Q. 5. A parallel plate capacitor with air between the plates has a capacitance of 8 pF (1 pF = 10^{-12} F). What will be the capacitance if the distance between the plates is reduced by half, and the space between them is filled with a substance of dielectric constant 6?

[NCERT Ex. Q. 2.5, Page 79]

Ans. Given that,

Capacitance between the parallel plates of the capacitor, C = 8 pF

Initially, the distance between the parallel plates = d

Dielectric constant of air, K = 1

As we know the capacitance, C is,

$$C=\frac{K\varepsilon_0 A}{d}$$

$$=\frac{\varepsilon_0 A}{d} \quad ...(i)$$

Where,

A = Area of each plate

ε_0 = Permittivity of free space

Now, If distance between the plates is reduced to half, then new distance, $d' = \frac{d}{2}$

Dielectric constant of the substance filled in between the plates, K' = 6

So, the new capacitance of the capacitor will be :

$$C'=\frac{K'\varepsilon_0 A}{d}=\frac{6\varepsilon_0 A}{\frac{d}{2}} \quad ...(ii)$$

Now, taking ratios of equations (i) and (ii),

$$C'=2\times6C$$

$$=12C=12\times8=96\ pF$$

So, the capacitance between the plates is 96 pF.

Q. 6. Three capacitors each of capacitance 9 pF are connected in series.

(a) What is the total capacitance of the combination?

(b) What is the potential difference across each capacitor if the combination is connected to a 120 V supply? **[NCERT Ex. Q. 2.6, Page 79]**

Ans. (a) Given that,

Capacitance of each of the three capacitors, C = 9 pF

Equivalent capacitance (C') of the combination of the capacitors is,

$$\frac{1}{C'}=\frac{1}{C}+\frac{1}{C}+\frac{1}{C}$$

$$=\frac{1}{9}+\frac{1}{9}+\frac{1}{9}=\frac{3}{9}=\frac{1}{3}$$

$$\therefore \quad C' = 3\ \mu F$$

So, total capacitance of the combination is 3 μF.

(b) Given that,

Supply voltage, V = 100 V

Potential difference (V') across each capacitor is equal to one-third of the supply voltage.

$$\therefore V'=\frac{V}{3}=\frac{120}{3}=40\ V$$

So, the potential difference across each capacitor is 40 V.

Q. 7. Three capacitors of capacitances 2 pF, 3 pF and 4 pF are connected in parallel.

(a) What is the total capacitance of the combination?

(b) Determine the charge on each capacitor if the combination is connected to a 100 V supply.

[NCERT Ex. Q. 2.7, Page 79]

Ans. (a) Given that,

C_1 = 2 pF

C_2 = 3 pF

C_3 = 4 pF

For the parallel combination of the capacitors, equivalent capacitor C' is the algebraic sum,

C' = 2+3+4 = 9 pF

So, total capacitance of the combination is 9 pF.

(b) Given that,

Supply voltage, V = 100 V

The voltage through all the three capacitors is same

$\Rightarrow V = 100\ V$

Charge on a capacitor of capacitance C and potential difference V is given by the relation,

$$q = VC \quad ...(i)$$

For C = 2 pF,

Charge = VC = 100×2 = 200 pC = 2×10^{-10} C

For C = 3 pF,

Charge = VC = 100×3 = 300 pC = 3×10^{-10} C

For C = 4 pF,

Charge = VC = 100×4 = 400 pC = 4×10^{-10} C

Q. 8. In a parallel plate capacitor with air between the plates, each plate has an area of 6 × 10^{-3} m² and the distance between the plates is 3 mm. Calculate the capacitance of the capacitor. If this capacitor is connected to a 100 V supply, what is the charge on each plate of the capacitor? **[NCERT Ex. Q. 2.8, Page 79]**

Ans. Given that,

Area of each plate of the parallel plate capacitor, $A = 6 \times 10^{-3}$ m²

Distance between the plates, $d = 3$ mm $= 3 \times 10^{-3}$ m

Supply voltage, $V = 100$ V

As we know the capacitance C of a parallel plate capacitor is given by,

$$C = \frac{\varepsilon_0 A}{d}$$

Where,

ε_0 = Permittivity of free space
$= 8.854 \times 10^{-12} N^{-1}m^{-2}C^2$

$$C = \frac{[8.854 \times 10^{-12} \times 6 \times 10^{-3}]}{3 \times 10^{-3}}$$

$$= 17.71 \times 10^{-12} F$$

$$V = \frac{q}{C}$$

$$\therefore q = CV$$

$$= 100 \times 17.71 \times 10^{-12} = 1.771 \times 10^{-9} C$$

So, the capacitance of the capacitor is 17.71 pF and charge on each plate is 1.771×10^{-9} C.

Q. 9. Explain what would happen if in the capacitor given in Q. 8, a 3 mm thick mica sheet (of dielectric constant = 6) were inserted between the plates,

(a) While the voltage supply remained connected.

(b) After the supply was disconnected.

[NCERT Ex. Q. 2.9, Page 80]

Ans. (a) Given that,

Dielectric constant of the mica sheet, $K = 6$

Initial capacitance,

$$C = 1.771 \times 10^{-11} F$$

Supply voltage, $V = 100$ V

New capacitance,

$$C' = KC$$
$$= 6 \times 1.771 \times 10^{-11}$$
$$= 10.6 \times 10^{-11} F$$

New charge, $q' = C'V = 100 \times 10.6 \times 10^{-11}$
$= 10.6 \times 10^{-9}$ C

As the capacitor is connected to supply, the potential across the plates remains 100 V.

(b) Dielectric constant, $K = 6$

Initial capacitance, $C = 1.771 \times 10^{-11}$ F

New capacitance, $C' = KC = 6 \times 1.771 \times 10^{-11} = 106$ pF

So, if supply voltage is removed, then there will be no effect on the amount of charge on the plates.

Charge $= 1.771 \times 10^{-9}$ C

Potential across the plates is given by,

$$\therefore V' = \frac{q}{C'}$$

$$= \frac{1.771 \times 10^{-9}}{106 \times 10^{-12}} = 16.7 V$$

Q. 10. A 12 pF capacitor is connected to a 50 V battery. How much electrostatic energy is stored in the capacitor?
[NCERT Ex. Q. 2.10, Page 80]

Ans. Given that,

Capacitor of the capacitance, $C = 12$ pF $= 12 \times 10^{-12}$ F

Potential difference, $V = 50$ V

As we know the, electrostatic energy stored in the capacitor is,

$$E = \frac{1}{2}CV^2$$

$$= \frac{1}{2} \times 12 \times 10^{-12} \times (50)^2$$

$$= 1.5 \times 10^{-8} J$$

So, the electrostatic energy stored in the capacitor is 1.5×10^{-8} J.

Q. 11. A 600 pF capacitor is charged by a 200 V supply. It is then disconnected from the supply and is connected to another uncharged 600 pF capacitor. How much electrostatic energy is lost in the process?

[NCERT Ex. Q. 2.11, Page 80]

Ans. Capacitance of the capacitor, $C = 600$ pF

Potential difference, $V = 200$ V

Electrostatic energy stored in the capacitor is given by,

$$E = \frac{1}{2}CV^2$$

$$= \frac{1}{2} \times 600 \times 10^{-12} \times 200^2$$

$$= 1.2 \times 10^{-5} J$$

If supply is disconnected from the capacitor and another capacitor of capacitance C = 600 pF is connected to it, then equivalent capacitance (C′) of the combination is given by,

$$\frac{1}{C'} = \frac{1}{C} + \frac{1}{C}$$

$$= \frac{1}{600} + \frac{1}{600} = \frac{2}{600} = \frac{1}{300}$$

New electrostatic energy can be calculated as

$$E' = \frac{1}{2} \times C' \times V^2$$

$$= \frac{1}{2} \times 300 \times 200^2$$

$$= 0.6 \times 10^{-5} J$$

Loss in electrostatic energy $= E - E'$

$$= 1.2 \times 10^{-5} - 0.6 \times 10^{-5}$$
$$= 0.6 \times 10^{-5}$$
$$= 6 \times 10^{-6} J$$

Therefore, the electrostatic energy lost in the process is 6×10^{-6} J.

□□

CHAPTER 3

CURRENT ELECTRICITY

Electric Current

- Electric current is defined as the rate of flow of charge, across the cross-section of conductor i.e.,

$$I = \frac{dq}{dt}$$

Scan to know more about this topic

Current Electricity

- When charge flows at a constant rate, the corresponding electric current can be written as:

$$I = \frac{q}{t}$$

- Conventional current in an external circuit flows from positive terminal to negative terminal.
- Free electrons flow from the negative terminal to the positive terminal in the external circuit.
- 1 Ampere current = 6.25×10^{18} electrons flowing per second.
- Direct current is unidirectional flow of electric charge.

Flow of Electric Charges in a Metallic Conductor

- When an electric field is applied to a metal at certain points, free electrons experience force and start moving.
- Without external applied emf, free electrons will move randomly through metal from one point to other giving zero net current.
- Motion of conducting electrons in electric field is a combination of motion due to random collisions.

Drift Velocity, Mobility and their Relation with Electric Current

- Drift velocity is an average velocity which is obtained by certain particle like electron due to the presence of electric field.
- Drift velocity is written as:

$$\vec{v}_d = -\frac{e\vec{E}}{m}\tau$$

where, relaxation time, $\tau = \frac{\lambda}{v}$, e = charge, m = mass, λ = mean free path

When electric current is set up in a conductor, electrons drift through the conductor with velocity v_d, is given as

$$v_d = \frac{I}{neA} \text{ or } I = neAv_d$$

where, I = electric current through conductor, n = number of free electrons per unit volume, A = area of cross-section, e = charge on electron

- Drift velocity of electrons under ordinary conditions is of the order of 0.1 mm/s.
- Mobility is the drift velocity of an electron when applied electric field is unity.

Mobility, $$\mu = \frac{v_d}{E}$$

or, $$\mu = \frac{e\tau E / m}{E} = \frac{e\tau}{m}$$

Electrical Resistivity and Conductivity

- Resistivity is the specific resistance that is given by the conductor having unit length and unit area of cross-section.

$$\rho = \frac{m}{ne^2\tau}$$

Conductivity is the reciprocal of resistivity, *i.e.*,

$$\sigma = \frac{1}{\rho} = \frac{ne^2\tau}{m}$$

Ohm's Law

- The flow of current through a conductor is directly proportional to the potential difference established across the ends of the conductor, provided physical conditions remain constant.

i.e., $$I \propto V$$

or, $$I = GV$$

Here, $$G = \frac{1}{R}$$

or, $$I = \frac{1}{R}V$$

or, $$V = IR$$

where, R = resistance of conductor

Electric Resistance

- It is an obstacle that is shown by a body during the flow of current:

$$R = \frac{V}{I} = \frac{m}{ne^2\tau}\frac{l}{A}$$

- The resistance of the conductor is given as:

$$R = \rho\frac{l}{A}$$

Current Electricity

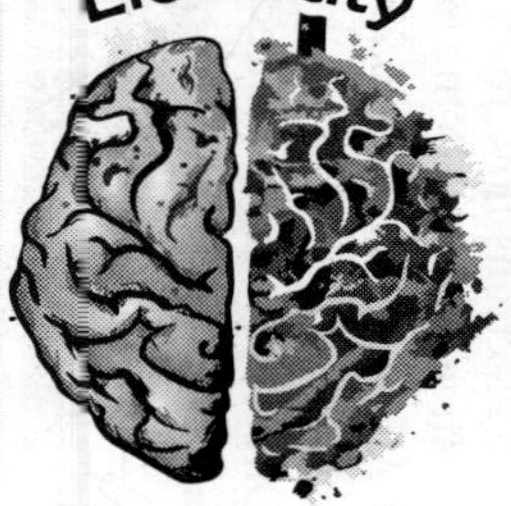

- **Electric Current**
  - Rate of flow of charge through an area,
    $i = \frac{Q}{t}$
    $i = \int \vec{J}.\vec{dS}$
- **Current density**
  - $\vec{J} = \frac{\Delta i}{\Delta s \cos\theta} = \sigma E$
  - ΔS = Area of cross-section
  - θ = Angle between Area vector and current flow
  - σ = Conductivity
- **Drift velocity**
  - $V_d = \frac{i}{neA} = \frac{J}{ne}$
- **Mobility**
  - $\mu = \frac{V_d}{E} = \frac{e\tau}{m}$
  - τ = Average collision time
- **Ohm's Law**
  - $J = \sigma E$ or $V = IR$
- **Resistivity**
  - $\rho = \frac{1}{\sigma} \Omega\,m$
- **Conductivity**
  - $\sigma = J/E$
- **Grouping of Resistors**
  - In series combination $R = R_1 + R_2 + R_3 + - - - + R_n$
    For two resistors, $R = R_1 + R_2$
  - In parallel combination $\frac{1}{R_{eq}} = \frac{1}{R_1} + \frac{1}{R_2} + - - - + \frac{1}{R_n}$
    For two resistors $R_{eq} = \frac{R_1 R_2}{R_1 + R_2}$
- **Temperature Dependence of Resistance**
  - $R = R_0 [1 + \alpha (T - T_0)]$
  - $\rho = \rho_0 [1 + \alpha (T - T_0)]$
  - R = Resistance at temperature T
  - R_0 = Resistance at temperature T_0
  - α = Temperature coefficient of resistivity
- **Wheatstone Bridge**
  - Condition for balanced wheatstone bridge
    If, $\frac{R_1}{R_2} = \frac{R_3}{R_4}$
  - $V_c = V_D$
    No current through G i.e., Ig > 0
- **Electric cell**
  - It is a device which maintains a potential difference between its two terminals.
  - EMF
    - emf $= E = \frac{W}{q}$
    - It is equal to the potential difference between the terminals when the they are not connected externally.
  - Internal Resistance
    - $V_A - V_B = E - ir$
    - r = Internal resistance of the cell
- **Grouping of cells**
  - Parallel grouping
    - $E_{eq} = \frac{E_1 r_2 + E_2 r_1}{r_1 + r_2}$, $i = \frac{E_{eq}}{R + \frac{r_1 r_2}{r_1 + r_2}}$
  - Series grouping
    - $i = \frac{E_1 + E_2}{R_1 + (r_1 + r_2)} = \frac{E_0}{R_1 + R_2}$
    - $E_0 = E_1 + E_2$, $R_2 = r_1 + r_2$
- **Kirchhoff's Rules**
  - Junction Rule
    - $i_1 + i_2 + i_4 = i_3 + i_5$
    - At any junction, the sum of currents entering the junction is equal to the sum of currents leaving the junction.
  - Loop Rule
    - The algebraic sum of all the potential difference along a closed loop is zero.
      $\Sigma E = 0$

Trace the Mind Map
▸ First Level ▸ Second Level ▸ Third Level

where, $\rho = \frac{m}{ne^2\tau}$ is specific resistance or resistivity of the material of conductor.

- In the series combination of resistances, the current is same throughout each resistor.
- In the parallel combination of resistances, the potential difference is same across each resistor.

V-I Characteristics (Linear and non-Linear)

V-I characteristics curve shows the relationship between the current flowing through an electronic device and applied voltage across its terminals.

- **Linear V-I Characteristics:**

❖ A linear V-I curve has a constant slope and hence a constant resistance. Carbon resistors and metals obey the Ohm's law and have a constant resistance. This means that the V-I curve is a straight line passing through the origin.

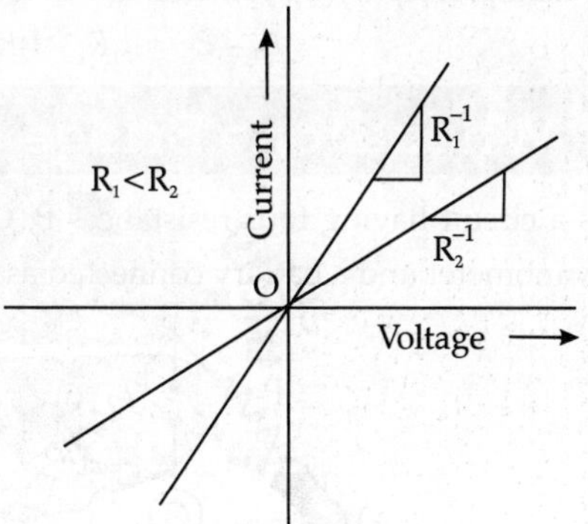

❖ An electronic component may exhibit linear characteristic only in a particular region. For example a diode shows linear behaviour mostly in its operating region.

- **Non-linear V-I Characteristics**

❖ A circuit component has a non-linear characteristic if the resistance is not constant throughout and is some function of voltage or current. The diode, for example, has varying resistance for different values of voltage.

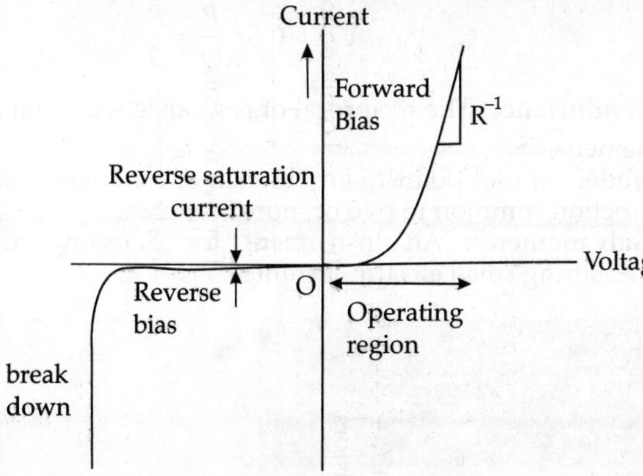

❖ However, it has linear characteristic for a narrow operating region. Note that in the graph above we can also see the maximum forward and reverse voltage in which the diode can be operated without causing breakdown and burning up of the diode.

Electrical Energy and Power

- Electrical energy is stored in the charged particles in an electric field.

$$E = V \times i \times t = i^2 \times R \times t = \frac{V^2}{R} \times t$$

were, E = Electrical energy, V = Potential difference, t = Time, i = Current, R = Resistance

- Power is the work done per unit time which is the rate of energy consumed in a circuit.

$$P = \frac{W}{t}$$

Since Voltage $V = \frac{W}{q}$,

So, $P = V\frac{q}{t} = VI \quad \left[\text{Here, } I = \frac{q}{t}\right]$

$$P = I^2R \text{ or } \frac{V^2}{R}$$

The unit of power is J/s or W (Watt).

Temperature Dependence of Resistivity

Temperature dependence of resistivity

- With small change in temperature, resistivity varies with temperature as:

$$\rho = \rho_0(1 + \alpha\, \Delta T)$$

where, α = temperature coefficient of resistivity.

Internal Resistance of Cell

- Cell is a device that maintains the potential difference that is present between the two electrodes as a result of chemical reaction.
- Internal resistance is the resistance of electrolyte that is present in a battery which resists the flow of current when connected to a circuit.
- emf (E) is the potential difference between the electrodes of cell, when no current flows through it.

Potential Difference and emf of a Cell

- **The emf and terminal potential difference of a cell:** Let emf of a cell be E and its internal resistance, r. If an external resistance R be connected across the cell through a key, then $IR = V =$ potential difference across the external resistance R. This is equal to the terminal potential difference across the cell.

$$E = V + Ir$$

$$\Rightarrow \quad I = \frac{E - V}{r}$$

So $\quad V = E - Ir$

$\therefore \quad V < E.$

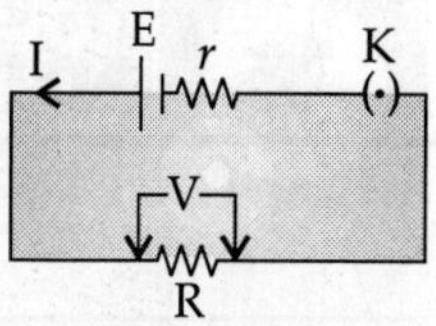

(if there is flow of current)

When current is drawn from a cell, its terminal potential difference is less than the emf.

Combination of cells in series and parallel

(i) Series combination of cells: This combination is used when an external resistance (R) of the circuit is larger as compared to the internal resistance (r) of the cell, i.e.,

$$R >> r$$

Let n cells, each of emf E and internal resistance r are connected in series across an external resistance R, then the current in the circuit will be

$$I_S = \frac{nE}{R+nr}$$

(ii) Parallel combination of cells: This combination is used when the external resistance R is smaller compared to the internal resistance (r) of the cell, i.e.,

$$R << r$$

When m cells are connected in parallel across a resistance R, then current through the resistance is given by

$$I_P = \frac{E}{R + r/m} = \frac{mE}{mR + r}$$

If m cells of emfs E_1, E_2, E_3,.....E_m and of internal resistances $r_1, r_2, r_3, ...r_m$ are connected in parallel across an external resistance R, then the current through the external resistance is given by

$$I_P = \frac{\frac{E_1}{r_1} + \frac{E_2}{r_2} + \frac{E_3}{r_3} ..... + \frac{E_m}{r_m}}{R + \left(\frac{1}{r_1} + \frac{1}{r_2} + \frac{1}{r_3} + ... + \frac{1}{r_m}\right)}$$

Kirchhoff's Laws

- Kirchhoff's Laws tell us about the relationship between voltages and currents in circuits.

Scan to know more about this topic

Introduction of Kirchhoff's Laws

- **First law**
  - Kirchhoff's first law is also known as junction law which states that for a given junction or node in a circuit, sum of the currents entering in a junction will be equal to sum of currents leaving that junction.

$$I_1 = I_2 + I_3$$

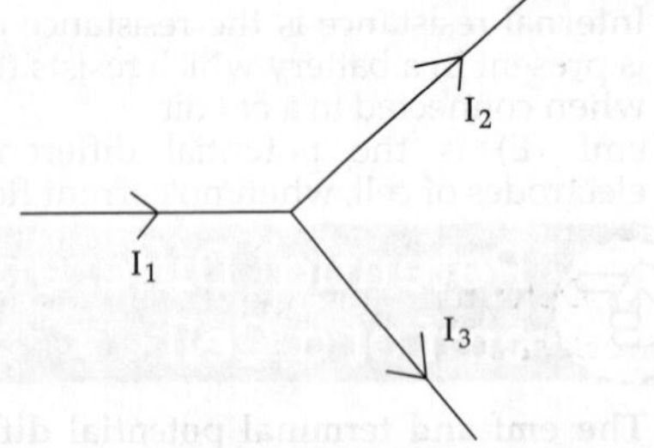

OR

- The algebraic sum of all currents meeting at a junction in a closed circuit is zero.

i.e., $\Sigma I = 0$

- This is called the law of conservation of charge.

- **Second Law**
  - Kirchhoff's second law also known as loop law shows that around any closed loop in a circuit, sum of the potential differences across all elements will be zero.

i.e., $\Sigma V = 0$

or $\Sigma V = \Sigma IR$

This is called the law of conservation of energy.

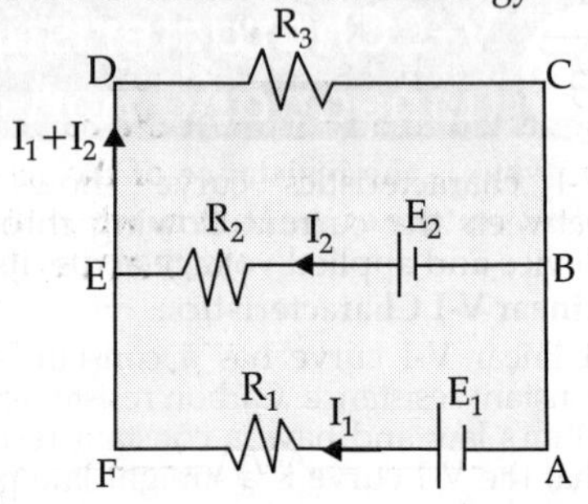

For example: Applying Junction law in loop AFEBA

$$E_1 - E_2 = I_1R_1 - I_2R_2$$

Wheatstone Bridge

- It is a circuit having four resistances P, Q, R and S, a galvanometer and a battery connected as shown.

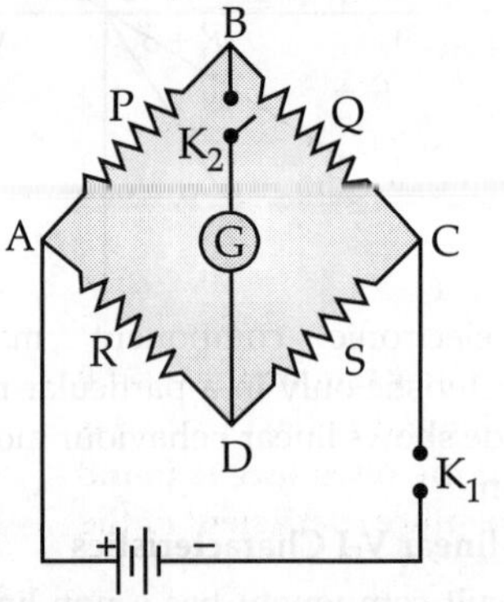

- It is a balanced bridge when there is no current passing through the galvanometer and potential at node B will be equal to potential at node D resulting as:

$$V_B \sim V_D = 0 \text{ or } \frac{P}{Q} = \frac{R}{S}$$

- **Conductance:** The reciprocal of resistance with unit as siemens, "S."
- **Node:** An end point to any branch of a network or a junction common to two or more branches.
- **Galvanometer:** An instrument for detecting and measuring small electric currents.

NCERT CORNER

Exercise Questions

Q. 1. The storage battery of a car has an emf of 12 V. If the internal resistance of the battery is 0.4 Ω, what is the maximum current that can be drawn from the battery? [NCERT Ex. Q. 3.1, Page no. 105]

Ans. The maximum current will be obtained when no external resistance is offered by wire joining the two terminals.

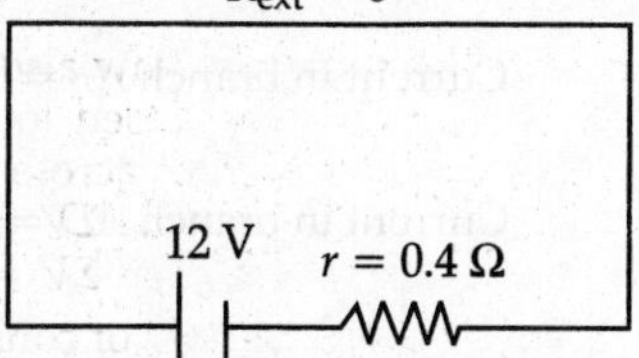

$$I = \frac{E}{R_{ext} + r}$$

$$\Rightarrow I = \frac{12}{0.4}$$

$$= 30\ A$$

$$(\because R_{ext} = 0)$$

Q. 2. A battery of emf 10 V and internal resistance 3 Ω is connected to a resistor. If the current in the circuit is 0.5 A, what is the resistance of the resistor? What is the terminal voltage of the battery when the circuit is closed?
[NCERT Ex. Q. 3.2, Page no. 105]

Ans. $I = \frac{E}{R+r}$

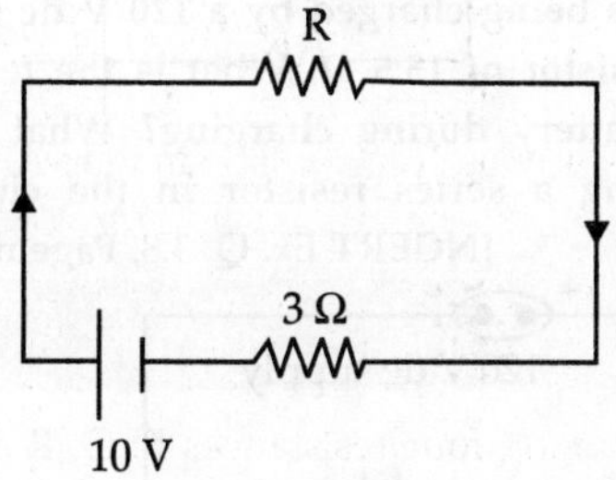

$$0.5 = \frac{10}{R+3}$$

$$R + 3 = 20$$

$$R = 17\ \Omega$$

Terminal voltage of the battery

$$V = E - Ir$$

$$V = 10 - 0.5 \times 3$$

$$= 8.5\ V$$

Q. 3. At room temperature (27.0 °C) the resistance of a heating element is 100 Ω. What is the temperature of the element if the resistance is found to be 117 Ω, given that the temperature coefficient of the material of the resistor is 1.70×10^{-4} °C^{-1}? [NCERT Ex. Q. 3.3, Page no. 105]

Ans. As $R_2 = R_1 [1 + \alpha(t_2 - t_1)]$

$\therefore$ $117 = 100[1 + 1.7 \times 10^{-4} (t - 27)]$

or $17 = 1.7 \times 10^{-2} (t - 27)$

or $1000 = t - 27$

$\therefore$ $t = 1027\ °C.$

Q. 4. A negligibly small current is passed through a wire of length 15 m and uniform cross-section 6.0×10^{-7} m^2, and its resistance is measured to be 5.0 Ω. What is the resistivity of the material at the temperature of the experiment? [NCERT Ex. Q. 3.4, Page no. 106]

Ans. We know the relation,

$$R = \rho \frac{l}{A}$$

$$5 = \rho \frac{15}{6 \times 10^{-7}}$$

$$\therefore \text{Resistivity, } \rho = \frac{30 \times 10^{-7}}{15}$$

$$= 2 \times 10^{-7}\ \Omega\ m$$

Q. 5. A silver wire has a resistance of 2.1 Ω, at 27.5 °C and a resistance of 2.7 Ω at 100 °C. Determine the temperature coefficient of resistivity of silver. [NCERT Ex. Q. 3.5, Page no. 106]

Ans. $T_1 = 27.5\ °C,$

$R_1 = 2.1\ \Omega,$

$T_2 = 100\ °C$

and $R_2 = 2.7\ \Omega$

Using the relation,

$R_2 = R_1[1 + \alpha(T_2 - T_1)]$, we have

Temperature coefficient of resistivity of silver,

$$\alpha = \frac{R_2 - R_1}{R_1(T_2 - T_1)}$$

$$= \frac{2.7 - 2.1}{2.1 \times (100 - 27.5)}$$

$$= \frac{0.6}{152.25}$$

$$= 3.94 \times 10^{-3}$$

or $= 0.0039\ °C^{-1}$

Q. 6. A heating element using nichrome wire connected to a 230 V supply draws an initial current of 3.2 A which settles after a few seconds to a steady value of 2.8 A. What is the steady temperature of the heating element if the room temperature is 27.0 °C? Temperature coefficient of resistance of nichrome averaged over the temperature range involved is 1.70×10^{-4} °C^{-1}.
[NCERT Ex. Q. 3.6, Page no. 106]

Ans. At room temperature 27 °C, the resistance of the heating element.

$$R_{27} = \frac{230}{3.2}$$

$$= 71.875\ \Omega$$

At the steady temperature t °C, the resistance.

$$R_t = \frac{230}{2.8}$$

$$= 82.143\ \Omega$$

Now, $R_2 = R_1[1 + \alpha(t_2 - t_1)]$

or $82.143 = 71.875\ [1 + 1.7 \times 10^{-4} (t - 27)]$

or, $t - 27 = \frac{82.143 - 71.875}{71.875 \times 1.7 \times 10^{-4}}$

or $840 = t - 27$

$\therefore$ $t = 867\ °C.$

Q. 7. Determine the current in each branch of the network shown in figure.

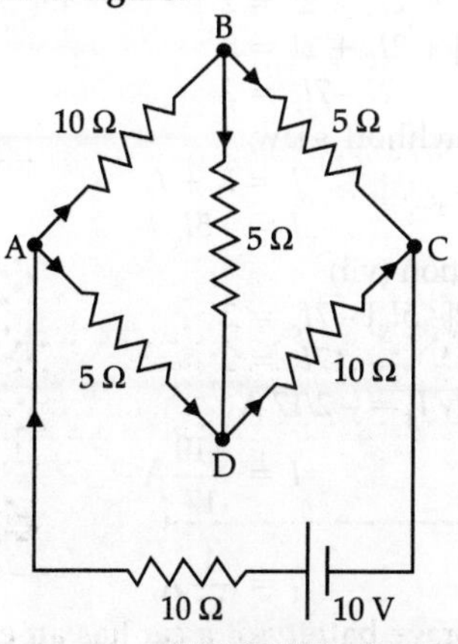

[NCERT Ex. Q. 3.7, Page no. 106]

Ans. Let us first distribute the current in different branches. Now, in different loops using Kirchhoff's IInd law,

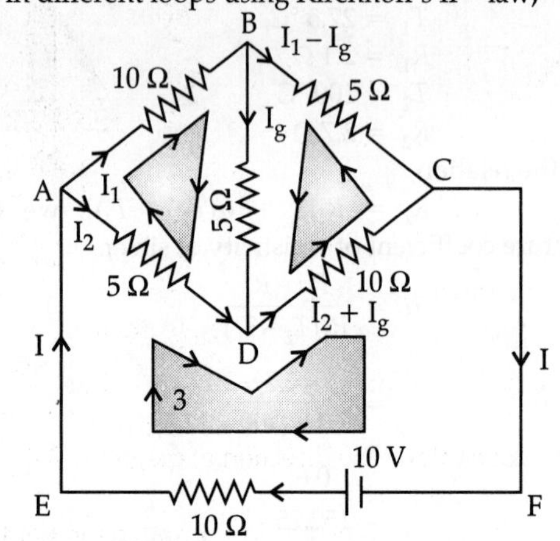

Loop 1 (ABDA)

$$\Sigma E = \Sigma IR$$

$$10I_1 + 5I_g - 5I_2 = 0$$

or $$2I_1 + I_g - I_2 = 0 \quad ...(i)$$

Loop 2 (BDCB)

$$\Sigma E = \Sigma IR$$

$$5I_g + 10[I_2 + I_g] - 5[I_1 - I_g] = 0$$

$$10I_2 + 20I_g - 5I_1 = 0$$

or $$2I_2 + 4I_g - I_1 = 0 \quad ...(ii)$$

Loop 3 (ABCFEA)

$$5I_2 + 10(I_2 + I_g) + 10I = 10$$

$$15I_2 + 10I_g + 10I = 10$$

or $$3I_2 + 2I_g + 2I = 2 \quad ...(iii)$$

Solving equations (i) and (ii)

$$2I_1 + I_g - I_2 = 0$$

$$[-I_1 + 4I_g + 2I_2 = 0] \times 2$$

or $$9I_g + 3I_2 = 0$$

or $$I_2 = -3I_g \quad ...(iv)$$

In the loop ABCDA

$$10I_1 + 5[I_1 - I_g] - 10[I_2 + I_g] - 5I_2 = 0$$

$$15I_1 - 15I_2 - 15I_g = 0$$

or $$I_1 - I_2 - I_g = 0 \quad ...(v)$$

Solving equations (ii) and (v)

$$2I_2 + 4I_g - I_1 = 0$$

or $$2(I_1 - I_2 - I_g = 0)$$

or $$2I_g + I_1 = 0$$

or $$I_1 = -2I_g \quad ...(vi)$$

Now using the result of (iv) and (vi) in equation (iii)

$$3I_2 + 2I_g + 2I = 2$$

$$-3[3I_g] + 2I_g + 2I = 2$$

or $$2I - 7I_g = 2 \quad ...(vii)$$

Using Kirchhoff's law,

$$I = I_1 + I_2$$

$$I = -5I_g$$

So, equation (vii)

$$2[-5I_g] - 7I_g = 2$$

or $$-17I_g = 2$$

So, finally $I_g = -2/17$ A

and $$I = \frac{+10}{17} \text{A}$$

Also $$I_1 = \frac{4}{17} \text{A},$$

$$I_2 = \frac{6}{17} \text{A}$$

Current in branch $AB = \frac{4}{17}$ A

Current in branch $AD = \frac{6}{17}$ A

Current in branch $BD = \frac{-2}{17}$ A

Current in branch $BC = \frac{6}{17}$ A

Current in branch $DC = \frac{4}{17}$ A

Q. 8. A storage battery of emf 8.0 V and internal resistance 0.5 Ω is being charged by a 120 V dc supply using a series resistor of 15.5 Ω. What is the terminal voltage of the battery during charging? What is the purpose of having a series resistor in the charging circuit? [NCERT Ex. Q. 3.8, Page no. 106]

Ans.

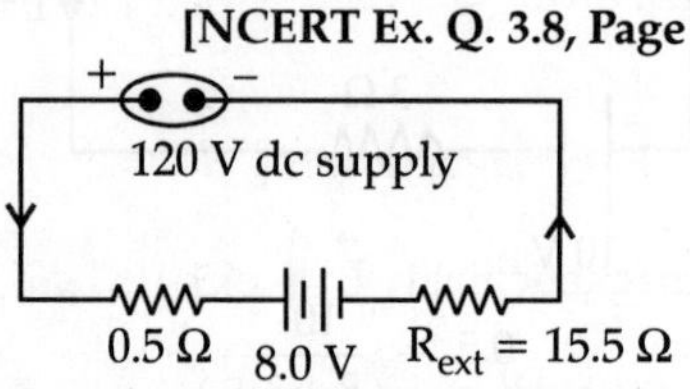

During charging, the electric current is sent into the 8.0 V battery.

The current in the circuit

$$I = \frac{E_1 - E_2}{R_{ext} + r}$$

$$= \frac{120 - 8}{15.5 + 0.5}$$

or $$I = \frac{112}{16}$$

$$= 7\,A$$

Now, terminal voltage of the battery during charging $V = E + Ir = 8 + 7(0.5) = 11.5$ V. A series resistance is joined in the charging circuit to limit the excessive current.

Q. 9. The number density of free electrons in a copper conductor estimated is 8.5 × 10[28] m[−3]. How long does an electron take to drift from one end of a wire 3.0 m long to its other end? The area of cross-section of the wire is 2.0 × 10[−6] m[2] and it is carrying a current of 3.0 A. [NCERT Ex. Q. 3.9, Page no. 106]

Ans. We can first calculate drift velocity of the electrons from the given data $I = Anev_d$

$$3 = 2 \times 10^{-6} \times 8.5 \times 10^{28} \times 1.6 \times 10^{-19} v_d$$

$$v_d = 0.11 \times 10^{-3} \text{ ms}^{-1}$$

Now time taken by an electron to drift a length of 3 m with drift speed is

$$t = \frac{l}{v_d}$$

$$= 27.27 \times 10^3 \text{ s.}$$

□□

MOVING CHARGES AND MAGNETISM

CHAPTER 4

Concept of Magnetic Field

- Magnetic field is a region around a magnet where force of magnetism acts which affects other magnets.
- Magnetic field also known as *B*-field can be pictorially represented by magnetic field lines.
- Magnetic fields are produced by electric currents, which can be macroscopic currents in wires, or microscopic currents associated with electrons in atomic orbits.
- **Lorentz Force:** When a charge q moving with velocity v enters a region where both magnetic fields and electric field exist, both field exert a force on it.

Lorentz Force, $\vec{F} = q[\vec{E} + \vec{v} \times \vec{B}]$

where, $\vec{F}$ = magnetic force, $\vec{q}$ = charge, $\vec{v}$ = velocity, $\vec{B}$ = magnetic field, $\vec{E}$ = electric field, $q\vec{E}$ = electric force on the charge, $q(\vec{v} \times \vec{B})$ = magnetic force on the charge

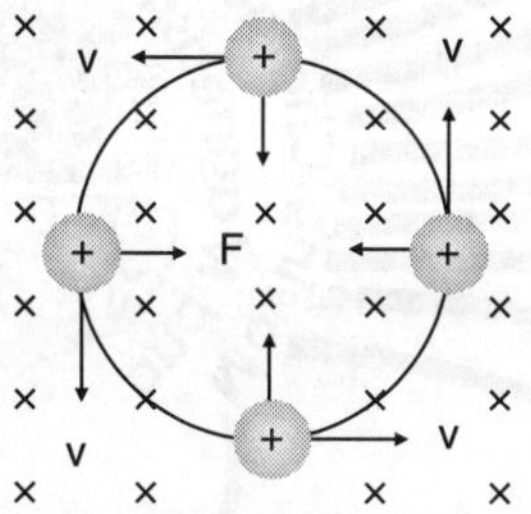

- SI unit of magnetic field is Tesla, while smaller magnetic fields are measured in terms of Gauss

$$1 \text{ Tesla} = 10^4 \text{ G}$$

- When a test charge q_0 enters a magnetic field $\vec{B}$ directed along negative *z*-axis with a velocity $\vec{v}$ making an angle θ with the *z*-axis, then,

$$\vec{F}_m = q_0(\vec{v} \times \vec{B}) = q_0 vB \sin\theta\, \hat{n}$$

Motion in a Magnetic Field

Characteristics of motion of particle in magnetic field

- Speed and kinetic energy of particle do not change, as force is always perpendicular to velocity.
- Direction of velocity will continuously change
- when θ = 0, no force will act on the particle, hence there will be no change in velocity.
- when θ = 90°, test charge describes a circle of radius $\frac{mv}{q_0 B}$,

Scan to know more about this topic

Magnetic effect of current

where, *m* is mass of the particle; larger the momentum, bigger the circle described.

- In case of θ being any other angle than 0° and 90° test charge will show circular path of radius $\frac{mv\sin\theta}{q_0 B}$ which moves along the direction of magnetic field with speed of $v\cos\theta$.
- Momentum along the direction of magnetic field will remain same.
- Angular speed of test charge $\frac{q_0 B}{m}$ is independent of initial speed of particle.
- Centripetal force on test charge $q_0 vB \sin\theta$ is independent of the mass of particle.
- When the particle enters the magnetic field with the same momentum, then radius of path will be,

$$r = \frac{mv}{q_0 B}$$

where, $r \propto \frac{1}{q_0}$

Oersted's Experiment

Oersted observed that:

- When there is no current, compass needle below a wire shows no deflection.
- When the flow of current is in single direction, then the compass needle deflects in particular direction.
- When the flow of current is reversed, deflection in compass needle occurs in opposite direction.
- From an experiment, it is concluded that an electrical current produces a magnetic field which surrounds the wire.

Biot-Savart's Law

- The magnetic field due to a current element at any nearby point is given by:

$$\vec{dB} = \left[\frac{\mu_0}{4\pi}\right] I \frac{\vec{ds} \times \vec{r}}{r^3}$$

where,

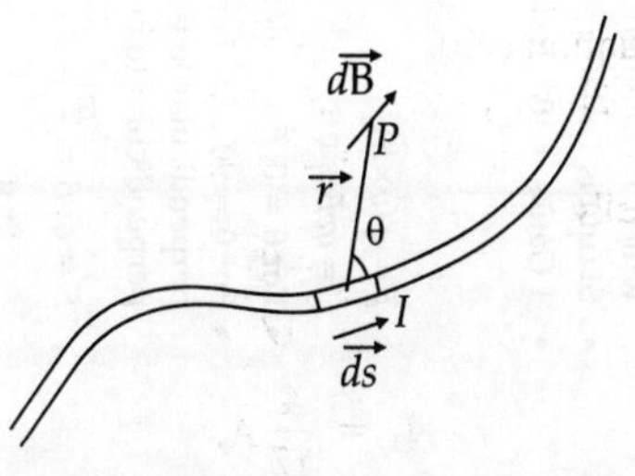

$\vec{dB}$ = Magnetic field produced by current element

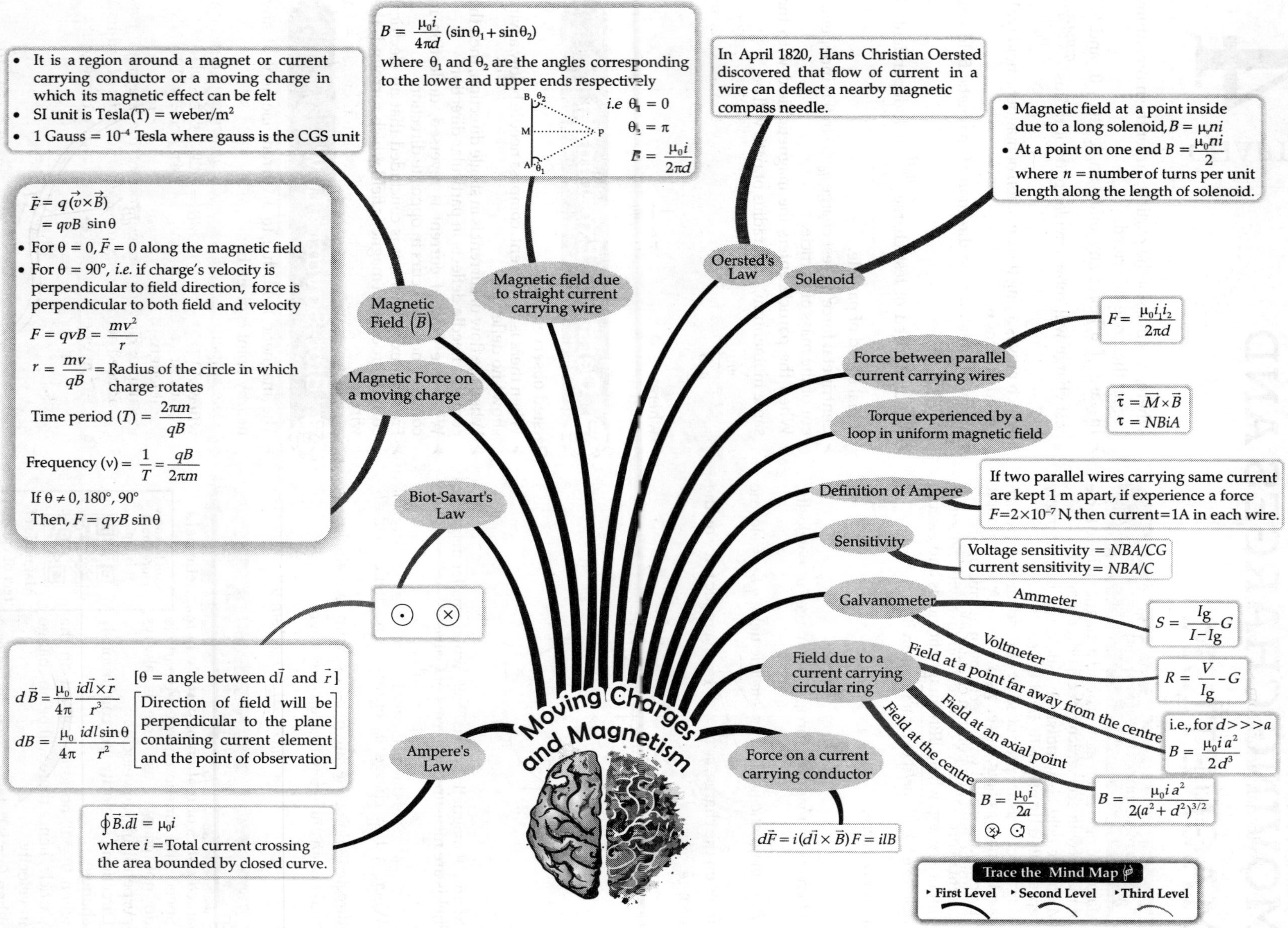
Moving Charges and Magnetism
Magnetic Field $(\vec{B})$
• It is a region around a magnet or current carrying conductor or a moving charge in which its magnetic effect can be felt
• SI unit is Tesla(T) = weber/m^2
• 1 Gauss = 10^{-4} Tesla where gauss is the CGS unit
Magnetic field due to straight current carrying wire
$B = \frac{\mu_0 i}{4\pi d}(\sin\theta_1 + \sin\theta_2)$
where θ_1 and θ_2 are the angles corresponding to the lower and upper ends respectively
B
M
P
A
i.e $\theta_1 = 0$
$\theta_2 = \pi$
$B = \frac{\mu_0 i}{2\pi d}$
Oersted's Law
In April 1820, Hans Christian Oersted discovered that flow of current in a wire can deflect a nearby magnetic compass needle.
Solenoid
• Magnetic field at a point inside due to a long solenoid, $B = \mu_0 ni$
• At a point on one end $B = \frac{\mu_0 ni}{2}$
where n = number of turns per unit length along the length of solenoid.
Magnetic Force on a moving charge
$\vec{F} = q(\vec{v} \times \vec{B})$
$= qvB \sin\theta$
• For $\theta = 0, \vec{F} = 0$ along the magnetic field
• For $\theta = 90°$, i.e. if charge's velocity is perpendicular to field direction, force is perpendicular to both field and velocity
$F = qvB = \frac{mv^2}{r}$
$r = \frac{mv}{qB}$ = Radius of the circle in which charge rotates
Time period $(T) = \frac{2\pi m}{qB}$
Frequency $(\nu) = \frac{1}{T} = \frac{qB}{2\pi m}$
If $\theta \neq 0, 180°, 90°$
Then, $F = qvB \sin\theta$
Force between parallel current carrying wires
$F = \frac{\mu_0 i_1 i_2}{2\pi d}$
Torque experienced by a loop in uniform magnetic field
$\vec{\tau} = \vec{M} \times \vec{B}$
$\tau = NBiA$
Definition of Ampere
If two parallel wires carrying same current are kept 1 m apart, if experience a force $F = 2\times10^{-7}$ N, then current = 1A in each wire.
Sensitivity
Voltage sensitivity = NBA/CG
current sensitivity = NBA/C
Galvanometer
Ammeter
$S = \frac{I_g}{I - I_g}G$
Voltmeter
$R = \frac{V}{I_g} - G$
Field due to a current carrying circular ring
Field at a point far away from the centre
i.e., for $d >> a$
$B = \frac{\mu_0 i a^2}{2d^3}$
Field at an axial point
$B = \frac{\mu_0 i a^2}{2(a^2 + d^2)^{3/2}}$
Field at the centre
$B = \frac{\mu_0 i}{2a}$
⊗ ⊙
Force on a current carrying conductor
$d\vec{F} = i(d\vec{l} \times \vec{B})\ F = ilB$
Biot-Savart's Law
⊙ ⊗
$d\vec{B} = \frac{\mu_0}{4\pi}\frac{id\vec{l} \times \vec{r}}{r^3}$
$dB = \frac{\mu_0}{4\pi}\frac{idl \sin\theta}{r^2}$
[θ = angle between $d\vec{l}$ and $\vec{r}$]
[Direction of field will be perpendicular to the plane containing current element and the point of observation]
Ampere's Law
$\oint \vec{B}.\vec{dl} = \mu_0 i$
where i = Total current crossing the area bounded by closed curve.
Trace the Mind Map
First Level
Second Level
Third Level

$\vec{ds}$ = Vector length of small section of wire in direction of current

$\vec{r}$ = Positional vector from section of wire to where magnetic field is measured

I = current in the wire

θ = Angle between $\vec{ds}$ & $\vec{r}$

μ_0 = permeability of free space and $\mu_0 = 4\pi \times 10^{-7}$ Wb/Am

The magnitude of magnetic field,

$$|\vec{dB}| = \left(\frac{\mu_0}{4\pi}\right)\frac{Idl\sin\theta}{r^2}$$

Applications of Biot-Savart's Law

➢ Magnetic field at a point in circular loop will be:

$$\vec{B} = \frac{\mu_0 IR^2}{2\left(R^2+x^2\right)^{3/2}}\vec{r} \qquad [\text{Here, } r^2 = R^2 + x^2]$$

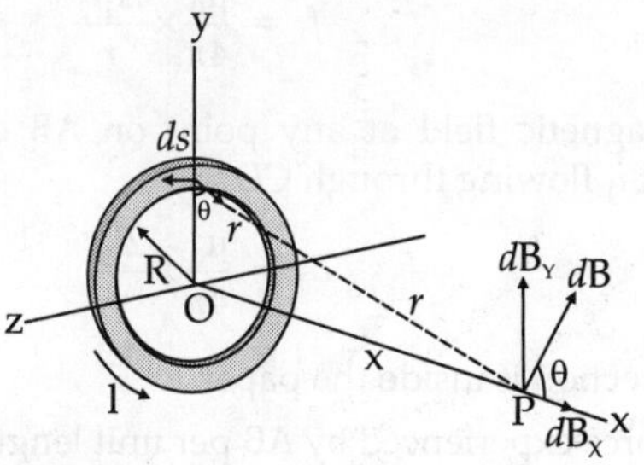

➢ Magnetic field at Centre of the coil:

$$\vec{B} = \frac{\mu_0 NI}{2R}\vec{r}, \qquad [x = 0]$$

➢ Magnetic field at very large distance from the centre :

$$B = \frac{2\mu_0 NiA}{4\pi x^3}$$

[Here, $R^2 << r^2$ or, $R^2 + x^2 \to x^2$]

where, A = area of circular loop $= \pi R^2$

➢ Magnetic field due to current carrying circular arc with centre O will be:

(i) $B = \frac{\mu_0}{4\pi}.\frac{\pi i}{r} = \frac{\mu_0 i}{4r}$

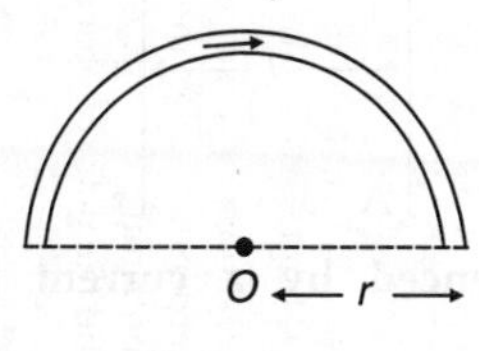

(ii) $B = \frac{\mu_0}{4\pi}.\frac{\theta i}{r}$

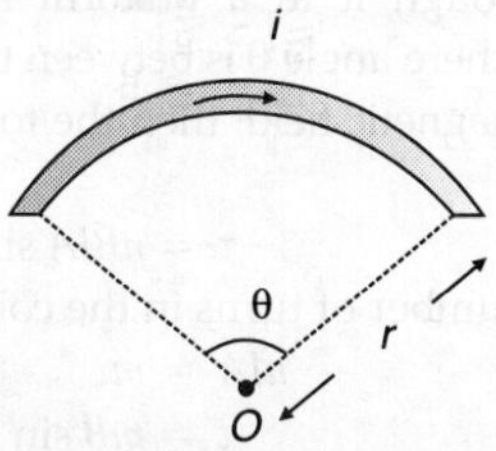

(iii) $B = \frac{\mu_0}{4\pi}.\frac{(2\pi-\theta)i}{r}$

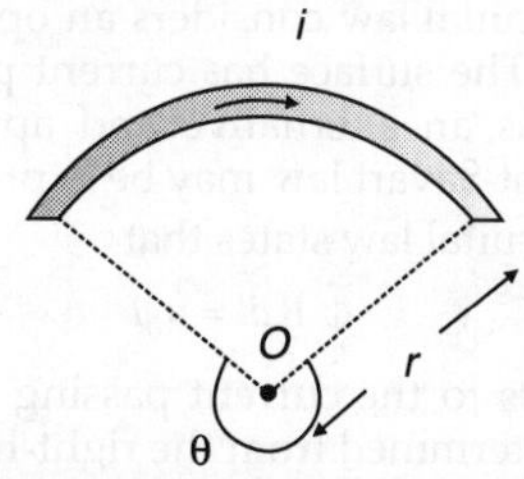

➢ Magnetic field at common centre of non-coplanar and concentric coils, where both coils are perpendicular to each other will be:

$$B = \sqrt{B_1^2 + B_2^2} = \frac{\mu_0}{2r}\sqrt{i_1^2 + i_2^2}$$

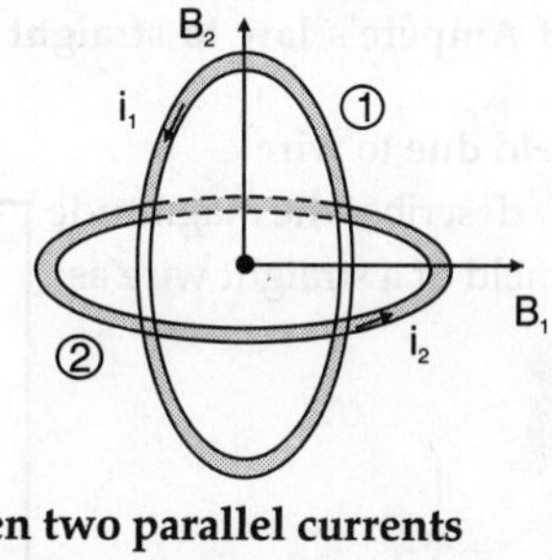

Forces between two parallel currents

➢ Two parallel wires separated by distance r having currents I_1 and I_2 where magnetic field strength at second wire due to current flowing in first wire is given as:

$$B = \frac{\mu_0 I_1}{2\pi r}$$

- In this, the field is orientated at right-angles to second wire where force per unit length on the second wire will be:

$$\frac{F}{l} = \frac{\mu_0 I_1 I_2}{2\pi r}$$

- Magnetic field-strength at first wire due to the current flowing in second wire will be:

$$B = \frac{\mu_0 I_2}{2\pi r}$$

➢ **Definition of ampere**

If the current in the parallel wires $i_1 = i_2 = 1$ A and the distance between them is $r = 1$m, then

$$f_1 = f_2 = \frac{\mu_0}{4\pi}\times\frac{2i_1 i_2}{r}$$

$$= 2 \times 10^{-7}\ \text{N}$$

One ampere current is the current which when flows through two infinitely long parallel wires placed 1 m apart, in vacuum, produces a force of 2×10^{-7} N per unit length.

Example: Find the magnitude of the magnetic field produced at the centre of a coil of 50 turns of radius 25 × 10^{-2} m due to a 10 A current flowing through it.

Ans. $B = \frac{\propto_0 Ni}{2R}$

Or, $B = \frac{4\pi\times10^{-7}\times50\times10}{2\times25\times10^{-2}}$

$\therefore$ $B = 1.256 \times 10^{-3}$ T

Ampere's Circuital Law

- Ampere's circuital law considers an open surface with a boundary. The surface has current passing through it. This law is an alternative and appealing way in which the Biot-Savart law may be expressed.
- Ampere's circuital law states that

$$\oint_c B.dl = \mu_0 I$$

where I refers to the current passing through S. The sign of I is determined from the right-hand rule.

- If B is directed along the tangent to every point on the perimeter L of a closed curve and is constant in magnitude along perimeter then,

$$BL = \mu_0 I_e$$

where I_e is the net current enclosed by the closed circuit.

Applications of Ampere's law to straight wire, straight solenoids:

(i) Magnetic Field due to wire

➢ Ampere's law describes the magnitude of magnetic field of a straight wire as:

$$B = \frac{\mu_0 I}{2\pi r}$$

Scan to know more about this topic

Ampere's circuital law

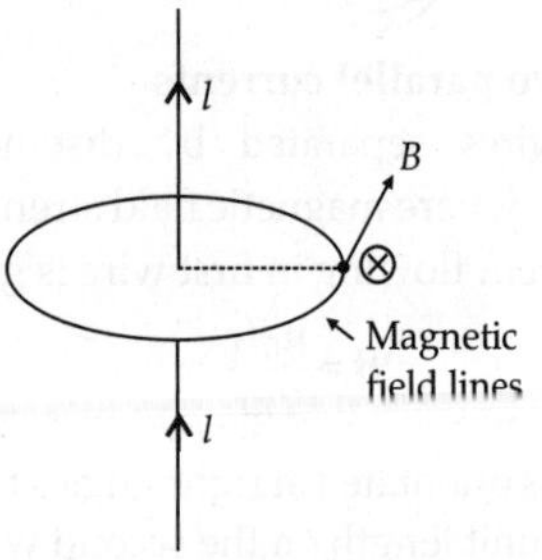

where,

- Field B is tangential to a circle of radius r centered on the wire.
- Magnetic field B and path length L will remain parallel where magnetic field travels.

(ii) Magnetic Field due to Solenoid

➢ **Solenoid:** An electromagnet that generates a controlled magnetic field.

➢ Solenoid is a tightly wound helical coil of wire whose diameter is small compared to its length.

➢ Magnetic field generated in the centre, or core of a current carrying solenoid is uniform and is directed along the axis of solenoid.

➢ Magnetic field due to a straight solenoid:

- at any point in the solenoid,

$$B = \mu_0 nI$$

- at the ends of solenoid,

$$B_{end} = \frac{\mu_0 nI}{2}$$

where, n = number of turns per unit length, I = current in the coil.

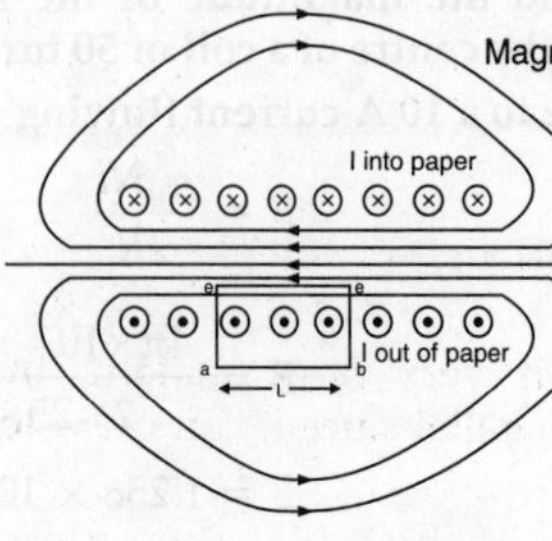

➢ Force between two infinitely long parallel current carrying conductors (Laws of parallel currents):

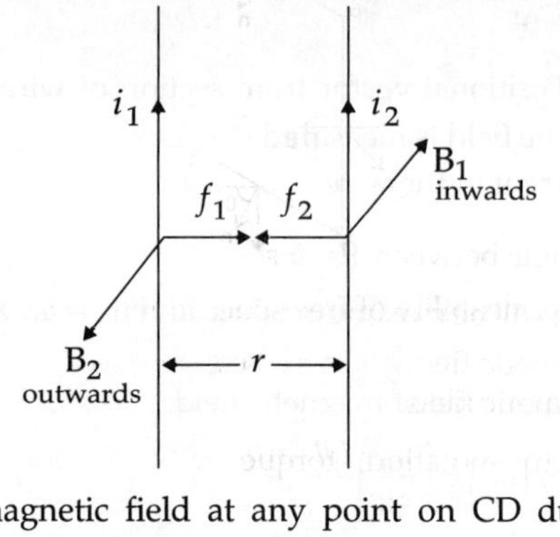

The magnetic field at any point on CD due to the current i_1 flowing through AB is

$$B_1 = \frac{\mu_0}{4\pi} \times \frac{2i_1}{r}$$

Now force experienced by CD per unit length

$$f_1 = \frac{\mu_0}{4\pi} \times \frac{2i_1 i_2}{r}$$

The magnetic field at any point on AB due to the current i_1 flowing through CD is

$$B_1 = \frac{\mu_0}{4\pi} \times \frac{2i_2}{r}$$

The direction is inside the paper.

Now force experienced by AB per unit length

$$f_2 = \frac{\mu_0}{4\pi} \times \frac{2i_2 i_2}{r}$$

Both f_1 and f_2 are of same magnitude but oppositely directed.

So, there will be an attraction.

If the current follows in opposite direction, then there will be a repulsion between them.

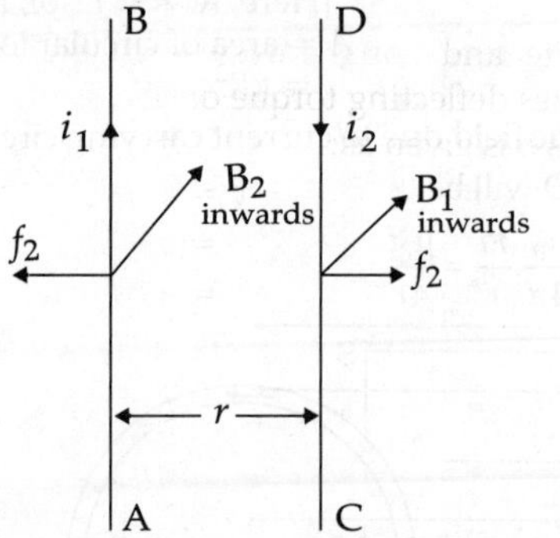

Torque experienced by a current loop in uniform magnetic field

➢ In a rectangular loop of length l, breadth b with current I flowing through it in a uniform magnetic field of induction B where angle θ is between the normal and in direction of magnetic field, then the torque experienced will be:

$$\tau = nBIA \sin\theta$$

where, n = number of turns in the coil

$$\therefore \quad nIA = m$$

Further $$\tau = mB \sin\theta$$

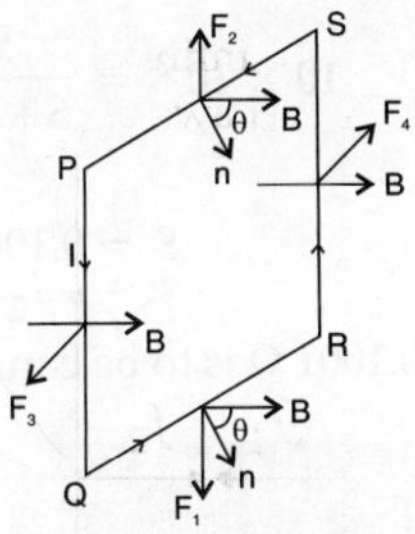

➢ Torque will be maximum when the coil is perpendicular to magnetic field and will be zero when coil is parallel to magnetic field.

➢ In vector notation, torque $\vec{\tau}$ experienced will be $\vec{\tau} = \vec{m} \times \vec{B}$

Moving Coil Galvanometer

➢ It is an instrument used for detection and measurement of small electric currents.

➢ In this, when a current carrying coil is suspended in uniform magnetic field, it experiences a torque which rotates the coil.

➢ The force experienced by each side of the galvanometer will be $F = BIl$ which are opposite in direction.

Scan to know more about this topic

Moving coil galvanometer

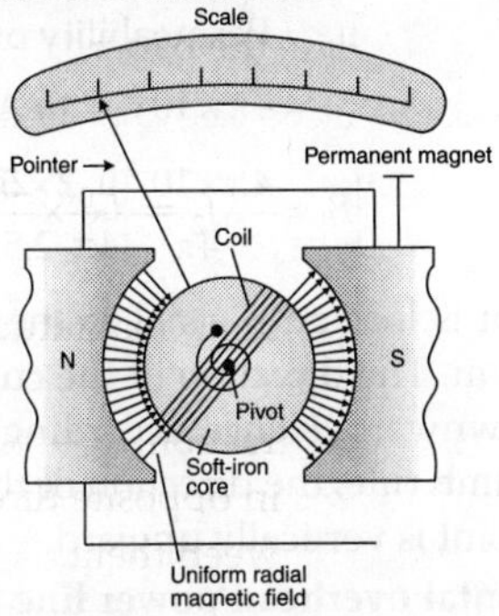

➢ Opposite and equal forces form the couple which generates deflecting torque on the coil having number of turns n is given as:

$$\tau = F \times b$$
$$= nBIl \times b$$
$$= nBIA$$

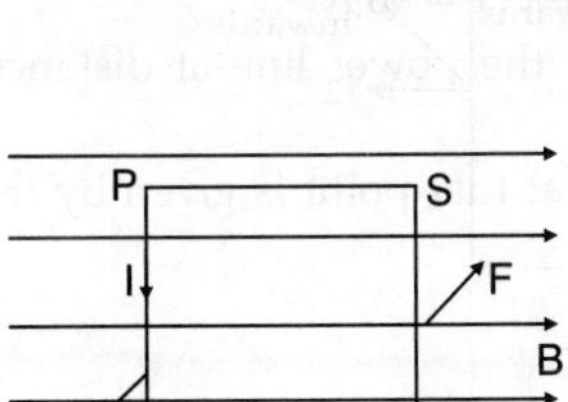

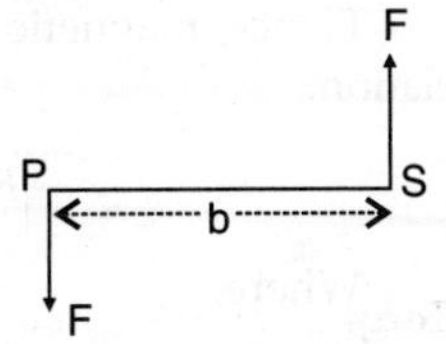

➢ In moving coil galvanometer, current in the coil will be directly proportional to the angle of the deflection of the coil,

$$I \propto \theta$$

i.e., where, θ is the angle of deflection.

Current and voltage sensitivity of galvanometer

➢ Current sensitivity of galvanometer is the deflection produced when unit current passes through the galvanometer. A galvanometer is said to be sensitive if it produces large deflection for a small current.

$$I = \frac{C}{nBA}\theta$$

$$\text{Current Sensitivity,} \quad \frac{\theta}{I} = \frac{nBA}{C}$$

➢ Voltage sensitivity of galvanometer is the deflection per unit voltage given as

$$\text{Voltage Sensitivity,} \quad \frac{\theta}{V} = \frac{\theta}{IG} = \frac{nBA}{CG}$$

where, G = galvanometer resistance, C = torsional constant.

➢ Increase in sensitivity of moving coil galvanometer depends on:
(i) number of turns, n **(ii)** magnetic field, B **(iii)** area of coil, A and **(iv)** torsional constant.

Conversion of galvanometer to ammeter

➢ Galvanometer can be converted into ammeter by connecting a low resistance known as shunt in parallel with the galvanometer coil.

➢ If i_g being the maximum current with full scale deflection that passes through galvanometer, then current through shunt resistance will be $i_s = (i - i_g)$ where, G = Galvanometer resistance, S = Shunt resistance and i = Current in circuit

➢ Now effective resistance of ammeter will be:

$$\frac{1}{R_a} = \frac{1}{G} + \frac{1}{S}$$

$$R_a = \frac{GS}{G+S}$$

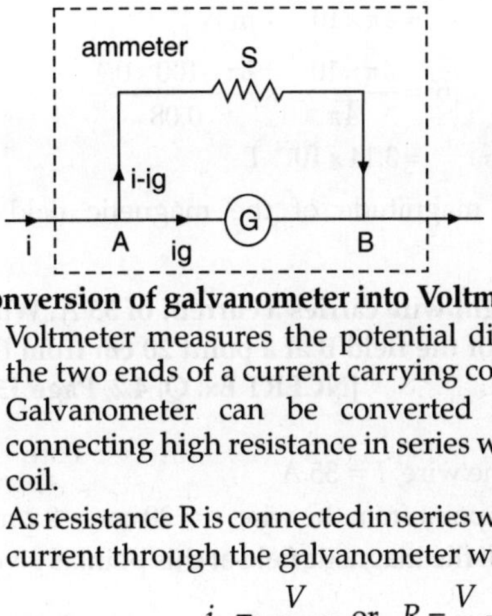

Conversion of galvanometer into Voltmeter

➢ Voltmeter measures the potential difference between the two ends of a current carrying conductor.

➢ Galvanometer can be converted to voltmeter by connecting high resistance in series with galvanometer coil.

➢ As resistance R is connected in series with galvanometer, current through the galvanometer will be,

$$i_g = \frac{V}{R+G} \quad \text{or,} \quad R = \frac{V}{i_g} - G$$

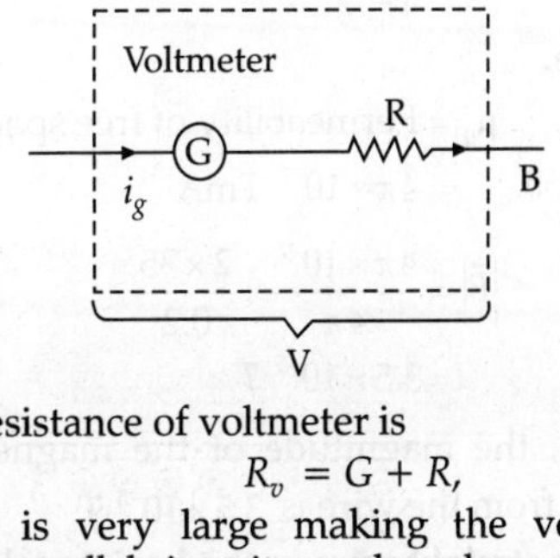

➢ Effective resistance of voltmeter is

$$R_v = G + R,$$

where, R_v is very large making the voltmeter to connect in parallel since it can draw less current from the circuit.

Example: A galvanometer shows full scale deflection for 10 mA current. How this galvanometer may be converted into an ammeter of range 10A? (Resistance of galvanometer is 100 Ω)

Ans:
$$I_G = \frac{S}{S+G} \times I$$

Or,
$$10 \times 10^{-3} = \frac{S}{S+100} \times 10$$

$\therefore$
$$S = 0.1001\ \Omega$$

So, a shunt of 0.1001 Ω is to be connected in parallel

NCERT CORNER

Exercise Questions

Q. 1. A circular coil of wire consisting of 100 turns, each of radius 8.0 cm carries a current of 0.40 A. What is the magnitude of the magnetic field B at the centre of the coil? [NCERT Ex. Q. 4.1, Page 134]

Ans. Given that,

Number of turns on the circular coil, $n = 100$

Radius of each turn, $r = 8.0\text{ cm} = 0.08\text{ m}$

Current flowing in the coil, $I = 0.4\text{ A}$

Magnitude of the magnetic field at the centre of the coil is given by the relation,

$$|\vec{B}| = \frac{\mu_0}{4\pi}\frac{2\pi nI}{r}$$

Where,

$$\mu_0 = \text{Permeability of free space} = 4\pi \times 10^{-7}\ \text{T m A}^{-1}$$

$$|\vec{B}| = \frac{4\pi \times 10^{-7}}{4\pi} \times \frac{2\pi \times 100 \times 0.4}{0.08} = 3.14 \times 10^{-4}\ T$$

Hence, the magnitude of the magnetic field is $3.14 \times 10^{-4}\ T$.

Q. 2. A long straight wire carries a current of 35 A. What is the magnitude of the field B at a point 20 cm from the wire? [NCERT Ex. Q. 4.2, Page 134]

Ans. Given that,

Current in the wire, $I = 35\text{ A}$

Distance of a point from the wire, $r = 20\text{ cm} = 0.2\text{ m}$

Magnitude of the magnetic field at this point is given as:

$$|\vec{B}| = \frac{\mu_0}{4\pi}\frac{2I}{r}$$

Where,

$$\mu_0 = \text{Permeability of free space} = 4\pi \times 10^{-7}\ \text{TmA}^{-1}$$

$$|\vec{B}| = \frac{4\pi \times 10^{-7}}{4\pi} \times \frac{2 \times 35}{0.2} = 3.5 \times 10^{-5}\ T$$

Hence, the magnitude of the magnetic field at a point 20 cm from the wire is 3.5×10^{-5} T.

Q. 3. A long straight wire in the horizontal plane carries a current of 50 A in north to south direction. Give the magnitude and direction of B at a point 2.5 m east of the wire. [NCERT Ex. Q. 4.3, Page 134]

Ans. Current in the wire, $I = 50$ A

A point is 2.5 m away from the East of the wire.

$\therefore$ Magnitude of the distance of the point from the wire, $r = 2.5$ m.

Magnitude of the magnetic field at that point is given by the relation,

$$|\vec{B}| = \frac{\mu_0}{4\pi}\frac{2I}{r}$$

Where,

$$\mu_0 = \text{Permeability of free space} = 4\pi \times 10^{-7}\ \text{T m A}^{-1}$$

$$|\vec{B}| = \frac{4\pi \times 10^{-7}}{4\pi} \times \frac{2 \times 50}{2.5} = 4 \times 10^{-6}\ \text{T}$$

The point is located normal to the wire length at a distance of 2.5 m. The direction of the current in the wire is vertically downward. Hence, according to the Maxwell's right hand thumb rule, the direction of the magnetic field at the given point is vertically upward.

Q. 4. A horizontal overhead power line carries a current of 90 A in east to west direction. What is the magnitude and direction of the magnetic field due to the current 1.5 m below the line? [NCERT Ex. Q. 4.4, Page 135]

Ans. Current in the power line, $I = 90$ A

Point is located below the power line at distance, $r = 1.5$ m

Hence, magnetic field at that point is given by the relation,

$$|\vec{B}| = \frac{\mu_0}{4\pi}\frac{2I}{r}$$

Where,

$$\mu_0 = \text{Permeability of free space} = 4\pi \times 10^{-7}\ \text{TmA}^{-1}$$

$$|\vec{B}| = \frac{4\pi \times 10^{-7}}{4\pi} \times \frac{2 \times 90}{1.5} = 1.2 \times 10^{-5}\ \text{T}$$

The current is flowing from East to West. The point is below the power line. Hence, according to Maxwell's right hand thumb rule, the direction of the magnetic field is towards the South.

Q. 5. What is the magnitude of magnetic force per unit length on a wire carrying a current of 8 A and making an angle of 30° with the direction of a uniform magnetic field of 0.15 T? [NCERT Ex. Q. 4.5, Page 135]

Ans. Given that,

Current in the wire, $I = 8$ A

Magnitude of the uniform magnetic field, $B = 0.15$ T

Angle between the wire and magnetic field, $\theta = 30°$

Magnetic force per unit length on the wire is given as:

$$F/l = BI \sin\theta$$
$$= 0.15 \times 8 \times 1 \times \sin 30°$$
$$= 0.6 \text{ Nm}^{-1}$$

Hence, the magnetic force per unit length on the wire is 0.6 Nm^{-1}.

Q. 6. A 3.0 cm wire carrying a current of 10 A is placed inside a solenoid perpendicular to its axis. The magnetic field inside the solenoid is given to be 0.27 T. What is the magnetic force on the wire? [NCERT Ex. Q. 4.6, Page 135]

Ans. Given that,

Length of the wire, $l = 3$ cm $= 0.03$ m

Current flowing in the wire, $I = 10$ A

Magnetic field, $B = 0.27$ T

Angle between the current and magnetic field, $\theta = 90°$

Magnetic force exerted on the wire is given as:

$$F = BIl \sin\theta$$
$$= 0.27 \times 10 \times 0.03 \sin 90°$$
$$= 8.1 \times 10^{-2} \text{ N}$$

Hence, the magnetic force on the wire is 8.1×10^{-2} N. The direction of the force can be obtained from Fleming's left hand rule.

Q. 7. Two long and parallel straight wires *A* and *B* carrying currents of 8.0 A and 5.0 A in the same direction are separated by a distance of 4.0 cm. Estimate the force on a 10 cm section of wire *A*. [NCERT Ex. Q. 4.7, Page 135]

Ans. Current flowing in wire *A*, $I_A = 8.0$ A

Current flowing in wire *B*, $I_B = 5.0$ A

Distance between the two wires, $r = 4.0$ cm $= 0.04$ m

Length of a section of wire *A*, $L = 10$ cm $= 0.1$ m

Force exerted on length L due to the magnetic field is given as:

$$F = \frac{\mu_0 I_A I_B L}{2\pi r}$$

Where, μ_0 = Permeability of free space $= 4\pi \times 10^{-7}$ T m A^{-1}

$$F = \frac{4\pi \times 10^{-7} \times 8 \times 5 \times 0.1}{2\pi \times 0.04} = 2 \times 10^{-5} N$$

The magnitude of force is 2×10^{-5} N. This is an attractive force normal to A towards B because the direction of the currents in the wires is the same.

Q. 8. A closely wound solenoid 80 cm long has 5 layers of windings of 400 turns each. The diameter of the solenoid is 1.8 cm. If the current carried is 8.0 A, estimate the magnitude of B inside the solenoid near its centre. [NCERT Ex. Q. 4.8, Page 135]

Ans. Length of the solenoid, $l = 80$ cm $= 0.8$ m

There are five layers of windings of 400 turns each on the solenoid.

∴ Total number of turns on the solenoid,

$$N = 5 \times 400 = 2000$$

Diameter of the solenoid, $D = 1.8$ cm $= 0.018$ m

Current carried by the solenoid, $I = 8.0$ A

Magnitude of the magnetic field inside the solenoid near its centre is given by the relation,

by the relation, $B = \frac{\mu_0 NI}{l}$

Where, μ_0 = Permeability of free space

$= 4\pi \times 10^{-7}$ TmA^{-1}

$$B = \frac{4\pi \times 10^{-7} \times 2000 \times 8}{0.8}$$
$$= 2.512 \times 10^{-2} \text{ T}$$

Hence, the magnitude of the magnetic field inside the solenoid near its centre is 2.512×10^{-2} T.

Q. 9. A square coil of side 10 cm consists of 20 turns and carries a current of 12 A. The coil is suspended vertically and the normal to the plane of the coil makes an angle of 30° with the direction of a uniform horizontal magnetic field of magnitude 0.80 T. What is the magnitude of torque experienced by the coil? [NCERT Ex. Q. 4.9, Page 135]

Ans. Length of a side of the square coil, $l = 10$ cm $= 0.1$ m

Current flowing in the coil, $I = 12$ A

Number of turns on the coil, $n = 20$

Angle made by the plane of the coil with magnetic field, $\theta = 30°$

Strength of magnetic field, $B = 0.80$ T

Magnitude of the magnetic torque experienced by the coil in the magnetic field is given by the relation,

$$\tau = n\, BIA \sin\theta$$

Where,

A = Area of the square coil

$= l \times l = 0.1 \times 0.1 = 0.01 \text{ m}^2$

So, $\tau = 20 \times 0.8 \times 12 \times 0.01 \times \sin 30°$

$= 0.96$ Nm

Hence, the magnitude of the torque experienced by the coil is 0.96 Nm.

Q. 10. Two moving coil meters, M_1 and M_2 have the following particulars:

$R_1 = 10\ \Omega$, $N_1 = 30$,

$A_1 = 3.6 \times 10^{-3}$ m², $B_1 = 0.25$ T

$R_2 = 14\ \Omega$, $N_2 = 42$,

$A_2 = 1.8 \times 10^{-3}$ m², $B_2 = 0.50$ T

(The spring constants are identical for the two meters). Determine the ratio of:

(a) current sensitivity and

(b) voltage sensitivity of M_2 and M_1. [NCERT Ex. Q. 4.10, Page 135]

Ans. For moving coil meter M_1:

Resistance, $R_1 = 10\ \Omega$

Number of turns, $N_1 = 30$

Area of cross-section, $A_1 = 3.6 \times 10^{-3}$ m²

Magnetic field strength, $B_1 = 0.25$ T

Spring constant $K_1 = K$

For moving coil meter M_2:

Resistance, $R_2 = 14\ \Omega$

Number of turns, $N_2 = 42$

Area of cross-section, $A_2 = 1.8 \times 10^{-3}$ m²

Magnetic field strength, $B_2 = 0.50$ T

Spring constant, $K_2 = K$

(i) Current sensitivity of M_1 is given as:

$$I_{S_1} = \frac{N_1 B_1 A_1}{K_1}$$

And, current sensitivity of M_2 is given as:

$$I_{S_2} = \frac{N_2 B_2 A_2}{K_2}$$

$$\therefore \text{Ratio } \frac{I_{S_2}}{I_{S_1}} = \frac{N_2 B_2 A_2 k_1}{N_1 B_1 A_1 k_2}$$

$$= \frac{42 \times 0.5 \times 1.8 \times 10^{-3} \times K}{K \times 30 \times 0.25 \times 3.6 \times 10^{-3}} = 1.4$$

Hence, the ratio of current sensitivity of M_2 to M_1 is 7 : 5.

(ii) Voltage sensitivity for M_2 is given as:

$$V_{S_2} = \frac{N_2 B_2 A_2}{K_2 R_2}$$

And, voltage sensitivity for M_1 is given as:

$$V_{S_1} = \frac{N_1 B_1 A_1}{K_1 R_1}$$

$$\therefore \text{Ratio } \frac{V_{S_2}}{V_{S_1}} = \frac{N_2 B_2 A_2 R_1 k_1}{N_1 B_1 A_1 R_2 k_2}$$

$$= \frac{42 \times 0.5 \times 1.8 \times 10^{-3} \times 10 \times K}{K \times 14 \times 30 \times 0.25 \times 3.6 \times 10^{-3}} = 1$$

Hence, the ratio of voltage sensitivity M_2 to M_1 is 1.

Q. 11. In a chamber, a uniform magnetic field of 6.5 G (1 G = 10^{-4} T) is maintained. An electron is shot into the field with a speed of 4.8 × 10^6 ms^{-1} normal to the field. Explain why the path of the electron is a circle. Determine the radius of the circular orbit. (e = 1.6 × 10^{-19} C, m_e = 9.1×10^{-31} kg)
[NCERT Ex. Q. 4.11, Page 135]

Ans. Magnetic field strength, B = 6.5 G = 6.5 × 10^{-4} T
Speed of the electron, v = 4.8 × 10^6 m/s
Charge on the electron, e = 1.6 × 10^{-19} C
Mass of the electron, m_e = 9.1 × 10^{-31} kg
Angle between the shot electron and magnetic field, θ = 90°

Magnetic force exerted on the electron in the magnetic field is given as: $F = evB \sin\theta$

This force provides centripetal force to the moving electron. Hence, the electron starts moving in a circular path of radius r.

Hence, centripetal force exerted on the electron,

$$F_e = \frac{mv^2}{r}$$

In equilibrium, the centripetal force exerted on the electron is equal to the magnetic force, that is,

$$F_e = F$$

$$\Rightarrow \quad \frac{mv^2}{r} = evB \sin\theta$$

$$\Rightarrow \quad r = \frac{mv}{eB\sin\theta}$$

So,

$$r = \frac{9.1 \times 10^{-31} \times 4.8 \times 10^6}{6.5 \times 10^{-4} \times 1.6 \times 10^{-19} \times \sin 90^\circ} = 4.2 \times 10^{-2} \text{m}$$

$$= 4.2 \text{ cm}$$

Hence, the radius of the circular orbit of the electron is 4.2 cm.

Q. 12. In the question 11, obtain the frequency of revolution of the electron in its circular orbit. Does the answer depend on the speed of the electron? Explain.
[NCERT Ex. Q. 4.12, Page 135]

Ans. Magnetic field strength, B = 6.5 × 10^{-4} T
Charge of the electron, e = 1.6 × 10^{-19} C
Mass of the electron, m_e = 9.1 × 10^{-31} kg
Velocity of the electron, v = 4.8 × 10^6 m/s
Radius of the orbit, r = 4.2 cm = 0.042 m
Frequency of revolution of the electron = ν
Angular frequency of the electron = $\omega = 2\pi\nu$

Velocity of the electron is related to the angular frequency as: $v = r\omega$

In the circular orbit, the magnetic force on the electron is balanced by the centripetal force.

Hence, we can write:

$$\frac{mv^2}{r} = evB$$

$$\Rightarrow \quad eB = \frac{mv}{r} = \frac{m(r\omega)}{r} = \frac{m(r \cdot 2\pi v)}{r}$$

$$\Rightarrow \quad v = \frac{Be}{2\pi m}$$

This expression for frequency is independent of the speed of the electron. On substituting the known values in this expression, we get the frequency as:

$$v = \frac{6.5 \times 10^{-4} \times 1.6 \times 10^{-19}}{2 \times 3.14 \times 9.1 \times 10^{-31}} = 1.82 \times 16^6 \ Hz \approx 18 \text{ MHz}$$

Hence, the frequency of the electron is around 18 MHz and is independent of the speed of the electron.

Q. 13. (a) A circular coil of 30 turns and radius 8.0 cm carrying a current of 6.0 A is suspended vertically in a uniform horizontal magnetic field of magnitude 1.0 T. The field lines make an angle of 60° with the normal of the coil. Calculate the magnitude of the counter torque that must be applied to prevent the coil from turning.

(b) Would your answer change, if the circular coil in (a) were replaced by a planar coil of some irregular shape that encloses the same area? (All other particulars are also unaltered.) **[NCERT Ex. Q. 4.13, Page 135]**

Ans. Number of turns on the circular coil, n = 30
Radius of the coil, r = 8.0 cm = 0.08 m
Area of the coil $\pi r^2 = \pi\,(0.08)^2$=0.0201 m^2
Current flowing in the coil, I = 6.0 A
Magnetic field strength, B = 1 T
Angle between the field lines and normal with the coil surface, θ = 60°

The coil experiences a torque in the magnetic field. Hence, it turns. The counter torque applied to prevent the coil from turning is given by the relation,

$$\tau = n\ IBA \sin\theta$$
$$= 30 \times 6 \times 1 \times 0.0201 \times \sin 60^\circ$$
$$= 3.133 \text{ Nm}$$

(b) It can be inferred from relation $\tau = nIBA \sin\theta$ that the magnitude of the applied torque is not dependent on the shape of the coil. It depends on the area of the coil. Hence, the answer would not change if the circular coil in the above case is replaced by a planar coil of some irregular shape that encloses the same area.

CHAPTER 5

MAGNETISM AND MATTER

Bar Magnet

- A bar magnet is a rectangular piece of an object, made up of iron, steel or any other ferromagnetic substance, that shows permanent magnetic properties.
- Bar magnet has two magnetic poles known as North pole and South pole each having strength m. If the separation between the poles known as magnetic length is $2l$, then bar magnet is said to have magnetic dipole moment which is

$$M = m \times 2l = 2ml$$

- Direction of magnetic dipole moment is from South Pole to North Pole of bar magnet.
- Lines of magnetic force run in closed loops and form continuous closed loops.

Scan to know more about this topic

Magnetic Field

➢ **Point lies on axis line of bar magnet:**

- If $2l$ is length of bar magnet, m is magnetic strength of each pole, M is magnetic dipole moment, then magnetic field at point P due to this bar magnet:

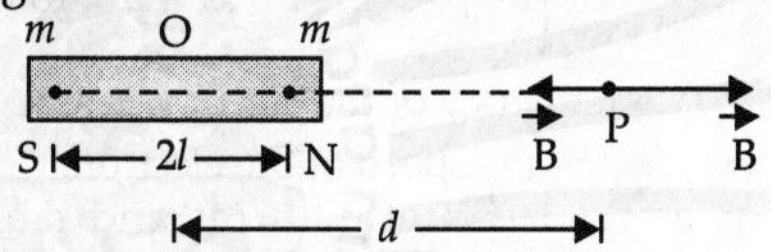

North pole of magnet (N)

$$B = \frac{\mu_0(+m)}{4\pi(d-l)^2}$$

South pole of magnet (S)

$$B = \frac{\mu_0(-m)}{4\pi(d+l)^2}$$

Here, resultant magnetic field at point P when $2l << d$,

$$B = \frac{\mu_0 2M}{4\pi d^3}$$

where, $M = m \times 2l.$

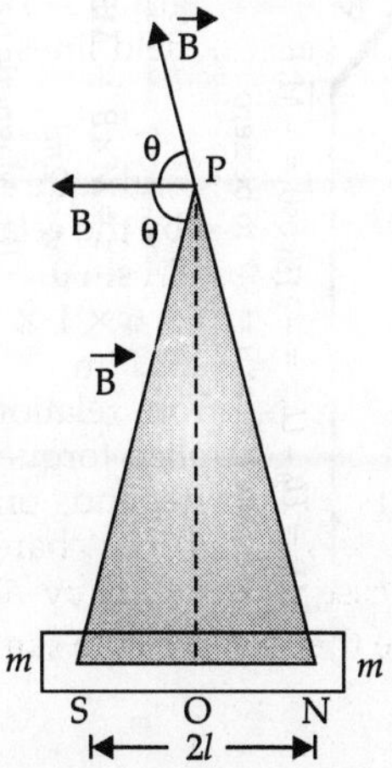

➢ **Point lies on equatorial line of bar magnet:**

- If $2l$ is magnet length of bar magnet, m is magnetic strength of each pole, μ_0 is permeability of free space, then magnetic field at point P due to,

N pole of magnet (direction N–P)

$$B = \frac{+\mu_0(m)}{4\pi(d^2+l^2)}$$

S pole of magnet (direction P–S)

$$B = \frac{-\mu_0 m}{4\pi(d^2+l^2)}$$

Hence resultant at point P when $2l << d$,

$$B = \frac{2\mu_0 M}{4\pi d^3}$$

where, $M = m \times 2l$

➢ **Torque on a magnetic dipole (bar magnet) in uniform magnetic field:**

- A bar magnet with length $2l$ and pole strength m in uniform magnetic field induction B at angle θ with force mB acting on North and South Pole along the direction opposite to magnetic field results as a couple, where, torque τ due to couple will be,

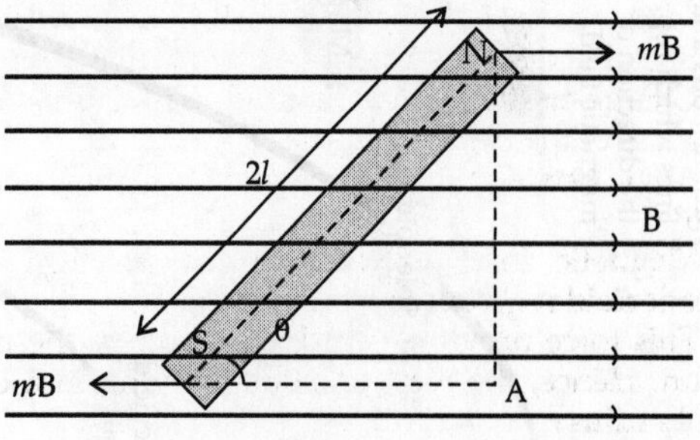

$$\tau = \text{Force} \times \text{perpendicular distance}$$

$$\tau = F \times NA$$

$$= mB \times NA$$

$$= mB \times 2l \sin\theta$$

$$= MB \sin\theta$$

where, $M = m \times 2l$

In vector form,

$$\vec{\tau} = \vec{M} \times \vec{B}$$

The direction of τ is perpendicular to plane containing M and B, so when $B = 1$ and $\theta = 90^0$,

$$\tau = M$$

- Magnetic moment M of the magnet will be equal to the torque required to keep the magnet at right angles to a magnetic field of unit magnetic induction.

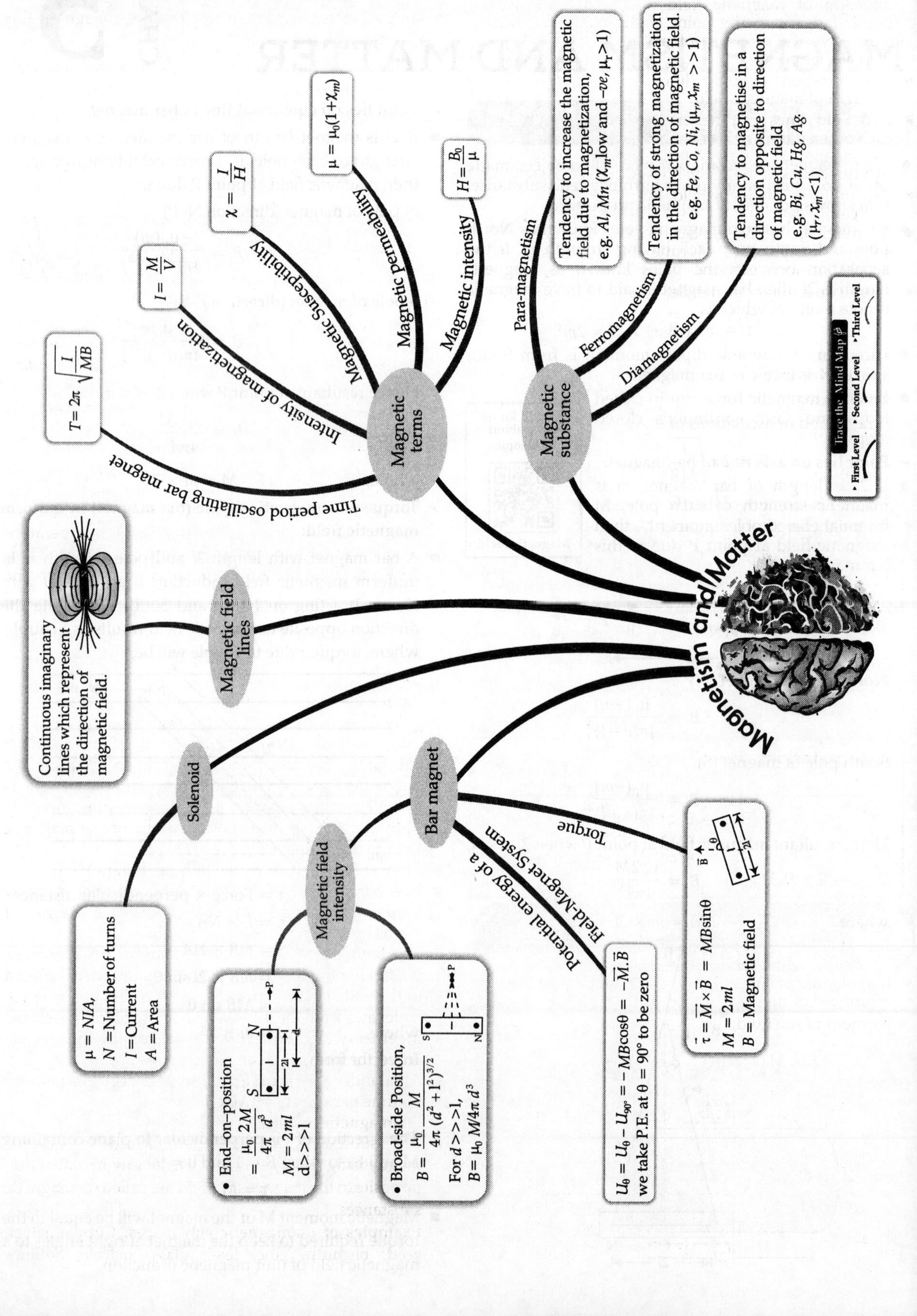
Magnetism and Matter
Magnetic terms
Time period oscillating bar magnet
$T = 2\pi\sqrt{\frac{I}{MB}}$
Intensity of magnetization
$I = \frac{M}{V}$
Magnetic Susceptibility
$\chi = \frac{I}{H}$
Magnetic permeability
$\mu = \mu_0(1+\chi_m)$
Magnetic intensity
$H = \frac{B_0}{\mu}$
Magnetic substance
Para-magnetism
Tendency to increase the magnetic field due to magnetization, e.g. Al, Mn (χ_m low and –ve, μ_r>1)
Ferromagnetism
Tendency of strong magnetization in the direction of magnetic field. e.g. Fe, Co, Ni, (μ_r, χ_m >>1)
Diamagnetism
Tendency to magnetise in a direction opposite to direction of magnetic field e.g. Bi, Cu, Hg, Ag (μ_r, χ_m<1)
Magnetic field lines
Continuous imaginary lines which represent the direction of magnetic field.
Solenoid
$\mu = NIA$, N = Number of turns, I = Current, A = Area
Bar magnet
Magnetic field intensity
• End-on-position $= \frac{\mu_0}{4\pi}\frac{2M}{d^3}$, $M = 2ml$, $d >> l$
• Broad-side Position, $B = \frac{\mu_0}{4\pi}\frac{M}{(d^2+l^2)^{3/2}}$ For $d >> l$, $B = \mu_0 M/4\pi d^3$
Torque
$\vec{\tau} = \vec{M} \times \vec{B} = MB\sin\theta$, $M = 2ml$, B = Magnetic field
Potential energy of a Field-Magnet System
$U_\theta = U_\theta - U_{90°} = -MB\cos\theta = -\vec{M}.\vec{B}$ we take P.E. at θ = 90° to be zero
Trace the Mind Map
First Level
Second Level
Third Level

Magnetic Field Lines

Scan to know more about this topic

Magnetic filed lines

- They are imaginary closed loops which continuously represent the direction of magnetic field at any point. Tangent at any point of these loops give the direction of magnetic field at that point.
- Concentration of field lines gives strength of magnetic field.
- Two field lines can never intersect each other. If they would, there will be two tangents at the point of intersection, which mean two directions of magnetic lines, which is impossible.
- In a 'uniform' magnetic field, the field lines are parallel and equidistant.
- If a magnetic needle is placed in a magnetic field and left, it will experience a torque and start oscillating in simple harmonic motion.
- Torque on a magnetic needle,

$$\vec{\tau} = \vec{M} \times \vec{B}$$

where, $\vec{B}$ is external magnetic field in which magnetic needle is kept.

- Time period of oscillations of magnetic needle

$$T = 2\neq\sqrt{\frac{I}{MB}}$$

where, I is moment of inertia of magnetic needle.

- Potential energy of a magnet in a magnetic field,

$$U = -\vec{M}.\vec{B}$$

MNEMONICS

Concept Name: Electric field due to Dipole

Mnemonics: Mr. **F**orbes of **D**ibrugarh flied from **B**agdogra to **B**engaluru

Interpretation: M → Magnatic
F → Field
D → Dipole
Ba → B on axis line
t → twice
Be → B on equitorial line

$B_{axial} = 2 \times B_{equitorial}$

Bar Magnet as an Equivalent Solenoid

- If a solenoid of length $2l$, radius a with current I having n number of turns per unit length, then the magnetic moment of solenoid,

$$M (= NIA), \quad B = \frac{\mu_0 2M}{4\pi d^3}$$

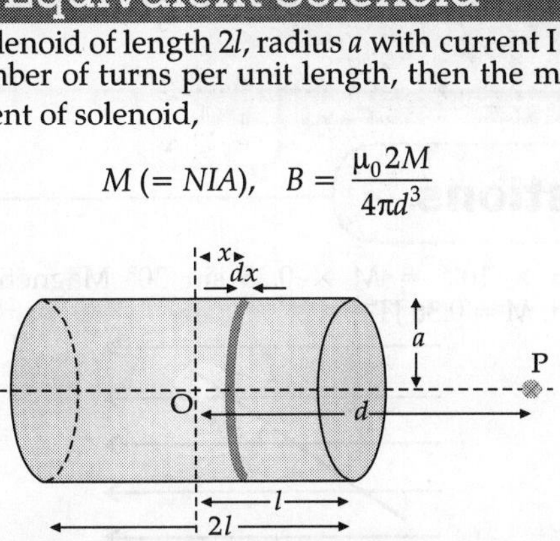

- Magnetic moment of a bar magnet is equal to magnetic moment of an equivalent solenoid that produces same magnetic field.

➤ **Gauss' Law for Magnetic Fields:**

- Gauss' law for magnetism applies to the magnetic flux through a closed surface.
- Gauss's law shows that no magnetic monopoles exist and total flux through closed surface will be zero.
- The Gauss's law for magnetic fields in integral form is given by

$$\phi = \int \vec{B}.d\vec{A} = 0$$

Magnetic Properties of Materials

Ferromagnetic Substances:

- The substances, which are placed in external magnetising field, get magnetised very strongly in the direction of the magnetising field are called ferromagnetic substances.
  Examples of ferromagnetic substances: iron, nickel, cobalt and certain alloys such as alnico.
- Ferromagnetism is not found in liquids and gases.
  Curie Point: The ferromagnetism depends on the temperature. If we raise temperature of the ferromagnetic substance, the domains may disintegrate and the substance turns paramagnetic. The temperature at which this happens is called **Curie point**. Thus, the Curie point is the temperature above which the ferromagnetic substance looses ferromagnetism and turns into a paramagnetic substance.
- Ferromagnetic substances are strongly magnetised and their induced dipole moment M is in the direction of the magnetising field H.
  For ferromagnetic substances, $\mu_r >> 1$
- χ_m of ferromagnetic substance is positive and large.
- The magnetic induction inside the ferromagnetic substances is much larger than that in vacuum. The magnetic induction for ferromagnetic substances is much larger than that for paramagnetic substances.
- They move from the weaker regions of the magnetic field to the stronger regions.
- They are strongly attracted by a bar magnet.
- If a bar magnet of ferromagnetic material is freely suspended between the pole pieces of a magnet, it aligns itself along the magnetic field.
  The liquids do not exhibit ferromagnetism. However, if a finely powdered ferromagnetic substance is placed in the watch glass kept on the pole pieces of a magnet, it elevates from the middle when pole pieces are closed together which suffers a depression in the middle when the pole pieces are far apart.
- Area under a B-H curve represents energy loss per unit volume per cycle.

➤ **Diamagnetic Substances:**

- The substances, which when placed in external magnetising field, get magnetised easily in a direction opposite to the magnetising field are called diamagnetic substances.
  Examples of diamagnetic substances: Copper, silver, gold, bismuth, zinc, lead, glass, marble, sodium

chloride, water and gases such as helium, argon, etc.

- Diamagnetic substances are feebly magnetised and their induced magnetic dipole moment is directed opposite to the magnetising field H.
- For diamagnetic substances,
$$0 \leq \mu_r < 1.$$
- χ_m of diamagnetic substances is negative and small,
$$-1 \leq \chi_m < 0.$$
- The magnetic field induction inside the diamagnetic materials is less than that in vacuum, because,
$$B = \mu_0(H + M)$$
$$B = \mu_0(H + \chi_m H)$$
$$= \mu_0(1 + \chi_m)H.$$
Because χ_m is negative, therefore B is less than H
$$B_0 = \mu_0 H$$
- They move from the stronger regions of magnetising field to the weaker regions
- They are repelled by a bar magnet.
- If a bar of diamagnetic material is suspended between the pole pieces of a magnet, it aligns itself perpendicular to the magnetic field of the magnet.
- Diamagnetic substances do not obey the Curie's law.
- Diamagnetic properties are independent of the temperature.

➢ **Paramagnetic Substances:**

- The substances which when placed in an external magnetising field, get weakly magnetised in the direction of magnetic field are called paramagnetic substances.
Examples of paramagnetic substances: Aluminium, antimony, platinum, manganese, sodium, chromium, liquid oxygen, etc.
- Paramagnetic substances are feebly magnetised and their induced magnetic dipole moment M is in the direction of the magnetising field H.
- For paramagnetic substance μ_r >1 but small ,
$$1 < \mu_r < 1 + \varepsilon.$$
- χ_m of paramagnetic substances is positive but small,
$$0 < \chi_m < \varepsilon.$$
- The magnetic field induction inside the paramagnetic materials is slightly more than that in vacuum.
- They move from the weaker regions of magnetic field to the stronger regions.
- They are attracted by a bar magnet.
- If a bar magnet of paramagnetic material is suspended between the poles of the magnet it aligns itself parallel to the magnetising field of the magnet.
- The paramagnetism depends on the temperature. As the temperature increases, magnetization tends to decrease.
- Paramagnetic substances obey the Curie's law, which states that the magnetic susceptibility is inversely proportional to the temperature in kelvin,
i.e., $$\chi_m \propto \frac{1}{T}$$
- Paramagnetism and ferromagnetism are associated with the intrinsic magnetic moment of spinning of electrons.
- In ferromagnetism, the magnetic effect is enhanced due to the formation of domains.
- Magnetic induction B and magnetic intensity H are related as
$$B = \mu H.$$
- Magnetic induction is expressed in Tesla (S.I.) and Gauss (C.G.S. system).
- Magnetic intensity in vacuum is expressed in Oersted (C.G.S. system) and Am^{-1} (SI unit).
- Diamagnetism originates from the magnetic moment associated with the orbital motion of electrons.

➢ **Curie's Law in Magnetism:** The intensity of magnetization I of a paramagnetic material is directly proportional to the strength of the external magnetic field H, called the magnetising field and is inversely proportional to absolute temperature of the material.
$$I \propto \frac{H}{T}$$
$$I = \frac{CH}{T}$$
$$\Rightarrow \quad \frac{I}{H} = \frac{C}{T}$$
or $$\chi = CT$$
where, C is known as Curie constant.

➢ **Magnetic Permeability:** Magnetic field exists in a vacuum. It can exist in other materials also. Magnetic permeability of a medium is defined as the ratio of magnetic intensity and the magnetising field,
i.e., $$\mu = \frac{B}{H}$$

- Magnetic permeability of a material decides the ability of the material to allow magnetic lines of force through it.

NCERT CORNER

Exercise Questions

Q. 1. A short bar magnet placed with its axis at 30° with a uniform external magnetic field of 0.25 T experiences a torque of magnitude equal to 4.5 × 10^{-2} J. What is the magnitude of magnetic moment of the magnet?

[NCERT Q.No. 5.1, Page 152]

Sol. Torque $\tau = MB \sin \theta$ or

$4.5 \times 10^{-2} = M \times 0.25 \sin 30°$ Magnetic dipole moment, $M = 0.36\ JT^{-1}$.

Q. 2. A short bar magnet of magnetic moment M = 0.32 JT^{-1} is placed in a uniform magnetic field of 0.15 T. If the bar is free to rotate in the plane of the field, which orientation would correspond to its (a) stable, and (b) unstable equilibrium? What is the potential energy of the magnet in each case? [NCERT Q.No. 5.2, Page 152]

Sol. (a) An equilibrium is stable, if on disturbing the magnet, it comes back to same initial state. Bar magnet is in stable equilibrium at $\theta = 0°$ Potential energy,

$$U = -M.B$$
$$= -MB\cos 0°$$
$$= -0.32 \times 0.15$$
$$= -0.048\text{ J}$$

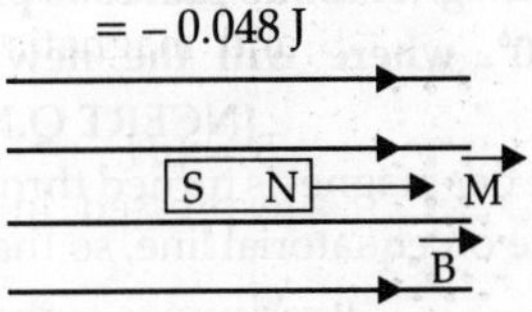

(b) A bar magnet is in unstable equilibrium, if on disturbing from its position, it does not come back to previous position of equilibrium. At θ = 180°, the equilibrium is unstable.

Potential energy,

$$U = -M.B$$
$$= -MB\cos 180°$$
$$= +MB$$
$$= +0.048\text{ J}$$

Q. 3. A closely wound solenoid of 800 turns and area of cross section 2.5 × 10^{-4} m^2 carries a current of 3.0 A. Explain the sense in which the solenoid acts like a bar magnet. What is its associated magnetic moment? [NCERT Q.No. 5.3, Page 152]

Sol.

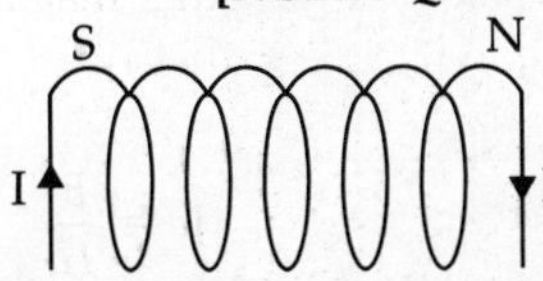

A current carrying closely wound solenoid acts like bar magnet. Each of the turn provide a dipole moment and all turns together provides the dipole moment of the magnet. Total magnetic moment,

$$M = NIA$$
$$= 800 \times 3 \times 2.5 \times 10^{-4}$$
$$= 0.6\text{ Am}^2$$

Q. 4. If the solenoid in the previous question is free to turn about the vertical direction and a uniform horizontal magnetic field of 0.25 T is applied, what is the magnitude of torque on the solenoid when its axis makes an angle of 30° with the direction of applied field? [NCERT Q.No. 5.4, Page 152]

Sol. The solenoid behaves as a bar magnet

so, torque, $\tau = MB\sin\theta$

$$\tau = 0.6 \times 0.25 \times \sin 30°$$
$$= 0.075\text{ Nm.}$$

Q. 5. A bar magnet of magnetic moment 1.5 JT^{-1} lies aligned with the direction of a uniform magnetic field of 0.22 T.

(a) What is the amount of work required by an external torque to turn the magnet so as to align its magnetic moment:

(i) normal to the field direction,

(ii) opposite to the field direction?

(b) What is the torque on the magnet in cases (i) and (ii)? [NCERT Q.No. 5.5, Page 152]

Sol. (a) Work required to turn the magnet

$$W = MB[\cos\theta_i - \cos\theta_f]$$

(i) $\theta_i = 0°$ and $\theta_f = 90°$

$$W = 1.5 \times 0.22\,[\cos 0° - \cos 90°]$$
$$= 0.33\text{ J}$$

(ii) $\theta_i = 0°$ and $\theta = 180°$

$$W = 1.5 \times 0.22\,[\cos 0° - \cos 180°]$$
$$= 0.66\text{ J}$$

(b) Torque when $\theta = 90°$

$$\tau_1 = MB\sin 90°$$
$$= 0.33\text{ J}$$

Torque when $\theta = 180°$

$$\tau_2 = MB\sin 180° = 0$$

Q. 6. A closely wound solenoid of 2000 turns and area of cross-section 1.6 × 10^{-4} m^2, carrying a current of 4.0 A, is suspended through its centre allowing it to turn in a horizontal plane.

(a) What is the magnetic moment associated with the solenoid?

(b) What is the force and torque on the solenoid if a uniform horizontal magnetic field of 7.5 × 10^{-2} T is set up at an angle of 30° with the axis of the solenoid? [NCERT Q.No. 5.6, Page 152]

Sol. (a) Magnetic moment associated with solenoid

$$M = NIA = 2000 \times 4 \times 1.6 \times 10^{-4} = 1.28\text{ Am}^2$$

(b) Force on the solenoid will be zero in uniform magnetic field.

Torque, $\tau = MB\sin\theta$

$$= 1.28 \times 7.5 \times 10^{-2} \times \sin 30°$$

or $\tau = 4.8 \times 10^{-2}$ Nm.

The torque tends to align the solenoid in the direction of magnetic field.

Q. 7. A short bar magnet has a magnetic moment of 0.48 JT^{-1}. Give the direction and magnitude of the magnetic field produced by the magnet at a distance of 10 cm from the centre of the magnet on (a) the axis, (b) the equatorial lines (normal bisector) of the magnet. [NCERT Q.No. 5.7, Page 152]

Sol.

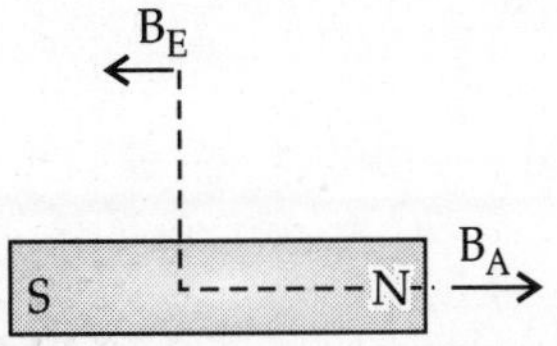

For short magnet

(i) $$B_{axial} = \frac{\mu_0}{4\pi}\frac{2M}{r^3}$$

$$B_{axial} = \frac{10^{-7} \times 2 \times 0.48}{(0.1)^3}$$

$$= 9.6 \times 10^{-5} \text{ T}$$

(along S-N direction)

(ii) $$B_{equatorial} = \frac{\mu_0}{4\pi}\frac{M}{r^3} = \frac{1}{2}B_{axial}$$

$$= 4.8 \times 10^{-5} \text{ T}$$

(along N-S direction)

Q. 8. A short bar magnet placed in a horizontal plane has its axis aligned along the magnetic north-south direction. Null points are found on the axis of the magnet at 14 cm from the centre of the magnet. The earth's magnetic field at the place is 0.36 G and the angle of dip is zero. What is the total magnetic field on the normal bisector of the magnet at the same distance as the null-point (i.e., 14 cm) from the centre of the magnet ? (At null points, field due to a magnet is equal and opposite to the horizontal component of earth's magnetic field.)

[NCERT Q.No. 5.8, Page 153]

Sol. Angle of dip is zero at the place, so earth's magnetic field is uniform with magnitude 0.36 G in the direction, geographical south to geographical north.

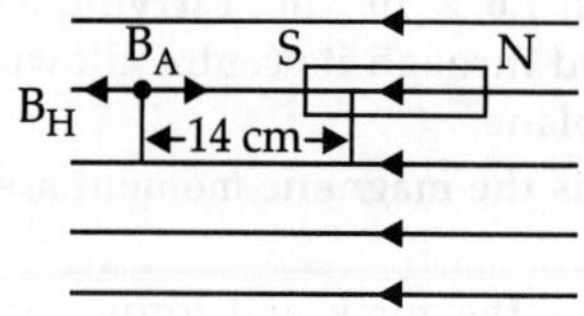

At axial position for null point

$$B_H = B_A$$

$$0.36 \text{ G} = B_A$$

At equatorial position the field due to bar magnet is $\frac{B_A}{2}$.

$$B_E = \frac{B_A}{2}$$

$$= 0.18 \text{ G}$$

Total magnetic field of earth and magnet adds at equatorial position

$$B_{Total} = B_H + B_E$$

$$= 0.36 \text{ G} + 0.18 \text{ G}$$

$$= 0.54 \text{ G.}$$

Q. 9. If the bar magnet in the previous problem is turned around by 180°, where will the new null points be located? **[NCERT Q.No. 5.9, Page 153]**

Sol. When the bar magnet is turned through 180°, neutral points would lie on equatorial line, so that

$$B_2 = \frac{\mu_0}{4\pi}\frac{M}{d_2^3} = B_H \quad \text{...(i)}$$

In the previous question,

$$B_1 = \frac{\mu_0}{4\pi}\frac{2M}{d_1^3} = B_H \quad \text{...(ii)}$$

From (i) and (ii),

$$\frac{\mu_0}{4\pi}\frac{M}{d_2^3} = \frac{\mu_0}{4\pi}\frac{2M}{d_1^3}$$

$$\therefore \quad d_2^3 = \frac{d_1^3}{2} = \frac{(14)^3}{2}$$

or $$d_2 = \frac{14}{2^{1/3}}$$

$$= 11.1 \text{ cm.}$$

□□

ELECTROMAGNETIC INDUCTION

CHAPTER 6

Magnetic Flux

- Magnetic flux through an enclosed area is the amount of field lines passing through a surface area *A* defined by unit area vector.
- The units for magnetic flux is weber, where, $1\ Wb = 1\ T/m^2$.
- Magnetic flux ϕ_B is related to number of field lines passing through a given area.
- If magnetic field is changing, then changing magnetic flux will be $\phi_B = NBA\cos\theta$, where angle θ is the angle between magnetic field and normal to the plane.

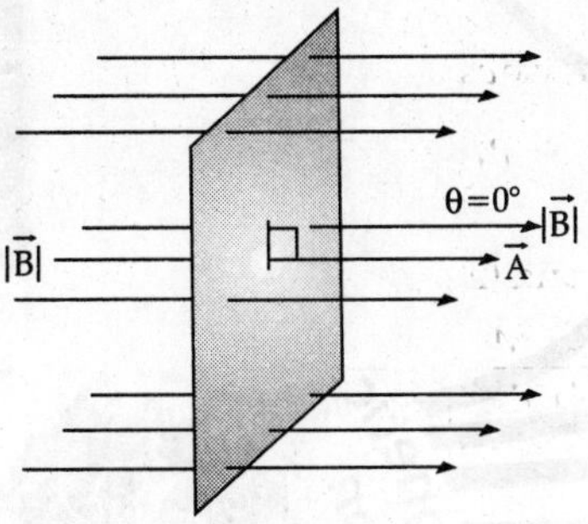

$\vec{B}$ parallel to A ($\theta = 0°$)
magnetic flux $\phi_B = BA$.

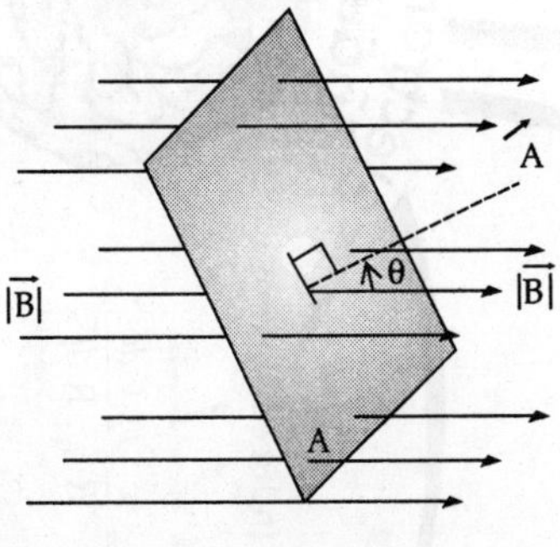

$\vec{B}$ at an angle ϕ with the perpendicular to A:
magnetic flux $\phi_B = BA\cos\theta$

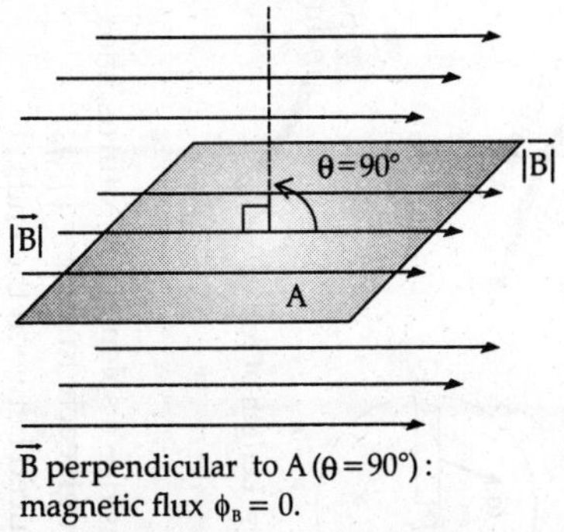

$\vec{B}$ perpendicular to A ($\theta = 90°$):
magnetic flux $\phi_B = 0$.

- **Electromagnetic Induction:** It is a process of generation of electric current in a closed coil due to change in magnetic flux through it.

The current generated is called induced current.
If the coil is open (not closed), an e.m.f. is induced in the coil due to change in magnetic flux through it.
The e.m.f. thus developed is called induced e.m.f.

Faraday's Law of Electromagnetic Induction

- **First Law:** Whenever a conductor is placed in varying magnetic field, an emf is induced which is known as induced emf and if the conductor circuit is closed, current is also induced which is called induced current.
- **Second Law:** The induced emf is equal to the rate of change of flux linkage where flux linkage is the product of number of turns in the coil and flux associated with the coil.

$$\varepsilon = -\frac{d\phi_B}{dt}$$

If the conductor is in the form of loop having N number of turns (all of same area) then,

$$\varepsilon = -N\frac{d\phi_B}{dt}$$

If each loop has an area A, placed in an uniform magnetic field B, making an angle θ, then the magnetic flux through the loop is $\phi_B = BA\cos\theta$

$$\therefore \quad \varepsilon = -N\frac{d}{dt}(BA\cos\theta)$$

Motional Electromotive Force

- The relationship between an induced emf ε in a wire moving at a constant speed *v* through a magnetic field *B* is given by:

$$\phi_B = Blx$$

$$\varepsilon = \frac{-d\phi_B}{dt} = \frac{-d}{dt}(Blx)$$

$$= -Bl\frac{dx}{dt}$$

$$= Blv \qquad \left(\frac{dx}{dt} = -v\right)$$

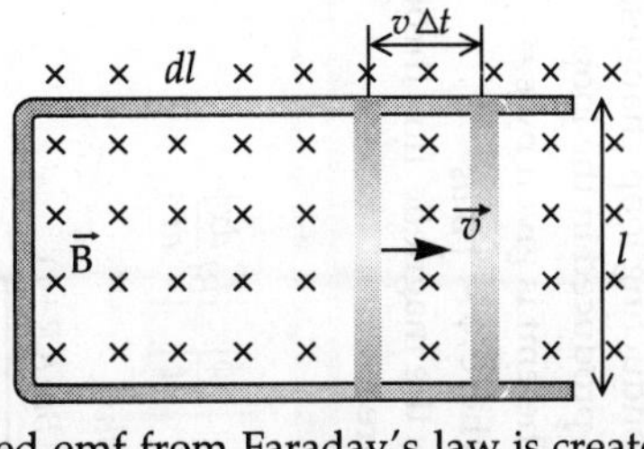

- An induced emf from Faraday's law is created from a motional emf that opposes the change in flux.
- Magnetic and electric forces on charges in a rod moving perpendicular to magnetic field is given as:

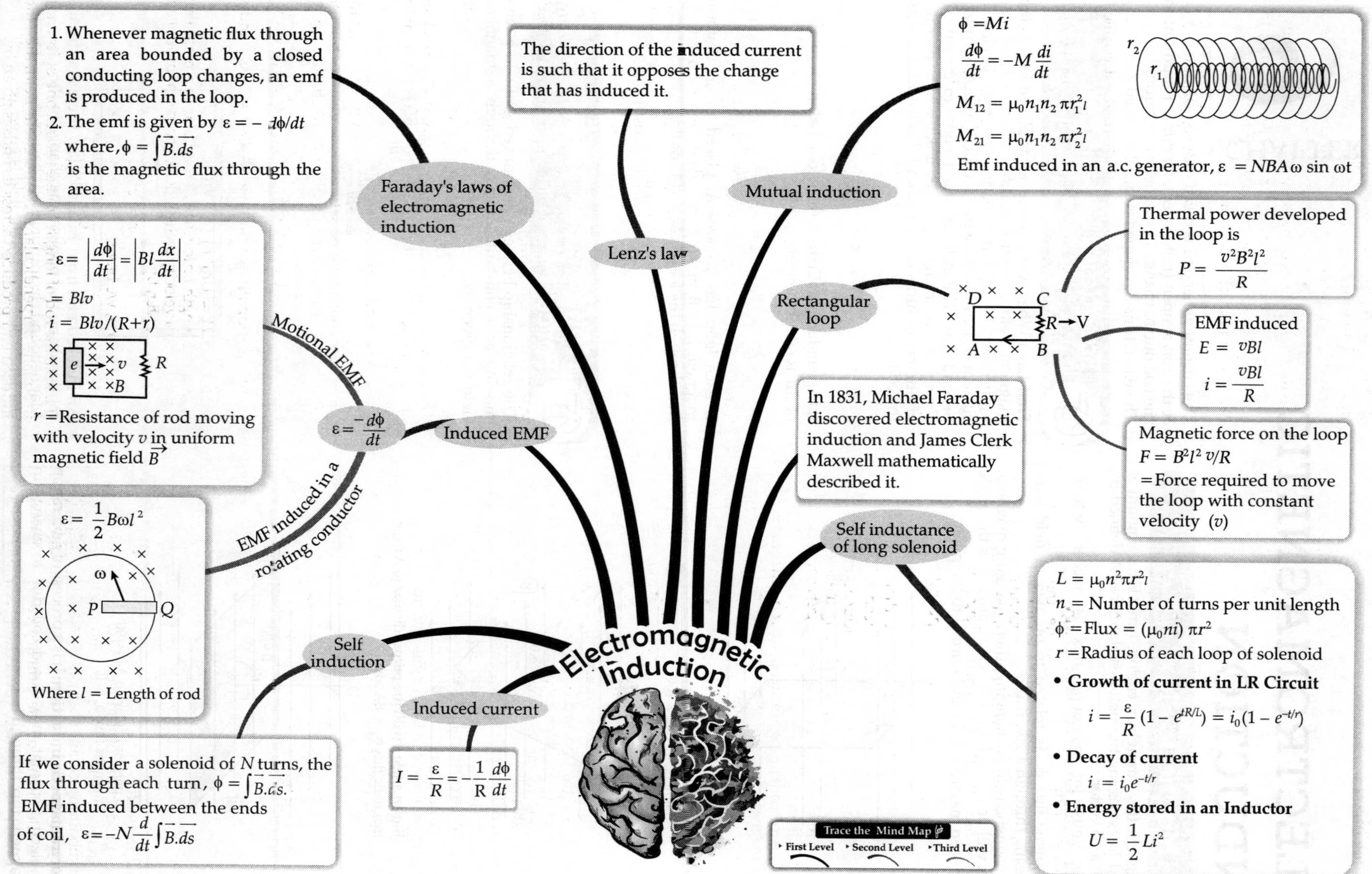
Electromagnetic Induction
Faraday's laws of electromagnetic induction
1. Whenever magnetic flux through an area bounded by a closed conducting loop changes, an emf is produced in the loop.
2. The emf is given by $\varepsilon = -d\phi/dt$ where, $\phi = \int \vec{B}.\vec{ds}$ is the magnetic flux through the area.
Lenz's law
The direction of the induced current is such that it opposes the change that has induced it.
Mutual induction
$\phi = Mi$
$\frac{d\phi}{dt} = -M\frac{di}{dt}$
$M_{12} = \mu_0 n_1 n_2 \pi r_1^2 l$
$M_{21} = \mu_0 n_1 n_2 \pi r_2^2 l$
Emf induced in an a.c. generator, $\varepsilon = NBA\omega \sin \omega t$
r_2
r_1
Rectangular loop
D
C
A
B
R→V
Thermal power developed in the loop is $P = \frac{v^2B^2l^2}{R}$
EMF induced $E = vBl$, $i = \frac{vBl}{R}$
Magnetic force on the loop $F = B^2l^2 v/R$ = Force required to move the loop with constant velocity (v)
In 1831, Michael Faraday discovered electromagnetic induction and James Clerk Maxwell mathematically described it.
Self inductance of long solenoid
$L = \mu_0 n^2 \pi r^2 l$
n = Number of turns per unit length
ϕ = Flux = $(\mu_0 ni)\pi r^2$
r = Radius of each loop of solenoid
• Growth of current in LR Circuit
$i = \frac{\varepsilon}{R}(1 - e^{-tR/L}) = i_0(1 - e^{-t/\tau})$
• Decay of current
$i = i_0 e^{-t/\tau}$
• Energy stored in an Inductor
$U = \frac{1}{2}Li^2$
Induced EMF
$\varepsilon = \frac{-d\phi}{dt}$
Motional EMF
$\varepsilon = \left|\frac{d\phi}{dt}\right| = \left|Bl\frac{dx}{dt}\right|$
$= Blv$
$i = Blv/(R+r)$
e
v
R
B
r = Resistance of rod moving with velocity v in uniform magnetic field $\vec{B}$
EMF induced in a rotating conductor
$\varepsilon = \frac{1}{2}B\omega l^2$
ω
P
Q
Where l = Length of rod
Induced current
$I = \frac{\varepsilon}{R} = -\frac{1}{R}\frac{d\phi}{dt}$
Self induction
If we consider a solenoid of N turns, the flux through each turn, $\phi = \int \vec{B}.\vec{ds}$.
EMF induced between the ends of coil, $\varepsilon = -N\frac{d}{dt}\int \vec{B}.\vec{ds}$
Trace the Mind Map
First Level
Second Level
Third Level

At equilibrium $F_E = F_B$

$$qE = qvB$$
$$E = vB$$
$$\frac{V}{l} = vB \qquad [\text{Here, } E = \frac{V}{l}]$$
$$V = Bvl$$

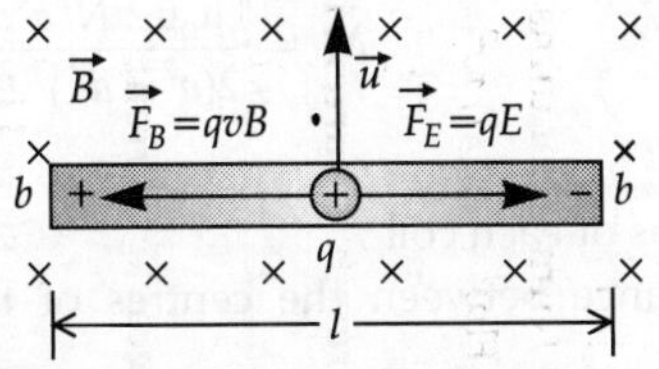

Lenz's Law and Conservation of Energy

- Lenz's law is used to determine the direction of induced magnetic fields, currents, and *emfs*.
- The direction of an induced emf always opposes the change in magnetic flux that causes the emf.
- It explains about the negative sign in Faraday's rule, $\varepsilon = -\frac{d\phi_B}{dt}$ showing that the polarity of induced emf tends to produce a current that opposes the change in magnetic flux that produced it.
- As per conservation of energy, induced emf opposes the cause which produces it making mechanical work to continue with the process which gets converted into electrical energy.
- Slide wire containing induced current, magnetic field and magnetic force:

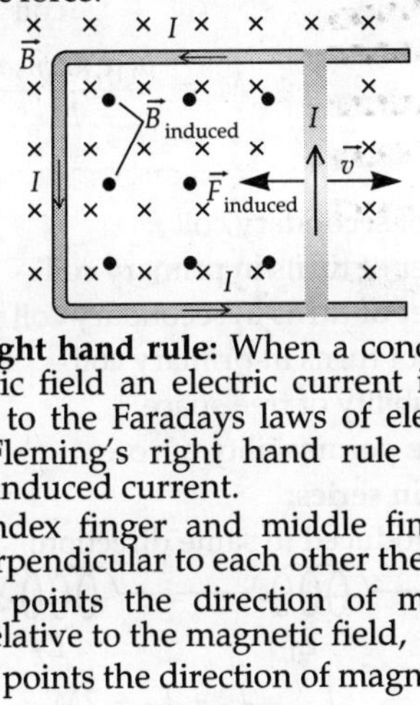

- **Fleming's right hand rule:** When a conductor moves in a magnetic field an electric current is induced in it according to the Faradays laws of electromagnetic induction. Fleming's right hand rule indicates the direction of induced current.
  If thumb, index finger and middle finger are held mutually perpendicular to each other then
  - The thumb points the direction of motion of the conductor relative to the magnetic field,
  - Index finger points the direction of magnetic field and,
  - Index finger points the direction of induced current.

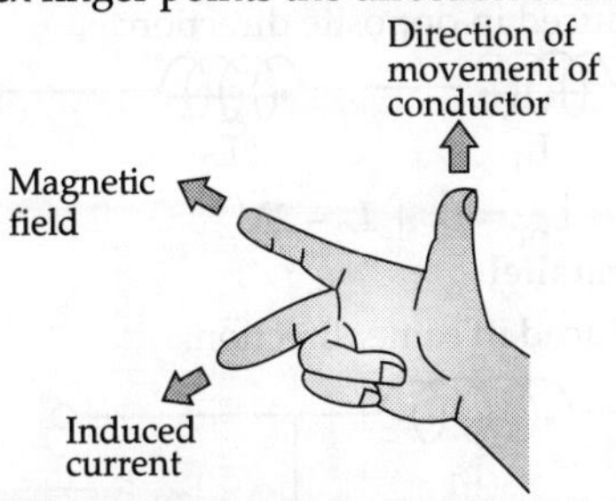

Mutual Induction

- The production of induced emf in a circuit, when the current in the neighbouring circuit changes is called **mutual induction.**

  When the circuit of the primary coil is closed or opened, deflection is produced in the galvanometer of the secondary coil. This is due to the mutual induction.

Scan to know more about this topic

Mutual inductance

- The mutual induction between two coils depends on the following factors:
  - The number of turns of primary and secondary coils.
  - The shape, size or geometry of the two coils. i.e., the area of cross-section and the length of the coils.

Coefficient of mutual induction:

- Suppose, the instantaneous current in the primary coil is I. Let the magnetic flux linked with the secondary coil be ϕ. It is found that the magnetic flux is proportional to the current. i.e.,

$$\phi \propto I \text{ or } \phi = MI \qquad \text{...(i)}$$

where, M is the constant of proportionality. It is called **coefficient of mutual induction.**

The induced emf ε in the secondary coil is given by

$$\varepsilon = -\frac{d\phi}{dt} = -M\frac{dI}{dt} \qquad \text{...(ii)}$$

The negative sign is in accordance with the Lenz's law i.e., the induced emf in the secondary coil opposes the variation of current in the primary coil.

From the equation (ii), we find

$$M = \frac{\varepsilon}{(dI/dt)}$$

Therefore, Unit of $M = \frac{V}{As^{-1}} = VA^{-1}s$

If n_1, n_2 be the number of turns in primary and secondary coils permit length and r be their radius, then coefficient of mutual inductance is given as

$$M = \pi_0 x_1 x_2 \pi r^2 l$$

Self-Induction

- The production of induced emf in a circuit, when the current in the same circuit changes is known as **self-induction.**

  Suppose the instantaneous current in the circuit is I and if the magnetic flux linked with the solenoid is ϕ, then it is found that:

$$\phi \propto I \text{ or } \phi = LI \qquad \text{...(i)}$$

where, L is the constant of proportionality. It is called **coefficient of self-induction.**

The induced emf ε in the coil is given by

$$\varepsilon = -\frac{d\phi}{dt} = -L\frac{dI}{dt} \qquad \text{...(ii)}$$

The negative sign is in accordance with the Lenz's law i.e., the induced emf opposes the variation of current in the coil.

From the equation (ii), we find :

$$L = \varepsilon / (dI/dt) \qquad \text{...(iii)}$$

Then, the coefficient of self-induction is the ratio of induced emf in the circuit to the rate of change of the current in the circuit.

Unit of L: The unit of self-induction is also called henry (symbol H).

From equation (ii), we find that if $dI/dt = 1\ As^{-1}$ and $\varepsilon = 1$ V,

then $L = 1\ H \Rightarrow$ Unit of $H = VA^{-1}s$

- If a rod of length l moves perpendicular to a magnetic field B with a velocity v, then the induced emf produced across it, is given by

$$\varepsilon = vBl$$

In general, we have,

$$\varepsilon = \vec{B}.(\vec{v} \times \vec{l})$$

- If a metallic rod of length l rotates about one of its ends in a plane perpendicular to the magnetic field, then the induced emf produced across its ends is given by

$$\varepsilon = \frac{B\omega l^2}{2} = \frac{B(2\pi)fl^2}{2} = BAf$$

Here, ω = angular velocity of rotation, $A = \pi l^2$ = area of circle and f = frequency of rotation.

- Inductance in the electrical circuit is equivalent to the inertia (mass) in mechanics.
- When a bar magnet is dropped into a coil, the electromagnetic induction in the coil opposes its motion, so the magnet falls with acceleration less than that due to gravity.
- The inductance of a coil depends on the following factors:
  - area of cross-section,
  - number of turns
  - permeability of the core.
- Unit of induction, $H = \frac{\text{Wb}}{\text{A}} = \frac{\text{Vs}}{\text{A}} = \Omega.\text{s}$
- The inductance of a circular coil is given by:

$$L = \frac{\phi}{I} = \frac{BAN}{I} = \frac{\mu}{4\pi}.\frac{(2\pi NI)}{rI} \times AN$$

$$\left[\because B = \frac{\mu}{4\pi}.\frac{2\pi NI}{r}\right]$$

$$L = \frac{\mu N^2}{2r}A = \frac{\mu N^2}{2r} \times \pi r^2$$

or $$L = \frac{\mu N^2 \pi r}{2}$$

- The inductance of a solenoid of length l is given by

$$L = \frac{\phi}{I} = \frac{BAN}{I} = \left(\frac{\mu NI}{l}\right)\frac{AN}{I}$$

$$\left[\because B = \frac{\mu NI}{l}\right]$$

or $$L = \frac{\mu N^2 A}{l} = \mu n^2 Al = \mu n^2 V$$

$$\left[\because n = \frac{N}{l}\right]$$

Here, $n = N/l$ = number of turns per unit length and $V = Al$ = volume of the solenoid.

- If two coils of inductance L_1 and L_2 are coupled together, then their mutual inductance is given by

$$M = k\sqrt{L_1 L_2}$$

where, k is called the coupling constant.

- The value of k lies between 0 and 1. For perfectly coupled coils, $k = 1$, it means that the magnetic flux of primary coil is completely linked with the secondary coil.
- Eddy currents do not cause sparking.
- If a current I is set up in a coil of inductance L, then the magnetic field energy stored in it is given by

$$U_m = \frac{1}{2}LI^2$$

- **Coefficient of Mutual Inductance of two identical, parallel and coaxial circular coils:**

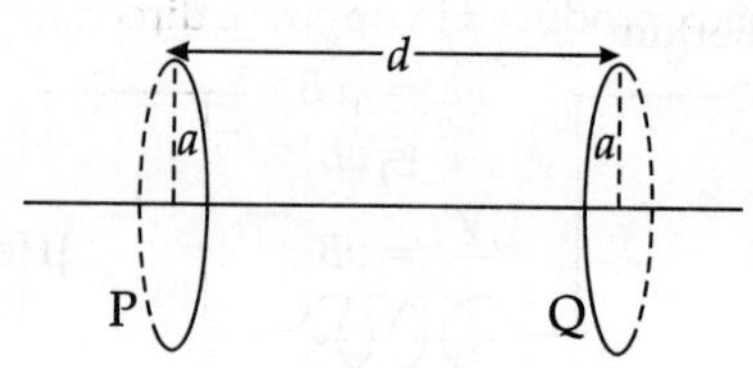

$$M = \frac{\mu_0 \mu_r \pi N^2 a^4}{2(a^2 + d^2)^{3/2}}$$

Where

a = Radius of each coil

d = distance between the centres of the two coils ($d >> a$)

N = Number of turns in each coil

μ_0 = Permeability of free space

μ_r = Relative permeability of core

- **Coefficient of Mutual Inductance of two solenoids tightly wound one over another:**

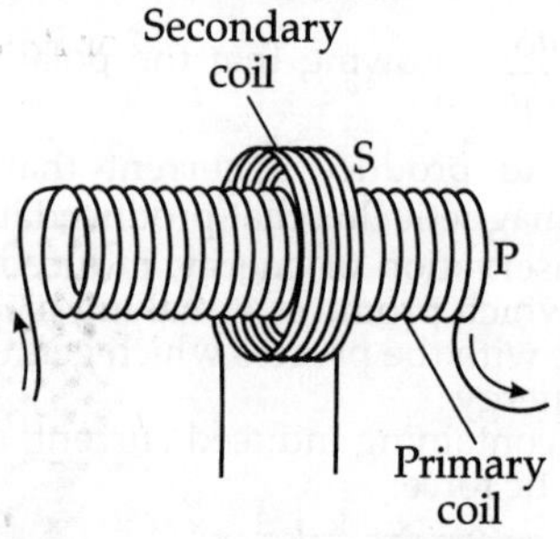

$$M = \frac{\mu_0 \mu_r \pi n_1 n_2 a^2}{l_1}$$

Where

a = Radius of secondary coil

n_1 = Number of turns in primary coil

n_2 = Number of turns in secondary coil

l_1 = Length of turns in primary coil

μ_0 = Permeability of free space

μ_r = Relative permeability of core

- **Inductance in series:**
  - When flux produced in same direction:

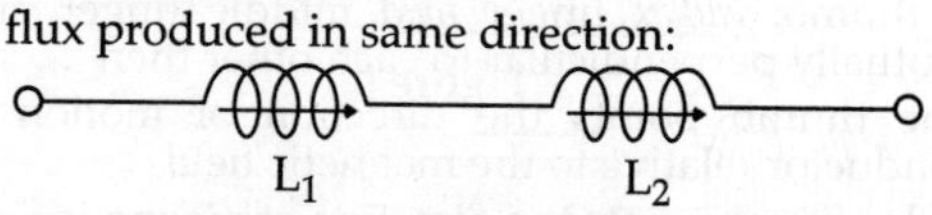

$$L_{eq} = L_1 + L_2 + 2M$$

- When flux produced in opposite direction:

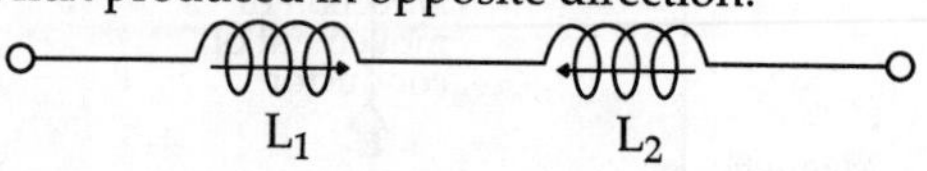

$$L_{eq} = L_1 + L_2 - 2M$$

- **Inductance in parallel:**
  - When flux produced in same direction:

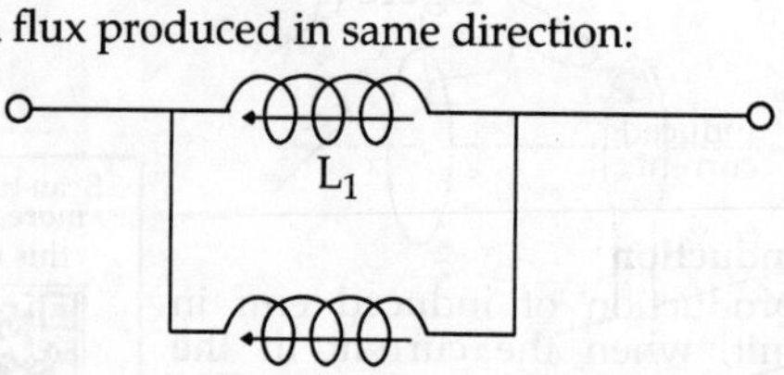

$$L_{eq} = \frac{L_1 L_2 - M^2}{L_1 + L_2 + 2M}$$

- When flux produced in opposite direction:

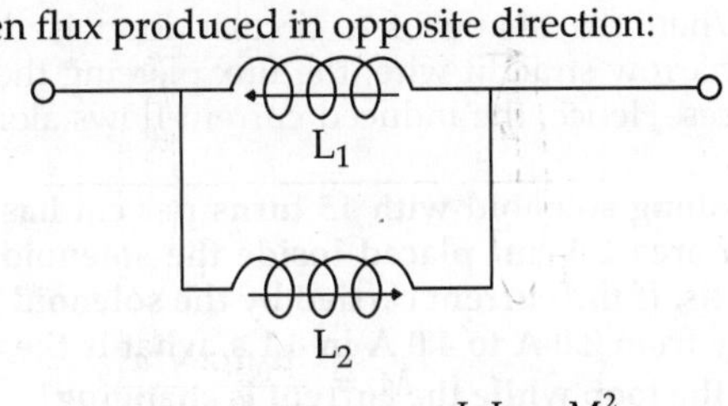

$$L_{eq} = \frac{L_1 L_2 - M^2}{L_1 + L_2 - 2M}$$

AC Generator

- ➢ It converts mechanical energy into electrical energy.
- ➢ It is based on the principle of mutual induction. It has mainly three components:
- **Rotator Coil:** It can rotate about an axis on a shaft.
- **Stator Coil:** It provides magnetic field.
- **Commutator:** It is pair of slip rings and carbon brushes. It will facilitate flow of current between moving coil and stationary circuit.

$$\phi_B = BA \cos\theta \text{ or } BA \cos\omega t \ (\theta = \omega t)$$

$$\varepsilon = -N\frac{d\phi_B}{dt}$$

$$\varepsilon = -N\frac{d(BA\cos\omega t)}{dt}$$

$$\varepsilon = NBA\omega \sin \omega t$$

Maximum value of emf, $\varepsilon_0 = NBA\,\omega$ (when $\sin \omega t = 1$)

$\therefore$ $\varepsilon = \varepsilon_0 \sin \omega t$

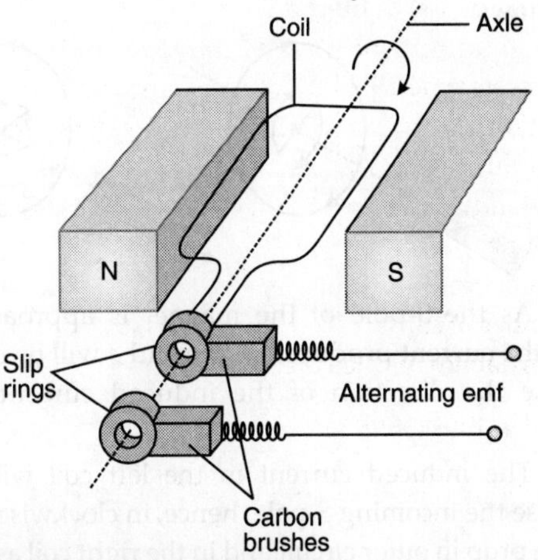

NCERT CORNER

Exercise Questions

Q. 1. Predict the direction of induced current in the situations described by the following figures (a) to (*f*).

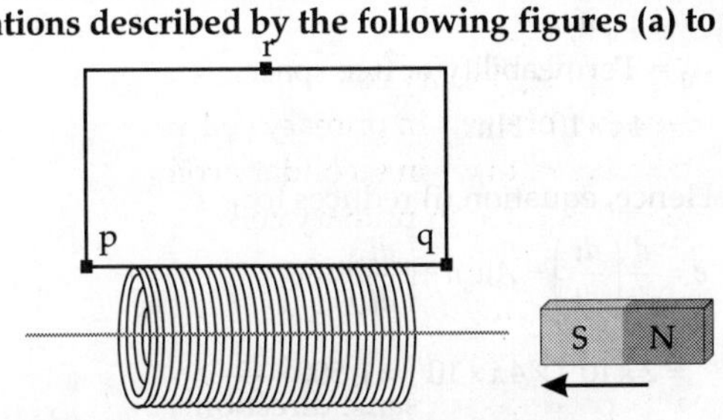

Figure (a)

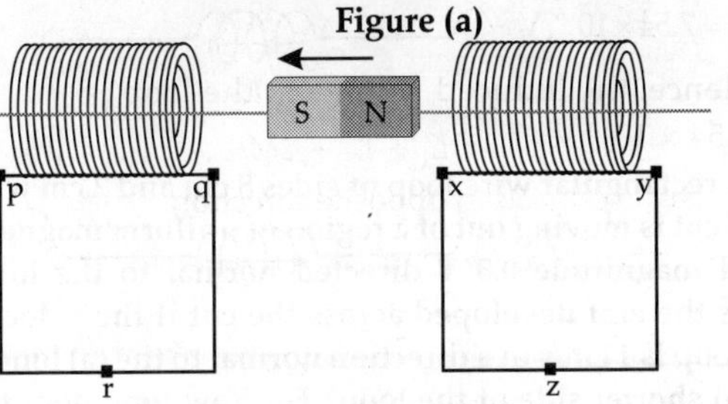

Figure (b)

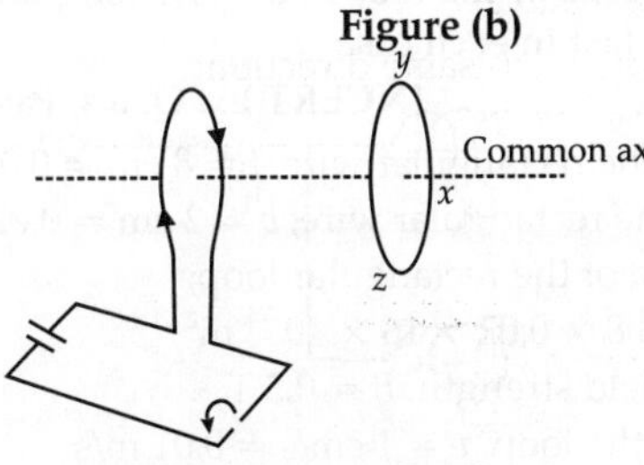

(Tapping key just closed)

Figure (c)

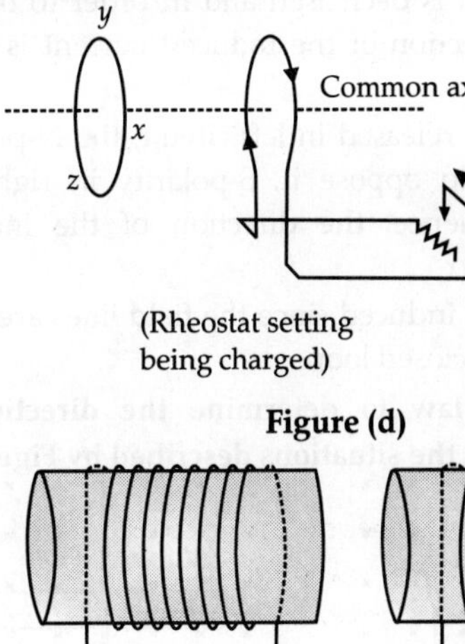

(Rheostat setting being charged)

Figure (d)

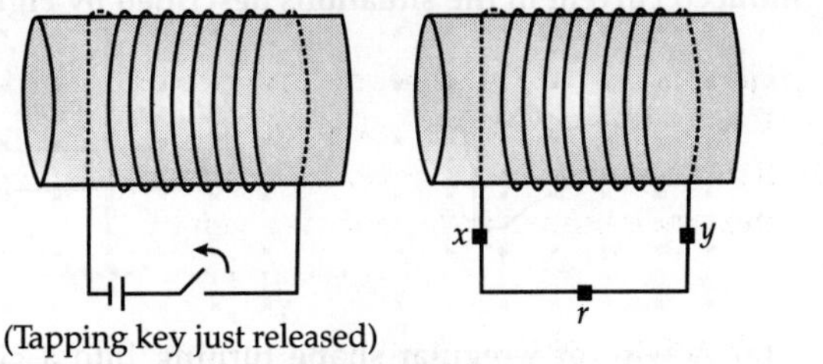

(Tapping key just released)

Figure (e)

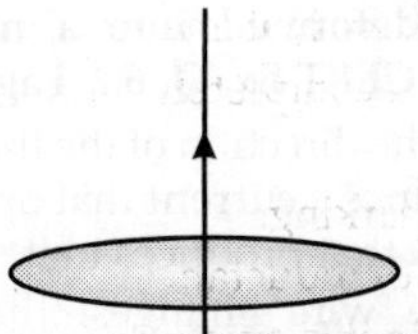

Current (*I*) decreasing at a steady rate

Figure (f) **[NCERT Ex. Q. 6.1, Page 174]**

Ans. The direction of the induced current in a closed loop is given by Lenz's law. The given pairs of figures show the direction of the induced current when the North Pole of a bar magnet is moved towards and away from a closed loop respectively. Using Lenz's rule, the direction of induced current in the given situations can be predicted as follows:

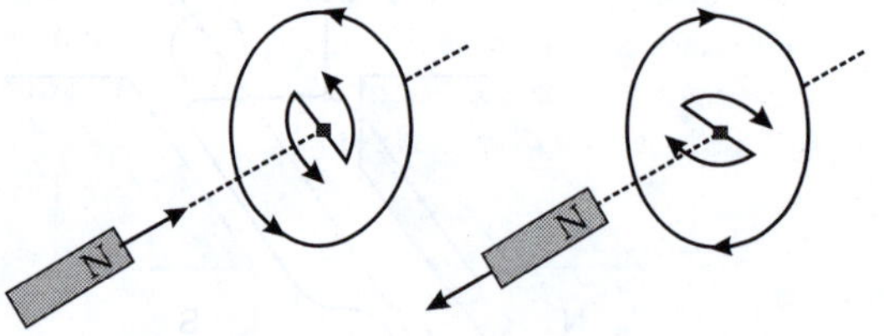

(a) As the S-pole of the magnet is approaching the coil, the current produced at the end *q* will be clockwise. Hence the direction of the induced current is along *qrpq*.

(b) The induced current in the left coil will flow to oppose the incoming S-pole, hence, in clockwise direction along prqp in outer circuit and in the right coil as N-pole is going away from it, hence it will induce S-pole hence the direction of the induced current in left coil is from *yzxy*.

(c) As the current is in clockwise direction due to which S-pole is produced and in order to oppose this, S-pole is produced and the direction of the induced current is along *yzxy*.

(d) As current in the right circuit, flowing in anti-clockwise direction is decreased and in order to oppose this cause the direction of the induced current is along *zyxz*.

(e) As the key is released in left circuit, the N-polarity decreases, hence to oppose it, S-polarity in right coil should increase hence, the direction of the induced current is along *xryx*.

(f) No current is induced since the field lines are lying in the plane of the closed loop.

Q. 2. Use Lenz's law to determine the direction of induced current in the situations described by Figure:

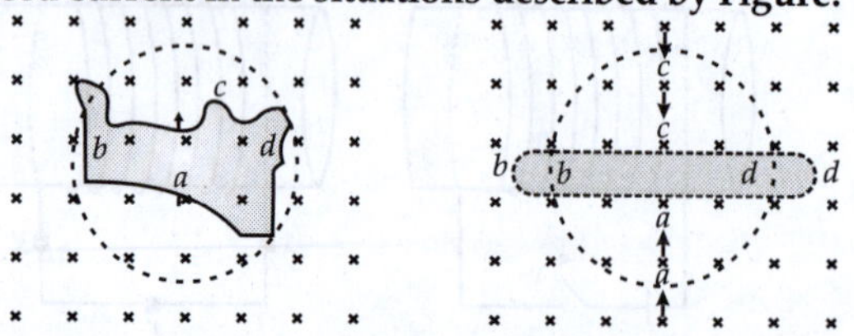

(a) A wire of irregular shape turning into a circular shape;

(b) A circular loop being deformed into a narrow straight wire. [NCERT Ex. Q. 6.2, Page 175]

Ans. According to Lenz's law, the direction of the induced emf is such that it tends to produce a current that opposes the change in the magnetic flux that produces in it.

(a) When the shape of the wire changes, the flux piercing through the unit surface area increases (or the number of magnetic fields line passing through the loop increases). As a result, the induced current produces an opposing flux. Hence, the induced current flows along *c*, *b*, *a* and *d*.

(b) When the shape of a circular loop is deformed into a narrow straight wire, the flux piercing the surface decreases. Hence, the induced current flows along *a*, *b*, *c* and *d*.

Q. 3. A long solenoid with 15 turns per cm has a small loop of area 2.0 cm² placed inside the solenoid normal to its axis. If the current carried by the solenoid changes steadily from 2.0 A to 4.0 A in 0.1 s, what is the induced emf in the loop while the current is changing?

[NCERT Ex. Q. 6.3, Page 176]

Ans. Given that,

Number of turns on the solenoid = 15 turns/cm = 1,500 turns/m

Number of turns per unit length, $n = 1{,}500$ turns

The solenoid has a small loop of area, $A = 2.0\text{ cm}^2 = 2\times10^{-4}\text{ m}^2$

Current carried by the solenoid changes from 2 A to 4 A.

∴ Change in current in the solenoid,

$$di = 4 - 2 = 2\text{ A}$$

Change in time, $dt = 0.1$ s

Induced *emf* in the solenoid is given by Faraday's law as:

$$e = \frac{d\phi}{dt} \qquad \text{...(i)}$$

Where,

ϕ = Induced flux through the small loop

$= BA$ ...(ii)

B = Magnetic field

$= \mu_0 ni$ ...(iii)

μ_0 = Permeability of free space

$= 4\pi\times10^{-7}\text{ Hm}^{-1}$

Hence, equation (i) reduces to:

$$e = \frac{d}{dt}\left(\frac{di}{dt}\right) = A\mu_0 n\times\left(\frac{di}{dt}\right)$$

$$= 2\times10^{-4}\times4\pi\times10^{-7}\times1{,}500\times\frac{2}{0.1}$$

$$= 7.54\times10^{-6}\text{ V}$$

Hence, the induced voltage in the loop is 7.54×10^{-6} V.

Q. 4. A rectangular wire loop of sides 8 cm and 2 cm with a small cut is moving out of a region of uniform magnetic field of magnitude 0.3 T directed normal to the loop. What is the emf developed across the cut if the velocity of the loop is 1 cm/s in a direction normal to the (a) longer side, (b) shorter side of the loop? For how long does the induced voltage last in each case?

[NCERT Ex. Q. 6.4, Page 176]

Ans. Length of the rectangular wire, $l = 8\text{ cm} = 0.08\text{ m}$

Width of the rectangular wire, $b = 2\text{ cm} = 0.02\text{ m}$

Hence, area of the rectangular loop,

$A = lb = 0.08\times0.02 = 16\times10^{-4}\text{ m}^2$

Magnetic field strength, $B = 0.3$ T

Velocity of the loop, $v = 1\text{ cm/s} = 0.01\text{ m/s}$

(a) Emf developed in the loop is given as:

$$e = Blv = 0.3\times0.08\times0.01 = 2.4\times10^{-4}\text{ V}$$

Time taken to travel along the width,

$$t = \frac{\text{Distance travelled}}{\text{Velocity}} = \frac{s}{v} = \frac{0.02}{0.01} = 2\text{ s}$$

Hence, the induced voltage is 2.4×10^{-4} V which lasts for 2 s.

(b) Emf developed, $e = Bbv = 0.3 \times 0.02 \times 0.01$
$= 0.6 \times 10^{-4}$ V

Time taken to travel along the length,

$$t = \frac{\text{Distance travelled}}{\text{Velocity}} = \frac{s}{v} = \frac{0.08}{0.01} = 8\text{ s}$$

Hence, the induced voltage is 0.6×10^{-4} V which lasts for 8 s.

Q. 5. A 1.0 m long metallic rod is rotated with an angular frequency of 400 radsec^{-1} about an axis normal to the rod passing through its one end. The other end of the rod is in contact with a circular metallic ring. A constant and uniform magnetic field of 0.5 T parallel to the axis exists everywhere. Calculate the emf developed between the centre and the ring.
[NCERT Ex. Q. 6.5, Page 176]

Ans. Length of the rod, l = 1 m

Angular frequency, ω = 400 rad/s

Magnetic field strength, B = 0.5 T

One end of the rod has zero linear velocity, while the other end has a linear velocity of $l\omega$.

Average linear velocity of the rod, $v = \frac{l\omega + 0}{2} = \frac{l\omega}{2}$

Emf developed between the centre and the ring,

$$e = Blv = \frac{Bl^2\omega}{2} = \frac{0.5 \times (1)^2 \times 400}{2} = 100\text{ V}$$

Hence, the emf developed between the centre and the ring is 100 V.

Q. 6. A horizontal straight wire 10 m long extending from east to west is falling with a speed of 5.0 m/sec, at right angles to the horizontal component of the earth's magnetic field, 0.30 × 10^{-4} Wbm^{-2}.

(a) What is the instantaneous value of the emf induced in the wire?

(b) What is the direction of the emf?

(c) Which end of the wire is at the higher electrical potential? [NCERT Ex. Q. 6.6, Page 176]

Ans. Given that,

Length of the wire, l = 10 m

Falling speed of the wire, v = 5.0 m/s

Magnetic field strength, $B = 0.3 \times 10^{-4}$ Wb m^{-2}

(a) Emf induced in the wire,

$$e = Blv = 0.3 \times 10^{-4} \times 5 \times 10 = 1.5 \times 10^{-3}\text{ V}$$

(b) Using Fleming's right hand rule, it can be inferred that the direction of the induced emf is from West to East end of the falling wire.

(c) The eastern end of the wire is at a higher potential.

Q. 7. Current in a circuit falls from 5.0 A to 0.0 A in 0.1 s. If an average emf of 200 V induced, give an estimate of the self-inductance of the circuit.
[NCERT Ex. Q. 6.7, Page 176]

Ans. Given that,

Initial current, I_1 = 5.0 A

Final current, I_2 = 0.0 A

Change in current, $dI = I_1\ I_2$ = 5 A

Time taken for the change, t = 0.1 s

Average emf, e = 200 V

For self-inductance (L) of the coil, we have the relation for average emf as:

$$e = L\left(\frac{di}{dt}\right)$$

$$L = \frac{e}{\left(\frac{di}{dt}\right)} = \frac{200}{\frac{5}{0.1}} = 4\text{ H}$$

Hence, the self-induction of the coil is 4 H.

Q. 8. A pair of adjacent coils has a mutual inductance of 1.5 H. If the current in one coil changes from 0 A to 20 A in 0.5 s, what is the change of flux linkage with the other coil? [NCERT Ex. Q. 6.8, Page 176]

Ans. Mutual inductance of a pair of coils, μ = 1.5 H

Initial current, I_1 = 0 A

Final current I_2 = 20 A

Change in current, $dI = I_2 - I_1 = 20 - 0 = 20$ A ...(1)

Time taken for the change, dt = 0.5 s

Induced emf, $e = \frac{d\phi}{dt}$ ...(2)

Where $d\phi$ is the change in the flux linkages with the coil.

Emf is related with mutual inductance as:

Equating (1) and (2), we get

$$\frac{d\phi}{dt} = \mu\frac{dI}{dt}$$

$$d\phi = 1.5 \times (20) = 30\text{ Wb}$$

□□

CHAPTER 7

ALTERNATING CURRENT

- Alternating current changes continuously in magnitude and periodically in direction.
- It is represented by sine curve or cosine curve as $I = I_0 \sin \omega t$ or $I = I_0 \cos \omega t$ where, I_0 is peak value of current and I is instantaneous value of current.
- Frequency of an alternating current supply f, is defined as the number of cycles which gets completed per second which is measured in Hertz (Hz). In India, the frequency is 50 Hz.
- The time period T, of an alternating supply, is time taken to complete one cycle.
- The behaviour of ohmic resistance R in ac circuit is the same as in dc circuit.
- Alternating current can be produced by using a device called ac generator.
- Different types of A.C. wave

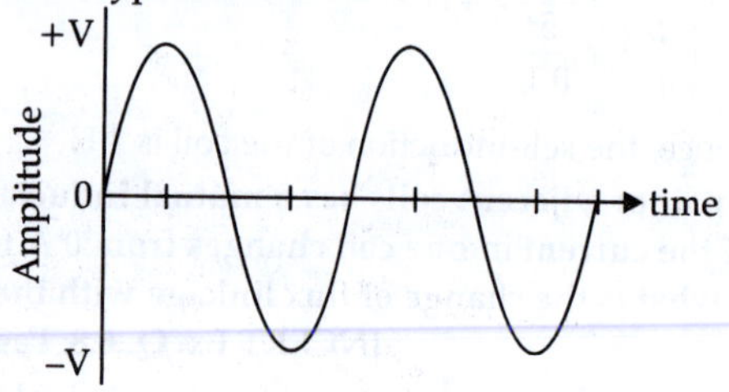

Sine wave

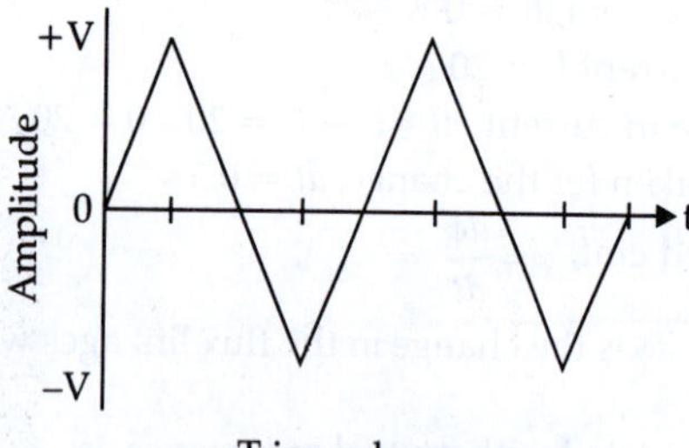

Triangular wave

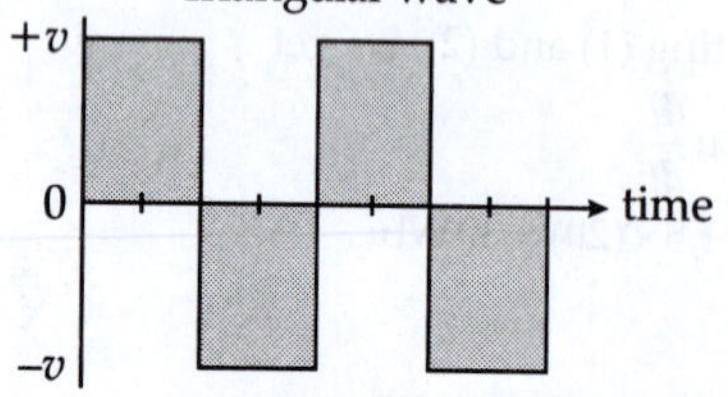

Square wave

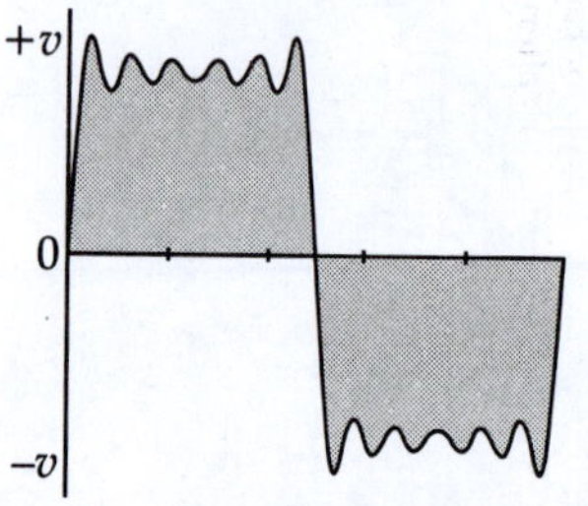

Complex wave

- **Peak and rms value of alternating current/voltage:**

A.C. Voltage	A.C. Current
Equation: $E = E_0 \sin\omega t$ Where $\omega = 2\pi f$ E_0 is the maximum value of peak value.	Equation: $i = i_0 \sin\omega t$ Where $\omega = 2\pi f$ i_0 is the maximum value of peak value. $i = \frac{E}{R} = \frac{E_0 \sin \omega t}{R}$ $= i_0 \sin\omega t$ where R = resistance
r.m.s. value: $E_{rms} = \frac{E_0}{\sqrt{2}}$ $= 0.707E_0$	r.m.s. value: $i_{rms} = \frac{i_0}{\sqrt{2}}$ $= 0.707 i_0$
Average value: E_{avg} $= \frac{2E_m}{\neq}$	Average value: $i_{avg} = \frac{2i_m}{\neq}$
Form factor: $\frac{E_{rms}}{E_{avg}}$	Form factor: $\frac{i_{rms}}{i_{avg}}$

Reactance and Impedance

- When an alternating current is passed through a resistance, a voltage drop is produced which is in phase with the current and is measured in ohms (Ω).
- Reactance is the inertia against the motion of electrons where an alternating current after passing through it produces a voltage drop which is 90° out of phase with the current.
- Reactance is shown by "X" and is measured in ohms (Ω).
- Reactances are of two types: inductive and capacitive.

* Inductive reactance is linked with varying magnetic field that surrounds a wire or a coil carrying a current. Inductive reactance (X_L) is the resistance offered by an inductor and is given by X_L

$X_L = \omega L = 2\pi f L$

Through a pure inductor, alternating current lags behind the alternating voltage by phase angle of 90°.

* Capacitive reactance is linked with changing electric field between two conducting surfaces separated from each other by an insulating medium.

Capacitive reactance (X_C) is the resistance offered by a capacitor and is given by

$X_C = 1/\omega C = 1/2\pi f C$

Through a pure capacitor, alternating current leads the alternating emf by a phase angle of 90°.

Alternating Current

A C Circuits

R–C circuit
- $I = I_0 \sin(\omega t + \phi)$
- $Z = \sqrt{R^2 + X_c^2}$
- $X_c = 1/\omega C$
- $\tan\phi = 1/\omega CR$
- $I_0 = E_0/Z$
- Power factor $\cos\phi = \dfrac{R^2}{\sqrt{R^2 + X_c^2}}$
- current leading.

Inductive (L) circuit
- $I = I_0 \sin\left(\omega t - \dfrac{\pi}{2}\right)$
- Phase difference between V & I, $\phi = \pi/2$
- Power factor $\cos(\phi) = 0$
- Voltage leads current by $\pi/2$
- $P = 0$

Capacitive (C) circuit
- $I = I_0 \sin\left(\omega t + \dfrac{\pi}{2}\right)$
- $\phi = \pi/2$ Power factor $\cos\phi = 0$
- Power $(P) = 0$
- Current leads the voltage by $\pi/2$

Resistive (R) circuit
- $I = I_0 \sin(\omega t)$
- $\phi = 0°$
- $\cos\phi = 1$
- $P = V_0 I_0/2$
- Current & voltage both are in same phase

L–C–R circuit
- $I = I_0 \sin(\omega t \pm \phi)$
- $Z = \sqrt{R^2 + (X_c - X_L)^2}$
- $X = X_c - X_L = \left(\dfrac{1}{\omega c} - \omega L\right)$
- $\tan\phi = \left(\dfrac{1}{\omega c} - \omega L\right)/R$, $I_0 = \dfrac{E_0}{Z}$
- At resonance: $X_L = X_C$
- Voltage and current are in phase

L–R circuit
- $I = I_0 \sin(\omega t + \phi)$
- $Z = \sqrt{R^2 + X_L^2}$
- $X_L = \omega L$
- $\tan\phi = \omega L/R$
- $I_0 = E_0/Z$
- power factor $= R/Z$
- voltage is leading

L–C circuit
- $I = I_0 \sin\left(\omega t \pm \dfrac{\pi}{2}\right)$
- $X = X_L - X_C$
- $\phi = \pi/2$
- Power factor = 0, Either voltage or current leading

Contribution
In 1883, Nikola Tesla invented AC motor, AC generator and AC transmission technology.

A C Generator
A device generating alternating current having elements magnet, armature and graphite brushes emf induced through coil

$E = NBA\omega \sin \omega t$

$I = E/R = NBA\omega \sin \omega t/R$

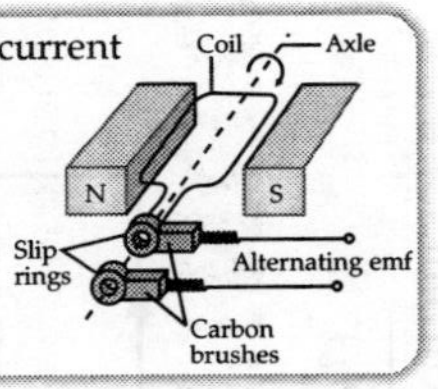

Transformer
It is used to obtain a high AC voltage from a Low–voltage AC source or vice–versa

Efficiency of a transformer
- η = output power/Input power
- 99% efficiency can easily achieved

Turns ratio
- $\dfrac{E_s}{E_p} = \dfrac{I_p}{I_s} = \dfrac{N_s}{N_p} = K$

For step-up transformer $N_s > N_p$,
For step-down transformer $N_p > N_s$,

Power in AC Circuit
$P = E_{rms} I_{rms} \cos\phi = \dfrac{E_0}{\sqrt{2}} \times \dfrac{I_0}{\sqrt{2}} \cos\phi = \dfrac{1}{2} E_0 I_0 \cos\phi$

Impedance
The ratio of emf applied and the current produced in an AC circuit $Z = E_0/I_0$ Ohm

Reactance
The hindrance offered by inductor or capacitor or both to the flow of alternating current

AC Current
Direction of current changes alternatively
$I = I_0 \sin\omega t$
$v = v_0 \sin\omega t$

RMS value or root mean square value
- $I_{rms} = I_0/\sqrt{2}$
- $V_{rms} = v_0/\sqrt{2}$

Mean value or Average value
- $I_{mean} = 2I_0/\pi$
- $V_{rms} = 2v_0/\pi$

Peak value or Maximum value
- $I_0 = \sqrt{2} I_{rms}$
- $V_0 = \sqrt{2} v_{rms}$

Trace the Mind Map
- First Level
- Second Level
- Third Level

- Impedance is the comprehensive expression of all forms of opposition to electron flow, including resistance and reactance in an A.C. circuit, where alternating voltage remains out of phase 90° with current.

$$Z = \sqrt{R^2 + X^2} = \sqrt{R^2 + (X_C \sim X_L)^2}$$

➢ **Pure resistive circuit:**

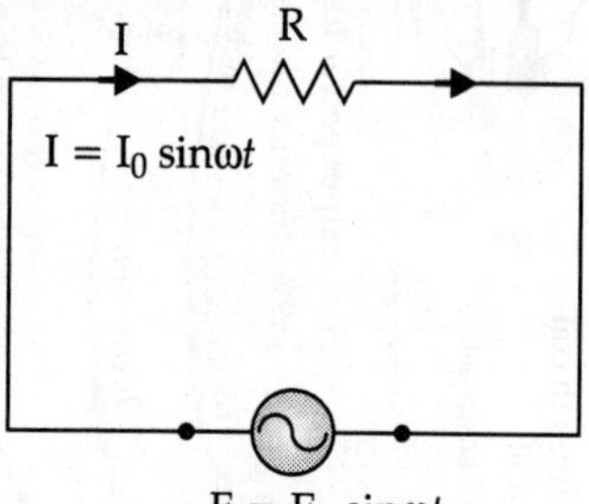

E = E_0 sinωt

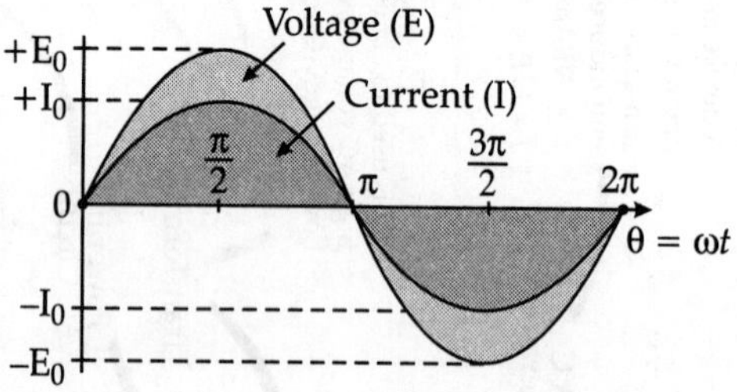

- No phase difference between voltage and current.

  $E = E_0\sin\omega t$

  $I = (E_0/R)\sin\omega t = i_0\sin\omega t$

- **Phasor diagram:**

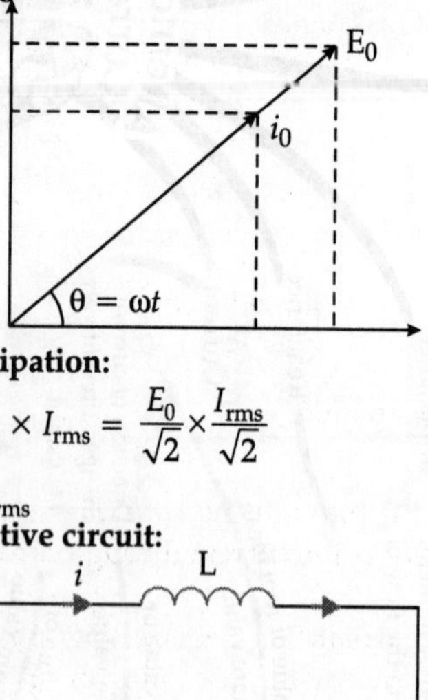

- **Power dissipation:**

$$P_{rms} = E_{rms} \times I_{rms} = \frac{E_0}{\sqrt{2}} \times \frac{I_{rms}}{\sqrt{2}}$$

$P_{avg} = ½ P_{rms}$

➢ **Pure inductive circuit:**

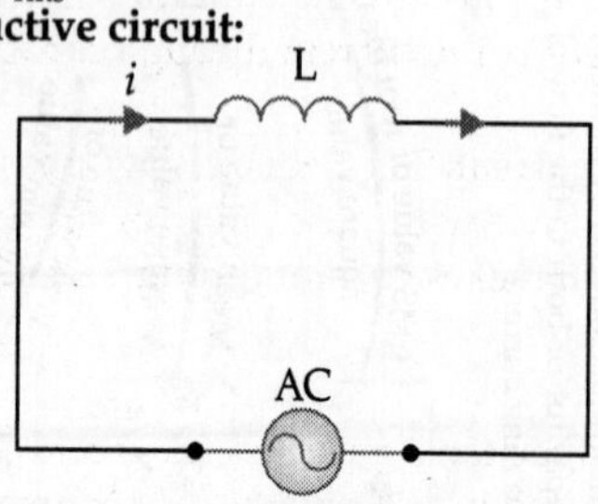

E = E_0 sinωt

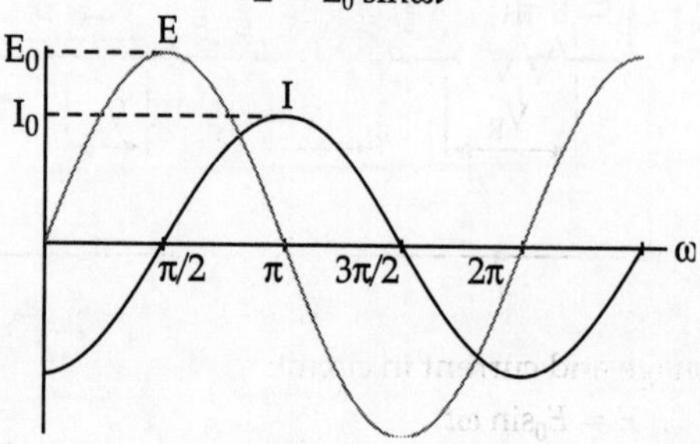

- **Voltage and current in circuit:**

  $E = E_0\sin\omega t$

$$I = -\left(\frac{E_0}{\omega L}\right)\cos\omega t = I_0 \sin\left(\omega t - \frac{\pi}{2}\right)$$

where, X_L = inductive reactance = ωL

Current lags behind voltage by 90°.

- Phasor diagram

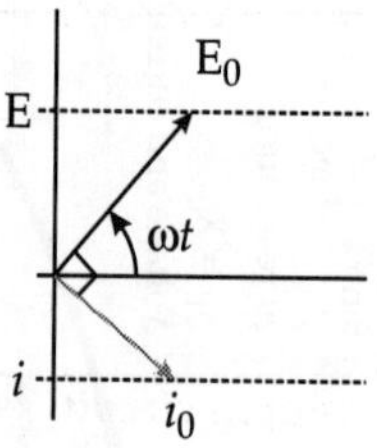

- **Power dissipation:**

  $P_{av} = 0$

➢ **Pure capacitive circuit:**

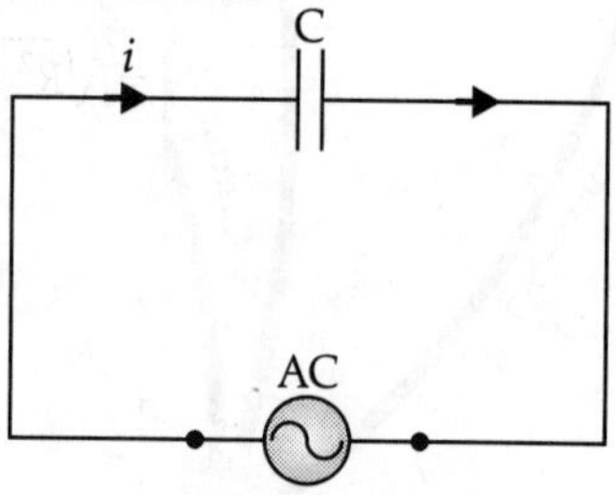

E = E_0 sinωt

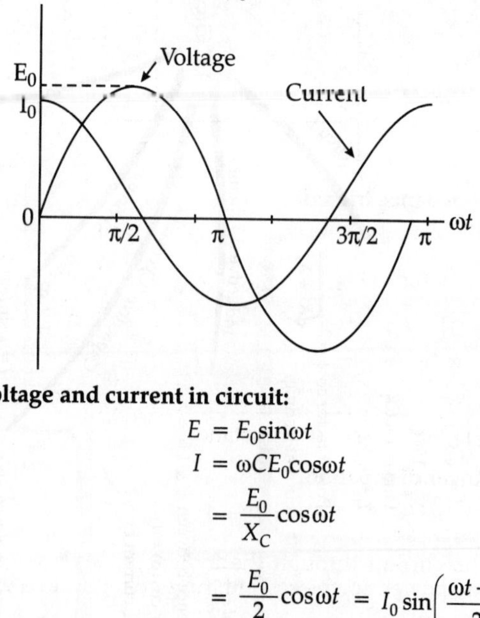

- **Voltage and current in circuit:**

$$E = E_0\sin\omega t$$

$$I = \omega C E_0 \cos\omega t$$

$$= \frac{E_0}{X_C}\cos\omega t$$

$$= \frac{\frac{E_0}{2}}{\omega C}\cos\omega t = I_0 \sin\left(\frac{\omega t + \pi}{2}\right)$$

where, X_L = inductive reactance = ωL

Current leads voltage by 90°.

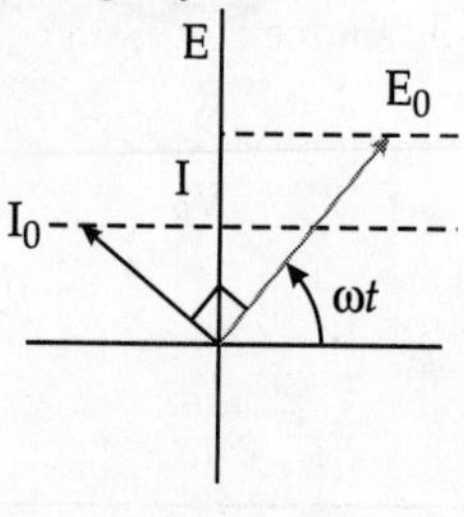

- Phasor Diagram:
- Power dissipation:

$P_{av} = 0$

LR Circuit

- A pure inductor and a pure resistor are connected in series with an ac source $E = E_0\sin\omega t$.

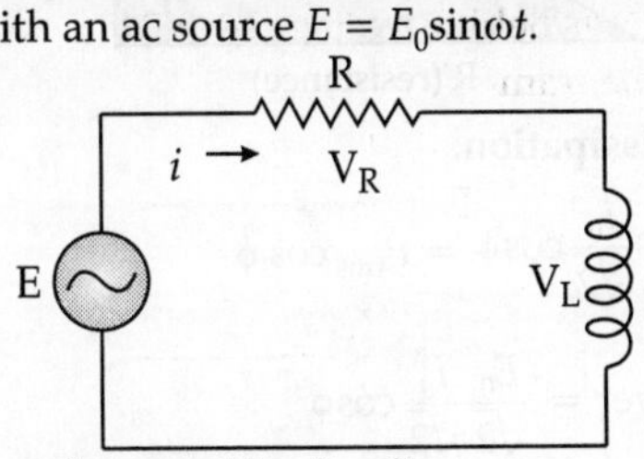

- **Voltage and current in circuit:**

$$E = E_0\sin\omega t$$

$$i = \left(\frac{E_0}{Z}\right)\sin(\omega t - \phi) = i_0\sin(\omega t - \phi)$$

where $$Z = \sqrt{R^2 + X_L^2} = \sqrt{R^2 + (\omega L)^2}$$

$$\phi = \tan^{-1}(\omega L/R)$$

Current lags behind voltage by ϕ.

$$0° < \phi < 90°$$

- **Phasor diagram:**

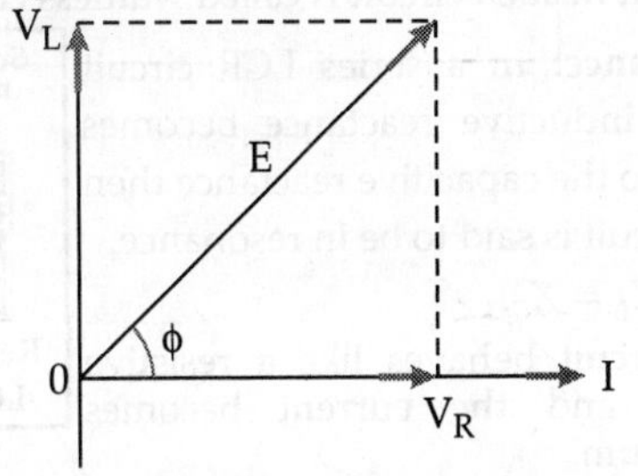

- **Impedance triangle:**

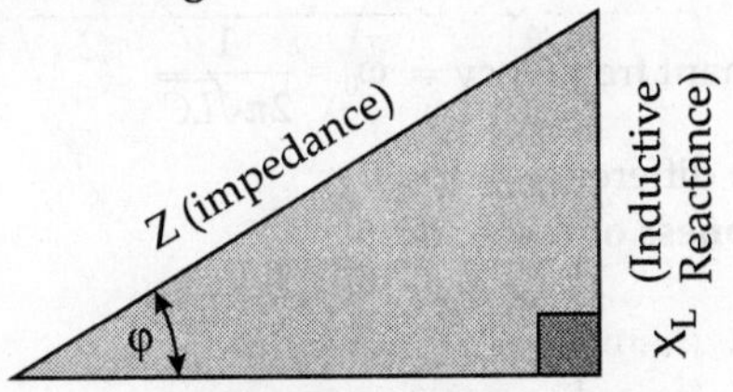

- **Power dissipation:**

$$P = I_{rms}^2 R$$

The current through the inductor does not dissipate any power. So, the current through inductor is wattless current.

CR Circuit

- A pure capacitor and a pure resistor are connected in series with an ac source $E = E_0\sin\omega t$.

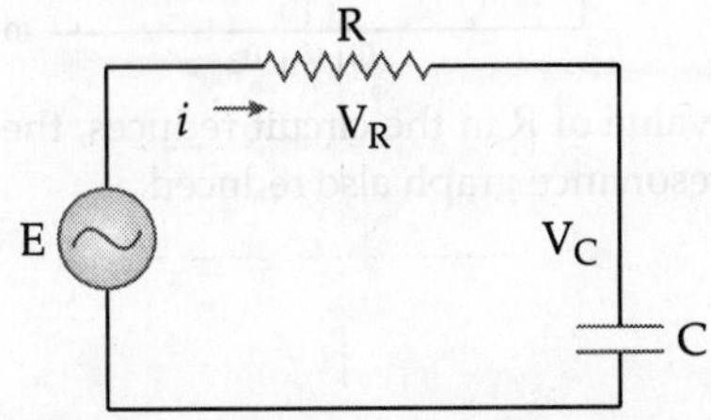

- Voltage and current in circuit:

$$E = E_0\sin\omega t$$

$$I = \left(\frac{E_0}{Z}\right)\sin(\omega t + \phi) = I_0\sin(\omega t + \phi)$$

where $$Z = \sqrt{R^2 + X_C^2} = \sqrt{R^2 + \left(\frac{1}{\omega C}\right)^2}$$

$$\phi = \tan^{-1}\left(\frac{1/\omega C}{R}\right)$$

$$= \tan^{-1}\left(\frac{1}{\omega CR}\right)$$

Current leads voltage by ϕ.

$$0° < \phi < 90°$$

- **Phasor diagram:**

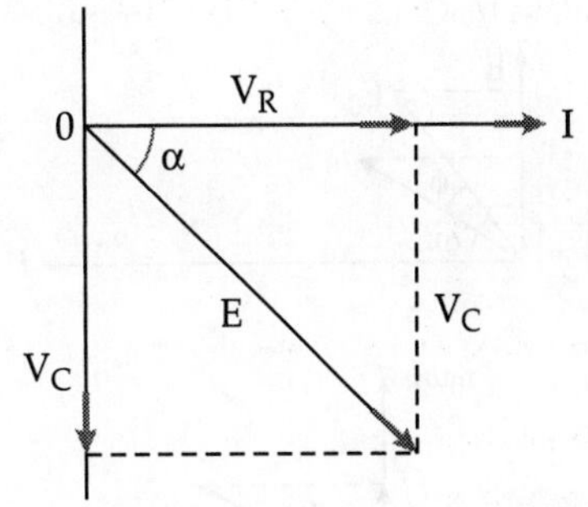

- **Impedance triangle:**

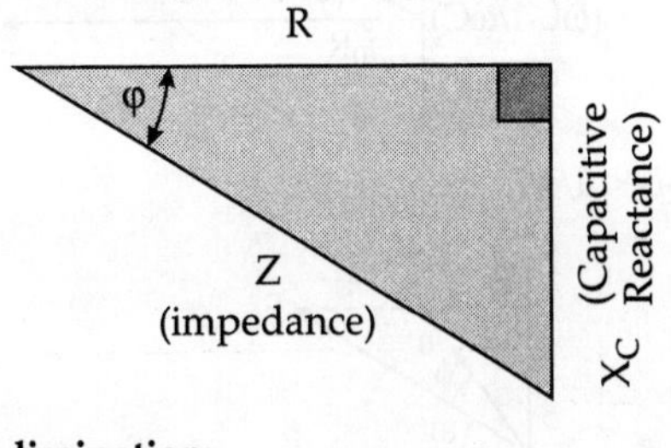

- **Power dissipation:**

$$P = I_{rms}^2 R$$

The current through the capacitor does not dissipate any power. So, the current through capacitor is wattless current.

➢ **Wattless current:** The average power associated over a complete cycle with pure inductor or pure capacitor is zero which makes current through L and C as wattless or idle current.

➢ **LCR circuit:**

- A pure capacitor, a pure inductor and a pure resistor are connected in series with an ac source $E = E_0\sin\omega t$.

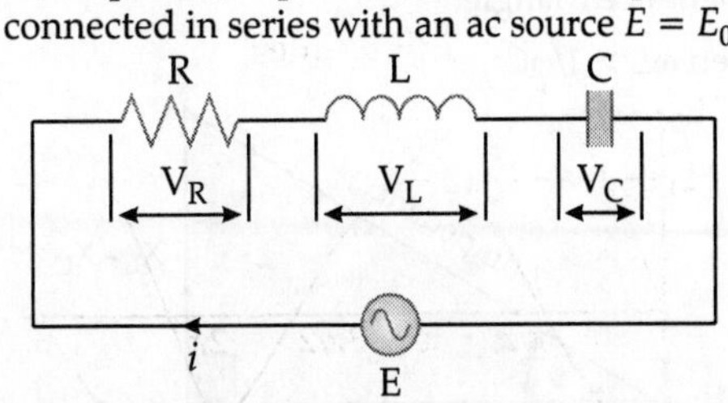

- Voltage and current in circuit:

$$E = E_0\sin\omega t$$

$$I = \frac{E_0}{\sqrt{R^2+(\omega L - 1/\omega C)^2}}\sin(\omega t - \phi)$$

or, $$I = \frac{E_0}{\sqrt{R^2+(X_L - X_C)^2}}\sin(\omega t - \phi)$$

or, $$I = \left(\frac{E_0}{Z}\right)\sin(\omega t - \phi)$$

$\therefore$ $$I = I_0 \sin(\omega t - \phi)$$

$$\phi = \tan^{-1}\frac{\omega L - 1/\omega C}{R} = \frac{X_L - X_C}{R}$$

If $\omega L > 1/\omega C$, Current lags behind voltage by ϕ.

If $\omega L < 1/\omega C$, Current leads voltage by ϕ.

$$0° < \phi < 90°$$

- **Phasor diagrams:**

When $\omega L > 1/\omega C$

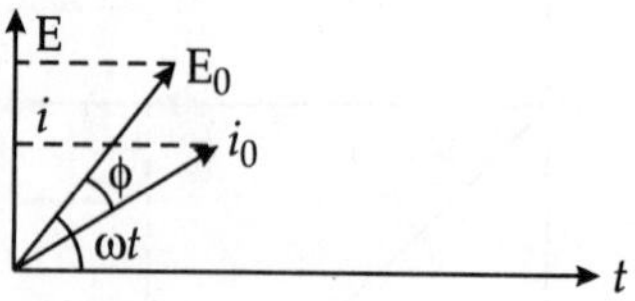

$i_0\omega L$

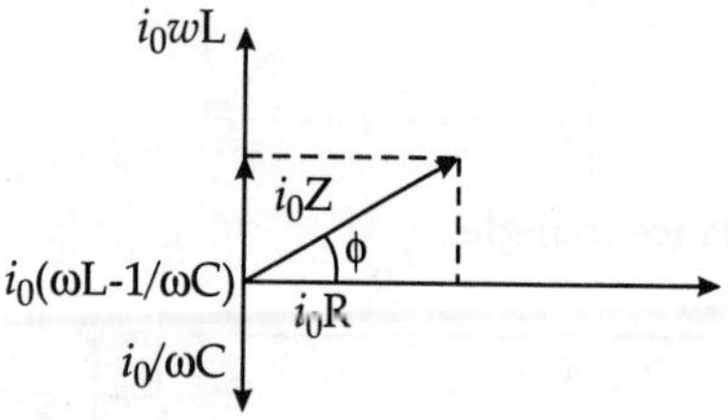

When $\omega L < 1/\omega C$

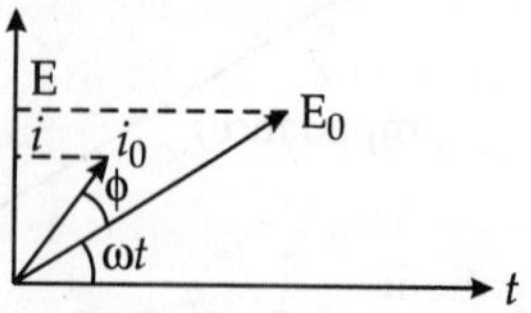

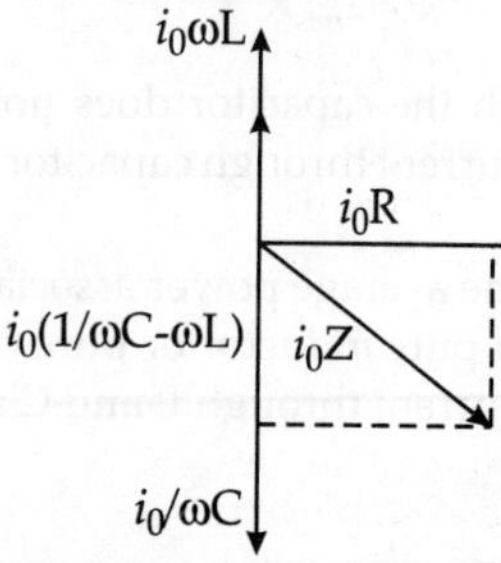

- **Impedance triangle:**

When $\omega L > 1/\omega C$

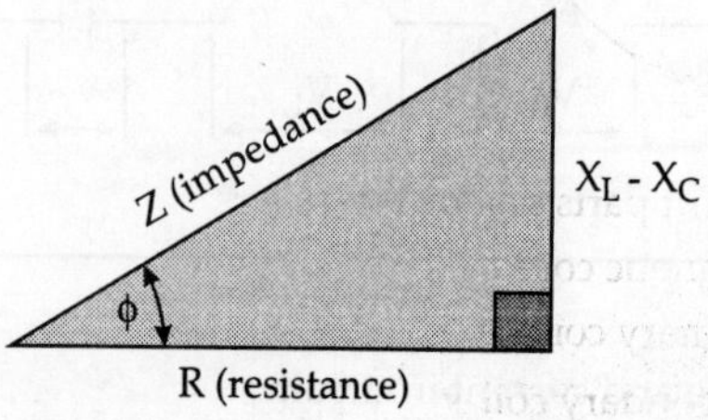

When $\omega L < 1/\omega C$

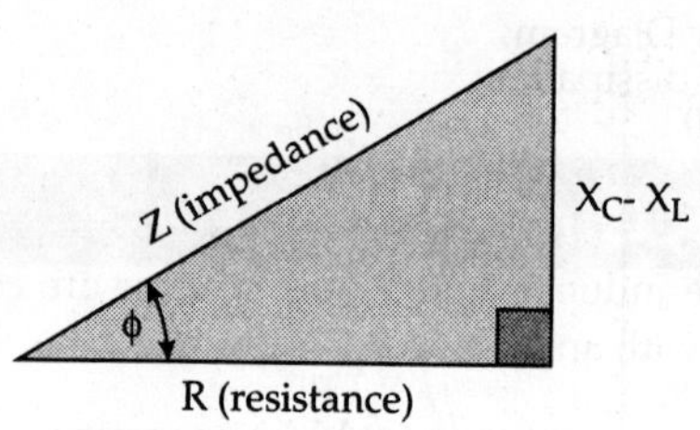

- **Power dissipation:**

$$P_{av} = \frac{E_0}{\sqrt{2}}\frac{i_0}{\sqrt{2}}\cos\phi = P_{rms}\cos\phi$$

$$\text{True power} = \frac{E_0}{\sqrt{2}}\frac{i_0}{\sqrt{2}}\cos\phi$$

$$\text{Apparent power} = P_{rms} = E_{rms} i_{rms}$$

- **Power factor**

Power factor = True power / apparent power = $\cos\phi = \frac{R}{Z}$

If $\phi = \frac{\neq}{2}$, then power factor is zero.

Current in such circuit is called wattless current.

> **Resonance:** In a series LCR circuit when inductive reactance becomes equal to the capacitive reactance then the circuit is said to be in resonance.

Scan to know more about this topic

Resonance of LCR circuit

Since $X_L = X_C$,

The circuit behaves like a resistive circuit and the current becomes maximum.

So, $Z = R$

$$\text{Resonant frequency} = \omega_0 = \frac{1}{2\pi\sqrt{LC}}$$

Phase difference = $\phi = 0$

- **Sharpness of resonance:**

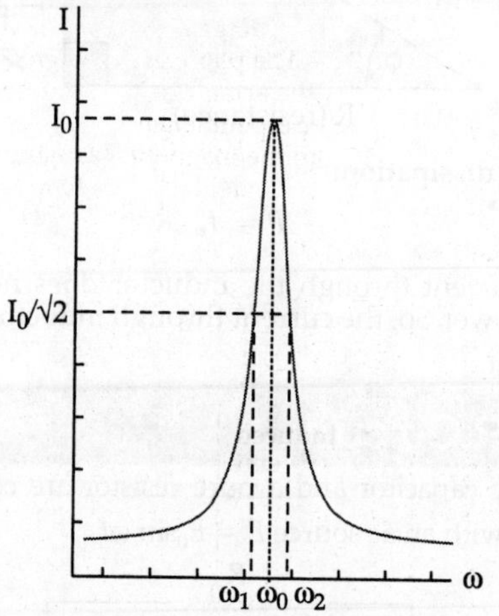

As the value of R in the circuit reduces, the sharpness of the resonance graph also reduced.

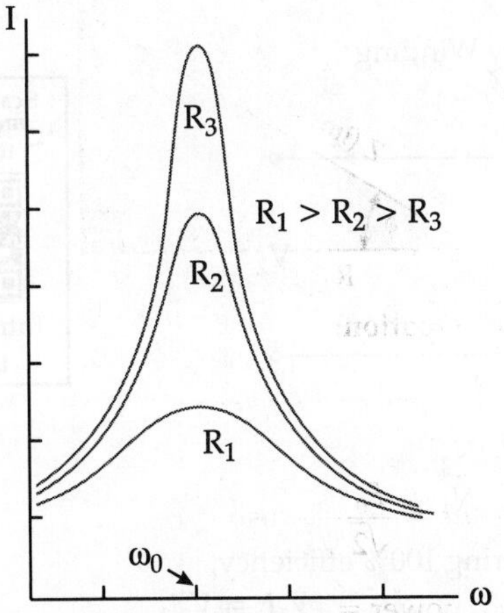

- Variation of impendance versus frequency:

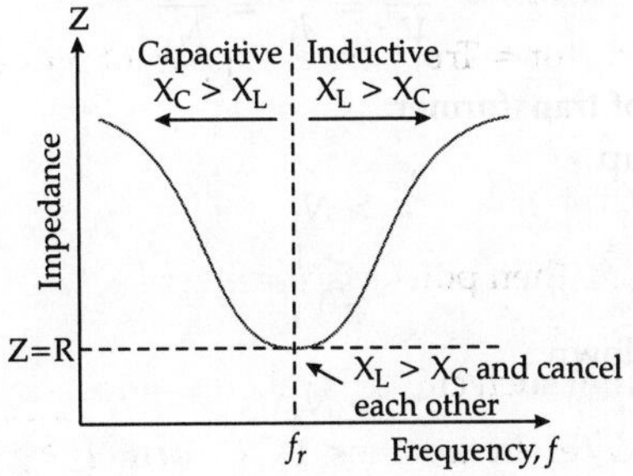

➢ Q-factor is the ratio of potential difference across the inductor or capacitor and the applied voltage.

$$Q \text{ factor} = \frac{V_L}{E} = \frac{V_C}{E}$$

$$\therefore Q \text{ factor} = \frac{\omega_0 L}{R} = \frac{1}{\omega_0 CR}$$

AC Circuit

- **Working principle:** It works on the principle of Faraday's laws of electromagnetic induction.
- **Output emf:**

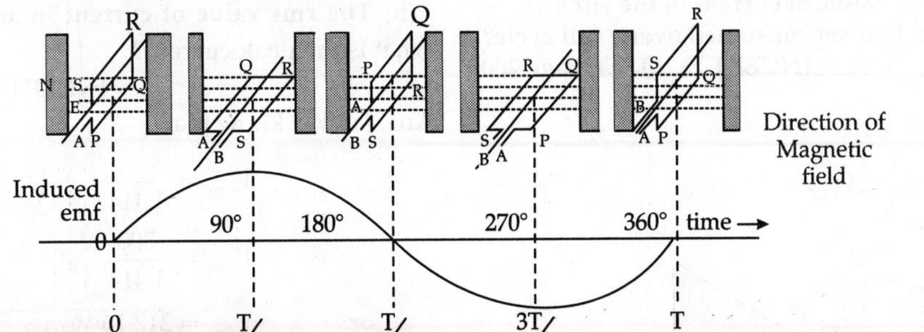

When armature rotates in between the magnetic poles, the flux linkage changes continuously and emf is induced in the armature.

If N is the number of turns of the armature, then flux throgh the coil = $\phi = NBA\cos\omega t$

Induced emf = $\varepsilon = -d\phi/dt = NBA\omega\sin\omega t$

Peak value of emf = $\varepsilon_0 = NBA\omega$

If T = time period of rotation and frequency is ν, then

$$\varepsilon = \varepsilon_0 \sin\frac{2\neq t}{T}$$

$$= \varepsilon_0 \sin\omega t$$

- Different parts of an AC generator
  (i) Permanent magnet (field magnet)
  (ii) Armature wound on soft iron core
  (iii) Slip ring
  (iv) Carbon brush
- **Diagram:**

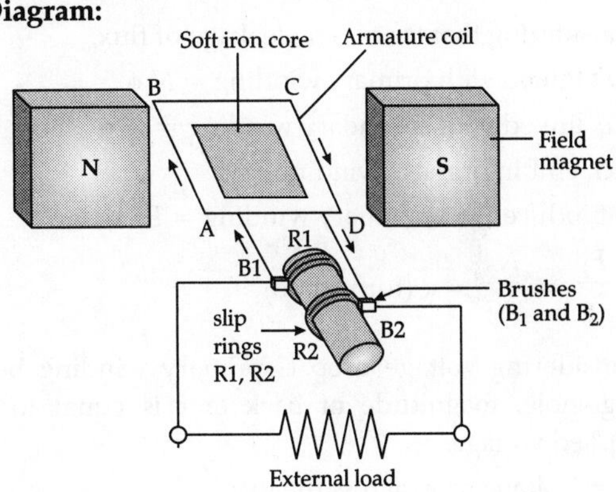

- **Working:**

  Turbine rotates the armature in between the poles of field magnet.

  The two ends of the armature is attached to two slip rings. Armature rotates with slip rings.

  Carbon brushes maintain contacts with the slip rings.

  External circuit is connected with the brushes.

Transformer

- Transformer is a static electrical device which converts low voltage ac to high voltage ac and vice versa.
- **Working principle:** It works on the principle of mutual induction between two magnetically coupled coils.
- Different parts of a transformer:
  (i) Magnetic core
  (ii) Primary coil
  (iii) Secondary coil

  The two coils are wound on the closed iron core.

- **Diagram:**

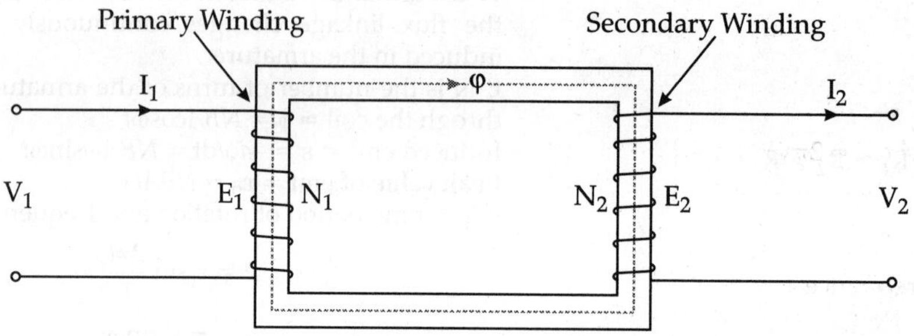

Scan to know more about this topic

Introduction to A.C.

- Working:

N_1 = number of turns ion primary winding

N_2 = Number of turns in secondary winding

V_1 = applied voltage in primary winding

ϕ = alternating flux in core

Considering that there is no leakage of flux,

Flux linked with primary winding = $N_1\phi$

Flux linked with secondary winding = $N_2\phi$

Back emf in primary winding = E_1

emf induced in secondary winding = E_2

$$\therefore \frac{E_2}{E_1} = \frac{N_2}{N_1} = \kappa \text{ (turns ratio)}$$

Considering voltage drop is primary winding being negligible, magnitude of back emf is equal to the applied voltage.

V_2 = Voltage drop across the load

Considering voltage drop is secondary winding being negligible, magnitude of induced emf is equal to the voltage across the load.

$$\therefore \frac{V_2}{V_1} = \frac{N_2}{N_1}$$

Considering 100% efficiency,

$$V_1I_1 = V_2I_2$$

$$\therefore \frac{V_2}{V_1} = \frac{I_2}{I_1} = \frac{N_2}{N_1}$$

- **Types of transformer:**

o Step up

$N_2 > N_1$

$\kappa > 1$

$V_2 > V_1$

o Step down

$N_1 > N_2$

$\kappa < 1$

$V_1 > V_2$

- **Different types of losses in transformer:**

(i) Eddy current loss

(ii) Hysteresis loss

(iii) Copper loss

(iv) Magnetic flux leakage loss

NCERT CORNER

Exercise Questions

Q. 1. A 100 Ω resistor is connected to a 220 V, 50 Hz ac supply.

(a) What is the rms value of current in the circuit?

(b) What is the net power consumed over a full cycle?

[NCERT Ex. Q. 7.1, Page 200]

Ans. Given that:

$R = 100$ Ohms

$V = 220$ V

$\nu = 50$ Hz

(a) We know that

$$I_{rms} = \frac{V_{rms}}{R}$$

Substituting the values,

$$I_{rms} = \frac{220}{100} = 2.2 \text{ A}$$

(b) Power $P = VI$

Or Power $= 220 \times 2.2$

Or Power $= 484$ W

Q. 2. (a) The peak voltage of an ac supply is 300 V. What is the rms voltage?

(b) The rms value of current in an ac circuit is 10 A. What is the peak current?

[NCERT Ex. Q. 7.2, Page 200]

Ans. (a) We know that

$$V_{rms} = \frac{V_{peak}}{1.414}$$

$$V_{rms} = \frac{300}{1.414}$$

or $V_{rms} = 212.16$ V

(b) Using above identity for current,

$$I_{peak} = 1.414 \times I_{rms}$$

or $I_{peak} = 1.414 \times 10 = 14.14$ A.

Q. 3. A 44 mH inductor is connected to 220 V, 50 Hz ac supply. Determine the rms value of the current in the circuit. [NCERT Ex. Q. 7.3, Page 200]

Ans. Given that

$$L = 44 \text{ mH}$$
$$V = 220 \text{ V}$$
$$\nu = 50 \text{ Hz}$$

Inductive reactance, $X_L = \omega L = 2\pi\nu L$

I_{rms} is given by, $\dfrac{V}{X_L}$

Determining inductive reactance

$$X_L = 2 \times 3.14 \times 50 \times 44 \times 10^{-3}$$
$$X_L = 13.82 \text{ ohms}$$

Therefore,

$$I_{rms} = 220/13.82$$

or $I_{rms} = 15.92$ A.

Q. 4. A 60 μF capacitor is connected to a 110 V, 60 Hz ac supply. Determine the rms value of the current in the circuit. [NCERT Ex. Q. 7.4, Page 200]

Ans. Given that

$$C = 60 \text{ microfarads}$$
$$V = 110 \text{ volts}$$
$$\nu = 60 \text{ Hz}$$
$$I_{rms} = \frac{V}{X_C}$$

Now, $X_C = \dfrac{1}{\omega_C}$

$$X_c = \frac{1}{2 \times 3.14 \times 60 \times 60 \times 10^{-6}}$$
$$X_c = 44.232 \text{ Ohms}$$

Hence $I_{rms} = \dfrac{110}{44.232} = 2.487$ A.

Q. 5. In Questions 7.3 and 7.4, what is the net power absorbed by each circuit over a complete cycle. Explain your answer. [NCERT Ex. Q. 7.5, Page 200]

Ans. Zero. As the phase difference between voltage and current in pure capacitive or inductive circuit is 90°. So, the average power is zero and power is absorbed only by resistance in the circuit.

Q. 6. A charged 30 μF capacitor is connected to a 27 mH inductor. What is the angular frequency of free oscillations of the circuit? [NCERT Ex. Q. 7.6, Page 200]

Ans. Given that

$C = 30$ μF

$L = 27$ mH

Angular frequency of free oscillations

$$\omega = \frac{1}{(LC)^{1/2}}$$

Substitution results,

Angular frequency = 1111.11 rad/s

$= 1.11 \times 10^3$ rad/s.

Q. 7. *A* series *LCR* circuit with *R* = 20 Ω, *L* = 1.5 H and *C* = 35 μF is connected to a variable-frequency 200 *V* ac supply. When the frequency of the supply equals the natural frequency of the circuit, what is the average power transferred to the circuit in one complete cycle? [NCERT Ex. Q. 7.7, Page 200]

Ans. Given that

$$R = 20 \text{ ohms}$$
$$L = 1.5 \text{ H}$$
$$C = 35\ \mu\text{F}$$
$$V = 200 \text{ volts}$$

$$\text{Natural frequency} = \frac{1}{(LC)^{1/2}} = 138 \text{ s}^{-1}.$$

At natural frequency,

$$Z = R$$

So, $I = \dfrac{V}{R} = \dfrac{200}{20} = 10\,A$

Thus

$$P = I^2R$$

Or, $P = 10 \times 10 \times 20 = 2{,}000$ W.

Q. 8. Figure shows a series *LCR* circuit connected to a variable frequency 230 V source. *L* = 5.0 H, *C* = 80 μF, *R* = 40 Ω.

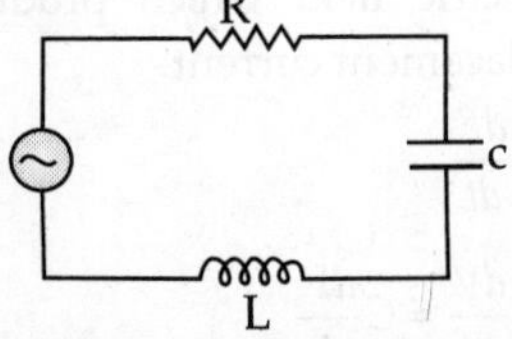

(a) Determine the source frequency which drives the circuit in resonance.

(b) Obtain the impedance of the circuit and the amplitude of current at the resonating frequency.

(c) Determine the rms potential drops across the three elements of the circuit. Show that the potential drop across the *LC* combination is zero at the resonating frequency. [NCERT Ex. Q. 7.8, Page 200]

Ans. Given that

$$V = 230 \text{ V}$$
$$L = 5 \text{ H}$$
$$C = 80\ \mu\text{F}$$
$$R = 40\ \Omega$$

(a) Source frequency at resonance $= \dfrac{1}{(LC)^{1/2}}$

Putting respective values, the frequency is 50 rad/s.

(b) At resonance,

Impedance (Z) = Resistance (*R*)

⇒ $Z = R = 40$ Ohms

Now, rms value of current, $I = \dfrac{V}{R}$

Or $I = \dfrac{230}{40}$

Hence, $I = 5.75$ A

Amplitude of this value of current

$= 1.414 \times I$

$= 1.414 \times 5.75 = 8.13$ A.

(c) Now taking into consideration the rms potential drops:

Across Resistance, $V_R = IR = 5.75 \times 40 = 230$ V.

Across Capacitance, $V_C = IX_C = 1437.5$ V.

Across Inductance, $V_L = IX_L = 5.75 \times 50 \times 5$

$= 1437.5$ V.

Across *LC* combination, $V_{LC} = I(X_L - X_C) = 0$ (at resonating frequency)

CHAPTER 8

ELECTROMAGNETIC WAVES

➢ Electric current produces a magnetic field. Logically James Clerk Maxwell showed that changing electric field must also produce a magnetic field. Since magnetic field was already known to be associated with electric current, Maxwell postulated that the rate of change of electric field should be proportional to a current known as displacement current.

➢ When a capacitor is charged or discharged, there is a flow of charge in the circuit. This flow of charge produces conduction current. But there is no flow of charge in between the plates. In between the plates there is changing electric field which produces a current known as displacement current.

$$I_D = \varepsilon_0 \frac{d(EA)}{dt} = \varepsilon_0 A \frac{dE}{dt}$$

$$= \varepsilon_0 A \frac{d}{dt}\left(\frac{V}{d}\right) = \frac{\varepsilon_0 A}{d}\frac{dV}{dt} = C\frac{dV}{dt}$$

where,
E = electric field between the plates of capacitor
V = potential difference
d = separation between the plates
A = area of the plates.

➢ While finding symmetry of the above 4 laws, James Clerk Maxwell noticed that there is some discrepancy in Ampere's circuital law. If the idea of displacement current is included in Ampere's circuital law then the 4 laws become symmetrical. From this symmetry, Maxwell developed the idea of electromagnetic waves which can even travel through vacuum as transverse wave.

Scan to know more about this topic

Electromagnetic waves

Maxwell's Equations in Vacuum

- $\oint E.dA = \frac{Q}{\varepsilon_0}$ (Gauss' Law for electricity)
- $\oint B.dA = 0$ (Gauss' Law for magnetism)
- $\oint E.dl = -\frac{d\phi_B}{dt}$ (Faraday's Law)
- $\oint B.dl = \mu_0 i_c + \mu_0\varepsilon_0 \frac{d\phi_E}{dt}$ (Ampere – Maxwell Law)

Electromagnetic Waves

➢ **Characteristics of electromagnetic waves:**

(i) Transverse waves.

(ii) Propagates such that oscillating electric field, oscillating magnetic field and direction of propagation are mutually perpendicular to each other.

(iii) Travels in vacuum with a speed

$$c = \frac{1}{\sqrt{\mu_0\varepsilon_0}} = 3\times10^8 \text{ m/s} \text{ along a straight line.}$$

(iv) Ratio of amplitude of electric and magnetic field is a constant, i.e., $E_0/B_0 = c$.

(v) Transports energy and momentum both.

(vi) Wavelength and frequency are related as $c = \nu\lambda$

➢ **Source of electromagnetic waves:**

Accelerated charge. Such as

- Electron jumping from its outer orbit to inner orbit.
- Electrical oscillations in LC circuit
- Electrical sparking

➢ **Nature of electromagnetic wave:**

In electromagnetic wave, electric and magnetic field vectors are perpendicular to each other and also to the direction of propagation.

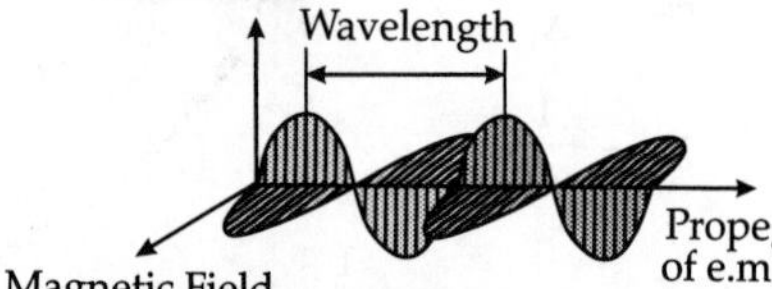

- A plane electromagnetic wave travelling in the x-direction is of the form

$E(x,t) = E_{max}\cos(kx - \omega t + \phi)$

$B(x,t) = B_{max}\cos(kx - \omega t + \phi)$

E is electric field, B is magnetic field

- A plane electromagnetic wave travelling in the z-direction may be in the form

$E = E_0\sin(kz - \omega t)$

$B = B_0\sin(kz - \omega t)$

➢ **Energy Density:**

Energy density due to electric field, $U_E = \frac{1}{2}\varepsilon_0 E^2$

Energy density due to magnetic field, $U_B = \frac{1}{2}\frac{B^2}{\propto_0}$

Total energy density, $U = \frac{1}{2}\varepsilon_0 E^2 + \frac{1}{2}\frac{B^2}{\propto_0}$

Since $E = \frac{B}{\sqrt{\varepsilon_0\mu_0}}$

$\therefore \quad U = \varepsilon_E E^2 = \frac{B^2}{\propto_0}$

➢ **Poynting vector** ($\vec{S}$): Energy transported by electromagnetic wave per unit area per second.

$$\vec{S} = \vec{E}\times\frac{\vec{B}}{\mu_0}$$

Electromagnetic Waves

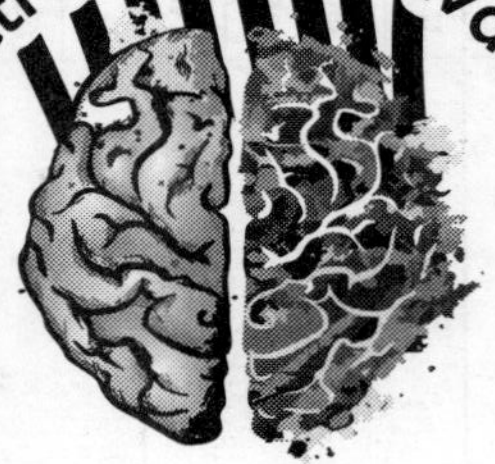

Contribution

In 1886, Heinrich Rudolf Hertz became the first person to transmit and receive controlled radio.

Conduction current

The current due to flow of charge is often called conduction current,

$$I_c = \frac{dq}{dt}$$

Displacement current

If there exists an electric current as well as a changing electric field, results magnetic field and causes displacement current,

$$I_d = \varepsilon_0 \frac{-d\phi_E}{dt}$$

Electromagnetic spectrum

- **Radio waves :** $\lambda > 10^8$ nm
  Use : radio, TV signal
- **Micro waves :** $10^8 > \lambda > 10^5$ nm
  Use : micro wave oven, radar
- **Infrared :** $10^6 > \lambda > 700$ nm
  Use : night vision
- **Visible light :** $700 > \lambda > 400$ nm
  Use : to observe world
- **UV rays :** $400 > \lambda > 1$ nm
  Use : destroying bacteria
- **X-rays :** $1 > \lambda > 0.001$ nm
  Use : detect bone break
- **γ rays :** $0.001 \text{ nm} > \lambda$
  Use : to treat cancer

Maxwell's equations

Gauss's law (electricity)

$$\oint \vec{E}.\vec{ds} = \frac{q_{in}}{\varepsilon_0}$$

Gauss's law (magnetism)

$$\oint \vec{B}.\vec{ds} = 0$$

Faraday's law

$$\oint \vec{E}.\vec{dl} = \frac{-d\phi_B}{dt}$$

Ampere's law

$$\oint \vec{B}.\vec{dl} = \mu_0 I + \mu_0\varepsilon_0 \frac{-d\phi_E}{dt}$$

Contribution

Combination of mutually perpendicular electric and magnetic fields is referred to as an electromagnetic wave

Characteristics of Electromagnetic waves

- Do not need any material medium for propagation
- Travel with speed of light $(c) = \frac{1}{\sqrt{\mu_0\varepsilon_0}}$
- Produced by accelerated charged particle
- Transverse in nature
- Oscillating electric & magnetic fields are in phase and their ratio is constant
  $(c) = \frac{E_0}{B_0}$

Energy density

- $U = \frac{1}{2}\varepsilon_0 E^2 + \frac{1}{2}\frac{B^2}{\mu_0}$ = Total energy per unit volume
- U_{av} over a long time

$$U_{av} = \frac{1}{4}\varepsilon_0 E_0^2 + \frac{1}{4}\frac{B_0}{\mu_0}$$

$$= \frac{1}{2}\varepsilon_0 E_0^2 \quad [\text{as } c = \frac{E_0}{B_0} \text{ and } \mu_0\varepsilon_0 = \frac{1}{c^2}]$$

$$= \frac{1}{2}\frac{B_0^2}{\mu_0}$$

Trace the Mind Map

- First Level
- Second Level
- Third Level

Since $\vec{E}$ and $\vec{B}$ are perpendicular to each other,

$$S = \frac{EB\sin\theta}{\mu_0}$$

➤ Electromagnetic wave travels in the direction $\vec{E}\times\vec{B}$ and $\vec{E}\perp\vec{B}$

Electromagnetic Spectrum

➤ Classification of electromagnetic waves based on their frequency or wavelength.

➤ Electromagnetic waves are classified as per frequency and wavelength of wave as

- Radio waves
- Microwaves
- Infrared radiation
- Visible light
- Ultraviolet radiation
- X-Rays
- Gamma Rays

Scan to know more about this topic

Electromagnetic spectrum

➤ **Frequency and wavelength range of Electromagnetic waves:**

Type of radiation	Subdivisions	Wavelength range	Frequency range
Radiowave	Extremely Low Frequency (ELF)	$> 1 \times 10^{-1}$ m	$< 3 \times 10^{9}$ Hz
	Infra Low Frequency (ILF)		
	Very low frequency (VLF)		
	Low Frequency (LF)		
	High Frequency (HF)		
	Very High Frequency (VHF)		
	Ultra High Frequency (UHF)		
Microwave	Super High Frequency (SHF)	1×10^{-3} m – 1×10^{-1} m	3×10^{9} Hz – 3×10^{11} Hz
	Extremely High Frequency (EHF)		
Infrared	Extreme Infrared	7×10^{-7} m – 1×10^{-3} m	3×10^{11} Hz – 4×10^{14} Hz
	Long wave Infrared		
	Mid wave infrared		
	Near infrared		
Visible	Red (700-650 nm)	4×10^{-7} m – 7×10^{-7} m	4×10^{14} Hz – 7.5×10^{14} Hz
	Orange (650-600 nm)		
	Yellow (600-650 nm)		
	Green (550-500 nm)		
	Blue (500-450 nm)		
	Violet (450-400 nm)		
Ultraviolet		1×10^{-9} m – 1×10^{-7} m	7.5×10^{14} Hz – 3×10^{17} Hz
X-rays		1×10^{-12} m – 1×10^{-9} m	3×10^{17} Hz – 3×10^{20} Hz
Gamma Ray		$< 1 \times 10^{-12}$ m	$> 3 \times 10^{20}$ Hz

➤ **Applications of electromagnetic waves:**

Band Designation	Application
Audible	Acoustics
Extremely Low Frequency (ELF) Radio	Electronics, Submarine Communications
Infra Low Frequency (ILF)	Not applicable
Very Low Frequency (VLF) Radio	Navigation, Weather
Low Frequency (LF) Radio	Navigation, Maritime Communications, Information and Weather Systems, Time Systems
Medium Frequency (MF) Radio	Navigation, AM Radio, Mobile Radio
High Frequency (HF) Radio	Citizens Band Radio, Mobile Radio, Maritime Radio
Very High Frequency (VHF) Radio	Amateur (Ham) Radio, VHF TV, FM Radio, Mobile Satellite, Mobile Radio, Fixed Radio
Ultra High Frequency (UHF) Radio	Microwave, Satellite, UHF TV, Paging, Cordless Telephone, Cellular and PCS Telephony, Wireless LAN (WiFi)

Super High Frequency (SHF) Radio	Microwave, Satellite, Wireless LAN (WiFi)
Extremely High Frequency (EHF) Radio	Microwave, Satellite, Radiolocation
Infrared Light (IR)	Wireless LAN Bridges, Wireless LANs, Fiber Optics Remote control
Visible Light	Photographic plate, photocells.
Ultraviolet (UV)	Photocells, kill bacteria and germs.
X-Rays	In medicell, Geiger tubes, ionisation chamber.
Gamma and Cosmic Rays	In medical (cancer cell killing)

➢ **Production and detection of electromagnetic waves:**

Type of Radiation	Production	Detection
Radio	Rapid acceleration and decelerations of electrons in aerials	Receiver's aerials
Microwave	Klystron valve or magnetron valve	Point contact diodes
Infra-red	Vibration of atoms and molecules	Thermopiles Bolometer, Infrared photographic film
Light	Electrons in atoms emit light when they move form one energy level to a lower energy level	The eyes, Photocells, Photographic film
Ultraviolet	Inner shell electrons in atoms moving from one energy level to a lower level	Photocells, Photographic film
X-rays	X-ray tubes or inner shell electrons	Photographic film, Geiger tubes, Ionisation chamber
Gamma rays	Radioactive decay of the nucleus	Photographic film, Geiger tubes Ionisation chamber

➢ **Health hazards of electromagnetic waves:**

Type of radiation	Health Hazards
Microwave	Internal heating of tissues
Infrared	Felt as heat, causes skin to burn
Ultraviolet	Severe sunburn, Damage of cell
X-rays	Damage cells, may cause cancer and cell death
Gamma Rays	Dame cells, may cause cancer, may cause mutation of gene

NCERT CORNER

Exercise Questions

Q. 1. Figure shows a capacitor made of two circular plates each of radius 12 cm, and separated by 5.0 cm. The capacitor is being charged by an external source (not shown in the figure). The charging current is constant and equal to 0.15 A.

(a) Calculate the capacitance and the rate of change of potential difference between the plates.

(b) Obtain the displacement current across the plates.

(c) Is Kirchhoff's first rule (junction rule) valid at each plate of the capacitor? Explain.

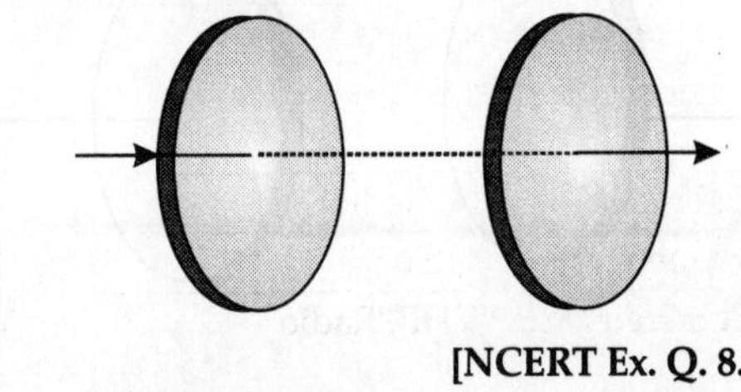

[NCERT Ex. Q. 8.1, Page 213]

Ans. According to question

Radius of each circular plate, $r = 12$ cm $= 0.12$ m

Distance between the plates, $d = 5$ cm $= 0.05$ m

Charging current, $I = 0.15\ A$

Permittivity of free space, $\varepsilon_0 = 8.85\times10^{-12}\ C^2N^{-1}m^{-2}$

(a) Capacitance between the two plates is given by the relation,

$$C = \frac{\varepsilon_0 A}{d}$$

where,

A = Area of each plate = πr^2

$$C = \frac{\varepsilon_0 \pi r^2}{d}$$

$$= \frac{8.85\times10^{-12}\times\pi(0.12)^2}{0.05}$$

$= 8.0032 \times 10^{-12}$ F

$= 8.0032$ pF

Charge on each plate, $q = CV$

where,

V = Potential difference across the plates

Differentiation on both sides with respect to time (t) gives:

$$\frac{dq}{dt} = C\frac{dV}{dt}$$

But, $\frac{dq}{dt}$ = Current (I)

$$\therefore \quad \frac{dV}{dt} = \frac{I}{C}$$

$$\Rightarrow \frac{0.15}{8.0032\times10^{-12}} = 1.87\times10^{8}\ \text{V/s}$$

Therefore, the change in potential difference between the plates is 1.87×10^8 V/s.

(b) The displacement current across the plates is the same as the conduction current. Hence, the displacement current, i_d is 0.15 A.

(c) Yes, Kirchhoff's first rule is valid at each plate of the capacitor provided that we take the sum of conduction and displacement for current.

Q. 2. A parallel plate capacitor made of circular plates each of radius R = 6.0 cm has a capacitance C = 100 pF. The capacitor is connected to a 230 V ac supply with a (angular) frequency of 300 rad s^{-1}.

(a) What is the rms value of the conduction current?

(b) Is the conduction current equal to the displacement current?

(c) Determine the amplitude of B at a point 3.0 cm from the axis between the plates.

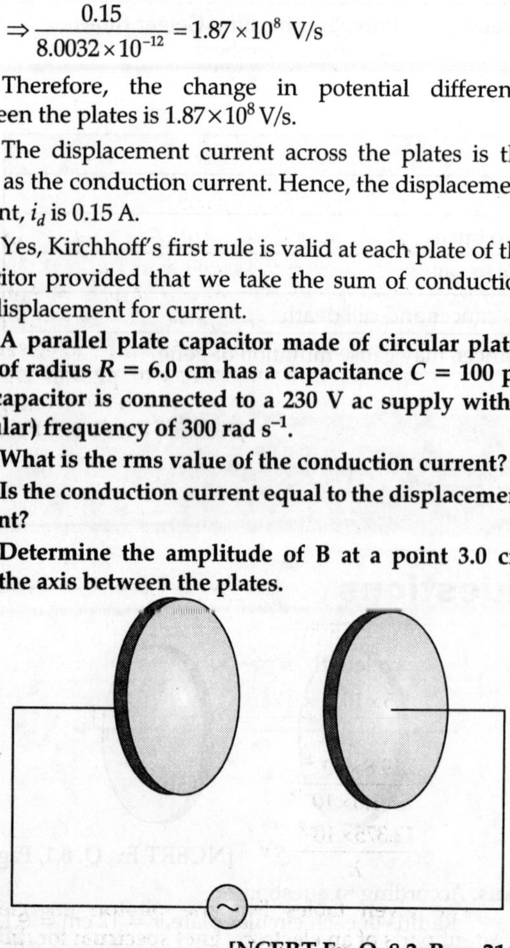

[NCERT Ex. Q. 8.2, Page 214]

Ans. Given that,

Radius of each circular plate, R = 6.0 cm = 0.06 m

Capacitance of a parallel plate capacitor,

C = 100 pF = 100×10^{-12} F

Supply voltage,

V = 230 V

Angular frequency, ω=300 rad s^{-1}

(a) RMS value of conduction current,

$$I = \frac{V}{X_c}$$

Where,

X_c = Capacitive reactance

$$X_c = \frac{1}{\omega C}$$

$$\therefore \quad I = V\times\omega C$$

$$= 230\times300\times100\times10^{-12}$$

$$= 6.9\times10^{-6}\ \text{A}$$

$$= 6.9\ \mu\text{A}$$

Hence, the RMS value of conduction current is 6.9 μA.

(b) Yes, conduction current is equivalent to displacement current.,

i.e., $i_c = i_d$

(c) Magnetic field is given as:

$$B = \frac{\mu_0 r}{2\pi R^2}I_0$$

where,

μ_0 = Permeability of free space = $4\pi\times10^{-7}$ TmA^{-1}

I_0 = Maximum value of current = $\sqrt{2}\ I$

r = Distance between the plates from the axis = 3.0 cm = 0.03 m

$$\therefore B = \frac{4\pi\times10^{-7}\times0.03\times\sqrt{2}\times6.9\times10^{-6}}{2\pi\times(0.06)^2}$$

$$= 1.63\times10^{-11}\ \text{T}$$

Hence, the magnetic field at that point is 1.63×10^{-11} T.

Q. 3. What physical quantity is the same for X-rays of wavelength 10^{-10} m, red light of wavelength 6800 Å and radio waves of wavelength 500 m?

[NCERT Ex. Q. 8.3, Page 214]

Ans. The speed of light (3×10^8 m/s) in vacuum is the same for all wavelengths. It is independent of the wavelength in the vacuum.

Q. 4. A plane electromagnetic wave travels in vacuum along z-direction. What can you say about the directions of its electric and magnetic field vectors? If the frequency of the wave is 30 MHz, what is its wavelength?

[NCERT Ex. Q. 8.4, Page 214]

Ans. The electromagnetic wave travels in a vacuum along the z-direction. The electric field (E) and the magnetic field (H) are in the x-y plane. They are mutually perpendicular. Frequency of the wave, ν = 30 MHz = 30×10^6 s^{-1}

Speed of light in vacuum, $c = 3\times10^8$ m/s

Wavelength of a wave is given as:

$$\lambda = \frac{c}{\nu}$$

$$= \frac{3\times10^8}{30\times10^6} = 10 \text{ m}$$

Q. 5. A radio can tune in to any station in the 7.5 MHz to 12 MHz band. What is the corresponding wavelength band? [NCERT Ex. Q. 8.5, Page 214]

Ans. A radio can tune to minimum frequency, ν_1=7.5 MHz = 7.5×10^6 Hz

Maximum frequency, ν_2=12 MHz = 12×10^6 Hz

Speed of light, $c = 3\times10^8$ m/s

Corresponding wavelength for ν_1 can be calculated as:

$$\lambda_1 = \frac{c}{\nu_1} = \frac{3\times10^8}{7.5\times10^6} = 40 \text{ m}$$

Corresponding wavelength for v_2 can be calculated as:

$$\lambda_2 = \frac{c}{\nu_2} = \frac{3\times10^8}{12\times10^6} = 25 \text{ m}$$

Thus, the wavelength band of the radio is 40 m to 25 m.

Q. 6. A charged particle oscillates about its mean equilirbium position with a frequency of 10^9 Hz. What is the frequency of the electromagnetic waves produced by the oscillator? [NCERT Ex. Q. 8.6, Page 214]

Ans. The frequency of an electromagnetic wave produced by the oscillator is same as that of a charged particle oscillating about its mean position, i.e., 10^9 Hz.

Q. 7. The amplitude of the electric field part of the harmonic electromagnetic wave in vacuum is B_0=510 nT. What is the amplitude of the electric field part of the wave? [NCERT Ex. Q. 8.7, Page 214]

Ans. Amplitude of magnetic field of an electromagnetic wave in vacuum,

B_0= 510 nT = 510×10^{-9} T

Speed of light in vacuum, $c = 3\times10^8$ m/s

Amplitude of electric field of an electromagnetic wave is given by the relation,

$E = cB_0 = 3\times10^8 \times 510 \times 10^{-9} = 153$ N/C

Therefore, the electric field part of the wave is 153 N/C.

Q. 8. Suppose that the electric field amplitude of an electromagnetic wave is E_0=120 N/C and that its frequency is ν = 50 MHz.

(a) Determine, B_0, ω, κ and λ.

(b) Find expressions for E and B.

[NCERT Ex. Q. 8.8, Page 214]

Ans. Given that,

Electric field amplitude, E_0= 120 N/C

Frequency of source, ν = 50 MHz = 50×10^6 Hz

Speed of light, $c = 3\times10^8$ m/s

(a) Magnitude of magnetic field strength is given as:

$$B_0 = \frac{E_0}{c}$$

$$= \frac{120}{3\times10^8}$$

$$= 4\times10^{-7} \text{ T} = 400 \text{ nT}$$

Angular frequency of source is given by:

$$\omega = 2\pi v = 2\pi\times50\times10^6$$

$$= 3.14\times10^8 \text{ rad/s}$$

Propagation constant is given as:

$$k = \frac{\omega}{c}$$

$$= \frac{3.14\times10^8}{3\times10^8} = 1.05 \text{ rad/m}$$

Wavelength of wave is given by:

$$\lambda = \frac{c}{\nu}$$

$$= \frac{3\times10^8}{50\times10^6} = 6.0 \text{ m}$$

(b) Suppose the wave is propagating in the positive x direction. Then, the electric field vector will be in the positive y-direction and the magnetic field vector will be in the positive z-direction. This is because all three vectors are mutually perpendicular.

Equation of electric field vector is given as:

$$\vec{E} = E_0 \sin(kx - \omega t)\hat{j}$$

$$= 120 \sin[1.05x - 3.14\times10^8 t]\hat{j}$$

$$\bar{B} = B_0 \sin(kx - \omega t)\hat{k}$$

$$\bar{B} = (4\times10^{-7})\sin(1.05x - 3.14\times10^8 t)\hat{k}$$

Q. 9. The terminology of different parts of the electromagnetic spectrum is given in the text. Use the formula $E = h\nu$ (for energy of a quantum of radiation photon) and obtain the photon energy in units of eV for different parts of the electromagnetic spectrum. In what way are the different scales of photon energies that you obtain related to the sources of electromagnetic radiation? [NCERT Ex. Q. 8.9, Page 214]

Ans. Energy of a photon is given as:

$$E = h\nu = \frac{hc}{\lambda}$$

Where,

h = Planck's constant = 6.6×10^{-34} Js

c = Speed of light = 3×10^8 m/s

λ = Wavelength of radiation

$$\therefore E = \frac{6.6\times10^{-34}\times3\times10^8}{\lambda} = \frac{19.8\times10^{-26}}{\lambda} \text{ J}$$

$$= \frac{19.8\times10^{-26}}{\lambda\times1.6\times10^{-19}}$$

$$= \frac{12.375\times10^{-7}}{\lambda} \text{ eV}$$

The given tables lists the photon energies for different parts of an electromagnet spectrum for different λ.

λ(m)	10^3	1	10^{-3}	10^{-6}	10^{-8}	10^{-10}	10^{-12}
E (eV)	12.375×10^{-10}	12.375×10^{-7}	12.375×10^{-4}	12.375×10^{-1}	12.375×10^{1}	12.375×10^{3}	12.375×10^{5}

The photon energies for the different parts of the spectrum of a source indicate the spacing of the relevant energy levels of the source.

Q. 10. In a plane electromagnetic wave, the electric field oscillates sinusoidally at a frequency of 2.0×10^{10} Hz and amplitude 48 Vm^{-1}.

(a) What is the wavelength of the wave?

(b) What is the amplitude of the oscillating magnetic field?

(c) Show that the average energy density of the *E* field equals the average energy density of the *B* field. [$c = 3\times10^8$ m s^{-1}.] [NCERT Ex. Q. 8.10, Page 214]

Ans. Given that,

Frequency of the electromagnetic wave,

$\nu = 2 \times 10^{10}$ Hz

Electric field amplitude, $E_0 = 48$ Vm^{-1}

Speed of light, $c = 3\times10^8$ m/s

(a) Wavelength of a wave is given as:

$$\lambda = \frac{c}{\nu} = \frac{3\times10^8}{2\times10^{10}} = 0.015 \text{ m}$$

(b) Magnetic field strength is given as:

$$B_0 = \frac{E_0}{c} = \frac{48}{3\times10^8} = 1.6\times10^{-7} \text{ T}$$

(c) Energy density of the electric field is given as:

$$U_E = \frac{1}{2}\varepsilon_0 E^2$$

And, energy density of the magnetic field is given as:

$$U_B = \frac{1}{2\mu_0} B^2$$

where,

ε_0 = Permittivity of free space

μ_0 = Permeability of free space

$$E = cB \quad \text{...(i)}$$

where,

$$c = \frac{1}{\sqrt{\varepsilon_0\mu_0}} B$$

Squaring on both sides, we get

$$E^2 = \frac{1}{\varepsilon_0\mu_0} B^2$$

$$\Rightarrow \quad \varepsilon_0 E^2 = \frac{B^2}{\mu_0}$$

Multiplying both sides by $\frac{1}{2}$

$$\frac{1}{2}\varepsilon_0 E^2 = \frac{1}{2}\frac{B^2}{\mu_0}$$

$$\Rightarrow \quad U_E = U_B$$

□□

CHAPTER 9

RAY OPTICS AND OPTICAL INSTRUMENTS

Reflection of Light

- When light is incident on the interface of two homogeneous medium of different densities, then a portion of light comes back to the first medium. This phenomenon is known as reflection of light.

➢ **Types of reflection:**

- **Regular:** When parallel rays of light incident on a reflecting surface, remains parallel after reflection.
- **Diffused:** When parallel rays of light incident on a reflecting surface, does not remain parallel after reflection.

➢ **Laws of reflection:**

- **Law-I:** Incident ray, reflected ray and normal drawn at the point of incidence on the reflecting surface lie on the same plane.
- **Law-II:** Angle of incidence = angle of reflection.

➢ **Image:**

- **Real:** When rays of light after reflection or refraction meet at a point.
- **Virtual:** When rays of light after reflection or refraction without meeting at a point, appear to diverge from a point.

Reflection of Light by Spherical Mirrors

➢ **Spherical Mirror:** Any reflecting surface which is the part of a hollow sphere is called the spherical mirror.

➢ **Types of spherical mirrors:** (i) Concave (ii) Convex.

➢ **Concave Mirror:** A spherical mirror, whose reflecting surface is curved inwards, i.e., the reflecting surface faces the center of the sphere of which it is a part.

➢ **Convex Mirror:** A spherical mirror whose reflecting surface is curved outwards i.e., the reflecting surface is away from the center of the sphere of which it is a part.

➢ **Important parts of a spherical mirror:**

- **Pole:** Mid point of the spherical mirror.
- **Centre of curvature:** Centre of the sphere of which the mirror is a part.
- **Principal axis:** The imaginary line joining the pole and the centre of curvature.
- **Radius of curvature:** Radius of the sphere of which the mirror is a part.
- **Aperture:** Line joining the two end of the reflecting surface.
- **Angular aperture:** Angle made by the two ends of the reflecting surface at the centre of curvature.
- **Principal focus:** A point on the principal axis at which the rays parallel to principal axis, after reflection, meet (for concave mirror) or appear to diverge from (for convex mirror).
- **Focal length:** Distance of focus from the pole.
- **Secondary focus:** A point at which the parallel rays, making an angle with the principal axis, after reflection by the mirror, meet (for concave mirror) or appear to diverge from (for convex mirror).

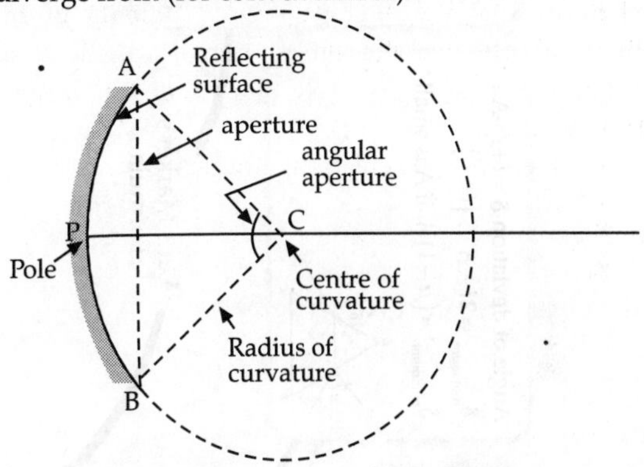

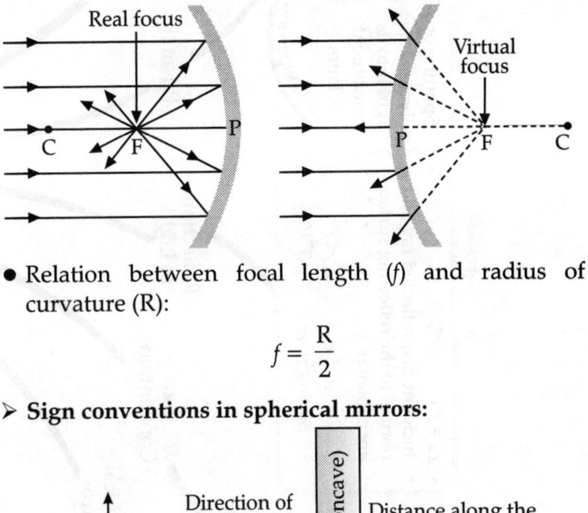

- Relation between focal length (f) and radius of curvature (R):

$$f = \frac{R}{2}$$

➢ **Sign conventions in spherical mirrors:**

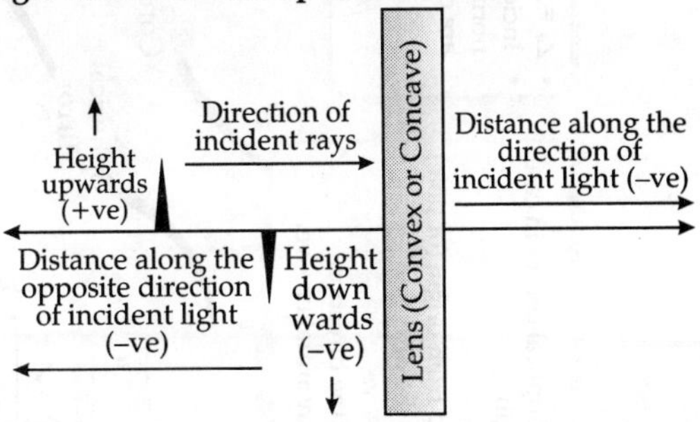

➢ **Mirror formula:**

- Relation between u, v and f

$$\frac{1}{v} + \frac{1}{u} = \frac{1}{f}$$

- **Linear Magnification:**

$$m = \frac{\text{Height of image}}{\text{Height of object}} = -\frac{v}{u}$$

Scan to know more about this topic

Reflection by spherical mirrors

Ray Optics & Optical Instruments

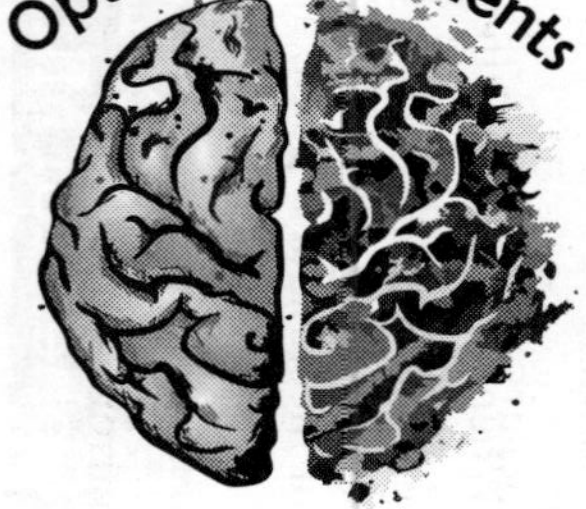

Sign Conventions

- Pole in case of mirror and optical centre in case of lenses are taken as origin
- Principle axis as the X-axis
- All distances are measured from origin (or pole)
- All distances measured in the direction of incident ray are taken + ve.
- All distances measured in the direction opposite to the incident ray are taken - ve.

Spherical Mirror

$\frac{1}{u}+\frac{1}{v}=\frac{2}{R}=\frac{1}{f}$

Lateral Magnification $=\frac{h_2}{h_1}=-\frac{v}{u}$

Reflection of Light

- $\angle i = \angle r$
- Incident ray, reflected ray and normal to the reflecting surface are coplanar

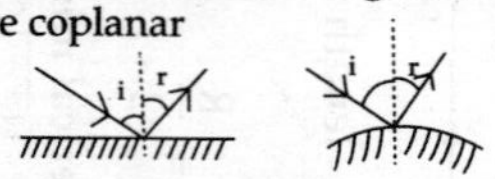

Refraction of light

$\frac{\sin i}{\sin r}=\frac{v_1}{v_2}=\frac{\mu_2}{\mu_1}$

$\mu=\frac{\text{real depth}}{\text{apparent depth}}$

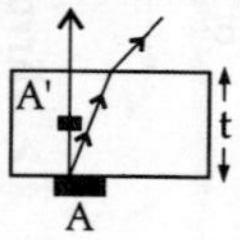

$\Delta t=\left(1-\frac{1}{\mu}\right)t$ = image shift

Total Internal reflection

When ray passes from optically denser to rarer medium, if incident angle (i) greater than critical angle, entire light is then reflected back to the denser medium again, this process is called T.I.R. It is used in optical fibre.

Critical Angle

- Incident angle (θ_c) for which angle of refraction is 90°

i.e., $\sin\theta_c=\frac{1}{\mu}$

$\theta_c=\sin^{-1}\left(\frac{1}{\mu}\right)$

When ray passes from optically denser to rarer medium.

Refraction on Spherical surface

$\frac{\mu_2}{v}-\frac{\mu_1}{u}=\frac{\mu_2-\mu_1}{R}$

Lateral Magnification

$m=\frac{h_2}{h_1}=\frac{\mu_1 v}{\mu_2 u}=\frac{R-v}{R-u}$

Prism

Angle of deviation $\delta=i+i'-A$

$\delta_{minimum}=2i-A \quad [i=i']$

$\delta_{minimum}=(\mu-1)A$, if A is small

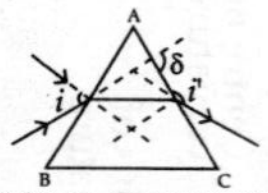

Dispersion

Splitting of polychromatic light into its constituent colours.

Lens Marker's Formula

$\frac{1}{v}-\frac{1}{u}=\frac{\mu_2-\mu_1}{\mu_1}\left(\frac{1}{R_1}-\frac{1}{R_2}\right)$

$\frac{1}{f}=\left(\frac{\mu_2}{\mu_1}-1\right)\left(\frac{1}{R_1}-\frac{1}{R_2}\right)$

$\frac{1}{f}=(\mu-1)\left(\frac{1}{R_1}-\frac{1}{R_2}\right)$ [If $\mu_2=\mu$, $\mu_1=1$ (air)]

$\frac{1}{f}=\frac{1}{v}-\frac{1}{u}$ (lens formula)

Lateral Magnification $=\frac{h_2}{h_1}=\frac{v}{u}$

Optical Instruments

Microscope

$M=1+\frac{D}{f}$ [image at near point]

$M=D/f$ [image at infinity]

Compound Microscope

$M=\frac{v}{u}\left[\frac{D}{f_e}\right]$ [normal adjustment]

$M=\frac{v}{u}\left(1+\frac{D}{f_e}\right)=-\frac{1}{f_o}\left(1+\frac{D}{f_e}\right)$

For final image at least distance

Telescope

$M=\frac{f_o}{f_e}\left(1+\frac{f_e}{D}\right)$ [image at near point]

$M=-\frac{fo}{fe}$ [image at infinity]

Power of a lens

$P=\frac{1}{f}$

[For combination of lens when they are in contact]

$P=\frac{1}{f_1}+\frac{1}{f_2}$

[For combination of lens when they are separated]

$P=\frac{1}{f_1}+\frac{1}{f_2}-\frac{d}{f_1 f_2}$

Trace the Mind Map

- First Level
- Second Level
- Third Level

➢ **Image formation by spherical mirrors:**

Type of mirror	Object distance (u)	Image distance (v)	Nature of image	Size of image compared to object
Concave	$u = \infty$	$v = f$	Real and inverted	Point sized
	$\infty > u > 2f$	$R > v > f$		Reduced
	$u = 2f$	$v = R$		Equal
	$2f > u > f$	$\infty > v > R$		Magnified
	$u = f$	$v = \infty$		Highly magnified
	$f > u > 0$	Behind the mirror	Virtual and erect	Magnified
Convex	$u = \infty$	$v = f$	Virtual and erect	Point sized
	$\infty > u > 0$	$f > v > 0$ Behind the mirror		Smaller

Example 1: A candle of 2.5 cm in size is placed at a distance 27 cm in front of a concave mirror of radius of curvature 36 cm. At what distance from the mirror should a screen be placed in order to obtain a sharp image? Describe the nature and size of the image. Draw a ray diagram of the same.

Sol.

Object size, $h = 2.5$ cm

Image size, $h' = ?$

Object distance, $u = -27$ cm

Image distance, v

Radius of curvature, $R = -36$ cm

Focal length, $f = \frac{R}{2}$

$$= -\frac{36}{2} = -18 \text{ cm}$$

Using mirror formula,

$$\frac{1}{v}+\frac{1}{u} = \frac{1}{f}$$

Or, $$\frac{1}{v} = \frac{1}{f}-\frac{1}{u}$$

Or, $$\frac{1}{v} = -\frac{1}{18}+\frac{1}{27}$$

Or, $$\frac{1}{v} = -\frac{1}{54}$$

$\therefore$ $v = -54$ cm

The screen is to be placed at a distance 54 cm in front of the mirror.

Magnification, $$m = \frac{h'}{h} = -\frac{v}{u}$$

Or, $$h' = h\times-\frac{v}{u}$$

Or, $$h' = 2.5\times-\frac{-54}{-27}$$

$\therefore$ $h' = -5$ cm

So, the image is real and inverted of height 5 cm.

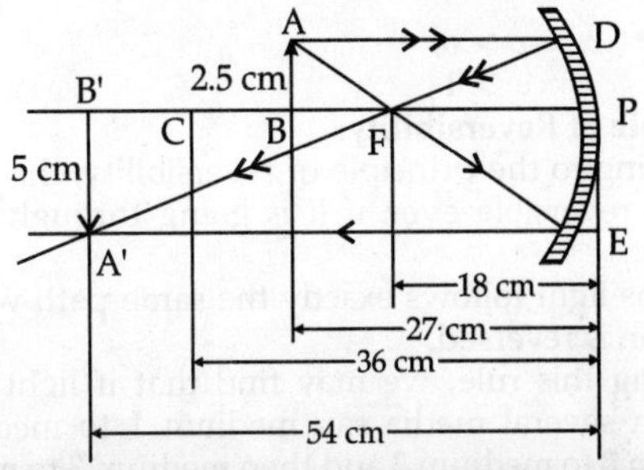

Refraction of Light

- Change of direction of a ray of light when it enters obliquely from one medium to another.

➢ **Change of direction of light ray when refracted:**

- **From denser to rarer medium:**
  The refracted ray moves away from the normal.

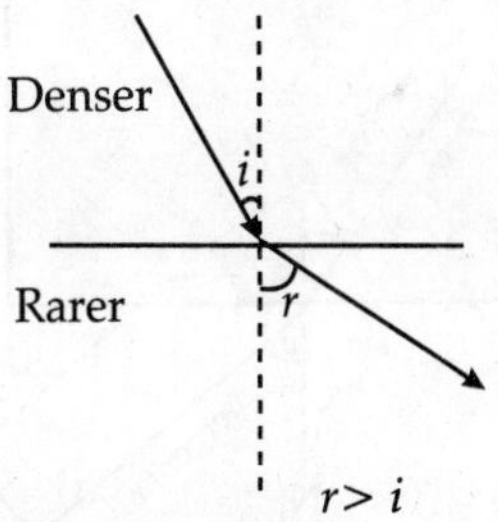

- **From rarer to denser medium:**
  The refracted ray moves towards the normal.

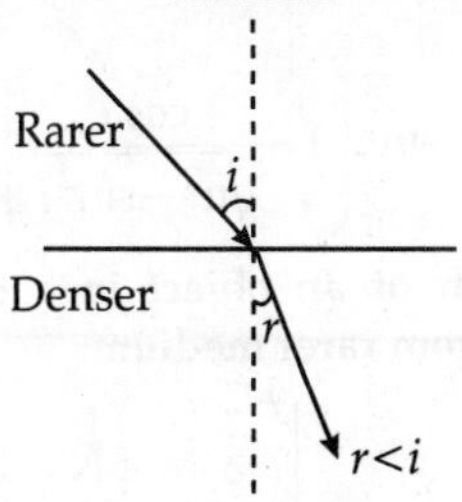

➢ **Laws of refraction:**

- **Law-I**
  The incident ray, the refracted ray and the normal drawn at the point of incidence on the surface of separation lie on the same plane.
- **Law-II (Snell's Law)**
  The ratio of sine of angle of incidence to the sine of angle of refraction is a constant, for the light of a given colour and for the given pair of media. This constant value is called the refractive index of the second medium with respect to the first medium.

$$\frac{\sin i}{\sin r} = {}_1\mu_2$$

$$\sin i = {}_1\mu_2 \sin r$$

If $\sin i = 0$, then $\sin r = 0$

Light rays do not deviate when they travel normally from one medium to another.

➤ **Absolute refractive index:** If the first medium is air or free space, then the refractive index is known as the absolute refractive index of the second medium. The absolute refractive index of a medium is expressed as

$$\mu_2 = \frac{\text{velocity of light in air or free space}}{\text{velocity of light in the medium}}$$

$$= \frac{c}{v}$$

since $c > v$,

so, $\mu > 1$

➤ **Principle of Reversibility:**

- According to the principle of reversibility, the path of light is reversible even if it is going through several media.
  It means light follows exactly the same path when its direction is reversed.
- Applying this rule, we may find that if light travels through several media say medium 1 to medium 2, medium 2 to medium 3 and then medium 3 to medium 1, then

$${}_1\mu_2 \times {}_2\mu_3 \times {}_3\mu_1 = 1$$

➤ **Refraction through glass slab:**

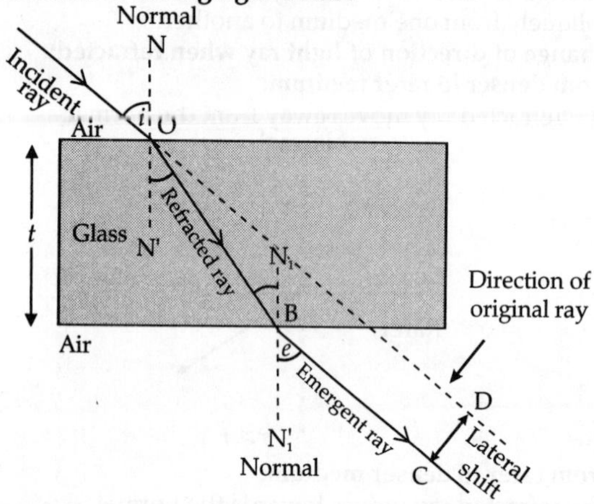

Emergent ray is parallel to the incident ray but it suffers lateral shift.

$$\text{Lateral shift} = t \sin i \left(1 - \frac{\cos i}{\sqrt{\mu^2 - \sin^2 i}}\right)$$

➤ **Apparent depth of an object in a denser medium when viewed from rarer medium:**

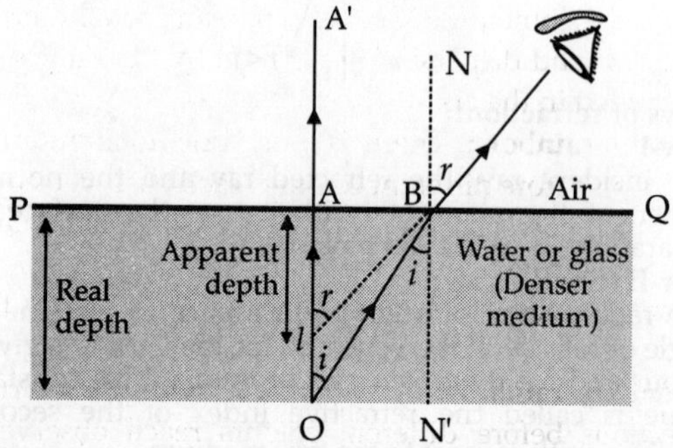

O is an object inside a denser medium. When it is viewed from a rarer medium,

Apparent rise of image = OI

$$= \text{Real depth} \times \left(1 - \frac{1}{\mu}\right)$$

➤ **Critical angle:** When light travels from denser to rarer medium,

$$\angle r > \angle i$$

As the angle of incidence increases, the angle of refraction also increases. For certain angle of incidence the angle of refraction becomes equal to 90°.

So, when light travels from denser to rarer medium, then the angle of incidence for which the angle of refraction is 90° is known as critical angle for that particular pair of medium.

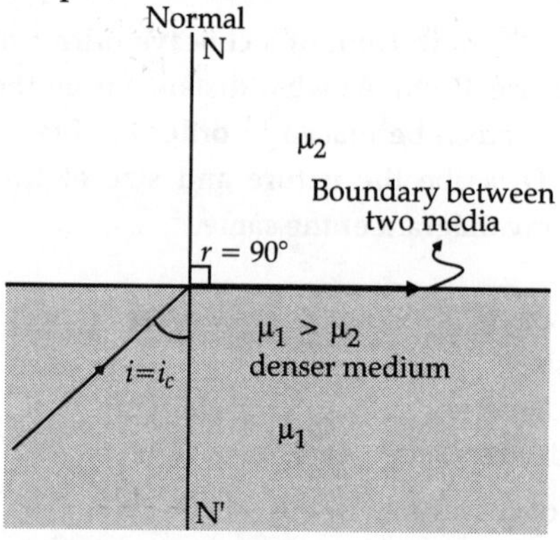

$$\frac{\sin i}{\sin r} = \frac{1}{{}_2\mu_1}$$

$$\therefore \quad \sin i_C = \frac{1}{{}_2\mu_1}$$

Total Internal Reflection

- If the angle of incidence in the denser medium is greater than the critical angle, for the pair of media, then the angle of refraction cannot be greater than 90° and so it reflects back to the denser medium. This phenomenon is known as total internal reflection.
- **Conditions for total internal reflection:**
  (a) Light should travel from denser to rarer medium.
  (b) Angle of incidence should be greater than critical angle for the pair of media.
- Why "total"?
  During normal reflection certain portion of incident light is refracted. But in case of total internal reflection no portion of incident light is refracted. Only certain portion of light is absorbed and rest portion is totally reflected.

➤ **Application of total internal reflection:**

Total internal reflection is used for communication through optical fibre. Optical fibre has 3 layers:

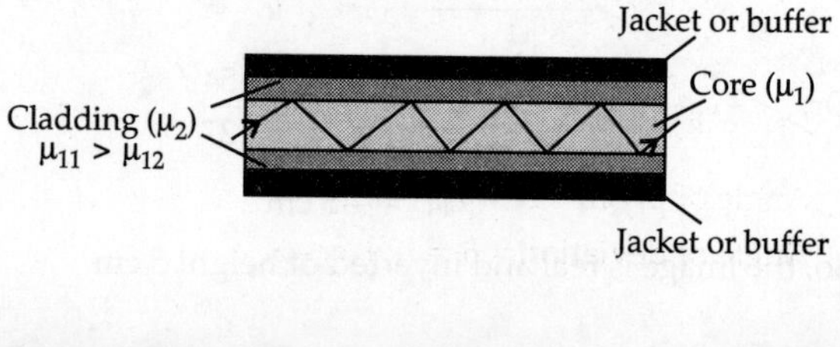

- **Core:** The innermost fibre made of transparent glass or plastic of high refractive index.
- **Cladding:** A layer surrounding the core. This layer has lower refractive index compared that of core.
- **Outer jacket or buffer:** A protective layer for protection. The angle of incidence in the fibre is so adjusted that it is greater than the critical angle for the core cladding pair of media. So, the total internal reflections take place and the signal travels from one end to other.

➢ **Total internal reflection through prism:**

Prisms are designed for 90° or 180° deviation by making use of total internal reflection.

Critical angle for Glass-air media pair is 420 approximately. So by using a 90° isosceles prism, the incident may be deviated by 90° or 180°.

- **90° deviation:**

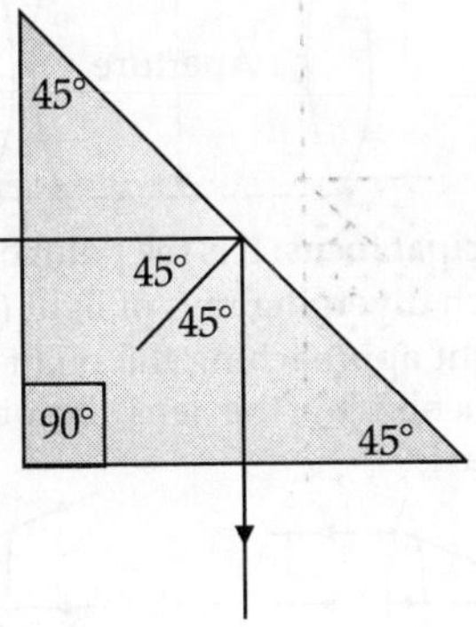

- **180° deviation:**

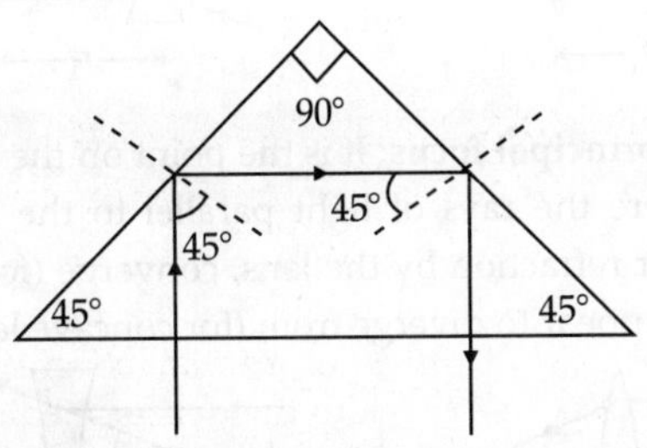

- **No angular deviation:**

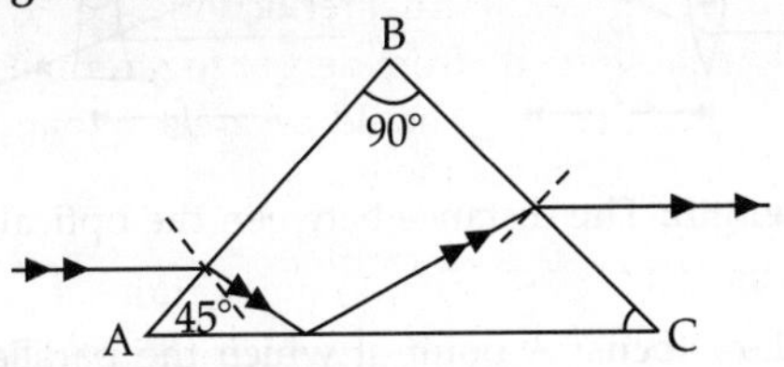

➢ **Refraction through prism:**

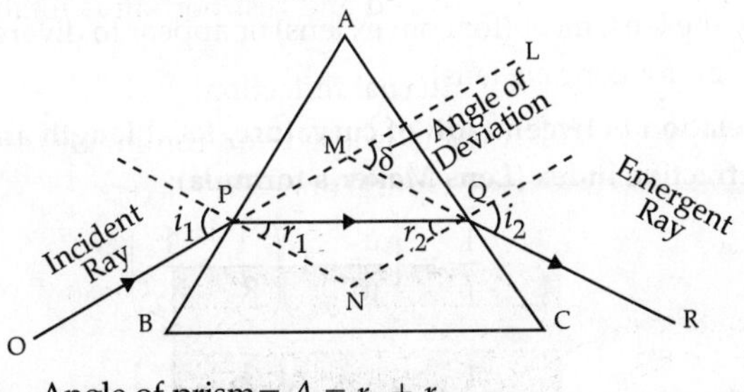

Angle of prism $= A = r_1 + r_2$

Angle of deviation $= \delta = i_1 + i_2 - A$

For minimum deviation,

$$i_1 = i_2 \text{ and } r_1 = r_2$$

$$\mu = \frac{\sin \frac{\delta_m + A}{2}}{\sin \frac{A}{2}}$$

➢ **Angle of deviation vs. angle of incidence graph for a prism:**

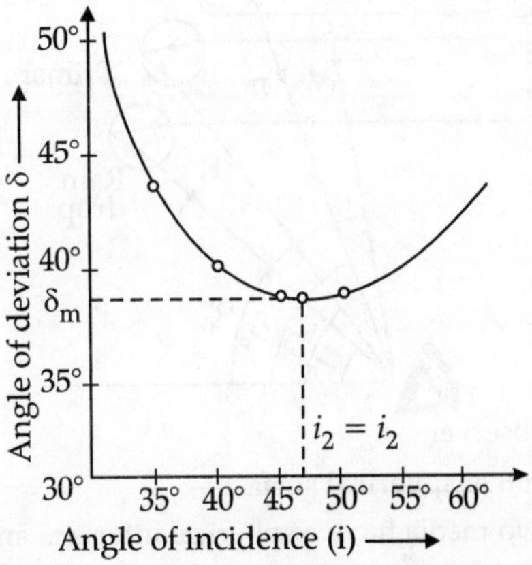

➢ **Dispersion of white light through Prism:** Splitting of white light into its constituent colours is known as dispersion of light. This is due to the different colours having different deviations.

- The seven colours are violet, indigo, blue, green, yellow, orange and red. The acronym of this colour band is VIBGYOR.
- Different colours of light have different wavelengths and different frequencies in medium. This is the cause of dispersion.

➢ **Angular dispersion:** Difference of deviations of two different colours after passing through a prism.

$$\delta_V - \delta_R = A(\mu_V - \mu_R)$$

➢ **Dispersive power:** Ratio of difference of deviations of red and violet colours and the deviation due to yellow light (mean colour) after passing through a prism.

$$\omega = \frac{\delta_V - \delta_R}{\delta}$$

$$= \frac{\mu_V - \mu_R}{\mu - 1}$$

➢ **Formation of rainbow:** Rainbow is the natural phenomenon of dispersion of light. After rain when sky is clear and sunny, we may observe a rainbow in a direction opposite to the direction of sun. It is caused due to the combined effect of refraction, total internal reflection and dispersion of sunlight by the raindrops suspended in the air.

- **Primary rainbow:** There is only one total internal reflection before different colours reach observer's eye. In this rainbow, observer watches red colour at top and violet at bottom.
  Primary rainbow is seen at an angle 41° – 43° on the sky.
- **Secondary rainbow:** In it there are two total internal reflections before different colours reach observer's

eye. In this rainbow, observer watches violet colour at top and red at bottom.

Secondary rainbow is seen at a higher (51° – 54°) angle on the sky. Its Intensity is lower than the primary rainbow.

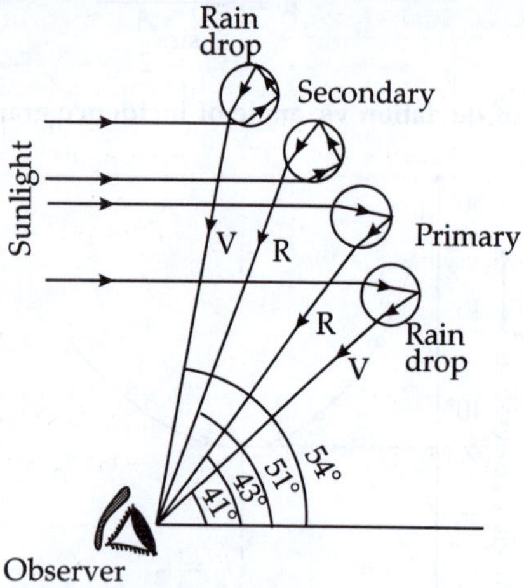

➢ **Refraction at spherical surface:**

- When two media have a spherical interface and ray of light is incident from medium of refractive index μ_1, to medium of refractive index μ_2, then

$$\frac{\mu_2}{v} - \frac{\mu_1}{u} = \frac{\mu_2 - \mu_1}{R} \qquad (\mu_2 > \mu_1)$$

R= Radius of curvature

u= Object distance

v= image distance

- When two media have a spherical interface and ray of light is incident from medium of refractive index μ_2, to medium of refractive index μ_1, then

$$\frac{\mu_1}{v} - \frac{\mu_2}{u} = \frac{\mu_1 - \mu_2}{R} \qquad (\mu_2 > \mu_1)$$

R= Radius of curvature

u= Object distance

v= image distance

Lens

- A piece of transparent medium which is bounded by two surfaces out of which at least one surface is spherical.

➢ **Types of lens:**

- **Convex lens:** A convex lens is one which is thinner at the edges and thicker at centre.
- **Concave lens:** A concave lens is one which is thicker at edges and thinner at centre.

➢ **Important parts of a lens:**

- **Centre of curvature:** Centres of the spheres of which it is a part.
- **Radius of curvature:** Radius of the spheres of which it is a part.
- **Principal axis:** The imaginary line joining the two centres of curvature.
- **Optical centre:** It is a point on the principal such that when light ray passes through the point, the incident ray and the refracted ray becomes parallel.
  (For thin lens, it is a point on the principal such that light ray passes through it undeviated)

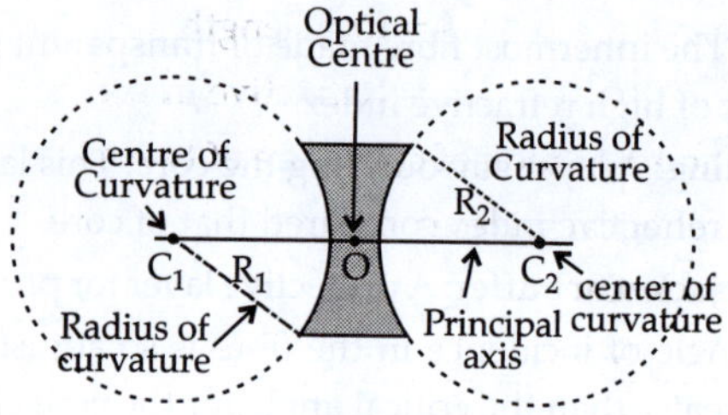

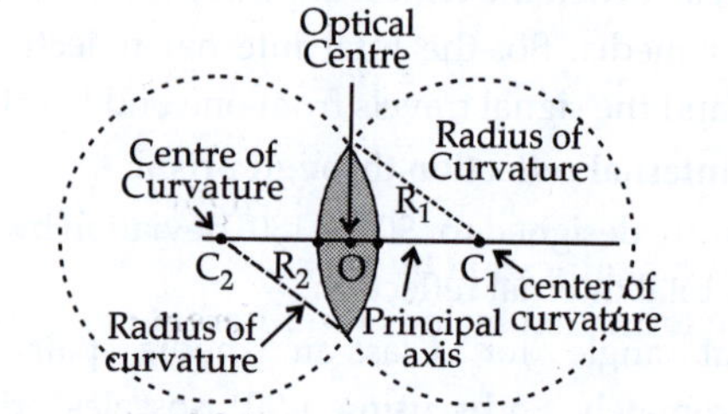

- **Aperture:** Effective diameter of light transmitting area.

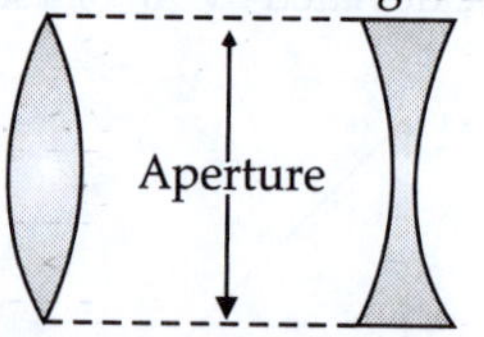

- **First principal focus:** It is the point on the principal axis from which diverging rays of light (for convex lens) or rays of light approaching the point (for concave lens), after refraction by the lens, become parallel to the principal axis.

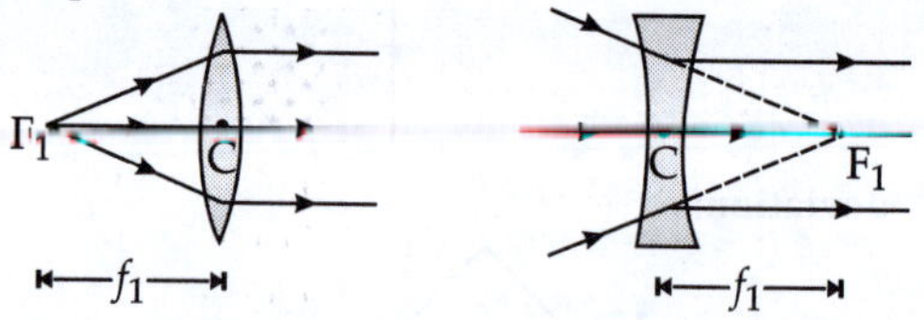

- **Second principal focus:** It is the point on the principal axis where the rays of light parallel to the principal axis, after refraction by the lens, converge (for convex lens) or appear to diverge from (for concave lens).

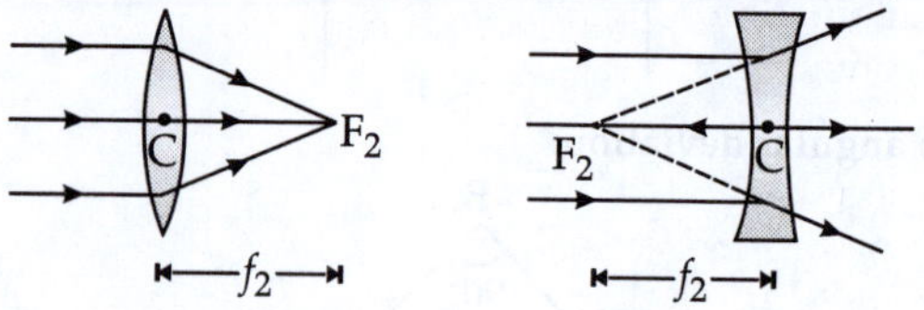

- **Focal length:** The distance between the optical centre and focus.
- **Secondary focus:** A point at which the parallel rays, making an angle with the principal axis, after refraction by the lens, meet (for convex lens) or appear to diverge from (for concave lens).

➢ **Relation between radii of curvature, focal length and refractive index (Lens Maker's formula):**

$$\frac{1}{f} = \left(\frac{\mu_2}{\mu_1} - 1\right)\left(\frac{1}{R_1} - \frac{1}{R_2}\right)$$

Or,

$$\frac{1}{f} = ({}_1\mu_2 - 1)\left(\frac{1}{R_1} - \frac{1}{R_2}\right)$$

where, f = focal length

$_1\mu_2$ = Refractive index

R_1 and R_2 = radii of curvature of two spherical surfaces.

➤ **Lens formula:**

- $$\frac{1}{v}-\frac{1}{u}=\frac{1}{f}$$

where, u = object distance

v = image distance

f = focal length

- **Linear magnification by lens:**

$$m=\frac{\text{Image height}}{\text{object height}}=\frac{v}{u}$$

➤ **Sign convention in lens:**

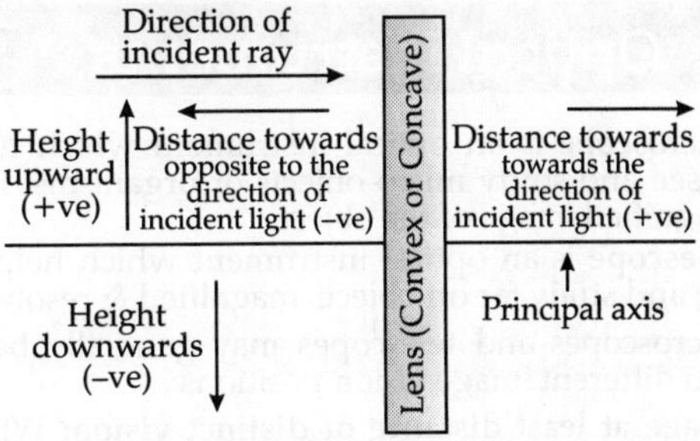

➤ **Image formation by lens for different object positions:**

Type of mirror	Object distance (u)	Image distance (v)	Nature of image	Size of image compared to object
Convex	$u=\infty$	$v=f$	Real and inverted	Point sized
	$\infty>u>2f$	$2f>v>f$		Reduced
	$u=2f$	$v=2f$		Equal
	$2f>u>f$	$\infty>v>2f$		Magnified
	$u=f$	$v=\infty$		Highly magnified
	$f>u>0$	Same side of the lens	Virtual and erect	Magnified
Concave	$u=\infty$	$v=f$	Virtual and erect	Point sized
	$\infty>u>0$	$f>v>0$ Same side of the lens		Smaller

Power of Lens

- Ability of a lens to diverge (for concave lens) or converge (for convex lens) parallel rays of light. It is the reciprocal of the focal length expressed in metre. SI unit of power is dioptre (D).

$$P=\frac{1}{f}$$

Scan to know more about this topic

Refraction of light

➤ **Combination of lens:** When lens are in contact:

$$\frac{1}{f_{eq}}=\frac{1}{f_1}+\frac{1}{f_2}+.....$$

$$P_{eq}=P_1+P_2+.....$$

Example 2: An object is placed at a distance 25 cm from a lens. Image is formed at a distance 100 cm on other side of the lens. If the object is moved 10 cm towards the lens what will be the shift of the image?

Sol. In 1st case,

$$u=-25\text{ cm}$$
$$v=100\text{ cm}$$

Applying lens formula,

$$\frac{1}{v}-\frac{1}{u}=\frac{1}{f}$$

Or, $$\frac{1}{100}+\frac{1}{25}=\frac{1}{f}$$

Or, $$\frac{1}{20}=\frac{1}{f}$$

$\therefore$ $$f=20\text{ cm}$$

So, the lens is convex lens.

In 2nd case,

$$u=-15\text{ cm}$$
$$f=15\text{ cm}$$

Applying lens formula,

$$\frac{1}{v}-\frac{1}{u}=\frac{1}{f}$$

Or, $$\frac{1}{v}+\frac{1}{15}=\frac{1}{20}$$

Or, $$\frac{1}{v}=-\frac{1}{60}$$

$\therefore$ $$v=-60\text{ cm}$$

So, the image is formed on the object side of the lens.

So, the shift of image is 100 + 60 = 160 cm

Example 3: Refractive index of the material of a equiangular prism is 1.5. A ray of light so passes through the prism so that the angle of incidence = angle of emergence = 3/4th of the angle of deviation. Find the angle of deviation.

Sol. Given, $$i_1=e=\frac{3}{4}\delta$$

$$A=60°$$ (since, the prism is equiangular)

$$\delta=i_1+e-A$$

or, $$\delta=\frac{3}{4}\delta+\frac{3}{4}\delta-60°$$

or, $\frac{\delta}{2} = 60°$

$\therefore$ $\delta = 120°$

Optical Instruments

➤ **Microscope** is an optical instrument which helps us to see and study micro objects or organisms. It forms magnified image of the object.

➤ **Telescope** is an optical instrument which helps us to see and study far off objects magnified & resolved.

➤ Microscopes and telescopes may generally be set at two different image vision positions:

- **Image at least distance of distinct vision:** When the image is formed at a distance of 25 cm from our eye.
- **Image at relaxed vision:** When the image is formed at infinite distance from our eye.
- Magnification at distinct vision is always greater than magnification at relaxed vision.

➤ **Simple Microscope:** Convex lens behaves as simple microscope.

➤ **The magnifying power of the simple microscope:**

(i) Magnification at least distance of distinct vision:

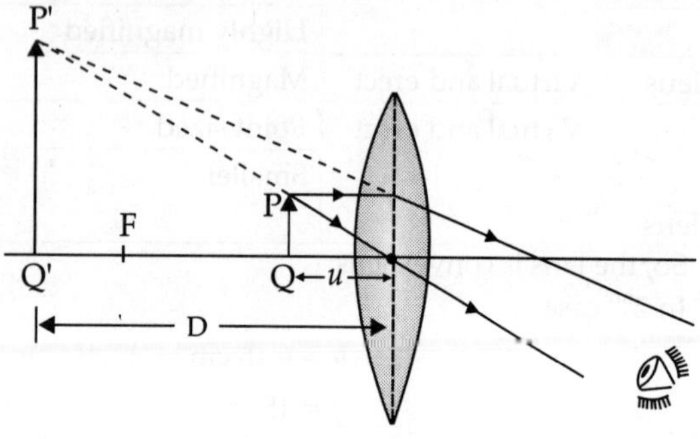

$$m = \frac{1+D}{f}$$

where, D is the least distance of distinct vision of the eye and f is focal length of the lens.

(ii) Magnification for relaxed eye:

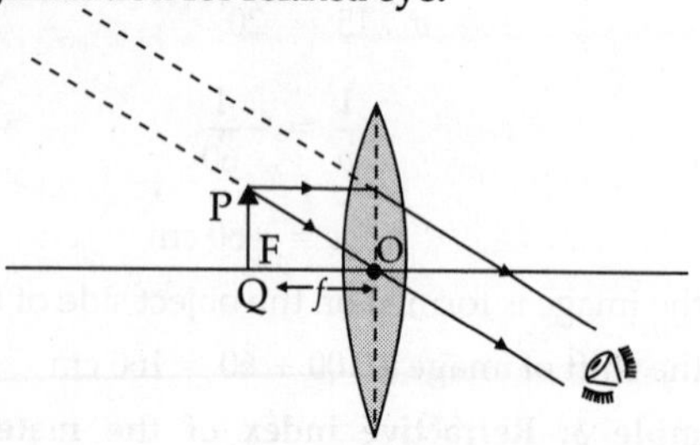

$$m = \frac{D}{f}$$

➤ **Compound Microscope:** For much larger magnification, compound microscope is used. It is a combination of two convex lenses when the magnification of each lens is compounded.

- The two lenses are placed co-axially and the distance between them is adjustable.
- The lens towards the object is called objective and towards the eye is called eyepiece.

Scan to know more about this topic
Ray diagram of compound microscope

- The final image formed by the compound microscope is magnified and inverted.

➤ **Compound Microscope (image at least distance of distinct vision):**

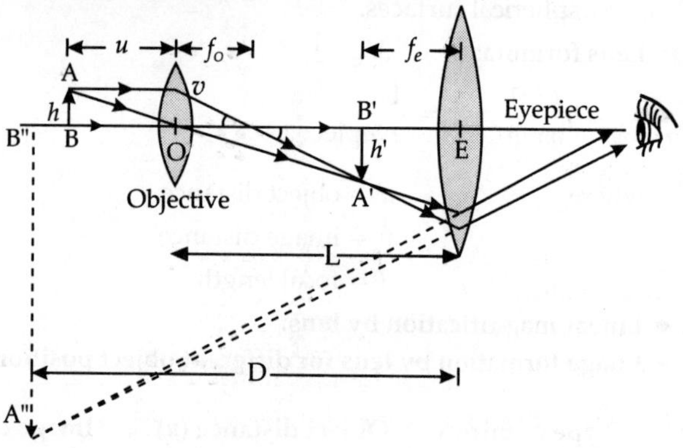

Magnification of objective, $m_o = \frac{v}{u} = \frac{v}{f_o} - 1$

Magnification of eyepiece, $m_e = \frac{1+D}{f_e}$

Total magnification, $m = m_0 \times m_e$

$$= \left(\frac{v}{f_o} - 1\right)\left(\frac{1+D}{f_e}\right)$$

Since $v \approx L$

$$m = \left(\frac{L}{f_o} - 1\right)\left(\frac{1+D}{f_e}\right)$$

since $L >> f_o$

$$m = \left(\frac{L}{f_o} - 1\right)\left(\frac{1+D}{f_e}\right)$$

where,

f_o = Focal length of objective
f_e = focal length of eyepiece
L = Length of tube
= Distance between objective and eyepiece.

➤ **Compound Microscope (image at infinity)**

This is also called normal adjustment or adjustment for relaxed eye.

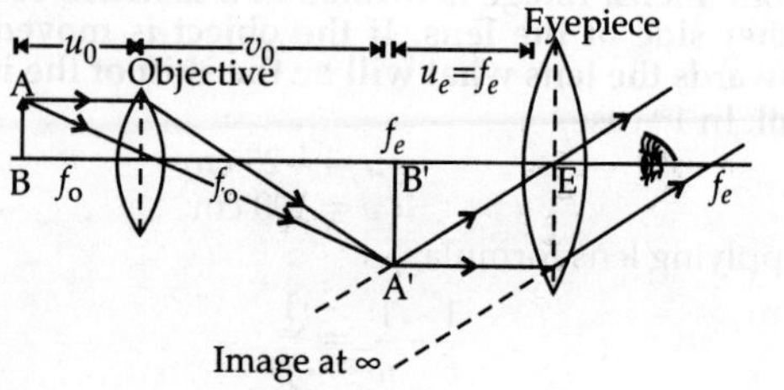

Here,

$$m_e = \frac{D}{f_e}$$

So, magnification, $m = \left(\frac{L}{f_o}\right)\left(\frac{D}{f_e}\right)$

➢ **Characteristics of compound microscope:**

- If the length of tube increases, magnification increases.

$$m \propto L$$

- If focal length of the objective decreases, magnification increases.

$$m \propto \frac{1}{f_o}$$

- If focal length of the eyepiece decreases, magnification increases.

$$m \propto \frac{1}{f_e}$$

(Normally $f_o > f_e$)

Telescope

- Telescope is an instrument to magnify and resolve far off objects.
- Far off objects make much smaller angle at our eye. Telescope makes that angle larger without much intensity loss.
- To maximise the intensity, aperture size of objective lens is quite large. It focuses a bright point size image at its focal plane.
- Now with eyepiece, this point size image is finally observed as final inverted magnified image. This type of telescope is known as astronomical telescope.

➢ **Telescope (image at least distance of distinct vision):**

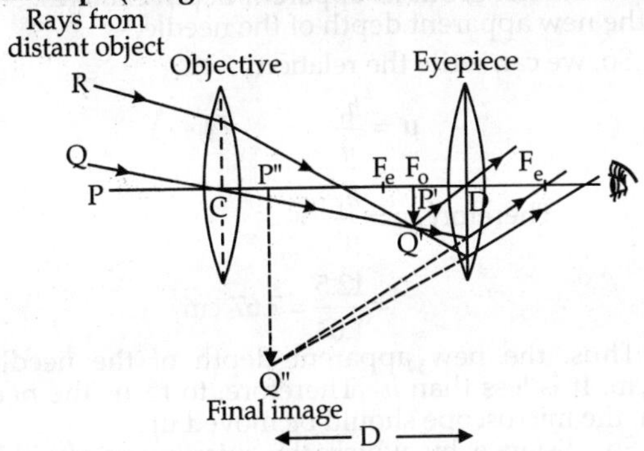

Magnification, $m = \left(\frac{f_o}{f_e}\right)\left(1+\frac{f_e}{D}\right)$

➢ **Telescope (image at infinity)**

This is also called normal adjustment or adjustment for relaxed eye.

Magnification, $m = \frac{\beta}{\alpha} = \frac{f_o}{f_e} = \frac{d_o}{d_e}$

where, d_o = Diameter of the objective

and d_e = Diameter of the eyepiece.

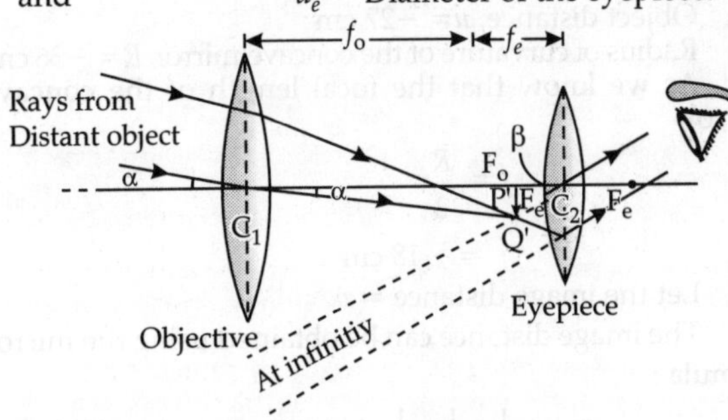

➢ **Characteristics of astronomical telescope:**

- For larger magnifying power, f_o should be large and f_e should be small.
- The length of the tube of an astronomical telescope is $L = f_o + f_e$ for relaxed vision adjustment.
- When the length of the tube of the telescope increases, f_o increases and magnifying power also increases.

➢ **Limitations of refractive telescope:**

- Manufacturing of large aperture objective lens is costly and its handling is also difficult.
- It has spherical and chromatic aberrations.

➢ **Modern Telescope (Reflecting Telescope):**

- Reflecting telescope consists of a concave mirror of large radius of curvature in place of objective lens.
- A secondary convex mirror is used to focus the incident light, which now passes through a hole in the objective primary mirror.

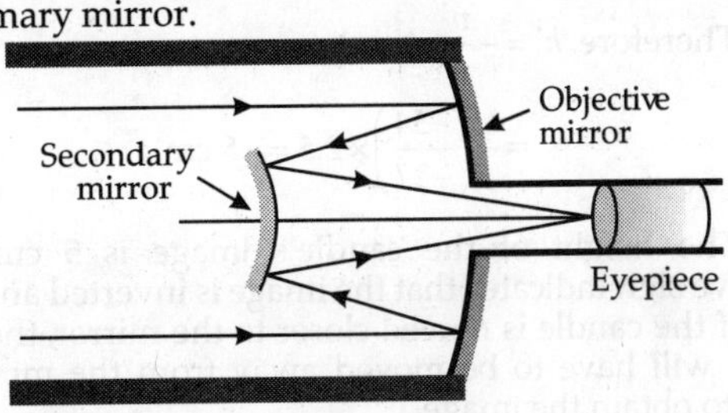

➢ **Magnifying power of the reflecting telescope:**

$$m = \frac{f_o}{f_e}$$

➢ **Advantages of reflecting telescope:**

- Very sharp image
- No spherical or chromatic aberrations.
- Cost effective
- Light and easy to handle.

➢ **Disadvantages of reflecting telescope:**

- The secondary mirror obstructs the incoming rays.

NCERT CORNER

Exercise Questions

Q. 1. A small candle, 2.5 cm in size is placed at 27 cm in front of a concave mirror of radius of curvature 36 cm. At what distance from the mirror should a screen be placed in order to obtain a sharp image? Describe the nature and size of the image. If the candle is moved closer to the mirror, how would the screen have to be moved?

[NCERT Ex. Q. 9.1, Page 249]

Ans. Given that,

Size of the candle, h = 2.5 cm

Image size = h'
Object distance, $u = -27$ cm
Radius of curvature of the concave mirror, $R = -36$ cm
As we know that the focal length of the concave mirror,

$$f = \frac{R}{2}$$

$$= -18 \text{ cm}$$

Let the image distance = v

The image distance can be obtained using the mirror formula :

$$\frac{1}{u} + \frac{1}{v} = \frac{1}{f}$$

$$\frac{1}{v} = \frac{1}{f} - \frac{1}{u}$$

$$= \frac{1}{-18} - \frac{1}{-27}$$

$$= \frac{-3+2}{54}$$

$$= -\frac{1}{54}$$

Hence, $v = -54$ cm

So, the screen should be placed 54 cm away from the mirror to obtain a sharp image.

The magnification of the image is:

$$m = \frac{h'}{h} = -\frac{v}{u}$$

Therefore, $h' = -\frac{v}{u} \times h$

$$= -\left(\frac{-54}{-27}\right) \times 2.5 = -5 \text{ cm}$$

The height of the candle's image is 5 cm. The negative sign indicates that the image is inverted and real.

If the candle is moved closer to the mirror, then the screen will have to be moved away from the mirror in order to obtain the image.

Q. 2. A 4.5 cm needle is placed 12 cm away from a convex mirror of focal length 15 cm. Give the location of the image and the magnification. Describe what happens as the needle is moved farther from the mirror. [NCERT Ex. Q. 9.2, Page 249]

Ans. Given that, Height of the needle, $h_1 = 4.5$ cm
Object distance, $u = -12$ cm
Focal length of the convex mirror, $f = 15$ cm
Let the image distance = v
As we know the mirror formula,

$$\frac{1}{u} + \frac{1}{v} = \frac{1}{f}$$

$$\frac{1}{v} = \frac{1}{f} - \frac{1}{u}$$

$$= \frac{1}{15} + \frac{1}{12} = \frac{4+5}{60} = \frac{9}{60}$$

Therefore, $v = \frac{60}{9} = 6.7$ cm

So, the image of the needle is 6.7 cm away from the mirror. Also, it is on the other side of the mirror.

The image size is given by the magnification formula:

$$m = \frac{h_2}{h_1} = -\frac{v}{u}$$

$$\therefore \quad h_2 = -\frac{v}{u} \times h_1 = \frac{-6.7}{-12} \times 4.5 = +2.5 \text{ cm}$$

Hence, magnification of the image,

$$m = \frac{h_2}{h_1} = \frac{2.5}{4.5} = 0.56$$

The height of the image is 2.5 cm. The positive sign indicates that the image is erect and virtual.

If the needle is moved farther from the mirror, the image will also move away from the mirror, and the size of the image will reduce gradually.

Q. 3. A tank is filled with water to a height of 12.5 cm. The apparent depth of a needle lying at the bottom of the tank is measured by a microscope to be 9.4 cm. What is the refractive index of water? If water is replaced by a liquid of refractive index 1.63 up to the same height, by what distance would the microscope have to be moved to focus on the needle again? [NCERT Ex. Q. 9.3, Page 249]

Ans. Given that,
Actual depth of the needle in water, $h_1 = 12.5$ cm
Apparent depth of the needle in water, $h_2 = 9.4$ cm
Refractive index of water

$$\mu = \frac{h_1}{h_2}$$

$$= \frac{12.5}{9.4} \approx 1.33$$

So, the refractive index of water is about 1.33.

Water is replaced by a liquid of refractive index, $\mu' = 1.63$

As we know that the actual depth of the needle remains the same, but its apparent depth changes. So, let y be the new apparent depth of the needle.

So, we can write the relation:

$$\mu' = \frac{h_1}{y}$$

Therefore, $y = \frac{h_1}{\mu'}$

$$= \frac{12.5}{1.63} = 7.67 \text{ cm}$$

Thus, the new apparent depth of the needle is 7.67 cm. It is less than h_2. Therefore, to focus the needle again, the microscope should be moved up.

So, distance by which the microscope should be moved up = 9.4 − 7.67 = 1.73 cm.

Q. 4. Figures (a) and (b) show refraction of a ray in air incident at 60° with the normal to a glass-air and water-air interface, respectively. Predict the angle of refraction in glass when the angle of incidence in water is 45° with the normal to a water-glass interface [Figure (c)].

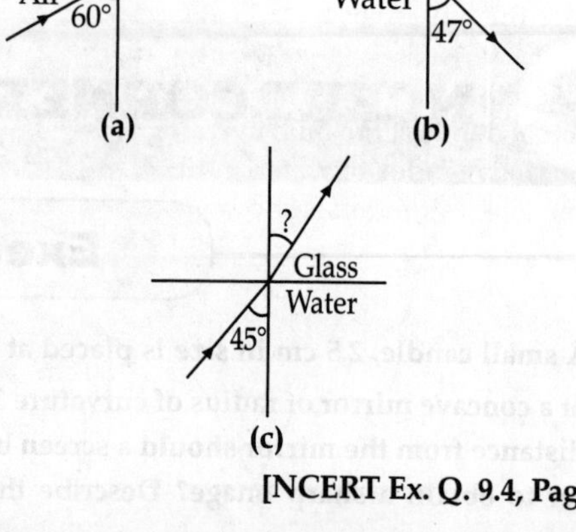

[NCERT Ex. Q. 9.4, Page 249]

Ans. Given that,

For the glass-air interface:

Angle of incidence, $i = 60°$

Angle of refraction, $r = 35°$

The relative refractive index of glass with respect to air,

$$ {}^{a}\mu_g = \frac{\sin i}{\sin r} = \frac{\sin 60°}{\sin 35°} = \frac{0.8660}{0.5736} = 1.51 \quad ...(i)$$

Given that,

For the air-water interface:

Angle of incidence, $i = 60°$

Angle of refraction, $r = 47°$

The relative refractive index of water with respect to air,

$$ {}^{a}\mu_w = \frac{\sin i}{\sin r} = \frac{\sin 60°}{\sin 47°} = \frac{0.8660}{0.7314} = 1.184 \quad ...(ii)$$

Using (i) and (ii), the relative refractive index of glass with respect to water,

$$\therefore \quad {}^{w}\mu_g = \frac{{}^{a}\mu_g}{{}^{a}\mu_w} = \frac{1.51}{1.184} = 1.275$$

The following figure shows the situation involving the glass-water interface.

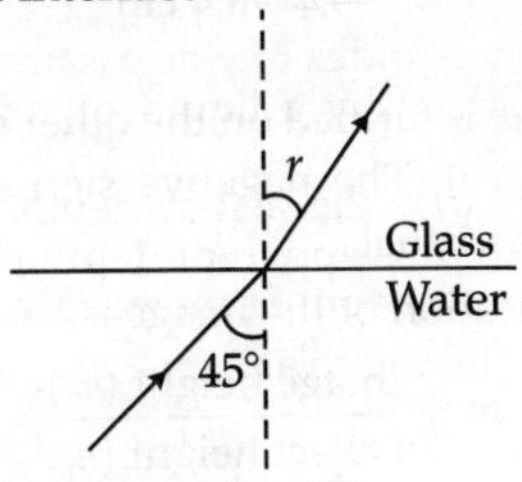

Angle of incidence, $i = 45°$

Angle of refraction $= r$

From Snell's law,

$$\frac{\sin i}{\sin r} = {}^{w}\mu_g$$

$$\frac{\sin 45°}{\sin r} = 1.275$$

$$\sin r = \frac{\frac{1}{\sqrt{2}}}{1.275} = 0.5546$$

$$\therefore \quad r = \sin^{-1}(0.5546) = 38.68°$$

Hence, the angle of refraction at the water-glass interface is 38.8°.

Q. 5. A small bulb is placed at the bottom of a tank containing water to a depth of 80 cm. What is the area of the surface of water through which light from the bulb can emerge out? Refractive index of water is 1.33. (Consider the bulb to be a point source.)

[NCERT Ex. Q. 9.5, Page 249]

Ans. Given that,

Actual depth of the bulb in water, $d = 80$ cm $= 0.8$ m

Refractive index of water, $\mu = 1.33$

The given situation is shown in the below figure:

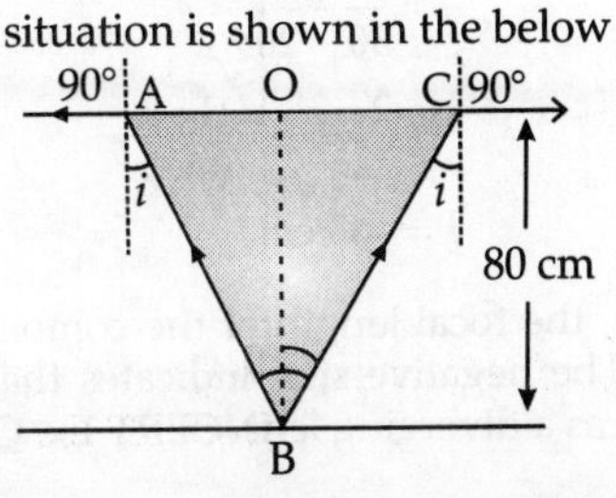

where,

i = Angle of incidence

r = Angle of refraction = 90°

Since the bulb is a point source, the emergent light can be considered as a circle of radius,

$$R = \frac{AC}{2} = AO = OB$$

$$\mu = \frac{\sin r}{\sin i}$$

$$1.33 = \frac{\sin 90°}{\sin i}$$

$$\therefore \quad i = \sin^{-1}\left(\frac{1}{1.33}\right) = 48.75°$$

Using the given figure, we have the relation:

$$\tan i = \frac{OC}{OB} = \frac{R}{d_1}$$

$$\therefore \quad R = \tan 48.75° \times 0.8 = 0.91 \text{ m}$$

$\therefore$ Area of the surface of water $= \pi R^2$

$= \pi (0.91)^2$

$= 2.61 \text{ m}^2$

Thus, the area of the surface of water through which the light from the bulb can emerge is approximately 2.61 m^2.

Q. 6. A prism is made of glass of unknown refractive index. A parallel beam of light is incident on a face of the prism. The angle of minimum deviation is measured to be 40°. What is the refractive index of the material of the prism? The refracting angle of the prism is 60°. If the prism is placed in water (refractive index 1.33), predict the new angle of minimum deviation of a parallel beam of light. **[NCERT Ex. Q. 9.6, Page 249]**

Ans. Given that,

Angle of minimum deviation, $\delta_m = 40°$

Angle of the prism, $A = 60°$

Refractive index of water, $\mu = 1.33$

Refractive index of the material of the prism $= \mu'$

The angle of deviation is related to refractive index as :

$$\mu' = \frac{\sin\left(\frac{A+\delta_m}{2}\right)}{\sin\frac{A}{2}} = \frac{\sin\left(\frac{60° + 40°}{2}\right)}{\sin\frac{60°}{2}} = \frac{\sin 50°}{\sin 30°} = 1.532$$

So, the refractive index of the material of the prism is 1.532.

Since the prism is placed in water, let δ'_m be the new angle of minimum deviation for the same prism.

The refractive index of glass with respect to water is given by the relation:

$$ {}^{w}\mu_g = \frac{\mu'}{\mu} = \frac{\sin\left(\frac{A+\delta'_m}{2}\right)}{\sin\left(\frac{A}{2}\right)}$$

$$\sin\left(\frac{A+\delta'_m}{2}\right) = \frac{\mu'}{\mu}\sin\left(\frac{A}{2}\right)$$

$$\sin\left(\frac{A+\delta'_m}{2}\right) = \frac{1.532}{1.33} \times \sin\left(\frac{60°}{2}\right) = 0.5759$$

$$\left(\frac{A+\delta'_m}{2}\right) = \sin^{-1} 0.5759 = 35.16°$$

$$60° + \delta'_m = 70.32°$$

$$\therefore \quad \delta'_m = 70.32° - 60° = 10.32°$$

So, the new minimum angle of deviation is 10.32°.

Q. 7. Double-convex lenses are to be manufactured from a glass of refractive index 1.55, with both faces of the same radius of curvature. What is the radius of curvature required if the focal length is to be 20 cm?

[NCERT Ex. Q. 9.7, Page 346]

Ans. Given that,

Refractive index of glass, $\mu = 1.55$

Focal length of the double-convex lens, $f = 20$ cm

Radius of curvature of one face of the lens = R_1

Radius of curvature of the other face of the lens = R_2

Radius of curvature of the double-convex lens = R

Therefore, $R_1 = R$ and $R_2 = -R$

The value of R can be calculated as:

$$\frac{1}{f} = (\mu - 1)\left[\frac{1}{R_1} - \frac{1}{R_2}\right]$$

$$\frac{1}{20} = (1.55 - 1)\left[\frac{1}{R} + \frac{1}{R}\right]$$

$$\frac{1}{20} = 0.55 \times \frac{2}{R}$$

$$\therefore \quad R = 0.55 \times 2 \times 20 = 22 \text{ cm}$$

Hence, the radius of curvature of the double-convex lens is 22 cm.

Q. 8. A beam of light converges at a point P. Now a lens is placed in the path of the convergent beam 12 cm from P. At what point does the beam converge if the lens is (a) a convex lens of focal length 20 cm, and (b) a concave lens of focal length 16 cm? **[NCERT Ex. Q. 9.8, Page 249]**

Ans. Given that,

According to the given situation, the object is virtual and the image formed is real.

Object distance, $u = +12$ cm

(a) Focal length of the convex lens, $f = 20$ cm

Image distance = v

According to the lens formula,

$$\frac{1}{v} - \frac{1}{u} = \frac{1}{f}$$

$$\frac{1}{v} - \frac{1}{12} = \frac{1}{20}$$

$$\frac{1}{v} = \frac{1}{20} + \frac{1}{12} = \frac{3+5}{60} = \frac{8}{60}$$

So, $$v = \frac{60}{8} = 7.5 \text{ cm}$$

Hence, the image is formed 7.5 cm away from the lens, towards its right.

(b) Focal length of the concave lens, $f = -16$ cm

Image distance = v

According to the lens formula,

$$\frac{1}{v} - \frac{1}{u} = \frac{1}{f}$$

$$\frac{1}{v} = -\frac{1}{16} + \frac{1}{12}$$

$$\frac{1}{v} = \frac{-3+4}{48} = \frac{1}{48}$$

So, $$v = 48 \text{ cm}$$

So, the image is formed 48 cm away from the lens, towards its right.

Q. 9. An object of size 3.0 cm is placed 14 cm in front of a concave lens of focal length 21 cm. Describe the image produced by the lens. What happens if the object is moved further away from the lens?

[NCERT Ex. Q. 9.9, Page 249]

Ans. Given that,

Size of the object, $h_1 = 3$ cm

Object distance, $u = -14$ cm

Focal length of the concave lens, $f = -21$ cm

Let the Image distance = v

According to the lens formula,

$$\frac{1}{v} - \frac{1}{u} = \frac{1}{f}$$

$$\frac{1}{v} = -\frac{1}{21} - \frac{1}{14}$$

$$= \frac{-2-3}{42} = \frac{-5}{42}$$

$$\therefore \quad v = -\frac{42}{5} = -8.4 \text{ cm}$$

So, the image is formed on the other side of the lens, 8.4 cm away from it. The negative sign shows that the image is erect and virtual.

The magnification of the image is:

$$m = \frac{\text{Image height } (h_2)}{\text{Object height } (h_1)} = \frac{v}{u}$$

$$\therefore \quad h_2 = \frac{-8.4}{-14} \times 3 = 0.6 \times 3 = 1.8 \text{ cm}$$

Thus, the height of the image is 1.8 cm.

If the object is moved further away from the lens, then the virtual image will move towards the focus of the lens, but not beyond it. So, the size of the image will decrease with the increase in the object distance.

Q. 10. What is the focal length of a convex lens of focal length 30 cm in contact with a concave lens of focal length 20 cm? Is the system a converging or a diverging lens? Ignore thickness of the lenses.

[NCERT Ex. Q. 9.10, Page 249]

Ans. Given that,

Focal length of the convex lens, $f_1 = 30$ cm

Focal length of the concave lens, $f_2 = -20$ cm

Focal length of the system of lenses = f

The equivalent focal length of a system of two lenses in contact is:

$$\frac{1}{f} = \frac{1}{f_1} + \frac{1}{f_2}$$

$$\frac{1}{f} = \frac{1}{30} - \frac{1}{20}$$

$$= \frac{2-3}{60} = -\frac{1}{60}$$

$$\therefore \quad f = -60 \text{ cm}$$

Thus, the focal length of the combination of lenses is 60 cm. The negative sign indicates that the system of lenses acts as a diverging lens.

Q. 11. A compound microscope consists of an objective lens of focal length 2.0 cm and an eyepiece of focal length 6.25 cm separated by a distance of 15 cm. How far from the objective should an object be placed in order to obtain the final image at (a) the least distance of distinct vision (25 cm), and (b) at infinity? What is the magnifying power of the microscope in each case?

[NCERT Ex. Q. 9.11, Page 250]

Ans. Given that,

Focal length of the objective lens, $f_1 = 2.0$ cm

Focal length of the eyepiece, $f_2 = 6.25$ cm

Distance between the objective lens and the eyepiece, $d = 15$ cm

(a) Least distance of distinct vision, $d' = 25$ cm

Image distance for the eyepiece, $v_2 = -25$ cm

Object distance for the eyepiece $= u_2$

According to the lens formula,

$$\frac{1}{v_2} - \frac{1}{u_2} = \frac{1}{f_2}$$

$$\frac{1}{u_2} = \frac{1}{v_2} - \frac{1}{f_2}$$

$$= \frac{1}{-25} - \frac{1}{6.25}$$

$$= \frac{-1-4}{25} = \frac{-5}{25}$$

$$\therefore \quad u_2 = -5 \text{ cm}$$

Image distance for the objective lens,

$$v_1 = d + u_2 = 15 - 5 = 10 \text{ cm}$$

Object distance for the objective lens $= u_1$

According to the lens formula,

$$\frac{1}{v_1} - \frac{1}{u_1} = \frac{1}{f_1}$$

$$\frac{1}{u_1} = \frac{1}{v_1} - \frac{1}{f_1} = \frac{1}{10} - \frac{1}{2}$$

$$= \frac{1-5}{10} = \frac{-4}{10}$$

$$\therefore \quad u_1 = -2.5 \text{ cm}$$

Magnitude of the object distance, $|u_1| = 2.5$ cm

The magnifying power of a compound microscope is:

$$m = \frac{v_1}{|u_1|}\left(1 + \frac{d'}{f_2}\right)$$

$$= \frac{10}{2.5}\left(1 + \frac{25}{6.25}\right)$$

$$= 4(1+4) = 20$$

(b) The final image is formed at infinity.

Therefore, image distance for the eyepiece, $v_2 = \infty$

Object distance for the eyepiece $= u_2$

According to the lens formula,

$$\frac{1}{v_2} - \frac{1}{v_2} = \frac{1}{f_2}$$

$$\frac{1}{\infty} - \frac{1}{u_2} = \frac{1}{6.25}$$

$$u_2 = -6.25 \text{ cm}$$

Image distance for the objective lens, $v_1 = d + u_2$

$= 15 - 6.25 = 8.75$ cm

Object distance for the objective lens $= u_1$

According to the lens formula,

$$\frac{1}{v_1} - \frac{1}{u_1} = \frac{1}{f_1}$$

$$\frac{1}{u_1} = \frac{1}{v_1} - \frac{1}{f_1} = \frac{1}{8.75} - \frac{1}{2.0} = \frac{2-8.75}{17.5}$$

$$\therefore \quad u_1 = -\frac{17.5}{6.75} = -2.59 \text{ cm}$$

Magnitude of the object distance, $|u_1| = 2.59$ cm

The magnifying power of a compound microscope,

$$m = \frac{v_1}{|u_1|}\left(\frac{d'}{|u_2|}\right) = \frac{8.75}{2.59} \times \frac{25}{6.25} = 13.51$$

Thus, the magnifying power of the microscope is 13.51.

Q. 12. A person with a normal near point (25 cm) using a compound microscope with objective of focal length 8.0 mm and an eyepiece of focal length 2.5 cm can bring an object placed at 9.0 mm from the objective in sharp focus. What is the separation between the two lenses? Calculate the magnifying power of the microscope. **[NCERT Ex. Q. 9.12, Page 250]**

Ans. Given that,

Focal length of the objective lens, $f_o = 0.8$ cm

Focal length of the eyepiece, $f_e = 2.5$ cm

Object distance for the objective lens,

$$u_o = -9.0 \text{ mm}$$

$$= -0.9 \text{ cm}$$

Least distance of distant vision, $d = 25$ cm

Image distance for the eyepiece, $v_e = -d = -25$ cm

Object distance for the eyepiece $= u_e$

Using the lens formula,

$$\frac{1}{v_e} - \frac{1}{u_e} = \frac{1}{f_e}$$

$$\frac{1}{u_e} = \frac{1}{v_e} - \frac{1}{f_e}$$

$$= \frac{1}{-25} - \frac{1}{2.5}$$

$$= \frac{-1-10}{25}$$

$$= \frac{-11}{25}$$

$$\therefore \quad u_e = -\frac{25}{11} = -2.27 \text{ cm}$$

We can also obtain the value of the image distance for the objective lens, v_o using the lens formula:

$$\frac{1}{v_o} - \frac{1}{u_o} = \frac{1}{f_o}$$

$$\frac{1}{v_o} = \frac{1}{f_o} - \frac{1}{u_o}$$

$$= \frac{1}{0.8} - \frac{1}{0.9}$$

$$= \frac{0.9-0.8}{0.72} = \frac{0.1}{0.72}$$

$$\therefore \quad v_o = 7.2 \text{ cm}$$

The distance between the objective lens and the eyepiece $= |u_e| + v_o$

$= 2.27 + 7.2$

$= 9.47$ cm

The magnifying power of microscope,

$$m = \frac{v_o}{|u_o|}\left(1 + \frac{d}{f_e}\right)$$

$$= \frac{7.2}{0.9}\left(1 + \frac{25}{2.5}\right) = 8(1+10) = 88$$

So, the magnifying power of the microscope is 88.

Q. 13. A small telescope has an objective lens of focal length 144 cm and an eyepiece of focal length 6.0 cm. What is the magnifying power of the telescope? What is the separation between the objective and the eyepiece?
[NCERT Ex. Q. 9.13, Page 250]

Ans. Given that,

Focal length of the objective lens, $f_o = 144$ cm

Focal length of the eyepiece, $f_e = 6.0$ cm

The magnifying power of the telescope,

$$m = \frac{f_o}{f_e}$$

$$= \frac{144}{6} = 24$$

The separation between the objective lens and the eyepiece,

$$f_o + f_e = 144 + 6 = 150 \text{ cm}$$

Thus, the magnifying power of the telescope is 24 D and the separation between the objective lens and the eyepiece is 150 cm.

Q. 14. (a) A giant refracting telescope at an observatory has an objective lens of focal length 15 m. If an eyepiece of focal length 1.0 cm is used, what is the angular magnification of the telescope?

(b) If this telescope is used to view the moon, what is the diameter of the image of the moon formed by the objective lens? The diameter of the moon is 3.48 × 10^6 m, and the radius of lunar orbit is 3.8 × 10^8 m.
[NCERT Ex. Q. 9.14, Page 346]

Ans. Given that,

Focal length of the objective lens,

$f_O = 15$ m $= 15 \times 100$ cm $= 1500$ cm

Focal length of the eyepiece, $f_e = 1.0$ cm

(a) The angular magnification of a telescope,

$$\alpha = \frac{f_O}{f_e}$$

$$= \frac{15 \times 10^2}{1.0} = 1500$$

Thus, the angular magnification of the given refracting telescope is 1500.

(b) Given that,

Diameter of the moon, $d = 3.48 \times 10^6$ m

Radius of the lunar orbit, $r_o = 3.8 \times 10^8$ m

Let 'd'' is the diameter of the image of the moon formed by the objective lens.

The angle subtended by the diameter of the moon is equal to the angle subtended by the image.

$$\frac{d}{r_0} = \frac{d'}{f_0}$$

$$\frac{3.48 \times 10^6}{3.8 \times 10^8} = \frac{d'}{15}$$

So, $d = \frac{3.48}{3.8} \times 10^{-2} \times 15$

$= 13.74 \times 10^{-2}$ m

$= 13.74$ cm

Thus, the diameter of the moon's image formed by the objective lens is 13.74 cm.

Q. 15. Use the mirror equation to deduce that

(a) an object placed between *f* and 2*f* of a concave mirror produces a real image beyond 2*f*.

(b) a convex mirror always produces a virtual image independent of the location of the object.

(c) the virtual image produced by a convex mirror is always diminished in size and is located between the focus and the pole.

(d) an object placed between the pole and focus of a concave mirror produces a virtual and enlarged image.
[NCERT Ex. Q. 9.15, Page 250]

Ans. (a) For a concave mirror, the focal length (*f*) is negative.

So, $f < 0$

When the object is placed on the left side of the mirror, the object distance (*u*) is negative.

So, $u < 0$

For image distance *v*, according to the lens formula:

$$\frac{1}{v} - \frac{1}{u} = \frac{1}{f}$$

$$\frac{1}{v} = \frac{1}{f} - \frac{1}{u} \quad \text{...(i)}$$

So the object lies between *f* and 2*f*.

$\therefore$ $2f < u < f$ ($\because$ *u* and *f* are negative)

$$\frac{1}{2f} > \frac{1}{u} > \frac{1}{f}$$

$$-\frac{1}{2f} < -\frac{1}{u} < -\frac{1}{f}$$

$$\frac{1}{f} - \frac{1}{2f} < \frac{1}{f} - \frac{1}{u} < 0 \quad \text{...(ii)}$$

Using equation (i), we get:

$$\frac{1}{2f} < \frac{1}{v} < 0$$

Since, $\frac{1}{v}$ is negative, *i.e.*, *v* is negative.

$$\frac{1}{2f} < \frac{1}{v}$$

$$2f > v$$

$$-v > -2f$$

Therefore, the image lies beyond 2*f*.

(b) For a convex mirror, the focal length (*f*) is positive.

$\therefore$ $f > 0$

When the object is placed on the left side of the mirror, the object distance (*u*) is negative.

$\therefore$ $u < 0$

For image distance v, according to the mirror formula:

$$\frac{1}{v}+\frac{1}{u}=\frac{1}{f}$$

$$\frac{1}{v}=\frac{1}{f}-\frac{1}{u}$$

Using equation (ii), we can conclude that:

$$\frac{1}{v}<0$$

$$v>0$$

Thus, the image is formed on the back side of the mirror.

So, a convex mirror always produces a virtual image, regardless of the object distance.

(c) For a convex mirror, the focal length (f) is positive.

So, $f>0$

When the object is placed on the left side of the mirror, the object distance (u) is negative,

Therefore, $u<0$

For image distance v, for this the mirror formula:

$$\frac{1}{v}+\frac{1}{u}=\frac{1}{f}$$

$$\frac{1}{v}=\frac{1}{f}-\frac{1}{u}$$

But we have $u<0$

Therefore, $\frac{1}{v}>\frac{1}{f}$

$$v<f$$

So, the image formed is diminished and is located between the focus (f) and the pole.

(d) For a concave mirror, the focal length (f) is negative.

So, $f<0$

When the object is placed on the left side of the mirror, the object distance (u) is negative.

So, $u<0$

It is placed between the focus (f) and the pole.

Therefore,

$$f>u>0$$

$$\frac{1}{f}<\frac{1}{u}<0$$

$$\frac{1}{f}-\frac{1}{u}<0$$

For image distance v, we have the mirror formula,

$$\frac{1}{v}+\frac{1}{u}=\frac{1}{f}$$

$$\frac{1}{v}=\frac{1}{f}-\frac{1}{u}$$

Therefore, $\frac{1}{v}<0$

$$v>0$$

The image is formed on the right side of the mirror. So that, it is a virtual image.

For $u<0$ and $v>0$,

$$\frac{1}{u}>\frac{1}{v}$$

So, $v>u$

Magnification, $m=\frac{v}{u}>1$

Therefore, the formed image is enlarged.

Q. 16 A small pin fixed on a table top is viewed from above from a distance of 50 cm. By what distance would the pin appear to be raised if it is viewed from the same point through a 15 cm thick glass slab held parallel to the table? Refractive index of glass = 1.5. Does the answer depend on the location of the slab?

[NCERT Ex. Q. 9.16, Page 250]

Ans. Given that,

Actual depth of the pin, d = 15 cm

Apparent depth of the pin = d'

Refractive index of glass, μ = 1.5

Ratio of actual depth to the apparent depth is equal to the refractive index of glass,

$$\mu=\frac{d}{d'}$$

$$d'=\frac{d}{\mu}$$

$$=\frac{15}{1.5}$$

$$= 10 \text{ cm}$$

The distance at which the pin appears to be raised $= d'-d$

$$= 15-10 = 5 \text{ cm}$$

For a small angle of incidence, this distance does not depend on the location of the slab.

Q. 17. (a) Figure shows a cross-section of a 'light pipe' made of a glass fibre of refractive index 1.68. The outer covering of the pipe is made of a material of refractive index 1.44. What is the range of the angles of the incident rays with the axis of the pipe for which total reflections inside the pipe take place, as shown the figure.

(b) What is the answer if there is no outer covering of the pipe?

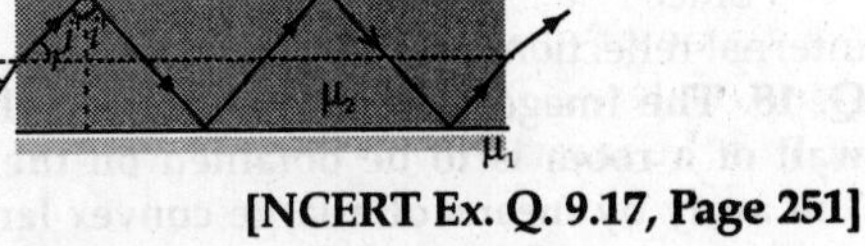

[NCERT Ex. Q. 9.17, Page 251]

Ans. (a) Given that,

Refractive index of the glass fibre, μ_1 = 1.68

Refractive index of the outer covering of the pipe, μ_2 = 1.44

Let the,

Angle of incidence = i

Angle of refraction = r

Angle of incidence at the interface = i'

So, the refractive index (μ) of the inner core-outer core interface is:

$$\mu=\frac{\mu_2}{\mu_1}$$

$$=\frac{1}{\sin i'}$$

$$\sin i'=\frac{\mu_1}{\mu_2}$$

$$=\frac{1.44}{1.68}$$

$$=0.8571$$

So, $i' = 59°$

For the critical angle, total internal reflection (TIR) takes place only when $i > i'$,

So, $i > 59°$

Maximum angle of reflection,

$$r_{max} = 90° - i'$$
$$= 90° - 59° = 31°$$

Let, i_{max} be the maximum angle of incidence.

The refractive index at the air-glass interface, $\mu_1 = 1.68$

We have the relation for the maximum angles of incidence and reflection as:

$$\mu_1 = \frac{\sin i_{max}}{\sin r_{max}}$$
$$\sin i_{max} = \mu_1 \sin r_{max}$$
$$= 1.68 \sin 31°$$
$$= 1.68 \times 0.5150$$
$$= 0.8652$$

Therefore, $i_{max} = \sin^{-1} 0.8652 \approx 60°$

So that, all the rays incident at angles lying in the range $0 < i < 60°$ will suffer total internal reflection.

(b) If the outer covering of the pipe is not present, then:

Refractive index of the outer pipe, μ_1 = refractive index of air = 1

For the angle of incidence $i = 90°$,

As we now the Snell's law at the air-pipe interface as:

$$\frac{\sin i}{\sin r} = \mu_2 = 1.68$$
$$\sin r = \frac{\sin 90°}{1.68} = \frac{1}{1.68}$$
$$r = \sin^{-1}(0.5952) = 36.5°$$
$$\therefore \quad i' = 90° - 36.5° = 53.5°$$

Since $i' > r$, So that all incident rays will suffer total internal reflection.

Q. 18. The image of a small electric bulb fixed on the wall of a room is to be obtained on the opposite wall 3 m away by means of a large convex lens. What is the maximum possible focal length of the lens required for the purpose? [NCERT Ex. Q. 9.18, Page 251]

Ans. Given that,

Distance between the object and the image, d = 3 m

Maximum focal length of the convex lens = f_{max}

For real images, the maximum focal length is given as:

$$f_{max} = \frac{d}{4} = \frac{3}{4} = 0.75 \text{ m}$$

So, for the required purpose, the maximum possible focal length of the convex lens is 0.75 m.

Q. 19. A screen is placed 90 cm from an object. The image of the object on the screen is formed by a convex lens at two different locations separated by 20 cm. Determine the focal length of the lens. [NCERT Ex. Q. 9.19, Page 251]

Ans. Given that,

Distance between the image (screen) and the object, D = 90 cm

Distance between two locations of the convex lens, d = 20 cm

Let the focal length of the lens = f

Focal length is related to d and D as:

$$f = \frac{D^2 - d^2}{4D}$$
$$= \frac{(90)^2 - (20)^2}{4 \times 90}$$
$$= \frac{770}{36}$$
$$= 21.39 \text{ cm}$$

So, the focal length of the convex lens is 21.39 cm.

Q. 20. (a) Determine the 'effective focal length' of the combination of the two lenses in Exercise 9.10, if they are placed 8.0 cm apart with their principal axes coincident. Does the answer depend on which side of the combination a beam of parallel light is incident? Is the notion of effective focal length of this system useful at all?

(b) An object 1.5 cm in size is placed on the side of the convex lens in the arrangement (a) above. The distance between the object and the convex lens is 40 cm. Determine the magnification produced by the two-lens system, and the size of the image. [NCERT Ex. Q. 9.20, Page 251]

Ans. Given that,

Focal length of the convex lens, f_1 = 30 cm

Focal length of the concave lens, f_2 = −20 cm

Distance between the two lenses, d = 8.0 cm

(a) (i) When the parallel beam of light is incident on the convex lens:

According to the lens formula,

$$\frac{1}{v_1} - \frac{1}{u_1} = \frac{1}{f_1}$$

where,

u_1 = Object distance = ∞

v_1 = Image distance

$$\frac{1}{v_1} = \frac{1}{30} - \frac{1}{\infty} = \frac{1}{30}$$
$$\therefore v_1 = 30 \text{ cm}$$

The image will act as a virtual object for the concave lens.

Applying lens formula to the concave lens,

$$\frac{1}{v_2} - \frac{1}{u_2} = \frac{1}{f_2}$$

where,

u_2 = Object distance
= (30 − d) = 30 − 8 = 22 cm

v_2 = Image distance

$$\frac{1}{v_2} = \frac{1}{22} - \frac{1}{20} = \frac{10-11}{220} = \frac{-1}{220}$$
$$\therefore \quad v_2 = -220 \text{ cm}$$

The parallel incident beam appears to diverge from a point that is

$$\left(220 - \frac{d}{2} = 220 - 4\right) = 216 \text{ cm}$$

from the centre of the combination of the two lenses.

(ii) When the parallel beam of light is incident, from the left, on the concave lens:

According to the lens formula,

$$\frac{1}{v_2} - \frac{1}{u_2} = \frac{1}{f_2}$$
$$\frac{1}{v_2} = \frac{1}{f_2} + \frac{1}{u_2}$$

where,
u_2 = Object distance = ∞
v_2 = Image distance

$$\frac{1}{v_2}=\frac{1}{-20}+\frac{1}{-\infty}=-\frac{1}{20}$$

$$\therefore \quad v_2=-20 \text{ cm}$$

The image will act as a real object for the convex lens.
Applying lens formula to the convex lens,

$$\frac{1}{v_1}-\frac{1}{u_1}=\frac{1}{f}$$

where,
u_1 = Object distance
= −(20 + *d*) = −(20+8) = −28 cm
And,
v_1 = Image distance

$$\frac{1}{v_1}=\frac{1}{30}+\frac{1}{-28}=\frac{14-15}{420}=\frac{-1}{420}$$

$$\therefore \quad v_1=-420 \text{ cm}$$

So, the parallel incident beam appears to diverge from a point that is (420 – 4 cm) = 416 cm from the left of the centre of the combination of the two lenses.

The answer does depend on the side of the combination at which the parallel beam of light is incident. The notion of effective focal length does not seem to be useful for this combination.

(b) Height of the image, *h* = 1.5 cm
Object distance from the side of the convex lens, u_1 = −40 cm

$$|u_1| = 40 \text{ cm}$$

According to the lens formula:

$$\frac{1}{v_1}-\frac{1}{u_1}=\frac{1}{f_1}$$

where,
v_1 = Image distance

$$\frac{1}{v_1}=\frac{1}{30}+\frac{1}{-40}=\frac{4-3}{120}=\frac{1}{120}$$

$$\therefore \quad v_1=120 \text{ cm}$$

$$\text{Magnification,} \quad m=\left|\frac{v_1}{u_1}\right| = \frac{120}{40}=3$$

So, the magnification due to the convex lens is 3.

The image formed by the convex lens acts as an object for the concave lens.

According to the lens formula:

$$\frac{1}{v_2}-\frac{1}{u_2}=\frac{1}{f_2}$$

where,
u_2 = Object distance
= +(120 − 8) = 112 cm.
v_2 = Image distance

$$\frac{1}{v_2}=\frac{1}{-20}+\frac{1}{112}=\frac{-112+20}{2240}=\frac{-92}{2240}$$

$$\therefore v_2=\frac{-2240}{92} \text{ cm}$$

$$\text{Magnification, } m'=\left|\frac{v_2}{u_2}\right|=\frac{2240}{92}\times\frac{1}{112}=\frac{20}{92}$$

The magnification produced by the combination of the two lenses is calculated as:

$$=m\times m'=3\times\frac{20}{92}=\frac{60}{92}=0.652$$

The magnification of the combination is given as :

$$\frac{h_2}{h_1}=0.652$$

$$h_2=0.652\times h_1$$

where,
h_1 = Object size = 1.5 cm
h_2 = Size of the image

$$\therefore h_2=0.652\times 1.5=0.98 \text{ cm}$$

So, the height of the image is 0.98 cm.

Q. 21. At what angle should a ray of light be incident on the face of a prism of refracting angle 60° so that it just suffers total internal reflection at the other face? The refractive index of the material of the prism is 1.524.
[NCERT Ex. Q. 9.21, Page 251]

Ans. The incident, refracted and emergent rays associated with a glass prism ABC are shown in the below figure.

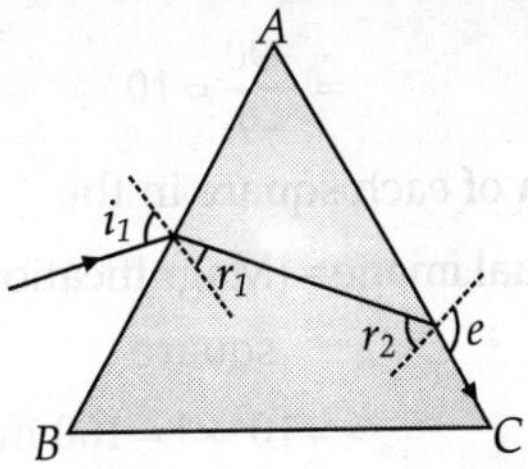

Given that,
Angle of prism, ∠*A* = 60°
Refractive index of the prism, μ = 1.524
i_1 = Incident angle
r_1 = Refracted angle
r_2 = Angle of incidence at the face *AC*
e = Emergent angle = 90°
According to Snell's law, for side *AC*,

$$\frac{\sin e}{\sin r_2}=\mu$$

$$\sin r_2=\frac{1}{\mu}\times\sin 90^\circ=\frac{1}{1.524}=0.6562$$

$$\therefore \quad r_2=\sin^{-1}0.6562\approx 41^\circ$$

It is clear from the figure that angle,

$$A=r_1+r_2$$

$$\therefore \quad r_1=A-r_2=60-41=19^\circ.$$

According to Snell's law,

$$\mu=\frac{\sin i_1}{\sin r_1}$$

$$\sin i_1=\mu\sin r_1=1.524\times\sin 19^\circ=0.496$$

$$i_1=29.75^\circ$$

So, the angle of incidence is 29.75°.

Q. 22. A card sheet divided into squares each of size 1 mm² is being viewed at a distance of 9 cm through a

magnifying glass (a converging lens of focal length 9 cm) held close to the eye.

(a) What is the magnification produced by the lens? How much is the area of each square in the virtual image?

(b) What is the angular magnification (magnifying power) of the lens?

(c) Is the magnification in (a) equal to the magnifying power in (b)? Explain. [NCERT Ex. Q. 9.22, Page 251]

Ans. (a) Given that,

Area of each square, $A = 1\ mm^2$

Object distance, $u = -9$ cm

Focal length of a converging lens, $f = 9$ cm

For image distance v, the lens formula can be written as:

$$\frac{1}{f} = \frac{1}{v} - \frac{1}{u}$$

$$\frac{1}{10} = \frac{1}{v} + \frac{1}{9}$$

$$\frac{1}{v} = -\frac{1}{90}$$

$$\therefore \quad v = -90 \text{ cm}$$

$$\text{Magnification, } m = \frac{v}{u}$$

$$= \frac{-90}{-9} = 10$$

∴ Area of each square in the virtual image $= (\text{Magnification})^2 \times$ Area of each square

$$= 10^2 \times 1 = 100\ mm^2 = 1\ cm^2$$

(b) Magnifying power of the lens

$$= \frac{d}{|u|} = \frac{25}{9} = 2.8$$

(c) The magnification in (a) is not the same as the magnifying power in (b).

The magnification magnitude is, $\left(\left|\frac{v}{u}\right|\right)$ and the magnifying power is, $\left(\frac{d}{|u|}\right)$.

The two quantities will be equal when the image is formed at the near point (25 cm).

Q. 23. (a) At what distance should the lens be held from the figure in Question 22 in order to view the squares distinctly with the maximum possible magnifying power?

(b) What is the magnification in this case?

(c) Is the magnification equal to the magnifying power in this case? Explain. [NCERT Ex. Q. 9.23, Page 251]

Ans. (a) Given that,

The maximum possible magnification is obtained when the image is formed at the near point ($d = 25$ cm).

Image distance, $v = -d = -25$ cm

Focal length, $f = 10$ cm

Let the object distance $= u$

According to the lens formula,

$$\frac{1}{f} = \frac{1}{v} - \frac{1}{u}$$

$$\frac{1}{u} = \frac{1}{v} - \frac{1}{f}$$

$$= \frac{1}{-25} - \frac{1}{10} = \frac{-2-5}{50} = -\frac{7}{50}$$

$$\therefore \quad u = -\frac{50}{7} = -7.14 \text{ cm}$$

So, to view the squares distinctly, the lens should be kept at 7.14 cm away from them.

(b) $\text{Magnification} = \left|\frac{v}{u}\right| = \frac{25}{\frac{50}{7}} = 3.5$

(c) $\text{Magnifying power} = \frac{d}{u} = \frac{25}{\frac{50}{7}} = 3.5$

Since the image is formed at the near point (25 cm), the magnifying power is equal to the magnitude of magnification.

Q. 24. What should be the distance between the object in Question 23 and the magnifying glass if the virtual image of each square in the figure is to have an area of 6.25 mm². Would you be able to see the squares distinctly with your eyes very close to the magnifier?

[NCERT Ex. Q. 9.24, Page 251]

Ans. Given that,

Area of the virtual image of each square, $A = 6.25\ mm^2$

Area of each square, $A = 1$ mm

So, the linear magnification of the object can be calculated as,

$$m = \sqrt{\frac{A}{A_0}} = \sqrt{\frac{6.25}{1}} = 2.5$$

But $\quad m = \frac{\text{Image distance } (v)}{\text{Object distance } (u)}$

$$\therefore \quad v = mu = 2.5\,u \quad \text{...(i)}$$

Focal length of the magnifying glass, $f = 10$ cm

According to the lens formula,

$$\frac{1}{f} = \frac{1}{v} - \frac{1}{u}$$

$$\frac{1}{10} = \frac{1}{2.5u} - \frac{1}{u} = \frac{1}{u}\left(\frac{1}{2.5} - \frac{1}{1}\right) = \frac{1}{u}\left(\frac{1-2.5}{2.5}\right)$$

$$\therefore \quad u = -\frac{1.5 \times 10}{2.5} = -6 \text{ cm}$$

And $v = 2.5\,u$

$$= 2.5 \times 6 = -15 \text{ cm}$$

The virtual image is formed at a distance of 15 cm, which is less than the near point (i.e., 25 cm) of a normal eye. Thus, it cannot be seen by the eyes distinctly.

Q. 25. Answer the following questions:

(a) The angle subtended at the eye by an object is equal to the angle subtended at the eye by the virtual image

produced by a magnifying glass. In what sense then does a magnifying glass provide angular magnification?

(b) In viewing through a magnifying glass, one usually position's one's eyes very close to the lens. Does angular magnification change if the eye is moved back?

(c) Magnifying power of a simple microscope is inversely proportional to the focal length of the lens. What then stops us from using a convex lens of smaller and smaller focal length and achieving greater and greater magnifying power?

(d) Why must both the objective and the eyepiece of a compound microscope have short focal lengths?

(e) When viewing through a compound microscope, our eyes should be positioned not on the eyepiece but a short distance away from it for best viewing. Why? How much should be that short distance between the eye and eyepiece?

[NCERT Ex. Q. 9.25, Page 252]

Ans. (a) Though the image size is bigger than the object, the angular size of the image is equal to the angular size of the object. A magnifying glass helps one see the objects placed closer than the least distance of distinct vision (i.e., 25 cm). A closer object causes a larger angular size. A magnifying glass provides angular magnification. Without magnification, the object cannot be placed closer to the eye. With magnification, the object can be placed much closer to the eye.

(b) Yes, the angular magnification changes. When the distance between the eye and a magnifying glass is increased, the angular magnification decreases a little. This is because the angle subtended at the eye is slightly less than the angle subtended at the lens. Image distance does not have any effect on angular magnification.

(c) The focal length of a convex lens cannot be decreased by a greater amount. This is because making lenses having very small focal lengths is not easy. Spherical and chromatic aberrations are produced by a convex lens having a very small focal length.

(d) The angular magnification produced by the eyepiece of a compound microscope is $\left[\left(\frac{25}{f_e}\right)+1\right]$.

where,

f_e = Focal length of the eyepiece

It can be inferred that if f_e is small, then angular magnification of the eyepiece will be large.

The angular magnification of the objective lens of a compound microscope is given as:

$$=\frac{1}{[|u_o| f_o]}$$

where,

u_o = Object distance for the objective lens

f_o = Focal length of the objective

The magnification is large when $u_o > f_o$.

In the case of a microscope, the object is kept close to the objective lens. So, the object distance is very little. Since u_o is small, f_o will be even smaller. Therefore, f_e and f_o are both small in the given condition.

(e) When we place our eyes too close to the eyepiece of a compound microscope, we are unable to collect much refracted light. As a result, the field of view decreases substantially.

So, the clarity of the image gets blurred.

The best position of the eye for viewing through a compound microscope is at the eye-ring attached to the eyepiece. The precise location of the eye depends on the separation between the objective lens and the eyepiece.

Q. 26. An angular magnification (magnifying power) of 30× is desired using an objective of focal length 1.25 cm and an eyepiece of focal length 5 cm. How will you set up the compound microscope? [NCERT Ex. Q. 9.26, Page 252]

Ans. Given that,

Focal length of the objective lens, f_o = 1.25 cm

Focal length of the eyepiece, f_e = 5 cm

Least distance of distinct vision, d = 25 cm

Angular magnification of the compound microscope = 30 ×

Total magnifying power of the compound microscope, m = 30

The angular magnification of the eyepiece is given by the relation,

$$m_e = \left(1+\frac{d}{f_e}\right) = \left(1+\frac{25}{5}\right) = 6$$

The angular magnification of the objective lens (m_o) is related to m_e as:

$$m = m_o \cdot m_e$$

$$m_e = \frac{m}{m_e} = \frac{30}{6} = 5$$

And we know that,

$$m_e = \frac{\text{Image distance for the objective lens } (v_o)}{\text{Object distance for the objective lens } (-u_o)}$$

$$5 = \frac{v_o}{-u_o}$$

$$\therefore v_o = -5u_o \quad \text{...(i)}$$

Applying the lens formula for the objective lens,

$$\frac{1}{f_o} = \frac{1}{v_o} - \frac{1}{u_o}$$

$$\frac{1}{1.25} = \frac{1}{-5u_o} - \frac{1}{u_o} = \frac{-6}{5u_o}$$

$$\therefore \quad u_o = \frac{-6}{5} \times 1.25 = -1.5 \text{ cm}$$

And $v_o = -5u_o$

$$= -5 \times (-1.5) = 7.5 \text{ cm}$$

The object should be placed 1.5 cm away from the objective lens to obtain the desired magnification.

Applying the lens formula for the eyepiece:

$$\frac{1}{v_e} - \frac{1}{u_e} = \frac{1}{f_e}$$

where,

v_e = Image distance for the eyepiece

$= -d = -25$ cm

u_e = Object distance for the eyepiece

$$\frac{1}{u_e} = \frac{1}{v_e} - \frac{1}{f_e}$$

$$=\frac{-1}{25}-\frac{1}{5}=-\frac{6}{25}$$

So,

$$u_e=-4.17 \text{ cm}$$

Separation between the objective lens and the eyepiece, $=|u_e|+|v_o|$

$$=4.17+7.5$$

$$=11.67 \text{ cm}$$

So, the separation between the objective lens and the eyepiece should be 11.67 cm.

Q. 27. A small telescope has an objective lens of focal length 140 cm and an eyepiece of focal length 5.0 cm. What is the magnifying power of the telescope for viewing distant objects when :

(a) the telescope is in normal adjustment (i.e., when the final image is at infinity)?

(b) the final image is formed at the least distance of distinct vision (25 cm)? [NCERT Ex. Q. 9.27, Page 252]

Ans. Given that,

Focal length of the objective lens, $f_o = 140$ cm

Focal length of the eyepiece, $f_e = 5$ cm

Least distance of distinct vision, $d = 25$ cm

(a) When the telescope is in normal adjustment, its magnifying power is given as:

$$m=\frac{f_o}{f_e}$$

$$=\frac{140}{5}=28$$

(b) When the final image is formed at d, the magnifying power of the telescope is given as:

$$\frac{f_o}{f_e}\left[1+\frac{f_e}{d}\right]=\frac{140}{5}\left[1+\frac{5}{25}\right]$$

$$=28[1+0.2]$$

$$=28\times 1.2$$

$$=33.6$$

Q. 28. (a) For the telescope described in Question 27, what is the separation between the objective lens and the eyepiece?

(b) If the telescope is used to view a 100 m tall tower 3 km away, what is the height of the image of the tower formed by the objective lens?

(c) What is the height of the final imge of the tower if it is formed at 25 cm? [NCERT Ex. Q. 9.28, Page 252]

Ans. Focal length of the objective lens, $f_O = 140$ cm

Focal length of the eyepiece, $f_e = 5$ cm

(a) The separation between the objective lens and the eyepiece = $f_O + f_e$ = 140 + 5 = 145 cm.

(b) Height of the tower, $h_1 = 100$ m

Distance of the tower from the telescope, u = 3 km = 3000 m.

The angle subtended by the tower at the telescope is given as:

$$\theta=\frac{h_1}{\mu}$$

$$=\frac{100}{3000}=\frac{1}{30}\text{rad}$$

The angle subtended by the image produced by the objective lens is given as:

$$\theta=\frac{h_2}{f_O}=\frac{h_2}{140}\text{ rad}$$

where h_2 = height of the image of the tower formed by the objective lens.

$$\frac{1}{30}=\frac{h_2}{140}$$

$$\therefore \quad h_2=\frac{140}{30}=4.7 \text{ cm}$$

Therefore, the objective lens forms a 4.7 cm tall image of the tower.

(c) Image is formed at a distance, $d = 25$ cm

The magnification of the eyepiece is given by the relation,

$$m=1+\frac{d}{f_e}$$

$$=1+\frac{25}{5}=1+5=6$$

Height of the final image = $mh_2 = 6 \times 4.7 = 28.2$ cm.

Hence, the height of the final image of the tower is 28.2 cm.

Q. 29. A Cassegrain telescope uses two mirrors as shown in Figure. Such a telescope is built with the mirrors 20 mm apart. If the radius of curvature of the large mirror is 220 mm and the small mirror is 140 mm, where will the final image of an object at infinity be?

[NCERT Ex. Q. 9.29, Page 252]

Ans. The following figure shows a Cassegrain telescope consisting of a concave mirror and a convex mirror.

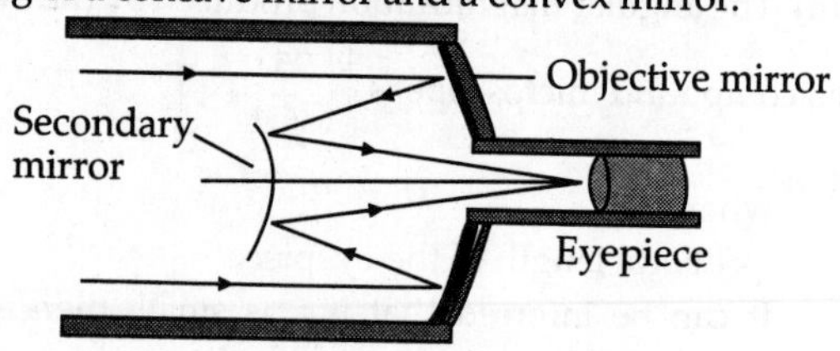

Given that,

Distance between the objective mirror and the secondary mirror, $d = 20$ mm

Radius of curvature of the objective mirror,

$$R_1 = 220 \text{ mm}$$

Radius of curvature of the secondary mirror,

$$R_2 = 140 \text{ mm}$$

So the focal length of the objective mirror,

$$f_1=\frac{R_1}{2}=110 \text{ mm}$$

Radius of curvature of the secondary mirror,

$$R_2 = 140 \text{ mm}$$

So the focal length of the secondary mirror,

$$f_2 = \frac{R_2}{2} = 70 \text{ mm}$$

The image of an object placed at infinity, formed by the objective mirror, will act as a virtual object for the secondary mirror.

Thus, the virtual object distance for the secondary mirror, $u = f_1 - d = 110 - 20 = 90$ mm

$$\frac{1}{v} + \frac{1}{u} = \frac{1}{f_2}$$

$$\frac{1}{v} = \frac{1}{f_2} - \frac{1}{u} = \frac{1}{70} - \frac{1}{90} = \frac{9-7}{630} = \frac{2}{630}$$

Therefore,

$$v = \frac{630}{2} = 315 \text{ mm}$$

So, the final image will be formed 315 mm away from the secondary mirror.

Q. 30. Light incident normally on a plane mirror attached to a galvanometer coil retraces backwards as shown in Figure. A current in the coil produces a deflection of 3.5° of the mirror. What is the displacement of the reflected spot of light on a screen placed 1.5 m away?

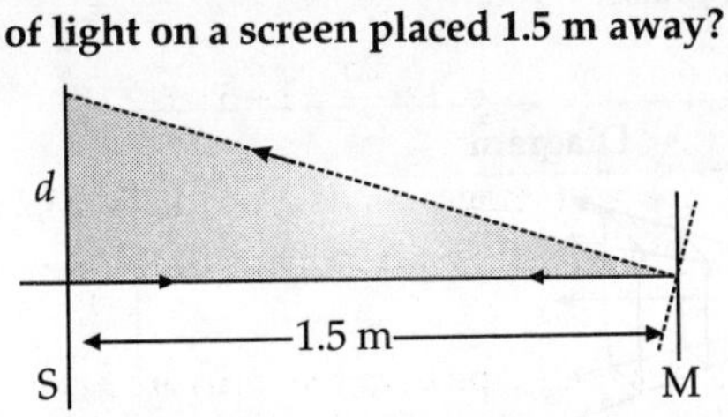

[NCERT Ex. Q. 9.30, Page 252]

Ans. Given that,

Angle of deflection, $\phi = 3.5°$

Distance of the screen from the mirror, $D = 1.5$ m

The reflected rays get deflected by an amount twice the angle of deflection, $2\theta = 7.0°$

The displacement (d) of the reflected spot of light on the screen is given as:

$$\tan 2\theta = \frac{d}{1.5}$$

$$\therefore \quad d = 1.5 \times \tan 7° = 0.184 \text{ m} = 18.4 \text{ cm}$$

So, the displacement of the reflected spot of light is 18.4 cm.

Q. 31. Figure shows an equi convex lens (of refractive index 1.50) in contact with a liquid layer on top of a plane mirror. A small needle with its tip on the principal axis is moved along the axis until its inverted image is found at the position of the needle. The distance of the needle from the lens is measured to be 45.0 cm. The liquid is removed and the experiment is repeated. The new distance is measured to be 30.0 cm. What is the refractive index of the liquid?

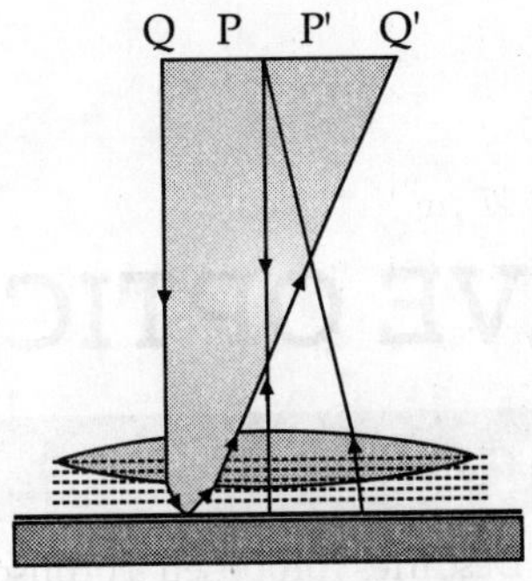

[NCERT Ex. Q. 9.31, Page 253]

Ans. Given that,

Focal length of the convex lens, $f_1 = 30$ cm

The liquid acts as a mirror. So, focal length of the liquid = f_2

Focal length of the system (convex lens + liquid), $f = 45$ cm

For a pair of optical systems placed in contact, the equivalent focal length is given as:

$$\frac{1}{f} = \frac{1}{f_1} + \frac{1}{f_2}$$

$$\frac{1}{f_2} = \frac{1}{f} - \frac{1}{f_1}$$

$$= \frac{1}{45} - \frac{1}{30} = \frac{1}{90}$$

$$\therefore \quad f_2 = -90 \text{ cm}$$

Let the refractive index of the lens be μ_1 and the radius of curvature of one surface be R. Therefore, the radius of curvature of the other surface is $-R$.

R can be obtained using the relation,

$$\frac{1}{f_1} = (\mu_1 - 1)\left(\frac{1}{R} - \frac{1}{-R}\right)$$

$$\frac{1}{30} = (1.5 - 1)\left(\frac{2}{R}\right)$$

$$\therefore \quad R = \frac{30}{0.5 \times 2} = 30 \text{ cm}$$

Let μ_2 be the refractive index of the liquid.

Radius of curvature of the liquid on the side of the plane mirror = ∞

Radius of curvature of the liquid on the side of the lens, $R = -30$ cm

The value of μ_2 can be calculated using the relation,

$$\frac{1}{f_2} = (\mu_2 - 1)\left(\frac{1}{-R} - \frac{1}{\infty}\right)$$

$$\frac{-1}{90} = (\mu_2 - 1)\left[\frac{1}{+30} - 0\right]$$

$$\mu_2 - 1 = \frac{1}{3}$$

$$\therefore \quad \mu_2 = \frac{4}{3} = 1.33$$

Therefore, the refractive index of the liquid is 1.33.

CHAPTER 10

WAVE OPTICS

Introduction

- In 1637, Descartes proposed corpuscular theory of light. This theory was able to explain reflection and refraction. But according to this theory the velocity of light in denser medium is higher as compared to rarer medium.
- Newton supported 'Descartes' corpuscular theory of light and developed it further.
- In 1678 Christiaan Huygens proposed wave theory of light. According to this theory, light travels in the form of longitudinal waves with uniform speed in a homogenous medium. Longitudinal and mechanical waves need medium to travel. So, Huygens assumed a hypothetical medium known as 'ether'. With this theory he was able to prove that velocity of light is higher in rarer medium compared to denser medium.
- Initially, Huygens' wave theory of light didn't get much success. The main point of its rejection was that it was considered as longitudinal wave which needs medium, but experimentally found that it could also travel in vacuum and there is no medium like ether.
- Later Maxwell's theory of electromagnetic waves and Young's famous double slit experiment firmly established this theory. Maxwell described light as an electromagnetic wave which does not need medium and its speed in vacuum is 3×10^8 m/s. Phenomenon of optical interference, diffraction and polarisation can be explained with wave nature of light.
- Huygens' wave theory can not explain photoelectric effect and Compton effect.
- Polarisation of light proves that light is not a longitudinal wave. It is a transverse wave.

Wavefront

- Wavefront is the locus of all points in which light waves are in same phase.

Types of wavefront:

Type of wave front	Source	Diagram
Spherical wavefront	Point source	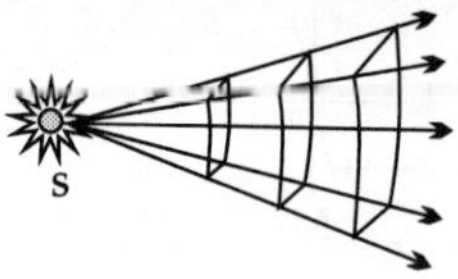
Cylindrical wavefront	Line source	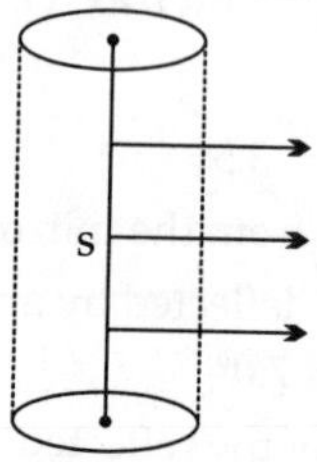
Plane wavefront	Point source at infinite distance	Source at infinite distance 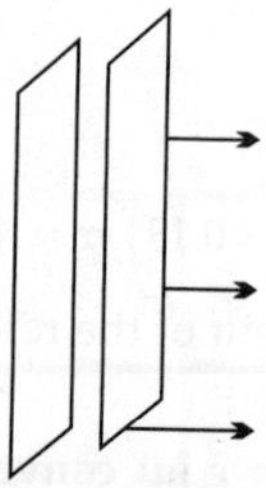

➢ **Properties of wavefront:**

- Phase is same at all points of a given wavefront.
- The direction in which wave advances is known as ray. Ray is a straight line perpendicular to the wavefront.

Huygens's Principle

- Every point on a given wavefront can be regarded as a source of secondary waves, known as wavelets.
- The secondary wavelets spread in all directions with the velocity of light.
- The new wavefront at any time is then the envelope of these wavelets in the forward direction.

➢ In Huygen's principle, there is no existence of wavefront propagating in backward direction. Voigt and Kirchhoff proved that the amplitude of secondary wavelets is proportional to $(1+\cos\theta)/2$.

Scan to know more about this topic

Huygen's principle

Electric Charges and Fields

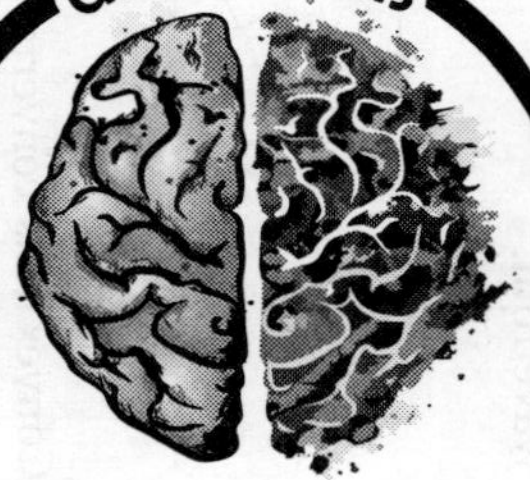

Electric charges

Electric field lines

- Always normal to conducting surface
- Lines originating from +ve charge
- Terminating at –ve charge
- Never intersect each other
- Do not form closed loop
- Are imaginary lines.

Quantization of charge

All charges must be a multiple of charge (e)

$Q = ne$

Where n is an integer

- Two kinds of charges + ve and – ve
- S.I. unit is Coulomb (C)
  1 C = charge flowing through a wire in 1s if current in it is 1A
- $e = 1.602 \times 10^{-19}$ C.

Conservation of charge

It is not possible to create or destroy net charge of an isolated system.

Electric Field

Electric field due to point charge

$\vec{E} = \frac{\vec{F}}{q} = k' \frac{Q}{r^2}$ (N/C)

$\because$ unit = N/C

- Due to discrete distribution of charges
  $\vec{E} = \sum_{i}^{n} \vec{E}_i$
- Due to continuous distribution of charge
  $\vec{E} = k' \int \frac{dQ}{r^3}\vec{r}$
  $|\vec{E}| = k' \int \frac{dQ}{r^2}$

Coulomb's Law

- Force between two charged particles
  $\vec{F} = \frac{k\, q_1\, q_2 \vec{r}}{r^3} = \frac{k q_1\, q_2 \hat{r}}{r^2}$, force is attractive when q_1 and q_2 are of opposite sign, otherwise repulsive
  $|\vec{F}| = \frac{k\, q_1\, q_2}{r^2}$
  $k = \frac{1}{4\pi\varepsilon_0} \approx 9 \times 10^9 \text{ Nm}^2\text{C}^{-2}$
- Force between multiple charges
  $\vec{F}_1 = \vec{F}_{12} + \vec{F}_{13} + \vec{F}_{14} + \vec{F}_{15} + ... = \frac{q_1}{4\pi\varepsilon_0} \sum_{i=2}^{n} \frac{q_i}{r_{1i}^2} \hat{r}_{1i}$
  where $\hat{r}$ is the unit vector along charge particle under consideration
  $\hat{r}_{1i}$ = distance between Ist and i^{th} particle

"The electric force with which two charges attract or repel one another are not affected by the presence of other charges". It is known as Superposition Principle.

In 1985, Charles Augustin de Coulomb gave Coulomb's law

Electric Dipole moment, $\vec{p} = q\vec{d}$

- Electric field due to dipole at axial position,
  $\vec{E} = \frac{1}{4\pi\varepsilon_0}\left(\frac{2p}{r^3}\right)\hat{r}$
- Electric field due to dipole at an equatorial position,
  $|E| = \frac{1}{4\pi\varepsilon_0}\left(\frac{p}{r^3}\right)$
- Torque on an electric dipole placed in an electric field $(\vec{E})$
  $\vec{\tau} = \vec{p} \times \vec{E} = p\,E \sin\theta$

Gauss' Theorem

$\oint \vec{E} \cdot \vec{ds} = q_{in}/\varepsilon_0 = \phi$

where, q_{in} = net charge enclosed

ϕ = flux through a closed surface

Applications of Gauss' Law

- Electric Field due to linear charge distribution
  $E = \lambda/2\pi\,\varepsilon_0 r$,
  λ = linear charge density
- Electric Field due to a plane sheet of charge
  $E = \sigma/2\varepsilon_0$,
  σ = charge per unit area
- Electric Field due to a charged conducting plate
  $E = \sigma/\varepsilon_0$,
  σ = charge per unit area
- Electric Field inside a conductor = 0

Electric field due to uniformly charged spherical shell at :

- Outside point,
  $E = Q/4\pi\varepsilon_0 r^2$
- Internal point,
  $E = 0$
- The surface,
  $E = Q/4\pi\varepsilon_0 R^2$

Electric flux

$\Delta\phi = \vec{E} \cdot \Delta\vec{S}$, $\Delta\vec{S}$ = area vector

$\vec{E}$ = electric field

$\phi = \int \vec{E} \cdot \vec{ds}$

Trace the Mind Map

- First Level
- Second Level
- Third Level

For wavelets in forward direction, $\theta = 0°$ and for backward direction $\theta = 180°$. For this reason the amplitude in backward direction is zero.

Refraction and Reflection of Plane Waves using Huygen's Principle

- Concave mirror converts plane wavefront into concave wavefront.

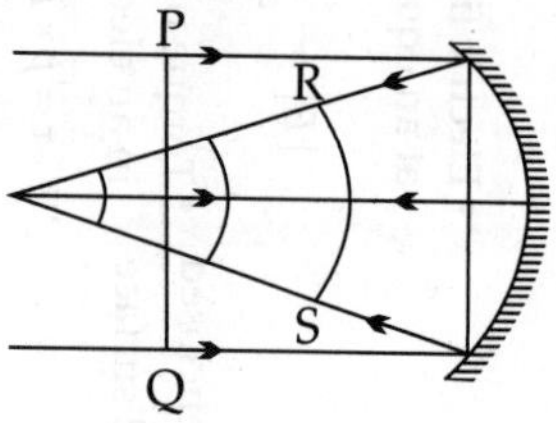

- Convex mirror converts plane wavefront into convex wavefront.

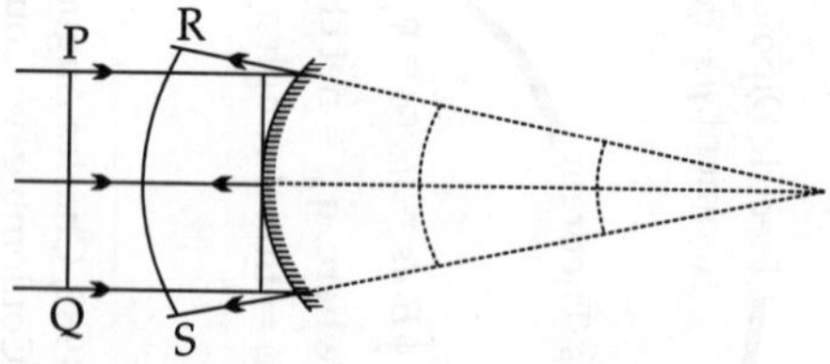

- Concave lens converts plane wavefront into convex wavefront.

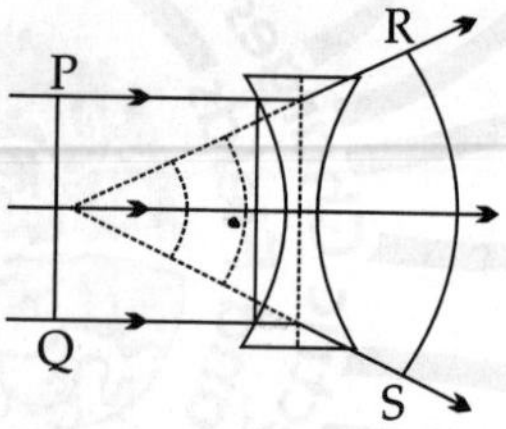

- Convex lens converts plane wavefront into concave wavefront.

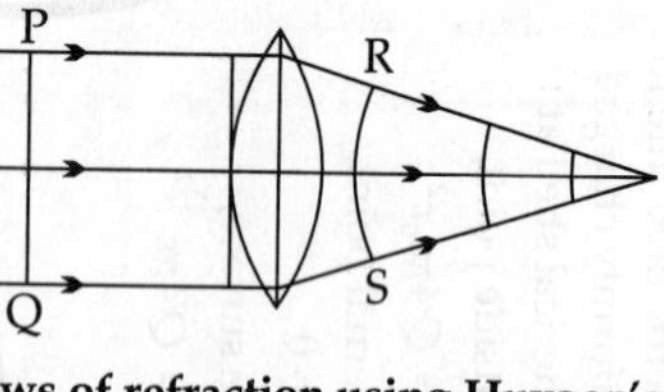

➢ **Proof of laws of refraction using Huygen's principle:**

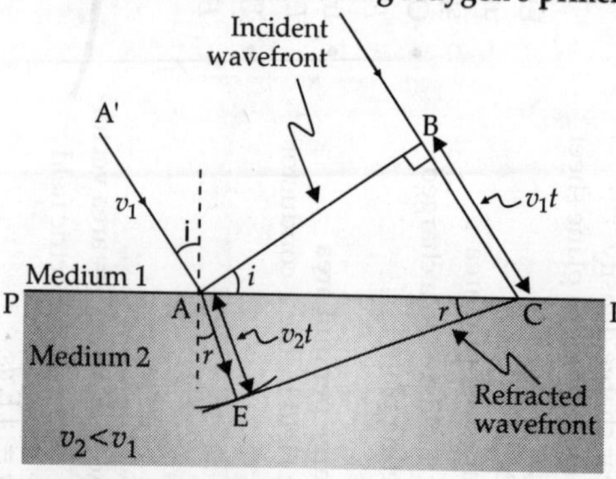

AB = incident wavefront

EC = refracted wavefront

$\angle i$ = angle between incident wavefront AB and interface PP'

$\angle r$ = angle between refracted wavefront EC and interface PP'

If medium 2 is optically denser than medium 1 and τ is the time in which disturbance from B reaches C. This is the same time t in which disturbance from A reaches E where distance

$$AE < BC$$

$$\Delta AEC \cong \Delta ABC$$

$$\sin i = \frac{BC}{AC}$$

$$\sin r = \frac{AE}{AC}$$

$$\therefore \quad \frac{\sin i}{\sin r} = \frac{BC}{AE}$$

BC = Distance travelled by wave at B in time t in medium 1

AE = Distance travelled by wave at A in time t in medium 2

$$\frac{\sin i}{\sin r} = \frac{v_1 t}{v_2 t}$$

$$\therefore \quad \frac{\sin i}{\sin r} = \frac{v_2}{v_1} = \text{constant.}$$

This is Snell's law of refraction.

➢ **Proof of laws of reflection using Huygen's principle:**

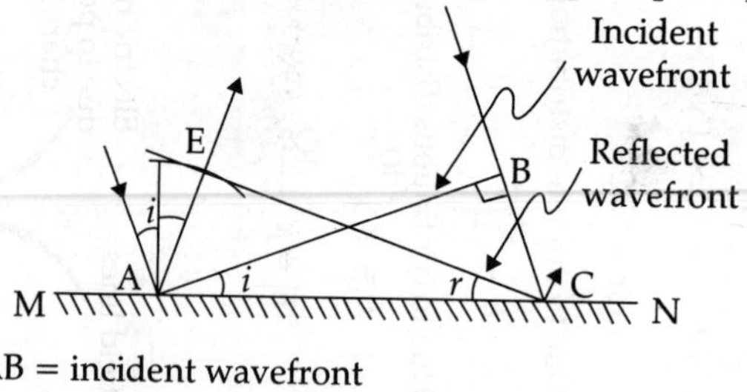

AB = incident wavefront

EC = reflected wavefront

$\angle i$ = angle between incident wavefront AB with the interface AC

$\angle r$ = angle between reflected wavefront EC with the interface AC

If disturbance at A is reflected from the interface AC, then disturbance at B and disturbance at A both travel in same medium. Thus, they will have travelled equal distance in time τ, where τ is the time in which disturbance from B reaches at C.

Now $AE = BC = v\tau$(distance travelled in same medium in same time)

$$\Delta AEC \cong \Delta ABC$$

$$\therefore \quad \angle i = \angle r$$

➢ **Superposition principle:** "At a particular point in a medium, the resultant displacement produced by a number of waves is the vector sum of the displacements produced by each wave".

If $\vec{y_1}$ and $\vec{y_2}$ be the displacement produced by two waves respectively, then the resultant displacement will be $\vec{y} = \vec{y_1} + \vec{y_2}$

➢ **Coherent sources:** The sources which emit light waves with same frequency, same wavelength and same phase or constant phase difference are known as coherent sources.

> **Interference:**

- When two or more light waves of same frequency and same wavelength superpose at a point in a medium, then the resultant amplitude may be enhanced or may be cancelled. This phenomenon is known as interference of light.

> **Types of interference**

- **Constructive Interference:** When two light waves superpose in such a way that the crest of one wave falls on the crest of the second wave and the trough falls on the trough of the second wave then constructive interference occurs.

  A bright fringe is obtained on the screen.

  The resultant amplitude of the wave is the sum of individual amplitudes.

- **Destructive Interference:** When two light waves superpose in such a way that the crest of one wave falls on the trough of the second wave then destructive interference occurs.

  A dark fringe is obtained on the screen.

  The resultant amplitude of the wave is the difference of individual amplitudes.

> Mathematical treatment of interference:

If the displacements of two waves emerging from two coherent sources, at any time t, be

$$y_1 = a_1 \sin \omega t$$

and $$y_2 = a_2 \sin \omega t$$

Then according to principle of superposition,

Resultant displacement,

$$y = y_1 + y_2 = a_1 \sin \omega t + a_2 \sin (\omega t + \theta)$$

Or, $$y = a_1 \sin \omega t + a_2 \sin \omega t \cos\theta + a_2 \cos \omega t \sin\theta$$

Or, $$y = (a_1 + a_2 \cos \theta) + a_2 \cos \omega t \sin \theta$$

Putting,

$$(a_1 + a_2 \cos\theta) = A \cos \phi \quad \text{...(i)}$$

$$a_2 \sin\theta = A \sin \phi \quad \text{...(ii)}$$

$$y = A \sin (\omega t + \phi)$$

where, A is the amplitude of the resultant wave and ϕ is the phase difference with the first wave.

From equations (i) and (ii),

$$A^2 = a_1^2 + a_2^2 + 2\, a_1 a_2 \cos \theta$$

Intensity being proportional to the square of amplitude,

$$I^2 = I_1 + I_2 + 2\sqrt{I_1 I_2} \cos\theta$$

where,

I is the resultant intensity

I_1 and I_2 are intensities of individual waves

> **Conditions of interference:**

- **Constructive interference:** Intensity will be maximum when $\cos \theta = 1$ i.e., $\theta = 2n\pi$

  where, $n = 0, 1, 2, ...$

  Phase difference, $\theta = \dfrac{2\pi}{\lambda} \times$ path difference

  $\therefore$ Path difference $= 2n \times \dfrac{\lambda}{2}$

  So, the constructive interference occurs when the path difference is the even multiple of $\dfrac{\lambda}{2}$.

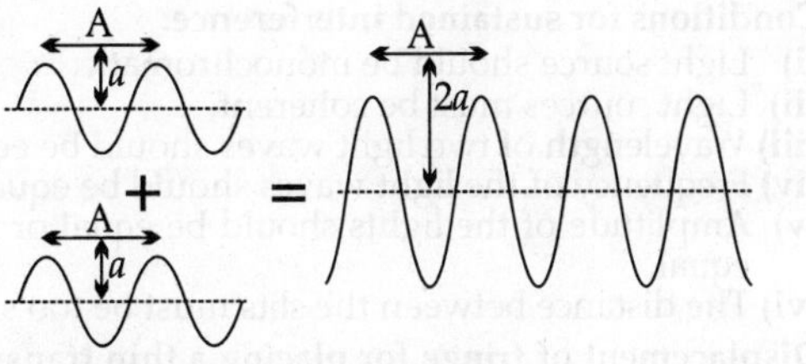

Constructive interferece

- **Destructive interference:** Intensity will be minimum when $\cos \theta = -1$, i.e., $\theta = (2n + 1)\pi$

  where, $n = 0, 1, 2, ...$

  Phase difference $\theta = \dfrac{2\pi}{\lambda} \times$ path difference

  $\therefore$ Path difference $= 2n{+}1 \times \dfrac{\lambda}{2}$

  So, the constructive interference occurs when the path difference is the odd multiple of $\dfrac{\lambda}{2}$.

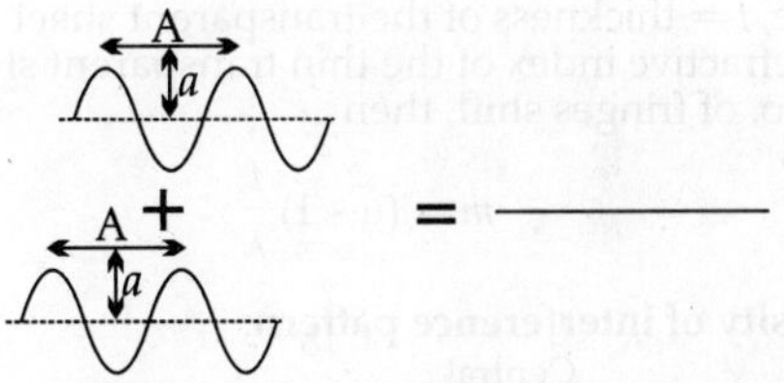

Destructive interference

Young's Double Slit Experiment

- **Experimental set-up:**

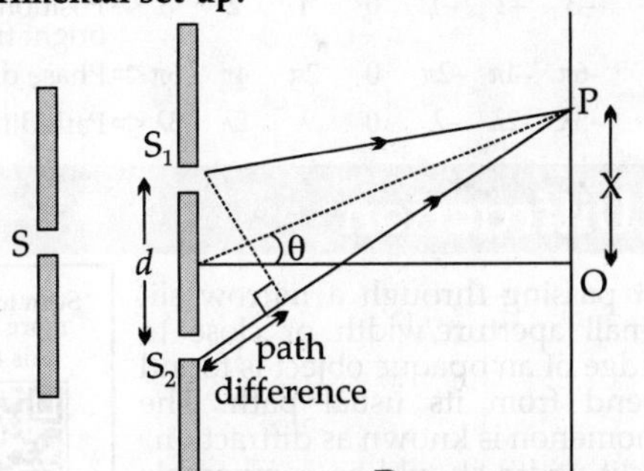

S is a monochromatic source of light.

S_1 are S_2 are two narrow slits function as two coherent sources.

$S_1S_2 = d$

A screen is placed at a distance D from the slits.

At point O, $S_1O = S_2O$. So, central bright fringe will form at O point on the screen.

- **Condition n^{th} bright fringe at P**

$$X_n = \frac{n\lambda D}{d}$$

- **Condition n^{th} dark fringe at P**

$$X_n = \frac{(2n+1)\lambda D}{d}$$

- **Fringe width**

$$\beta = \frac{\lambda D}{d}$$

- **Conditions for sustained interference:**
  (i) Light source should be monochromatic.
  (ii) Light sources must be coherent.
  (iii) Wavelength of two light waves should be equal.
  (iv) Frequency of the light waves should be equal.
  (v) Amplitude of the lights should be equal or nearly equal.
  (vi) The distance between the slits must be too small.
- **Displacement of fringe for placing a thin transparent sheet in one of the light paths:**

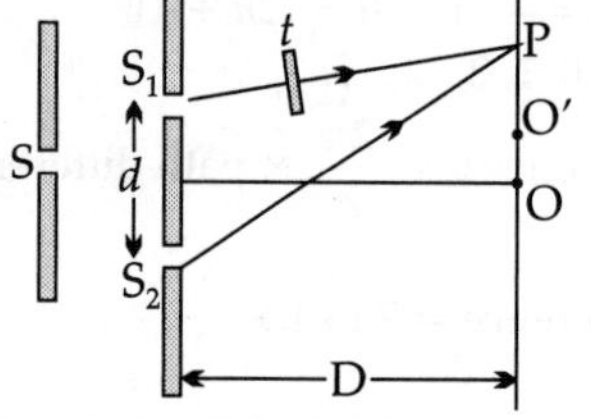

$$\text{Shift} = \frac{\beta}{\lambda}(\mu - 1)t$$

where, t = thickness of the transparent sheet
μ = refractive index of the thin transparent sheet
If m no. of fringes shift, then

$$m = (\mu - 1)\frac{t}{\lambda}$$

- **Intensity of interference pattern:**

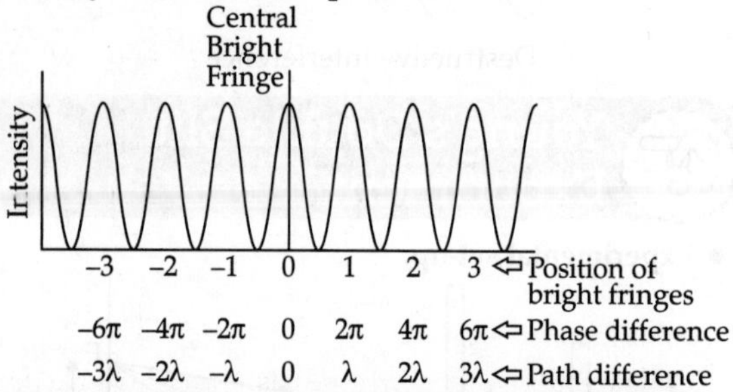

Diffraction

- Light passing through a narrow slit of small aperture/width or close to the edge of an opaque object is found to bend from its usual path. The phenomenon is known as diffraction. The slit width should be comparable to the wavelength of light (i.e., 4000 Å to 8000 Å) for diffraction.

Scan to know more about this topic

Diffraction

➢ **Types of diffraction:**
- Fresnel diffraction
  Related with spherical wavefront.
- Fraunhoffer diffraction:
  Related with plane wavefront.

➢ **Diffraction due to single slit:**

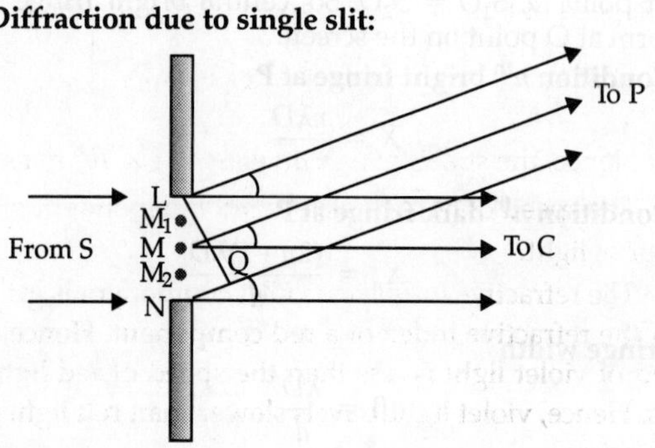

The slit LN is illuminated by monochromatic light.

The basic idea is to divide the slit into much smaller parts and then add their contributions at P with proper phase difference.

According to Huygens' principle, each point of the slit behaves as a source of secondary wavelet. So, the slit may be divided into much smaller parts and then add their contributions at P with proper phase difference.

Path difference between the rays coming from two edges of the slit, $a \sin\theta = a\,\theta$ [for small θ]

- **Central bright fringe (central maxima):** At point O, all path difference and phase difference are zero.
- For n^{th} secondary dark fringe (secondary minima): $\theta_n = \frac{n\lambda}{a}$, where, n = 1, 2, 3, ...
- **For secondary bright fringe (secondary maxima):**

$$\theta_n = (2n+1)\frac{\lambda}{2a}, \text{ where, } n = 1, 2, 3, ...$$

- **Width of central maxima:** $\frac{2D\lambda}{a}$
- **Width of secondary maxima:** $\frac{D\lambda}{a}$
- **Width of secondary minima:** $\frac{D\lambda}{a}$
- The intensity of secondary maxima decreases with the increase of value of n.
- **Single slit diffraction pattern:**

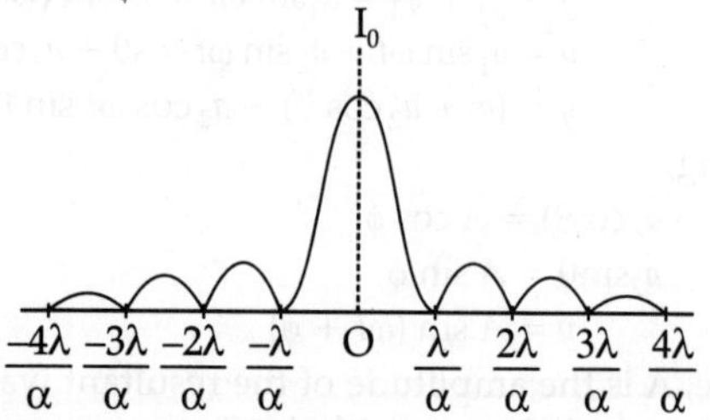

Example 1: In Young's double slit experiment the separation d between the slits is 2 mm, the wavelength λ of the light used is 5896 Å and distance D between the screen and slits is 100 cm. It is found that the angular width of the fringes is 0.20°. To increase the fringe angular width to 0.21° (with same λ and D) what should be the separation between the slits ?

Ans. $\theta = \frac{\beta}{D}$

Or, $\theta = \frac{\lambda D/d}{D}$

Or, $\theta = \frac{\lambda}{d}$

Or, $\lambda = \theta d$

∴ $\theta_1 d_1 = \theta_2 d_2$

Or, $d_2 = (\theta_1/\theta_2) \times d_1$

Or $d_2 = (0.20/0.21) \times 2\text{ mm}$

∴ $d_2 = 1.9\text{ mm}$

NCERT CORNER

Exercise Questions

Q. 1. Monochromatic light having a wavelength of 589 nm from the air is incident on a water surface. Find the frequency, wavelength and speed of
(a) reflected and (b)refracted light (Refractive index of water is 1.33). [NCERT Ex. Q. 10.1, Page 273]

Ans. Monochromatic light incident having wavelength, $\lambda = 589 \text{ nm} = 589 \times 10^{-9}$ m

Speed of light in air, $c = 3 \times 10^8 \text{ ms}^{-1}$

Refractive index of water, $\mu = 1.33$

(a) In the same medium through which incident ray passed the ray will be reflected back.

Therefore, the wavelength, speed and frequency of the reflected ray will be the same as that of the incident ray.

Frequency of light can be found from the relation:

$$v = \frac{c}{\lambda} = \frac{3\times10^8}{589\times10^{-9}} = 5.09\times10^{14} \text{ Hz}$$

Hence, the speed, frequency and wavelength of the reflected light are:

$c = 3 \times 10^8 \text{ ms}^{-1}$, 5.09×10^{14} Hz and 589 nm, respectively.

(b) The frequency of light, which is travelling, never depends upon the property of the medium. Therefore, the frequency of the refracted ray in water will be equal to the frequency of the incident or reflected light in air.

Refracted frequency, $\nu = 5.09 \times 10^{14}$ Hz

Speed of light in water is related to the refractive index of water as:

$$v = \frac{c}{\mu} \Rightarrow v = \frac{3\times10^8}{1.33} = 2.26\times10^8 \text{ ms}^{-1}$$

Wavelength of light in water can be found by the relation:

$$\lambda = \frac{v}{\nu} = \frac{2.26\times10^8}{5.09\times10^{14}}$$

$$= 444.007\times10^{-9}\ m$$

$$= 444.01 \text{ nm}$$

Hence the speed, frequency and wavelength of refracted light are: 2.26×10^8 m/s, 5.09×10^{14} Hz and 444.01 nm respectively.

Q. 2. Find the shape of the wavefront in each of the following cases:
(a) Light diverging from a point source.
(b) Light emerging out of a convex lens when a point source is placed at its focus.
(c) The portion of the wavefront of light from a distant star intercepted by the Earth.
[NCERT Ex. Q. 10.2, Page 273]

Ans. (a) The shape of a wavefront is spherical in case of a light diverging from a point source is spherical. The wavefront is shown in the figure:

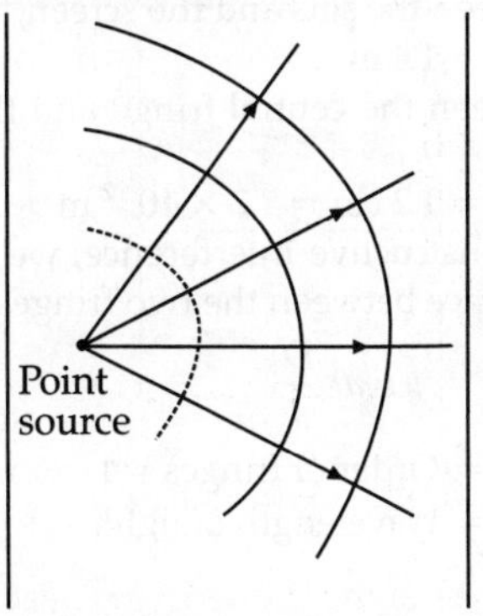

(b) The shape of a wavefront is a parallel grid in the case of a light emerging out of a convex lens when a point source is placed at its focus.

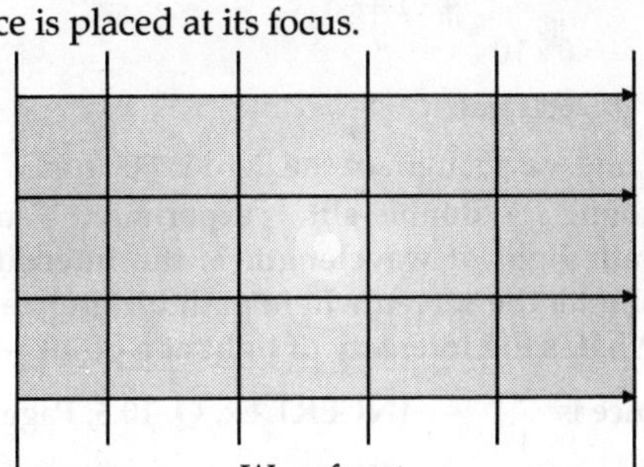

(c) The shape of the wavefront is a plane when a portion of the wavefront of light from a distant star intercepted by the Earth.

Q. 3. (a) The refractive index of glass is 1.5. What is the speed of light in glass? Speed of light in vacuum is $3.0\times10^8 \text{ ms}^{-1}$.
(b) Is the speed of light in glass independent of the colour of light? If not, which of the two colours red and violet travels slower in a glass prism?
[NCERT Ex. Q. 10.3, Page 273]

Ans. (a) Refractive index of glass, $\mu = 1.5$

Speed of light, $c = 3 \times 10^8$ m/s

Speed of light in glass is given by the relation,

$$v = \frac{c}{\mu} = \frac{3\times10^8}{1.5} = 2\times10^8 \text{ m/s}$$

Hence, the speed of light in glass is 2×10^8 m/s.

(b) The speed of light in glass is not independent of the colour of light.

The refractive index of a violet component is greater than the refractive index of a red component. Hence, the speed of violet light is less than the speed of red light in glass. Hence, violet light travels slower than red light in a glass prism.

Q. 4. In a Young's double-slit experiment, the slits are separated by 0.28 mm and the screen is placed 1.4 m away. The distance between the central bright fringe and the fourth bright fringe is measured to be 1.2 cm. Determine the wavelength of light used in the experiment? [NCERT Ex. Q. 10.4, Page 273]

Ans. Distance between the slits, $d = 0.28$ mm
$= 0.28 \times 10^{-3}$ m

Distance between the slits and the screen,
$D = 1.4$ m

Distance between the central fringe and the fourth ($n = 4$) fringe,

$u = 1.2 \text{ cm} = 1.2 \times 10^{-2}$ m

In case of a constructive interference, we have the relation for the distance between the two fringes as:

$$u = n\lambda\frac{D}{d}$$

where, n = Order of fringes $=4$
λ = Wavelength of light

$$\therefore \quad \lambda = \frac{ud}{nD}$$
$$= \frac{1.2\times 10^{-2}\times 0.28\times 10^{-3}}{4\times 1.4}$$
$$= 6\times 10^{-7}$$
$$= 600 \text{ nm}$$

Hence, the wavelength of the light is 600 nm.

Q. 5. In Young's double-slit experiment using monochromatic light of wavelength λ, the intensity of light at a point on the screen where path difference is λ, is K units. What is the intensity of light at a point where path difference is $\frac{\lambda}{3}$? [NCERT Ex. Q. 10.5, Page 273]

Ans. Let I_1 and I_2 be the intensities of the two light waves. Their resultant intensities can be obtained as:

$$I' = I_1 + I_2 + 2\sqrt{I_1 I_2}\cos\phi$$

Where,
ϕ = Phase difference between the two waves

For monochromatic light waves:

$$I_1 = I_2$$

Therefore $\quad I' = I_1 + I_2 + 2\sqrt{I_1 I_2}\cos\phi$
$$= 2I_1 + 2I_1\cos\phi$$

$$\text{Phase difference} = \frac{2\pi}{\lambda}\times \text{Path difference}$$

Since path difference $= \lambda$, Phase difference, $\phi = 2\pi$ and $I' = K$ [Given]

$$\therefore \quad I_1 = \frac{K}{4} \quad ...(i)$$

When path difference $= \frac{\lambda}{3}$

Phase difference, $\phi = \frac{2\pi}{3}$

Hence, resultant intensity,

$$I = I_1 + I_1 + 2\sqrt{I_1 I_1}\cos\frac{2\pi}{3}$$

Using equation (i), we can write:

$$I' = I_1 = \frac{K}{4}$$

Hence, the intensity of light at a point, which has path difference ($\frac{\lambda}{3}$), is $\frac{K}{4}$ units.

Q. 6. A beam of light consisting of two wavelengths, 650 nm and 520 nm, is used to obtain interference fringes in a Young's double-slit experiment.

(a) Find the distance of the third bright fringe on the screen from the central maximum for wavelength 650 nm.

(b) What is the least distance from the central maximum where the bright fringes due to both the wavelengths coincide? [NCERT Ex. Q. 10.6, Page 273]

Ans. Wavelength of the light beam, $\lambda_1 = 650$ nm
Wavelength of another light beam, $\lambda_2 = 520$ nm
Distance of the slits from the screen $= D$
Distance between the two slits $= d$

(a) Distance of the nth bright fringe on the screen from the central maximum is given by the relation,

$$x = n\lambda_1\frac{D}{d}$$

If the third bright firnge i.e., $n = 3$

So, $\quad x = 3\times 650\frac{D}{d}$
$$= 1950\frac{D}{d} \text{ nm}$$

(b) Let, the nth bright fringe due to wavelength λ_2 and $(n-1)^{th}$ bright fringe due to wavelength λ_1 coincide on the screen. We can equate the conditions for bright fringes as:

$$n\lambda_2 = (n-1)\lambda_1$$
$$520n = 650n - 650$$
$$650 = 130\,n$$

Therefore, $\quad n = 5$

Hence, the least distance from the central maximum can be obtained by the relation:

$$x = n\lambda_2\frac{D}{d}$$
$$= 5\times 520\frac{D}{d}$$
$$= 2600\frac{D}{d}\text{nm}$$

[Note: The values of d and D are not given in question.]

□□

DUAL NATURE OF RADIATION AND MATTER

CHAPTER 11

Photoelectric Effect

- The phenomenon of emission of electrons from metals by light is known as photoelectric effect.

Discovery:

- **Hertz's Experiment:** Hertz in 1887 was experimenting on electromagnetic waves. He observed that a spark across the gap of an induction coil passed more easily when the negative terminal was illuminated with UV light.
- **Hallwach's Experiment:** Hallwach in 1888 observed that a negatively charged zinc plate lost charge quickly when exposed to UV light. But no such effect was observed with positively charged plate.
- **Lenard's experiment:** Lenard in 1889 measured the value of e/m for the particles emitted from illuminated metals and proved that these particles are electrons.

➢ **Theory to explain photoelectric effect:** Wave theory of light could not explain the photoelectric effect.

But the quantum theory of light could explain the effect properly. Discovery of photoelectric effect established the fact that the light has two natures – wave and particle.

Electron Emission

- Electrons are bound in atom by the attractive force of the nucleus. To eject these electrons a minimum amount of energy is to be supplied. Energy may be supplied in form of heat, radiation or strong electric field.

➢ **Work function:** The minimum amount of energy required for ejection of electron. This is represented by W_0 or ϕ_0 and expressed in eV unit.

1 eV = 1.6×10^{-19} J

➢ **Types of electron emission:**

- **Thermionic emission:** When electron emission occurs by rising the temperature of the metal, then it is known as thermionic emission. Emitted electrons are called thermionic electrons.
- **Field emission:** When electron emission occurs by applying strong electric field, then it is known as field emission and emitted electrons are called field electrons.
- **Photoelectric emission:** When electron emission is occurred by illuminating the metal by light of suitable frequency, then it is known as photoelectric emission. Here, emitted electrons are called photo electrons.

Experimental Study of Photoelectric Effect

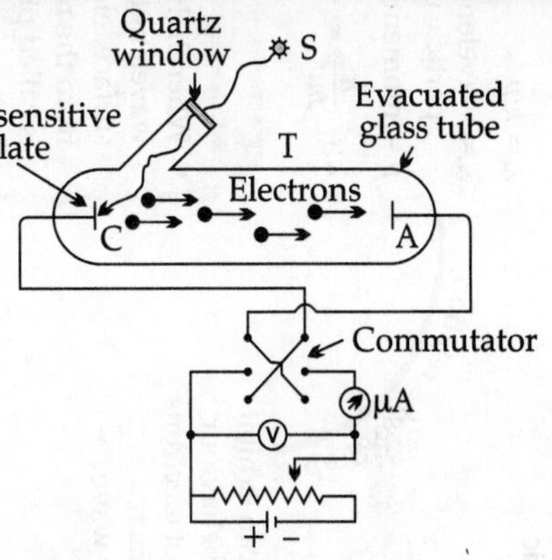

T is an evacuated tube.

C is a photosensitive plate used as cathode.

A is anode.

A is maintained at opposite potential compared to C.

When radiation is incident on C, it emits electrons.

The current due to the flow of electrons is measured by a micro-ammeter.

When A is maintained at positive potential it repels the electrons and for a definite value of negative potential, the flow of electrons stop. This potential is known as stopping potential.

➢ **Characteristics/laws of photoelectric effect:**

- It is an instantaneous process. The time difference between the incidence of light and emission of electrons is 10^{-9} s or less, no matter how weak the light intensity is.
- **Threshold frequency:** The emission of photoelectrons does not take place below a certain minimum frequency known as threshold frequency (ν_0) , no matter how intense the light is.
- **Threshold wavelength:** The emission of photoelectrons does not take place above a certain maximum wavelength known as threshold wavelength, no matter how intense the light is.
- **Stopping potential:** The anode potential with respect to cathode at which the photoelectric current is completely cut off is known as stopping potential. It is a measure of the kinetic energy of the most energetic electron.

  Maximum kinetic energy,

$$K_{\text{max}} = \frac{1}{2} m{v^2}_{\text{max}} = eV_s$$

  (where, v_{max} is the velocity of fastest electron and V_S is the stopping potential.)

- **Number of photoelectrons emitted and intensity of light:** When frequency of light is greater than the threshold frequency, then the electrons ejected per second is proportional to the intensity of light.

Dual Nature of Radiation & Matter

Dual Nature of Radiation

- Light has both wave character as well as particle nature
- Interference and diffraction can be explained by wave nature
- When light is of sufficiently small wavelength, it behaves as particle
- Light particles having definite energy and definite linear momentum are called "photons"
  Energy of each photon, $E = h\nu = h\nu/\lambda$
  Momentum of each photon, $p = h/\lambda = E/c$

Contribution

Einstein, after an average academic career put forward quantum theory of light in 1905 while working as a grade III technical officer in a patent office.

Matter waves

All matter can exhibit wave–like behaviour e.g., beam of electrons can be diffracted like a water wave

de-Broglie relation

$\lambda = h/p$

λ = wavelength associated with particle or de-Broglie wavelength

p = momentum

$$\lambda = \frac{h}{mv} = \frac{h}{\sqrt{2m\,K_{max}}}$$

Photoelectric Effect

- When light of sufficient small wavelength is incident on metal surface, electrons are ejected from the metal, the phenomenon is called photoelectric effect.
- Ejected electrons are called photoelectrons.
- Minimum energy equal to work function (ϕ) must be given to an electron so as to bring it out of the metal surface.

Hertz and Lenard's Observation

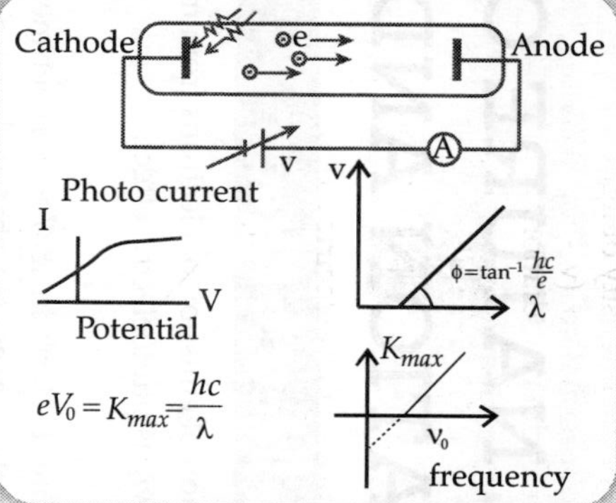

$eV_0 = K_{max} = \frac{hc}{\lambda}$

Einstein's Photoelectric equation

- If $\lambda = \lambda_0 = hc/\phi$
  $K_{max} = 0$, i.e.,
  Electron may just come out onto the surface
- If $\lambda > \lambda_0$
  i.e., $E < \phi$
  no electron will come out
- If $\lambda \leq \lambda_0$.
  Photoelectric effect takes place
- λ_0 = depends on metal used

- $K_{max} = E - \phi = eV_0$
  $= \frac{hc}{\lambda} - \phi$, V_0 = stopping potential
  K_{max} = maximum kinetic energy of ejected electrons

Here, $\lambda_0 = hc/\phi$
λ_0 = Threshold Wavelength
$\lambda_0 = c/\nu_0 = \phi/h$
ν_0 = Threshold frequency
$K_{max} = \lambda(\nu - \nu_0)$

Trace the Mind Map
- First Level
- Second Level
- Third Level

- **Dependence of kinetic energy of fastest electron:**
  (i) Independent of the intensity of light
  (ii) Directly proportional to $(\nu - \nu_0)$. Where ν is the frequency of the incident radiation.

Graphs related to Photoelectric Effect

- **Intensity of light vs. photoelectric current:**

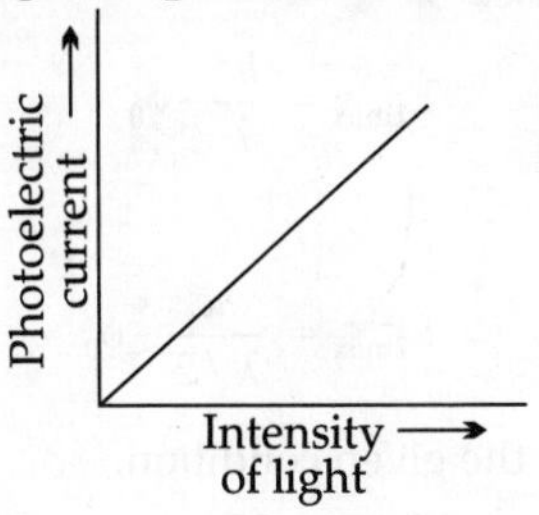

- **Potential difference vs. photoelectric current for different intensities of light:**

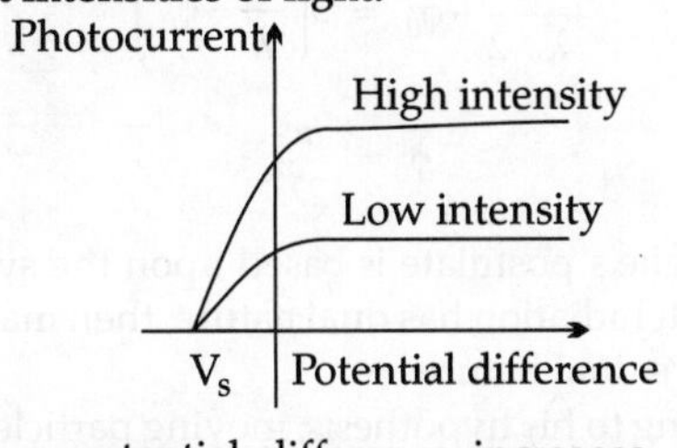

Initially as potential difference increases, the photo current increases. Finally it reaches a saturation. As intensity of light increases, the value of saturation current also increases.

- **Potential difference vs. photoelectric current for different frequencies of light:**

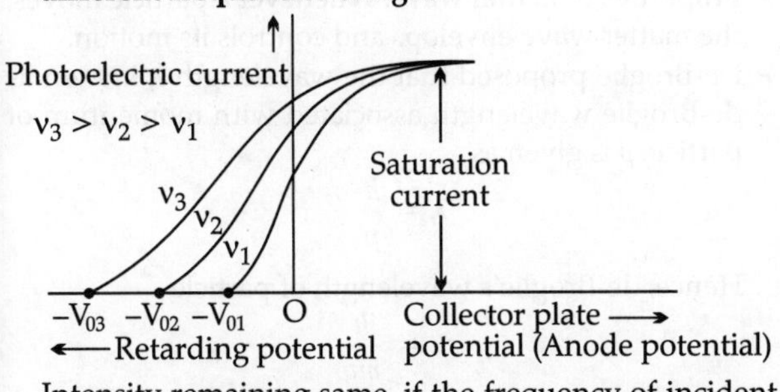

Intensity remaining same, if the frequency of incident light increases, the magnitude of stopping potential increases. Saturation current does not depend on the frequency of light.

- **Frequency of incident light vs. stopping potential:**

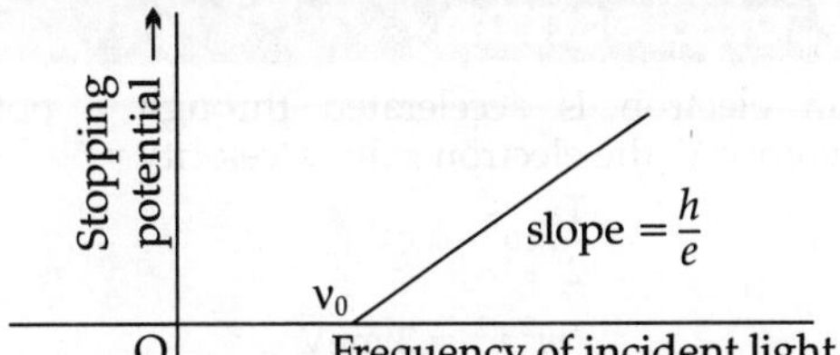

The stopping potential is directly proportional to the frequency of incident light.

Slope of the graph $= \frac{h}{e}$.

So, from the slope of the graph the value of h (Planck's constant) can be determined.

- **Highest kinetic energy of electron vs. frequency of light:**

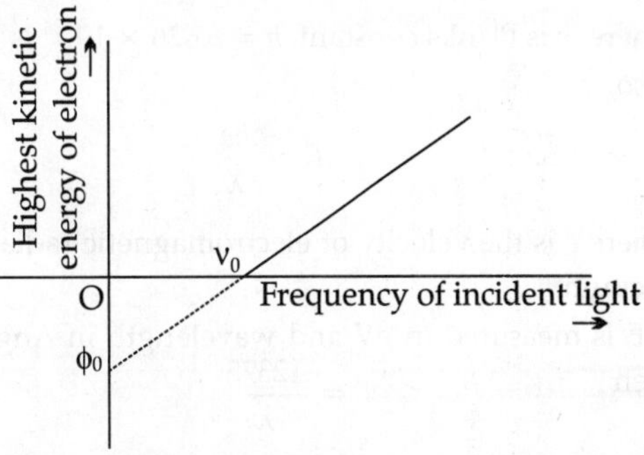

The graph is a straight line. The highest kinetic energy of the photoelectrons is proportional to the frequency of light.
The point at which the extended line intersects the x-axis is the work function of the material.

- **Photo-current vs. frequency of light with constant intensity:**
  For $\nu < \nu_0$, $i = 0$
  For $\nu \geq \nu_0$, i is constant, if intensity is constant.

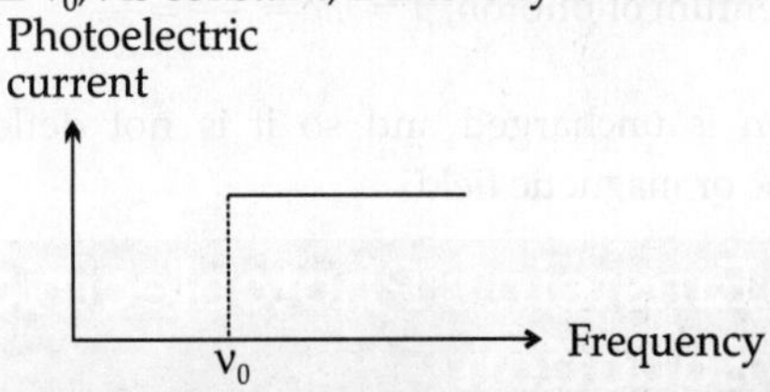

Shortcomings of Wave Theory

Wave theory was inadequate or failed to explain the photoelectric effect due to the following reasons:

- According to wave theory, higher amplitude means higher energy but experiments show that even higher amplitude (higher intensity) of light below threshold frequency can not exhibit photoelectric effect.
- According to wave theory, same intensity of different colour should have same energy but experiment shows that energy depends upon frequency, not amplitude.
- According to wave theory, wavefront should take some time to transfer energy to electron but experimentally it was found that ejection of electron is instantaneous.

Particle Nature of Light and Planck's Quantum Theory

- Max Planck in 1900 proposed that in electromagnetic radiation energy is emitted or absorbed discontinuously in indivisible packets energy $h\nu$. h is called Planck's constant and its value is 6.626×10^{-34} Js. These are called quanta.
- From Planck's concept of quanta, Einstein built up the idea of photon particle and explained the photoelectric effect.

➢ **Properties of Photon:**

- Photons are indivisible packets of electromagnetic energy.
- Energy of a photon is proportional to the frequency of the radiation.

$$E \propto \nu$$

Or, $E = h\nu$

where, h is Planks constant. $h = 6.626 \times 10^{-34}$ Js

Also, $c = \lambda\nu$

$$\therefore \quad E = \frac{hc}{\lambda}$$

where c is the velocity of electromagnetic radiation in vacuum.

If E is measured in eV and wavelength in Angstrom, then $E = \frac{12375}{\lambda}$

Energy of photon does not depend on intensity.

Number of photons depends on intensity.

- Velocity of photon is equal to that of light.
  Rest mass of photon is zero.
  Working mass of photon, $m = \frac{E}{c^2} = \frac{h\nu}{c^2} = \frac{h}{c\lambda}$.
  Momentum of photon, $p = mc = \frac{h\nu}{c} = \frac{h}{\lambda}$.
- Photon is uncharged and so it is not deflected by electric or magnetic field.

Einstein's Photoelectric Equation

$$E_{max} = h\nu - h\nu_0$$

$$\text{Or, } \frac{1}{2} mv_{max}^2 = h\nu - \phi_0$$

ν = Frequency of incident photon

h = Planck's constant

$h\nu$ = Energy of incident photon

ϕ_0 = Work function of the material

ν_0 = Threshold frequency of the photosensitive material

v_{max} = Maximum velocity of ejected electron

m = mass of electron.

E_{max} = Maximum kinetic energy of ejected photoelectron

➢ **Explanation of photoelectric effect with Einstein's equation:**

- When light is incident on a photoelectric substance, an elastic collision occurs between photon and electron of the substance.
- The electron will either absorb the whole energy of the photon or will not absorb any energy.
- If energy of incident photon ($h\nu$) is greater than the work function ($h\nu_0$) of the substance, then only electron will eject. The process is instantaneous.
- $h\nu - h\nu_0$ amount of energy increases the kinetic energy of ejected electron.
- Since electrons are distributed in different energy levels, so ejected electrons due to light of same frequency may have different kinetic energies.
- One photon is capable to eject one electron only.

Example 1: Two lights of wavelengths λ and $\frac{\lambda}{2}$ are incident on the surface of a photosensitive metal. If the maximum energy of the ejected photoelectron in the second case is three times that of the first case then find the expression for the work function of the metal.

Ans. In 1st case,

$$E_{1max} = \frac{hc}{\lambda} - \phi_0$$

In 2nd case,

$$E_{2max} = \frac{hc}{\lambda/2} - \phi_0$$

According to the given condition,

$$E_{2max} = 3E_{1max}$$

$$\text{Or, } \frac{hc}{\lambda/2} - \phi_0 = 3\left(\frac{hc}{\lambda} - \phi_0\right)$$

$$\therefore \quad \phi_0 = \frac{hc}{2\lambda}$$

➢ de- Broglie's postulate is based upon the symmetry of nature. If radiation has dual nature, then matter should also have dual nature.

➢ According to his hypothesis, moving particles of matter should display wave nature under suitable conditions. He named the wave as matter wave. It is a third type of wave. It is different from mechanical wave and electromagnetic wave.

➢ **Properties of matter wave:** Whenever a particle moves, the matter wave envelops and controls its motion.

➢ De-Broglie proposed that the wavelength λ known as de-Broglie wavelength associated with momentum of particle p is given as

$$\lambda = \frac{h}{p}$$

Hence, de-Broglie's wavelength of particle

$$\lambda = \frac{h}{mv}$$

where, h is Planck's constant, m is the mass of the particle and v is the velocity.

de-Broglie Wavelength of Electron

If an electron is accelerated through a potential difference V, the electron gains a velocity v.

$$\text{Then, } \frac{1}{2}mv^2 = \text{eV}$$

$$\text{Or, } m^2v^2 = 2\text{ meV}$$

$$\therefore \quad mv = \sqrt{2meV}$$

So, the wavelength of electron,

$$\lambda = \frac{h}{\sqrt{2meV}} \text{ metre}$$

$$\text{Or, } \lambda = \frac{6.63 \times 10^{-34}}{\sqrt{2 \times 9.1 \times 10^{-31} \times 1.6 \times 10^{-19} \times V}}$$

$$\therefore \quad \lambda = \frac{12.27\times10^{-10}}{\sqrt{V}} \text{ metre}$$

$$= \frac{12.27}{\sqrt{V}} \text{ Å}$$

➢ **λ vs. $\frac{1}{\sqrt{V}}$ graph for different masses:**

Since $\lambda = \frac{h}{\sqrt{2meV}}$, the graph will be a straight line passing through the origin.

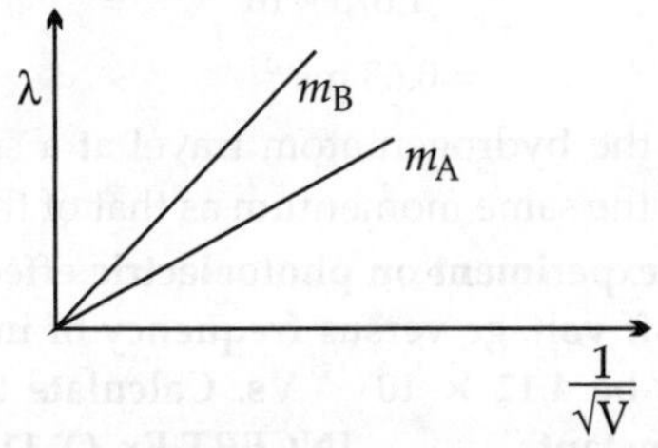

➢ **Characteristics of matter wave:**

- Matter wave represents the probability of finding a particle in space.
- Matter wave is not electromagnetic wave.
- Matter wave is not a mechanical wave. It can move through vacuum.
- Matter weave is independent of charge on the particle.
- Matter wave depends on the applied potential difference.
- Phase velocity of matter wave is greater than the velocity of light.

➢ **Application:** Electron microscope works on the basis of de-Broglie wave.

Example 2: An electron is accelerated under a potential difference of 150 V. What is the de-Broglie wavelength associated with the electron?

Ans. $\lambda = \frac{h}{\sqrt{meV}}$

Or, $\lambda = \frac{6.6\times10^{-34}}{\sqrt{2\times9.1\times10^{-31}\times1.6\times10^{-19}\times150}}$

$\therefore \quad \lambda = 1\text{Å}$

NCERT CORNER

Exercise Questions

Q. 1. Find the
(a) maximum frequency, and
(b) minimum wavelength of X-rays produced by 30 kV electrons. **[NCERT Ex. Q. 11.1, Page 288]**

Ans. Potential of the electrons, $V = 30 \text{ kV} = 3 \times 10^4 \text{ V}$

Hence, energy of the electrons, $E = 3 \times 10^4 \text{ eV}$

where,

e = Charge on an electron = 1.6×10^{-19} C

(a) Maximum frequency produced by the X-rays = ν

The energy of the electrons is given by the relation:

$$E = h\nu$$

where,

h = Planck's constant = 6.626×10^{-34} Js

So, $\nu = \frac{E}{h}$

$$= \frac{1.6\times10^{-19}\times3\times10^{4}}{6.626\times10^{-34}}$$

$$= 7.24\times10^{18} \text{ Hz}$$

Hence, the maximum frequency of X-rays produced is 7.24×10^{18} Hz.

(b) The minimum wavelength produced by the X-rays is given as:

$$\lambda = \frac{c}{v}$$

$$= \frac{3\times10^{8}}{7.24\times10^{18}}$$

$$= 4.14\times10^{-11} \text{ m}$$

$$= 0.0414 \text{ nm}$$

Hence, the minimum wavelength of X-rays produced is 0.0414 nm.

Q. 2. The work function of caesium metal is 2.14 eV. When light of frequency 6×10^{14} Hz is incident on the metal surface, photoemission of electrons occurs. What is the
(a) maximum kinetic energy of the emitted electrons,
(b) Stopping potential, and
(c) maximum speed of the emitted photoelectrons?
[NCERT Ex. Q. 11.2, Page 289]

Ans. Work function of caesium metal, ϕ_0 = 2.14 eV

Frequency of light, $\nu = 6.0 \times 10^{14}$ Hz

(a) The maximum kinetic energy is given by the photoelectric effect as:

$$K = h\nu - \phi_0$$

where,

h = Planck's constant = 6.626×10^{-34} Js

$$\therefore \quad K = \frac{6.626\times10^{-34}\times6\times10^{14}}{1.6\times10^{-19}} - 2.14$$

$$= 0.345 \text{ eV}$$

Hence, the maximum kinetic energy of the emitted electrons is 0.345 eV.

(b) For stopping potential, V_0 we can write the equation for kinetic energy as:

$$K = eV_0$$

$$\therefore \quad V_0 = \frac{K}{e} = \frac{0.345 \times 1.6 \times 10^{-19}}{1.6 \times 10^{-19}}$$

$$= 0.345 \text{ V}$$

Hence, the stopping potential of the material is 0.345 V.

(c) Maximum speed of the emitted photoelectrons = v

Hence, the relation for kinetic energy can be written as:

$$K = \frac{1}{2}mv^2$$

where,

m = Mass of an electron = 9.1×10^{-31} kg

$$v = \sqrt{\frac{2K}{m}} = \sqrt{\frac{2 \times 0.345 \times 1.6 \times 10^{-19}}{9.1 \times 10^{-31}}}$$

$$\therefore \quad v = 3.323 \times 10^5 \text{ m/s}$$

Hence, the maximum speed of the emitted photoelectrons is 3.323 m/s.

Q. 3. The photoelectric cut-off voltage in a certain experiment is 1.5 V. What is the maximum kinetic energy of photoelectrons emitted?

[NCERT Ex. Q. 11.3, Page 289]

Ans. Photoelectric cut-off voltage, $V_0 = 1.5$ V

The maximum kinetic energy of the emitted photoelectrons is given as :

$$K_e = eV_0$$

where,

e = Charge on an electron = 1.6×10^{-19} C

$\therefore K_e = 1.6 \times 10^{-19} \times 1.5 = 2.4 \times 10^{-19}$ J

Therefore, the maximum kinetic energy of the photoelectrons emitted in the given experiment is 2.4×10^{-19} J.

Q. 4. Monochromatic light of wavelength 632.8 nm is produced by a helium-neon laser. The power emitted is 9.42 mW.

(a) Find the energy and momentum of each photon in the light beam.

(b) How many photons per second, on the average, arrive at a target irridated by this beam? (Assume the beam to have uniform cross-section which is less than the target area), and

(c) How fast does a hydrogen atom have to travel in order to have the same momentum as that of the photon?

[NCERT Ex. Q. 11.4, Page 289]

Ans. Given,

Wavelength of monochromatic light, λ = 632.8 nm = 632.8×10^{-9} m

$$\therefore \text{ Frequency, } v = \frac{c}{\lambda} = \frac{3 \times 10^8}{632.8 \times 10^{-9}} \text{ Hz}$$

$$= 4.74 \times 10^{14} \text{ Hz}$$

(a) Energy of a photon, $E = h\nu$

$$= 6.63 \times 10^{-34} \times 4.74 \times 10^{14} \text{ J}$$

$$= 3.14 \times 10^{-19} \text{ J}$$

Momentum of each photon,

$$p_{momentum} = \frac{h}{\lambda} = \frac{6.63 \times 10^{-34}}{632.8 \times 10^{-9}}$$

(b) Power emitted, P = 9.42 mW = 9.42×10^{-3} W

Now $P = nE$

This implies $n = \dfrac{P}{E} = \dfrac{9.42 \times 10^{-3} \text{ W}}{3.14 \times 10^{-19} \text{ J}}$

$$= 3 \times 10^{16} \text{ photons/sec.}$$

Thus, 3×10^{16} photons/sec. arrive at a target.

(c) Velocity of hydrogen atom

$$= \frac{\text{Momentum 'p' of } H_2 \text{ atom (mv)}}{\text{Mass of } H_2 \text{ atom}}$$

$$v = \frac{1.05 \times 10^{-27}}{1.673 \times 10^{-27}} \text{ ms}^{-1}$$

$$= 0.63 \text{ ms}^{-1}$$

Thus, the hydrogen atom travel at a speed of 0.63 m/s to have the same momentum as that of the proton.

Q. 5. In an experiment on photoelectric effect, the slope of the cut-off voltage versus frequency of incident light is found to be 4.12×10^{-15} Vs. Calculate the value of Planck's constant. **[NCERT Ex. Q. 11.5, Page 289]**

Ans. The slope of the cut-off voltage (V) versus frequency (ν) of an incident light is given as:

$$\frac{V}{v} = 4.12 \times 10^{-15} \text{ Vs}$$

V is related to frequency by the equation:

$$h\nu = eV$$

where,

e = Charge on an electron = 1.6×10^{-19} C

h = Planck's constant

$$\therefore \quad h = \frac{eV}{\nu}$$

$$= 1.6 \times 10^{-19} \times 4.12 \times 10^{-15}$$

$$= 6.592 \times 10^{-34} \text{ Js}$$

Therefore, the value of Planck's constant is 6.592×10^{-34} Js.

Q. 6. The threshold frequency for a certain metal is 3.3×10^{14} Hz. If light of frequency 8.2×10^{14} Hz is incident on the metal, predict the cut-off voltage for the photoelectric emission. **[NCERT Ex. Q. 11.6, Page 289]**

Ans. Threshold frequency of the metal,

$$\nu_0 = 3.3 \times 10^{14} \text{ Hz}$$

Frequency of light incident on the metal,

$$\nu = 8.2 \times 10^{14} \text{ Hz}$$

Charge on an electron, $e = 1.6 \times 10^{-19}$ C

Planck's constant, $h = 6.626 \times 10^{-34}$ Js

Cut-off voltage for the photoelectric emission from the metal = V_0

The equation for the cut-off energy is given as:

$$eV_0 = h(\nu - \nu_0)$$

$$\therefore \quad V_0 = \frac{h(\nu - \nu_0)}{e}$$

$$= \frac{6.626 \times 10^{-34} \times (8.2 \times 10^{14} - 3.3 \times 10^{14})}{1.6 \times 10^{-19}}$$

$$= 2.0292 \text{ V}$$

Therefore, the cut-off voltage for the photoelectric emission is 2.0292 V.

Q. 7. The work function for a certain metal is 4.2 eV. Will this metal give photoelectric emission for incident radiation of wavelength 330 nm?

[NCERT Ex. Q. 11.7, Page 289]

Ans. No Work function of the metal, $\phi_0 = 4.2$ eV

Charge on an electron, $e = 1.6 \times 10^{-19}$ C

Planck's constant, $h = 6.626 \times 10^{-34}$ Js

Wavelength of the incident radiation,

$$\lambda = 330 \text{ nm}$$
$$= 330 \times 10^{-9} \text{ m}$$

Speed of light, $= 3 \times 10^8$ m/s

The energy of the incident photon is given as:

$$\therefore \quad E = \frac{hc}{\lambda}$$
$$= \frac{6.626\times10^{-34}\times3\times10^{8}}{330\times10^{-9}}$$
$$= 6.0\times10^{-19} \text{ J}$$
$$E = \frac{6.0\times10^{-19}}{1.6\times10^{-19}}$$
$$= 3.76 \text{ eV}$$

It can be observed that the energy of the incident radiation is less than the work function of the metal. Hence, no photoelectric emission will take place.

Q. 8. Light of frequency 7.21×10^{14} Hz is incident on a metal surface. Electrons with a maximum speed of 6.0×10^5 m/s are ejected from the surface. What is the threshold frequency for photoemission of electrons?

[NCERT Ex. Q. 11.8, Page 289]

Ans. Frequency of the incident photon, $\nu = 488$ nm

$= 488 \times 10^{-9}$ m

Maximum speed of the electrons, $v = 6.0 \times 10^5$ m/s

Planck's constant, $h = 6.626 \times 10^{-34}$ Js

Mass of an electron, $m = 9.1 \times 10^{-31}$ kg

For threshold frequency ν_0, the relation for kinetic energy is written as:

$$\frac{1}{2}mv^2 = h(\nu - \nu_0)$$
$$\therefore \quad \nu_0 = \nu - \frac{mv^2}{2h}$$
$$\nu_0 = 7.21\times10^{14} - \frac{9.1\times10^{-31}\times(6\times10^{5})^2}{2\times6.626\times10^{-34}}$$
$$= 7.21\times10^{14} - 2.472\times10^{14}$$
$$= 4.738\times10^{14} \text{ Hz}$$

Therefore, the threshold frequency for the photoemission of electrons is 4.738×10^{14} Hz.

Q. 9. Light of wavelength 488 nm is produced by an argon laser which is used in the photoelectric effect. When light from this spectral line is incident on the emitter, the stopping (cut-off) potential of photoelectrons is 0.38 V. Find the work function of the material from which the emitter is made. **[NCERT Ex. Q. 11.9, Page 289]**

Ans. Wavelength of light produced by the argon laser,

$$\lambda = 488 \text{ nm} = 488 \times 10^{-9} \text{ m}$$

Stopping potential of the photoelectrons, $V_0 = 0.38\ V$

$$1\ eV = 1.6 \times 10^{-19} \text{ J}$$
$$V_0 = \frac{0.38}{1.6\times10^{-19}} \text{ eV}$$

Planck's constant, $h = 6.6 \times 10^{-34}$ Js

Charge on an electron, $e = 1.6 \times 10^{-19}$ C

Speed of light, $c = 3 \times 10^8$ m/s

From Einstein's photoelectric effect, we have the relation involving the work function ϕ_0 of the material of the emitter as:

Let ϕ be work function.

$$eV_0 = \left(\frac{hc}{\lambda}\right) - \phi$$
$$\phi = \frac{hc}{\lambda} - eV_0$$
$$\Rightarrow \quad = \frac{6.6\times10^{-34}\times3\times10^{8}}{488\times10^{-9}\times1.6\times10^{-19}} - \frac{0.38}{1.6\times10^{-19}}$$
$$\Rightarrow \quad \phi = 2.16 \text{ eV}$$

Therefore, the material with which the emitter is made has the work function of 2.16 eV.

Q. 10. What is the de Broglie wavelength of

(a) a bullet of mass 0.040 kg travelling at the speed of 1.0 km/s,

(b) a ball of mass 0.060 kg moving at a speed of 1.0 m/s, and

(c) a dust particle of mass 1.0×10^{-9} kg drifting with a speed of 2.2 m/s? **[NCERT Ex. Q. 11.10, Page 289]**

Ans. (a) Mass of the bullet, $m = 0.040$ kg

Speed of the bullet, $v = 1.0$ km/s $= 1000$ m/s

Planck's constant, $h = 6.6 \times 10^{-34}$ Js

de-Broglie wavelength of the bullet is given by the relation:

$$\lambda = \frac{h}{mv}$$
$$= \frac{6.626\times10^{-34}}{0.040\times1000}$$
$$= 1.65\times10^{-35} \text{ m}$$

(b) Mass of the ball, $m = 0.060$ kg

Speed of the ball, $v = 1.0$ m/s

de-Broglie wavelength of the ball is given by the relation:

$$\lambda = \frac{h}{mv}$$
$$= \frac{6.626\times10^{-34}}{0.060\times1}$$
$$= 1.1\times10^{-32} \text{ m}$$

(c) Mass of the dust particle, $m = 1 \times 10^{-9}$ kg

Speed of the dust particle, $v = 2.2$ m/s

de-Broglie wavelength of the dust particle is given by the relation:

$$\lambda = \frac{h}{mv}$$

$$= \frac{6.626 \times 10^{-34}}{2.2 \times 1 \times 10^{-9}}$$

$$= 3.0 \times 10^{-25} \text{ m}$$

Q. 11. Show that the wavelength of electromagnetic radiation is equal to the de-Broglie wavelength of its quantum (photon). [NCERT Ex. Q. 11.11, Page 289]

Ans. The momentum of a photon having energy (hv) is given as:

$$p = \frac{hv}{c} = \frac{h}{\lambda}$$

$$\lambda = \frac{h}{p} \quad ...(i)$$

where,

λ = Wavelength of the electromagnetic radiation

c = Speed of light

h = Planck's constant

de-Broglie wavelength of the photon is given as :

$$\lambda = \frac{h}{mv}$$

But $p = mv$

$$\therefore \quad \lambda = \frac{h}{p} \quad ...(ii)$$

where, m = Mass of the photon

v = Velocity of the photon

Hence, it can be inferred from equations (i) and (ii) that the wavelength of the electromagnetic radiation is equal to the de-Broglie wavelength of the photon.

□□

ATOMS

CHAPTER 12

Introduction

- **Contribution of Indian philosopher Kanaad and Greek philosopher Democritus:**
  Matter is composed of very small, indivisible, solid, fundamental particles.
  Democritus called the particles "atomos". The greek word "atomos" means indivisible.
- **Contribution of John Dalton (in 1800's):**
  Adapted the idea of Democritus.
  All matter consists of tiny, indestructible, unchangeable particles called atom.
- **Contribution of J.J. Thomson (in 1890's):**
  Discovered electron and established the fact that atom is divisible.

Thomson's Plum Pudding model of atom:

- ♦ Each atom is a sphere positively charged fluid. This resembles to the "jam" of a "pudding".
- ♦ Negatively charged particles (electrons) are suspended in the fluid. This resembles to the "plum" of the "pudding".

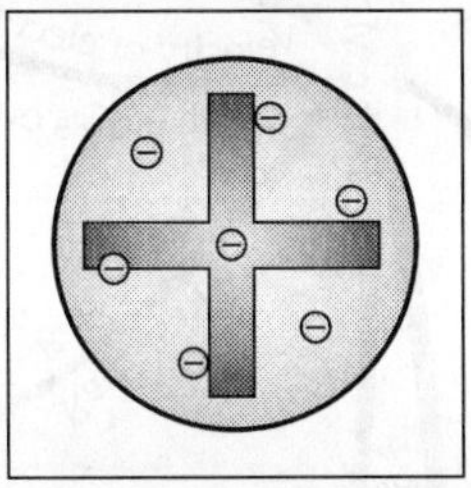

- **Contribution of Ernest Rutherford(in 1910's):**
  Not convinced with the Model described by J.J. Thomson.
  Performed alpha-particle scattering experiment.
  Rutherford's planetary model of atom:
- ♦ Nucleus at the centre of atom is a dense mass of positively charged particles.
- ♦ Electrons orbit the nucleus.
- ♦ Most of the space in atom is vacant.

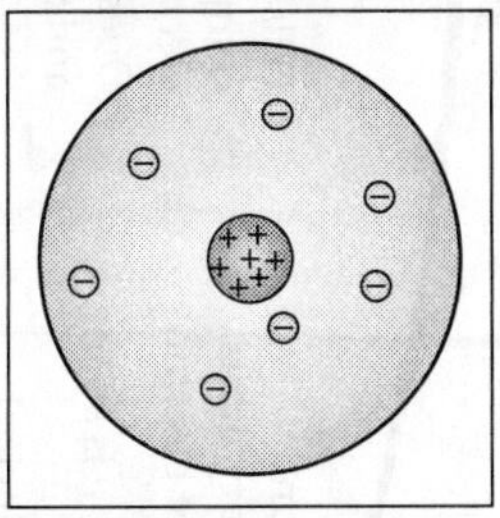

- **Contribution of Neils Bohr (in 1910's):**
  Accepted the idea of planetary model of atom but pointed a flaw.
  He modified the model which is known as Bohr-Rutherford model.
  Bohr's model of atom:
- ♦ Nucleus at the centre of atom is a dense mass of positively charged particles.
- ♦ Electrons orbit the nucleus in some specified orbits / energy levels only.

➢ **Alpha-particle Scattering and Rutherford's Nuclear Model of Atom**

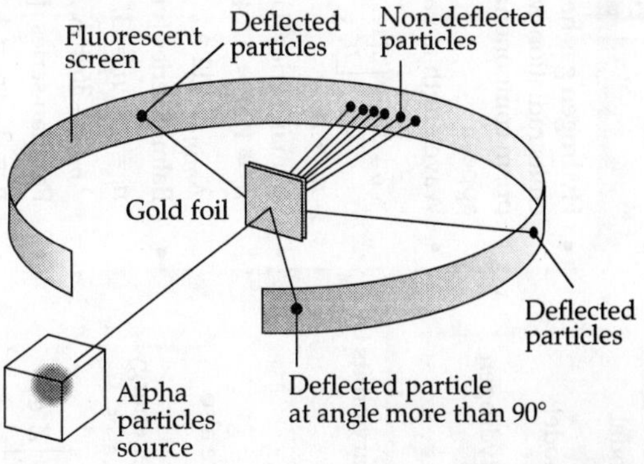

Set-up:

- Radioactive element $^{214}_{83}Bi$ was taken as alpha-particles generating source.
- Gold foil of thickness 2.1×10^{-7} m was taken as target metal. The selection of gold was based upon its two important characteristics:
- ♦ Highest malleability providing very thin foil possible to make. Gold foil that was used in experiment was almost transparent.
- ♦ Gold is a heavy metal, hence it helped in discovery of nucleus.
- Lead bricks absorbed the alpha-particles which were not towards the direction of gold foil. They worked as collimator.
- The detector was made from ZnS.

Scan to know more about this topic

Rutherford alpha particle Scattering Experiment

Observations:

- Most of the α-particles passed the gold foil roughly in straight line (within 1°) without deviation.
- A very small number of α-particles were scattered at an angle more than 90°. (1 out of 8000).
- In very rare cases, the α-particles were scattered at an angle 180°.
- **Scattering angle vs. no. of scattered alpha particle graph:**

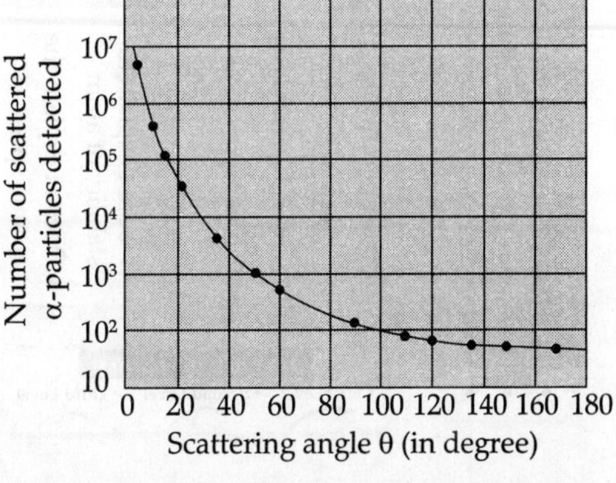

Atoms

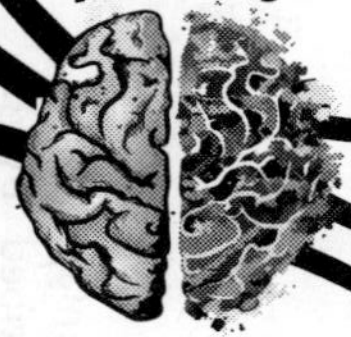

Contribution

In 1898, J.J Thomson proposed the first model of atom known as plum-pudding model.
In 1911, Rutherford prepared planetary model of atom.
In 1913, Niels Bohr prepared a model of Hydrogen atom based on quantum theory.

α – particle scattering experiment

- α- particle bombarded on thin gold foil
- Most of α– particles passed undeviated or with a small angle
- 1 out of 8000 α– particles were deflected by scattering angle

Impact parameter

$$b = \frac{Ze^2 \cot \theta / 2}{4\pi\varepsilon_0 \left(\frac{1}{2} mv^2\right)}$$

Rutherford's Model

Drawbacks

- Doesn't explain the stability of atom
- Doesn't explain the atomic spectra

Postulates

- Atoms have a central, massive, positively charged core called nucleus around which electrons revolve.
- Size of nucleus ≈ 1 fermi = 10^{-15} m

Energy Level

Energy of electron in each stationary orbits is

Given by $E_n = -13.6 \frac{Z^2}{n^2}$ eV

Where $n = 1, 2, 3....$

Z = atomic number of atom

- These stationary energy orbits are also called energy levels.
- When electron jumps from higher energy level to lower energy level, it releases energy.

$$\Delta E = E_f - E_i = 13.6\left[\frac{1}{n_i^2} - \frac{1}{n_f^2}\right] Z^2 \text{eV}$$

Hydrogen Spectrum

- Hydrogen gas heated in a sealed tube emits radiation when passed through prism components of different wavelength appear.
- Wavelength in each series given by

$$\bar{v} = \frac{1}{\lambda} = R\left[\frac{1}{n_i^2} - \frac{1}{n_f^2}\right]$$

$n_f > n_i$

- Lyman series [U.V. region]
  $n_i = 1, n_f = 2, 3, 4....$
  $\lambda_{min} = 912$ Å, $\lambda_{max} = 1216$ Å
- Balmer series [visible region]
  $n_i = 2 \quad n_f = 3, 4, 5.....$
  $\lambda_{min} = 3648$ Å, $\lambda_{max} = 6563$ Å
- Paschan series [IR region]
  $n_i = 3 \quad n_f = 4, 5, 6.....$
  $\lambda_{min} = 8208$ Å, $\lambda_{max} = 18761$ Å
- Brackett series [IR region]
  $n_i = 4 \quad n_f = 5, 6, 7...$
  $\lambda_{min} = 14592$ Å $\quad \lambda_{max} = 40533$ Å
- P fund [IR region]
  $n_i = 5 \quad n_f = 6, 7, 8......$
  $\lambda_{min} = 23850$ Å $\quad \lambda_{max} = 74618$ Å

Bohr Model

Postulates

- Electron revolves around the nucleus in stationary orbits.
- Angular momentum of electron

  $mvr_n = n \times \frac{h}{2\pi}$ where, n is an integer

  It is also known as principal Quantum Number.
- It explains spectrums of hydrogen or hydrogen like [He^+, Li^{++}] atoms.

Limitations

- Fails to explain spectrum of complex atoms/ions of multi electron system.
- Doesn't explain Zeeman's and Stark's effect.

Radius of nth Bohr's orbit

$$R_n = \frac{\varepsilon_0 h^2}{\pi me^2}\left(\frac{n^2}{Z}\right)$$

$$= 0.53 \frac{n^2}{Z} \text{ Å}$$

Velocity of electron in n^{th} Bohr's orbit

$$v_n = \frac{e^2}{2\varepsilon_0 h}\left(\frac{Z}{n}\right)$$

$$= 2.2 \times 10^6 \frac{Z}{n} \text{ m/s}$$

Potential Energy

$$U_n = -\frac{KZe^2}{r_n}$$

$$= \frac{-me^4}{4\varepsilon_0^2 h^2}\left(\frac{Z^2}{n^2}\right)$$

$$= \frac{-27.2 Z^2}{n^2} eV$$

Kinetic Energy

$$E_k = \frac{KZe^2}{2r_n}$$

$$= \frac{me^4}{8\varepsilon_0^2 h^2} \frac{Z^2}{n^2}$$

$$= \frac{13.6}{n^2} Z^2 \text{ eV}$$

Total Energy

$$E = U_n + E_k$$

$$= -\frac{KZe^2}{2r_n}$$

$$= \frac{-13.6 Z^2}{n^2} \text{eV}$$

$$= \frac{U_n}{2} = -E_K$$

Trace the Mind Map
- First Level
- Second Level
- Third Level

Conclusions:

- Most of the space in the atom is mostly empty.
- All positively charged particles are concentrated at the centre. It is called nucleus. Therefore, it has capability to reflect heavy positive α-particles.
- Force experienced by alpha particle

$$F = \frac{1}{4\pi\varepsilon_0}\frac{(2e)(Ze)}{r^2}$$

- Size of nucleus calculated to be about 10^{-14} m.

Alpha particle trajectory:

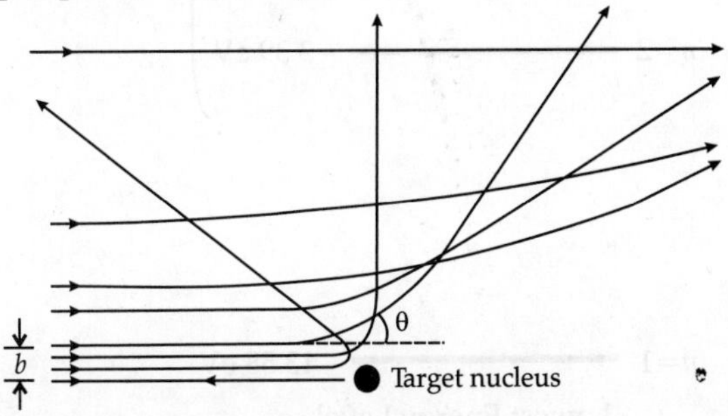

- **Impact parameter:** It is the perpendicular distance between direction of given alpha-particle and centre of nucleus. It is represented by 'b'.

$$b = \frac{Ze^2 \cot\frac{\theta}{2}}{4\pi\varepsilon_0\left(\frac{1}{2}mv^2\right)}$$

- **Distance of closest approach:**

As the alpha particle approaches the nucleus, due to Coulombian repulsion the kinetic energy goes on decreasing. At a point its total kinetic energy is converted into potential energy, the particle momentarily stops and then returns back. Distance of this point from the nucleus is known as distance of closest approach and is represented by r_0.

$$r_0 = \frac{1}{4\pi\varepsilon_0} \times \frac{2Ze^2}{\frac{1}{2}mv^2}$$

- **Estimated radius of nucleus:**

$$r = r_0 A^{1/3}$$

where, $r_0 = 1.4 \times 10^{-15}$ m

- **Volume and density of nucleus:**

Radius of nucleus $= r = r_0A^{1/3}$

Volume of nucleus $= V = \frac{4}{3}\pi r^3$

Or, $V = \frac{4}{3}\pi(r_0A^{1/3})^3$

Or, $V = \frac{4}{3}\pi A r_0^3$

Density $= \rho = \frac{\text{mass}}{\text{volume}}$

Or, $\rho = \frac{mA}{\left(\frac{4}{3}\pi A r_0^3\right)}$

[where, m is the average mass of nucleons]

$$\therefore \quad \rho = \frac{3m}{4\pi r_0^3}$$

So, density of nucleus is independent of mass no.

Rutherford's Atomic Model

- Similar to the planetary model of solar system.
- Almost the total mass of an atom is concentrated at the nucleus at the centre of atom which is positively charged.
- Electrons revolve around the nucleus in circular orbits.
- Radius of atom is around 10^{-10} m and the radius of nucleus is around 10^{-15} m.
- Most of the space in atom is vacant.
- Number of positively charged particle in nucleus is equal to the number of negatively charged electrons.

➤ **Drawbacks of Rutherford's model:**

- The model is unstable:

According to classical electromagnetic theory, an accelerated electron radiates electromagnetic radiation. As a result its total energy decreases. Radius of its orbit gradually decreases and it ultimately hits the nucleus.

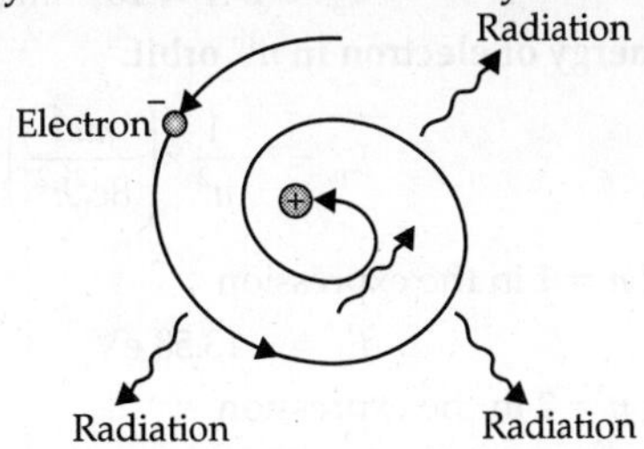

- Unable to explain the emission of line spectrum:

Spiral motion of electron should radiate continuous electromagnetic radiation. But it is not the fact. Hydrogen emits line spectrum.

Bohr's Postulates

- **Postulate-I:** An electron in an atom can revolve in certain stable orbits without the emission of radiant energy, contrary to the predictions of electromagnetic theory. These are called the stationary states of the atom.
- **Postulate-II:** The electron revolves around the nucleus only in those orbits for which the angular momentum is some integral multiple of $\frac{h}{2\pi}$ where, h is the Planck's constant,

$$h = 6.6 \times 10^{-34} \text{ Js}$$

Thus the angular momentum (L) of the orbiting electron is quantised.

i.e., $$L = \frac{nh}{2\pi}$$

- **Postulate-III:** An electron might make a transition from one of its specified non-radiating orbits to another of lower energy. When it does so, a photon is emitted having energy equal to the energy difference between the initial and final states. The frequency of the emitted photon is then given by

$$h\nu = E_f - E_i$$

where, E_i and E_f are the energies of the initial and final states and $E_i < E_f$.

Bohr Model of Hydrogen Atom

- Simplest atom having only one electron.
- **Radius of nth orbit of electron:**

$$r_n = \frac{\varepsilon_0 h^2 n^2}{\pi m e^2}$$

$$n = 1, 2, 3, 4 \ldots\ldots\ldots$$

n is called principal quantum number.

➤ **Radius of orbit of electron in Hydrogen similar atoms/ions:**

$$r_n = \frac{\varepsilon_0 h^2 n^2}{\pi m Z e^2}.$$

Putting $n = 1$ in the expression of r_n

$r_1 = 5.3 \times 10^{-11}$ m. This is also known as Bohr radius.

Putting $n = 2$

$$r_2 = 21.1 \times 10^{-11} \text{ m}$$

$$r_3 = 47.1 \times 10^{-11} \text{ m and so on.}$$

- **Total energy of electron in n^{th} orbit:**

$$E_n = -\frac{1}{n^2} \times \left(\frac{me^4}{8\varepsilon_0^2 h^2}\right)$$

Putting $n = 1$ in the expression

$$E_1 = -13.58 \text{ eV}$$

Putting $n = 2$ in the expression

$$E_2 = \frac{-13.58}{4} = -3.39 \text{ eV}$$

Putting $n = 3$ in the expression

$$E_3 = \frac{-13.58}{9} \text{ eV} = -1.31 \text{ eV}$$

Putting $n = \infty$ in the expression

$$E_\infty = 0$$

In general,

$$E_n = \frac{-13.58}{n^2} \text{ eV}$$

Energy of electron in n^{th} orbit of Hydrogen similar atoms/ions:

$$E_n = -\frac{1}{n^2} \times \left(\frac{mZ^2 e^4}{8\varepsilon_0^2 h^2}\right)$$

Due to this negative energy, electron is bound to nucleus and revolves around it. This energy is known as binding energy of electron.

From the above equation, it is clear that if energy is zero then radius is infinity. Practically, if we provide this amount of energy to this electron, it gets free.

- Relation between kinetic energy, potential energy and total energy:

$$KE = -TE$$

$$PE = -2KE$$

- **Energy level diagram for Hydrogen atom:**

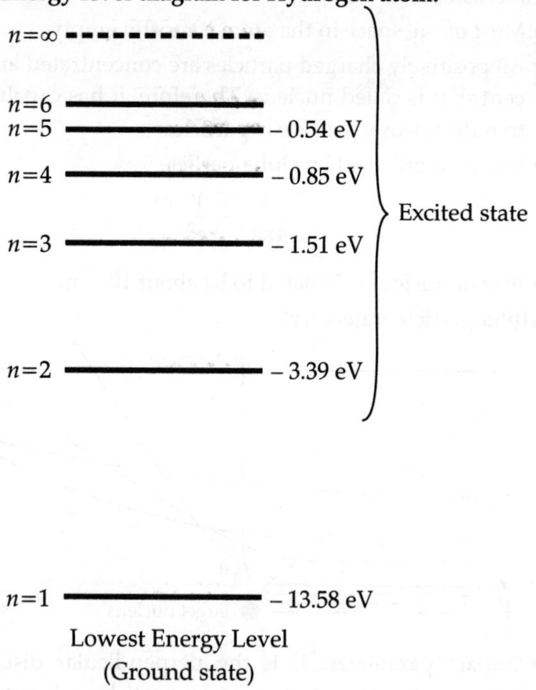

- Velocity of electron in n^{th} orbit:

$$v_n = \frac{e^2}{2\varepsilon_0 nh}$$

➤ **Velocity of electron in n^{th} orbit of Hydrogen similar atoms/ions:**

$$v_n = \frac{Ze^2}{2\varepsilon_0 nh})$$

Atomic Spectra

The spectrum of electromagnetic radiation emitted or absorbed by electron during transition from one energy level to another.

- Absorption spectra is observed when electron transits from lower to higher energy level.
- Emission spectra is observed when electron transits from higher to lower energy level.

➤ **Spectral series of Hydrogen:**

There are 4 spectral series for Hydrogen. If λ is the wavelength of the radiation emitted, then

$$\frac{1}{\lambda} = R\left(\frac{1}{n_i^2} - \frac{1}{n_f^2}\right)$$

where, $$R = \frac{me^4}{8\varepsilon_0^2 ch^3}$$

= Rydberg constant
= 1.09×10^7 m^{-1}

- **Lyman series:**

$n_i = 1, n_f = 2, 3, 4, \ldots..$

$$\frac{1}{\lambda} = R\left(\frac{1}{1^2} - \frac{1}{n_f^2}\right)$$

- **Balmer series:**

$n_i = 2, n_f = 3, 4, 5, \ldots..$

$$\frac{1}{\lambda} = R\left(\frac{1}{2^2} - \frac{1}{n_f^2}\right)$$

- **Paschen series:**

$n_i = 3, n_f = 4, 5, 6, \ldots$

$$\frac{1}{\lambda} = R\left(\frac{1}{3^2} - \frac{1}{n_f^2}\right)$$

- **Brackett series:**

$n_i = 4, n_f = 5, 6, 7, \ldots$

$$\frac{1}{\lambda} = R\left(\frac{1}{4^2} - \frac{1}{n_f^2}\right)$$

- **Pfund series:**

$n_i = 5, n_f = 6, 7, 8, \ldots$

$$\frac{1}{\lambda} = R\left(\frac{1}{5^2} - \frac{1}{n_f^2}\right)$$

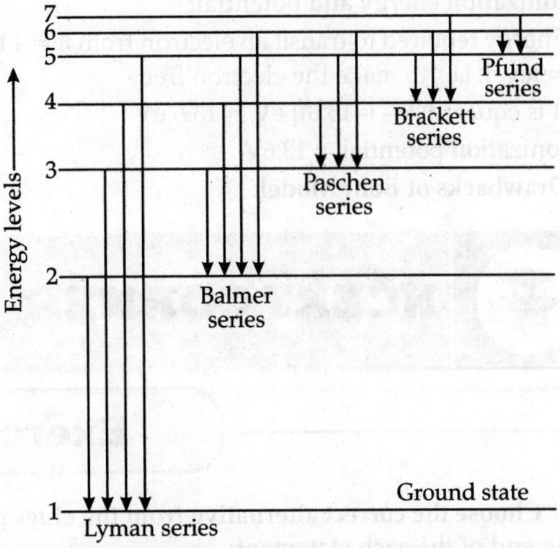

Name of series	Lower energy level	Upper energy level	Lowest wavelength	Highest wavelength	Position in electromagnetic spectrum
Lyman	1	2, 3, 4, 5....	$\frac{1}{\lambda_{min}} = R\left(\frac{1}{1^2} - \frac{1}{\infty^2}\right)$ $\lambda_{min} = 912$ Å	$\frac{1}{\lambda_{max}} = R\left(\frac{1}{1^2} - \frac{1}{2^2}\right)$ $\lambda_{max} = 1216$ Å	UV
Balmer	2	3, 4, 5, 6....	$\frac{1}{\lambda_{min}} = R\left(\frac{1}{2^2} - \frac{1}{\infty^2}\right)$ $\lambda_{min} = 3648$ Å	$\frac{1}{\lambda_{max}} = R\left(\frac{1}{2^2} - \frac{1}{3^2}\right)$ $\lambda_{max} = 6566$ Å	Visible
Paschen	3	4, 5, 6, 7....	$\frac{1}{\lambda_{min}} = R\left(\frac{1}{3^2} - \frac{1}{\infty^2}\right)$ $\lambda_{min} = 8208$ Å	$\frac{1}{\lambda_{max}} = R\left(\frac{1}{3^2} - \frac{1}{4^2}\right)$ $\lambda_{max} = 18761$ Å	IR
Brackett	4	5, 6, 7, 8....	$\frac{1}{\lambda_{min}} = R\left(\frac{1}{4^2} - \frac{1}{\infty^2}\right)$ $\lambda_{min} = 14592$ Å	$\frac{1}{\lambda_{max}} = R\left(\frac{1}{4^2} - \frac{1}{5^2}\right)$ $\lambda_{max} = 40533$ Å	IR
Pfund	5	6, 7, 8, 9....	$\frac{1}{\lambda_{min}} = R\left(\frac{1}{5^2} - \frac{1}{\infty^2}\right)$ $\lambda_{min} = 22800$ Å	$\frac{1}{\lambda_{max}} = R\left(\frac{1}{5^2} - \frac{1}{6^2}\right)$ $\lambda_{max} = 74618$ Å	Far IR

➢ **Absorption spectrum of Hydrogen:**

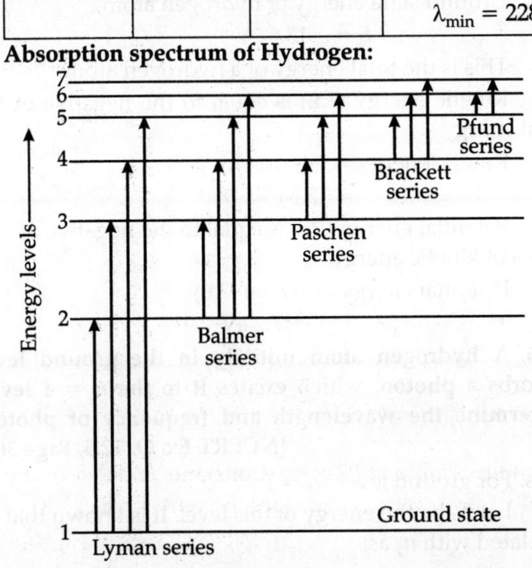

➢ **Excitation energy and potential of Hydrogen:**

Energy required to transit an electron from its ground level to an excited energy level.

- 1st excitation energy = energy required to transit an electron from $n = 1$ to $n = 2$ level.

  It is equal to [– 3.4 – (–13.6)] eV = 10.2 eV

  1st excitation potential = 10.2 V

- 2nd excitation energy = energy required to transit an electron from $n = 1$ to $n = 3$ level.

  It is equal to [– 1.5 – (–13.6)] eV = 12.1 eV

  2nd excitation potential = 12.1 V

- 3rd excitation energy = energy required to transit an electron from $n = 1$ to $n = 4$ level.

  It is equal to [– 0.85 – (–13.6)] eV = 12.75 eV

  3rd excitation potential = 12.75 V

- **Ionization energy and potential:**
  Energy required to transit an electron from $n = 1$ to $n = \infty$ level, i.e., to make the electron free.
  It is equal to [0 – (–13.6)] eV = 13.6 eV
  Ionization potential = 13.6V
- **Drawbacks of Bohr Model:**
  - It cannot explain the spectrum of multi-electron atoms
  - It cannot explain the splitting of spectral lines into a group of lines .
  - It cannot explain why the orbits of electrons are circular
  - It does not explain the distribution of electrons in different orbits in atom.

NCERT CORNER

Exercise Questions

Q. 1. Choose the correct alternative from the clues given at the end of the each statement:

(a) The size of the atom in Thomson's model is .... the atomic size in Rutherford's model. (much greater than/no different from/much less than.)

(b) In the ground state of .... electrons are in stable equilibrium, while in .... electrons always experience a net force. (Thomson's model/ Rutherford's model.)

(c) A classical atom based on .... is doomed to collapse. (Thomson's model/ Rutherford's model.)

(d) An atom has a nearly continuous mass distribution in .... but has a highly non-uniform mass distribution in .... (Thomson's model/ Rutherford's model.)

(e) The positively charged part of the atom possesses most of the mass in .... (Rutherford's model/both the models.) [NCERT Ex. Q. 12.1, Page 305]

Ans. (a) The sizes of the atoms taken in Thomson's model is **no different from** the atomic size in Rutherford's model.

(b) In the ground state of **Thomson's model,** electrons are in stable equilibrium, while in **Rutherford's** model electrons always experience a net force.

(c) A classical atom based on **Rutherford's model** is doomed to collapse.

(d) An atom has a nearly continuous mass distribution in **Thomson's model,** but has a highly non-uniform mass distribution in **Rutherford's model.**

(e) The positively charged part of the atom possesses most of the mass in **both the models.**

Q. 2. Suppose you are given a chance to repeat the alpha-particle scattering experiment using a thin sheet of solid hydrogen in place of the gold foil. (Hydrogen is a solid at temperatures below 14 K.) What results do you expect? [NCERT Ex. Q. 12.2, Page 305]

Ans. In the alpha-particle scattering experiment, if a thin sheet of solid hydrogen is used in place of a gold foil, then the scattering angle would not be large enough.

This is because the mass of hydrogen (1.67×10^{-27} kg) is less than the mass of incident α-particles (6.64×10^{-27} kg).

Here in this experiment, the mass of the scattering particle is more than the mass of target nucleus (hydrogen). Hence, the α-particles would not bounce back if solid hydrogen is used in the α-particle scattering experiment.

Q. 3. A difference of 2.3 eV separates two energy levels in an atom. What is the frequency of radiation emitted when the atom make a transition from the upper level to the lower level? [NCERT Ex. Q. 12.3, Page 305]

Ans. Separation of two energy levels in an atom,

$$E = 2.3 \text{ eV}$$
$$= 2.3 \times 1.6 \times 10^{-19}$$
$$= 3.68 \times 10^{-19} \text{ J}$$

Let ν be the frequency of radiation emitted when the atom transits from the upper level to the lower level.

As, the relation for energy is:

$$E = h\nu$$

where, h = Planck's constant
$= 6.62 \times 10^{-34}$ J-s

$$\therefore \quad \nu = \frac{E}{h}$$

$$\text{Or,} \quad \nu = \frac{3.68 \times 10^{-19}}{6.62 \times 10^{-34}}$$

$$\therefore \quad \nu = 5.6 \times 10^{14} \text{ Hz}$$

So, the frequency of the radiation is 5.6×10^{14} Hz.

Q. 4. The ground state energy of hydrogen atom is –13.6 eV. What are the kinetic and potential energies of the electron in this state? [NCERT Ex. Q. 12.4, Page 305]

Ans. Given that,

Ground state energy of hydrogen atom,

$$E = -13.6 \text{ eV}$$

This is the total energy of a hydrogen atom.

Kinetic energy (KE) is equal to the negative of the total energy.

Kinetic energy $= -(-13.6)$
$= 13.6$ eV

Potential energy (PE) is equal to the negative of two times of kinetic energy.

Potential energy $= -2 \times (13.6)$
$= -27.2$ eV

Q. 5. A hydrogen atom initially in the ground level absorbs a photon, which excites it to the $n = 4$ level. Determine the wavelength and frequency of photon. [NCERT Ex. Q. 12.5, Page 305]

Ans. For ground level, $n_1 = 1$

Let E_1 be the energy of this level. It is known that E_1 is related with n_1 as:

$$E_1 = \frac{-13.6}{n_1^2} \text{ eV}$$

where, $n_1 = 1$

$$\therefore \quad E_1 = \frac{-13.6}{1^2} = -13.6 \text{ eV}$$

The atom is excited to a higher level, $n^2 = 4$

Let E_2 be the energy of this level.

$$\therefore \quad E_2 = \frac{-13.6}{4^2} = \frac{-13.6}{16} \text{ eV}$$

The amount of energy absorbed by the photon is given as:

$$E = E_2 - E_1$$

Or,
$$E = \frac{-13.6}{16} - (-13.6)$$

$$\therefore \quad E = 2.04 \times 10^{-18} \text{ J}$$

For a photon of wavelength λ, the expression of energy is written as:

$$E = \frac{hc}{\lambda}$$

Or,
$$\lambda = \frac{hc}{E}$$

Or,
$$\lambda = \frac{6.6\times10^{-34}\times3\times10^{8}}{2.04\times10^{-18}}$$

$$\therefore \quad \lambda = 9.7 \times 10^{-8} \text{ m}$$

Frequency of photon is

$$\nu = \frac{c}{\lambda}$$

or,
$$\nu = \frac{3\times10^{8}}{9.7\times10^{-8}}$$

$$\therefore \quad \nu = 3.1 \times 10^{15}$$

So, the wavelength of the photon is 97 nm while the frequency is 3.1×10^{15} Hz;

Q. 6. (a) Using the Bohr's model calculate the speed of the electron in a hydrogen atom in the *n* = 1, 2, and 3 levels.

(b) Calculate the orbital period in each of these levels.

[NCERT Ex. Q. 12.6, Page 305]

Ans. (a) Let v_1 be the orbital speed of the electron in a hydrogen atom in the ground state level, $n_1 = 1$.

For charge (*e*) of an electron, v_1 is given by the relation,

$$v_1 = \frac{e^2}{n_1 4\pi\varepsilon_0 \left(\frac{h}{2\pi}\right)}$$

$$= \frac{e^2}{2\varepsilon_0 h}$$

or
$$v_1 = \frac{(1.6\times10^{-19})^2}{2\times8.85\times10^{-12}\times6.62\times10^{-34}}$$

$$\therefore \quad v_1 = 2.18 \times 10^{6} \text{ m/s}$$

For level $n_2 = 2$, we can write the relation for the corresponding orbital speed as:

$$v_2 = \frac{e^2}{2\varepsilon_0 h n_2}$$

or,
$$v_2 = \frac{(1.6\times10^{-19})^2}{2\times2\times8.85\times10^{-12}\times6.62\times10^{-34}}$$

$$\therefore \quad v_2 = 1.09 \times 10^{6} \text{ m/s}$$

For level $n_3 = 3$, we can write the relation for the corresponding orbital speed as:

$$v_3 = \frac{e^2}{2\varepsilon_0 h n_3}$$

or,
$$v_3 = \frac{(1.6\times10^{-19})^2}{2\times3\times8.85\times10^{-12}\times6.62\times10^{-34}}$$

$$\therefore \quad v_3 = 7.27 \times 10^{5} \text{ m/s}$$

(b) Let T_1 be the orbital period of the electron when it is in level $n_1 = 1$.

Orbital period is related to orbital speed as:

$$T_1 = \frac{2\pi r_1}{v_1}$$

where, r_1 = radius of the orbit = $\frac{n_1^2 h^2 \varepsilon_0}{\pi m_e e^2}$

$$\therefore \quad T_1 = \frac{2\pi\times1^2\times(6.62\times10^{-34})^2\times8.85\times10^{-12}}{2.18\times10^{6}\times\pi\times9.1\times10^{-31}\times(1.6\times10^{-19})^2}$$

$$= 1.527 \times 10^{-16} \text{ s}$$

Orbital period of the electron when it is in level $n_2 = 2$.

$$T_2 = \frac{2\pi\times2^2\times(6.62\times10^{-34})^2\times8.85\times10^{-12}}{2.18\times10^{6}\times\pi\times9.1\times10^{-31}\times(1.6\times10^{-19})^2}$$

$$= 1.22 \times 10^{-15} \text{ s}$$

Orbital period of the electron when it is in level $n_3 = 3$.

$$T_2 = \frac{2\pi\times3^2\times(6.62\times10^{-34})^2\times8.85\times10^{-12}}{2.18\times10^{6}\times\pi\times9.1\times10^{-31}\times(1.6\times10^{-19})^2}$$

$$= 4.12 \times 10^{-15} \text{ s}$$

Q. 7. The radius of the innermost electron orbit of a hydrogen atom is 5.3×10^{-11} m. What are the radii of the *n* = 2 and *n* = 3 orbits? [NCERT Ex. Q. 12.7, Page 305]

Ans. The radius of the innermost orbit of a hydrogen atom, $r_1 = 5.3 \times 10^{-11}$ m

Let r_2 be the radius of the orbit at $n = 2$. It is related to the radius of the innermost orbit as:

$$r_2 = (n)^2 r_1$$

$$\therefore r_2 = 4 \times 5.3 \times 10^{-11} = 2.12 \times 10^{-10} \text{ m}$$

For $n = 3$, we can write the corresponding electron radius as:

$$r_3 = (n)^2 r_1$$

$$\therefore \quad r_3 = 9 \times 5.3 \times 10^{-11}$$

$$= 4.77 \times 10^{-10} \text{ m}$$

So, the radii of an electron for $n = 2$ and $n = 3$ orbits are 2.12×10^{-10} m and 4.77×10^{-10} m, respectively.

Q. 8. A 12.5 eV electron beam is used to bombard gaseous hydrogen at room temperature. What series of wavelengths will be emitted?

[NCERT Ex. Q. 12.8, Page 305]

Ans. Given that,

The energy of the electron beam used to bombard gaseous hydrogen at room temperature is 12.5 eV. Also, the energy of the gaseous hydrogen in its ground state at room temperature is −13.6 eV.

And, When gaseous hydrogen is bombarded with an electron beam, the energy of the gaseous hydrogen becomes −13.6 + 12.5 eV (i.e., −1.1 eV).

Orbital energy is related to orbit level (n) as:

$$E = \frac{-13.6}{n^2} \text{ eV}$$

For $n = 3$,

$$E = \frac{-13.6}{9} = -1.5 \text{ eV}$$

This energy is approximately equal to the energy of gaseous hydrogen. It can be concluded that the electron has jumped from $n = 1$ to $n = 3$ level.

During its de-excitation, the electrons can jump from $n = 3$ to $n = 1$ directly, which forms a line of the Lyman series of the hydrogen spectrum.

$$\frac{1}{\lambda} = R\left(\frac{1}{1^2} - \frac{1}{n^2}\right)$$

For $n = 3$

$$\frac{1}{\lambda} = R\left(\frac{1}{1^2} - \frac{1}{3^2}\right) = \frac{8R}{9}$$

$$\therefore \quad \lambda = \frac{9}{8R}$$

$$\text{Or,} \quad \lambda = \frac{9}{8 \times 1.097 \times 10^7}$$

$$\therefore \quad \lambda = 102.55 \text{ nm}$$

If the electron jumps from $n = 2$ to $n = 1$, then

$$\frac{1}{\lambda} = R\left(\frac{1}{1^2} - \frac{1}{2^2}\right) = \frac{3R}{4}$$

$$\therefore \quad \lambda = \frac{4}{3R}$$

$$\text{Or,} \quad \lambda = \frac{4}{3 \times 1.097 \times 10^7}$$

$$\therefore \quad \lambda = 121.51 \text{ nm}$$

If the transition takes place from $n = 3$ to $n = 2$, the

$$\frac{1}{\lambda} = R\left(\frac{1}{2^2} - \frac{1}{3^2}\right)$$

$$\therefore \quad \lambda = \frac{36}{5R}$$

$$\text{Or,} \quad \lambda = \frac{36}{5 \times 1.097 \times 10^7}$$

$$\therefore \quad \lambda = 656.33 \text{ nm}$$

This radiation corresponds to the Balmer series c the hydrogen spectrum.

So, in Lyman series, two wavelengths (i.e., 102.5 nm and 121.5 nm) are emitted. And in the Balmer series, on wavelength (i.e., 656.33 nm) is emitted.

Q. 9. In accordance with the Bohr's model, fin the quantum number that characterises the earth' revolution around the sun in an orbit of radiu 1.5×10^{11} m with orbital speed 3×10^4 m/s. (Mass of eart $= 6.0 \times 10^{24}$ kg.) **[NCERT Ex. Q. 12.9, Page 305]**

Ans. Given that,

Radius of the orbit of the Earth around the Sun,

$$r = 1.5 \times 10^{11} \text{ m}$$

Orbital speed of the Earth,

$$v = 3 \times 10^4 \text{ m/s}$$

Mass of the Earth,

$$m = 6.0 \times 10^{24} \text{ kg}$$

According to Bohr's model, angular momentum i quantised and given as:

$$mvr = \frac{nh}{2\pi}$$

where, h = Planck's constant
$= 6.62 \times 10^{-34}$ J-s
n = Quantum number

As we know that,

$$n = \frac{mvr2\pi}{h}$$

$$\text{or,} \quad n = \frac{2\pi \times 6 \times 10^{24} \times 3 \times 10^4 \times 1.5 \times 10^{11}}{6.62 \times 10^{-34}}$$

$$\therefore \quad n = 2.6 \times 10^{74}$$

So, the quantum number that characterises the Earth's revolution is 2.6×10^{74}.

CHAPTER 13

NUCLEI

Nuclei

- All mass and positive charge of an atom is concentrated in its centre known as nucleus.
- Chadwick discovered a new sub-particle in nucleus known as neutron. It is electrically neutral in nature. Mass of neutron,

$$m_n = 1.00866$$
$$u = 1.6749 \times 10^{-27}\text{ kg}$$

- The composition of a nucleus can now be described using the following terms and symbols:

  Z = atomic number = number of protons (equal to the number of electrons)

  N = neutron number = number of neutrons

  A = atomic mass number = $(Z + N)$ = total number of protons and neutrons
- An atom is represented by ${}^{A}_{Z}X$ where

  X = Symbol of element

  A = Atomic mass number

  Z = Atomic number
- As per Rutherford scattering experiment, it is established that radius of atom is 10^4 times of its nucleus. Hence, volume of nucleus is 10^{-12} times smaller than atom. This concludes that atom is almost empty.
- If an atom is enlarged to the size of a classroom, the nucleus would be of the size of pinhead.
- For measuring atomic mass and its sub-particles, new unit of mass is introduced as atomic mass unit '*u*'.

$$1\,u = \frac{\text{mass of one } {}^{12}_{6}\text{C atom}}{12}$$

$$1\,u = 1.660539 \times 10^{-27}\text{ kg}$$

- Atomic mass unit is not an integral multiple of u due to presence of isotopes (atoms of same element with different atomic masses).

➢ **Isotopes:** Two atoms of an element having same atomic number (Z is same) but different atomic mass number (due to the different number of neutrons) are said to be isotopes.

➢ **Isobars:** Two atoms of different elements having same mass number but different atomic numbers are said to be isobars.

➢ **Isotones:** Two atoms of different elements having different mass numbers and atomic numbers such that their difference is same are said to be isotones. It means they have same number of neutrons.

Size of the Nucleus

- A nucleus of mass number A has a radius

$$R = R_0 A^{1/3};$$

where, $R_0 = 1.2 \times 10^{-15}$ m
- Nuclear matter density = 2.3×10^{17} kgm^{-3}

- Earlier it was believed that anything in the universe can be classified into matter or radiation. Einstein proposed that there are two forms of energy which are inter convertible.

$$E = mc^2;$$

where, c is speed of light.

With this relation we may calculate 1 u = 931.5 MeV

Scan to know more about this topic

Nuclei

Mass-Energy and Nuclear Binding Energy

➢ **Mass Defect:** The difference in mass of a nucleus and its constituents, ΔM is called the mass defect, and is given by

$$\Delta M = [Zm_p + (A - Z)m_n] - M$$

➢ **Binding Energy**

Binding energy of a nucleus is that quantity of energy which when given to nucleus, its nucleons will become free and will leave the nucleus. It is having negative sign.

$$E_b = \Delta Mc^2$$

where, E_b is binding energy.

- **Binding energy per nucleons (E_b /A):** A measure of the binding between the constituents of the nucleus is the binding energy per nucleon, E_{bn} or E_b/A, which is the ratio of the binding energy E_b of a nucleus to the number of the nucleons, A, in that nucleus.

$$E_{bn} = \frac{E_b}{A}$$

- **Relation between E_b/A and Stability of elements**

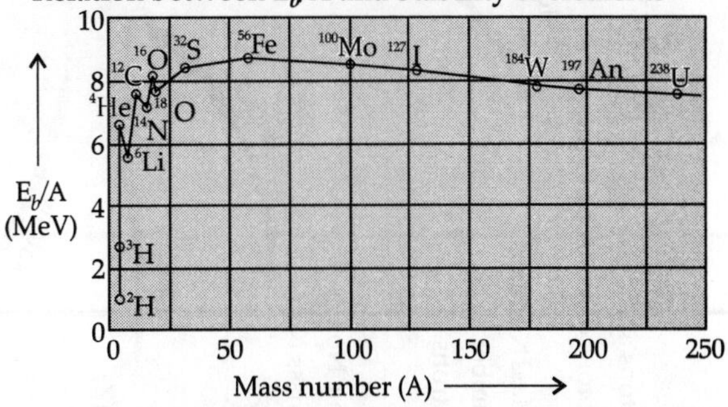

- Higher the binding energy per nucleons, more stable is the element. High binding energy per nucleon means we have to supply more energy to free nucleons or difficult to break the nucleus.
- Most of the atoms where atomic mass number are in the range 30 < A < 200, the Binding Energy per Nucleon is fairly constant and quite high. It is maximum for A = 56 about 8.75 MeV.
- For A < 30 and A > 170; Binding Energy per Nucleon is quite low.

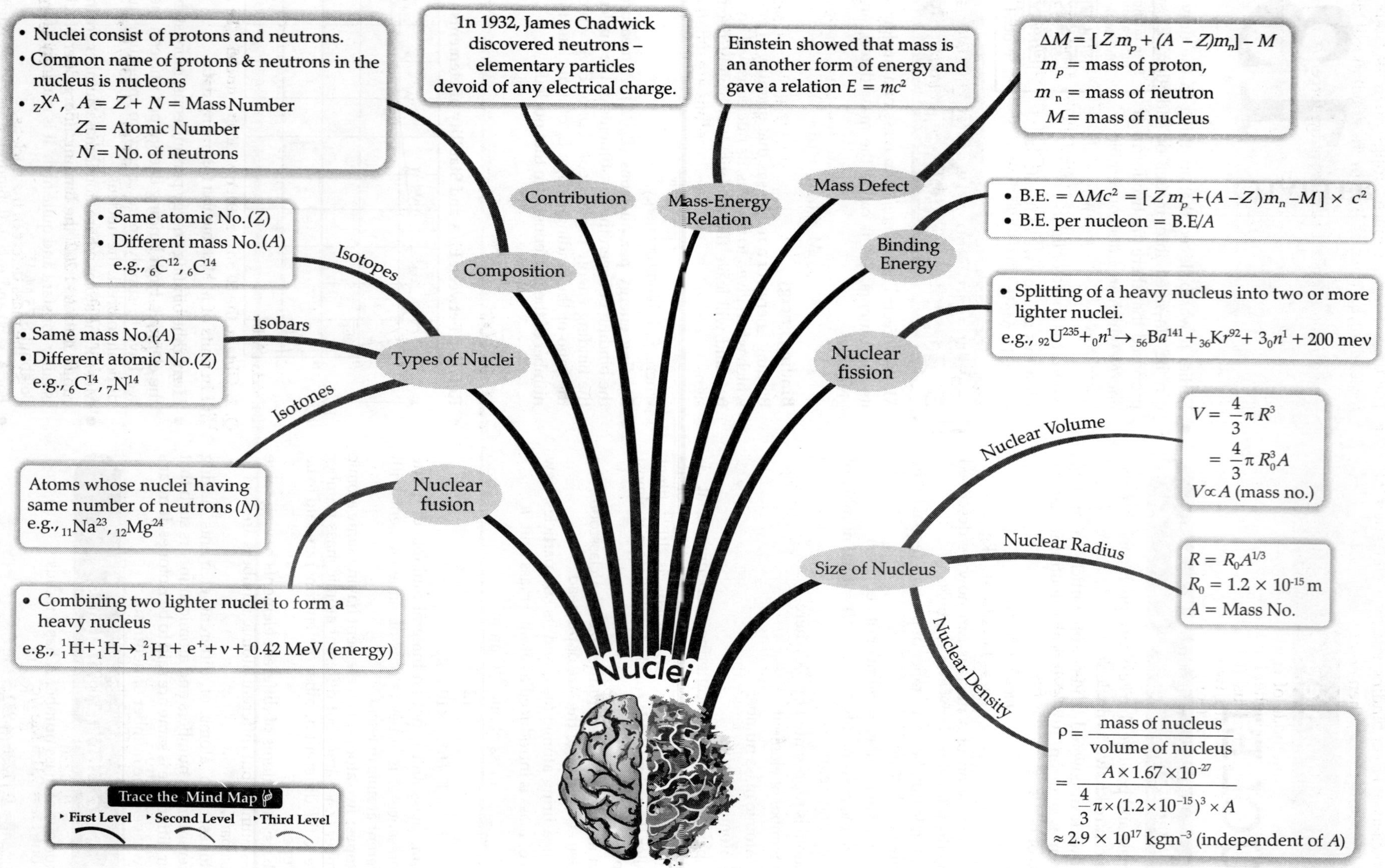
Nuclei
Composition
• Nuclei consist of protons and neutrons.
• Common name of protons & neutrons in the nucleus is nucleons
• ${}_ZX^A$, $A = Z + N$ = Mass Number
Z = Atomic Number
N = No. of neutrons
Contribution
In 1932, James Chadwick discovered neutrons – elementary particles devoid of any electrical charge.
Mass-Energy Relation
Einstein showed that mass is an another form of energy and gave a relation $E = mc^2$
Mass Defect
$\Delta M = [Zm_p + (A - Z)m_n] - M$
m_p = mass of proton,
m_n = mass of neutron
M = mass of nucleus
Binding Energy
• B.E. = $\Delta Mc^2 = [Zm_p + (A - Z)m_n - M] \times c^2$
• B.E. per nucleon = B.E/A
Nuclear fission
• Splitting of a heavy nucleus into two or more lighter nuclei.
e.g., ${}_{92}U^{235} + {}_0n^1 \rightarrow {}_{56}Ba^{141} + {}_{36}Kr^{92} + 3{}_0n^1 + 200$ mev
Types of Nuclei
Isotopes
• Same atomic No. (Z)
• Different mass No. (A)
e.g., ${}_6C^{12}$, ${}_6C^{14}$
Isobars
• Same mass No. (A)
• Different atomic No. (Z)
e.g., ${}_6C^{14}$, ${}_7N^{14}$
Isotones
Atoms whose nuclei having same number of neutrons (N)
e.g., ${}_{11}Na^{23}$, ${}_{12}Mg^{24}$
Nuclear fusion
• Combining two lighter nuclei to form a heavy nucleus
e.g., ${}_1^1H + {}_1^1H \rightarrow {}_1^2H + e^+ + \nu + 0.42$ MeV (energy)
Size of Nucleus
Nuclear Volume
$V = \frac{4}{3}\pi R^3$
$= \frac{4}{3}\pi R_0^3 A$
$V \propto A$ (mass no.)
Nuclear Radius
$R = R_0 A^{1/3}$
$R_0 = 1.2 \times 10^{-15}$ m
A = Mass No.
Nuclear Density
$\rho = \frac{\text{mass of nucleus}}{\text{volume of nucleus}}$
$= \frac{A \times 1.67 \times 10^{-27}}{\frac{4}{3}\pi \times (1.2 \times 10^{-15})^3 \times A}$
$\approx 2.9 \times 10^{17}$ kgm^{-3} (independent of A)
Trace the Mind Map
First Level
Second Level
Third Level

- If a nucleus of lower binding energy is converted into higher binding energy then energy is released.

Nuclear Energy

- There are two methods of converting lower binding energy nucleons into higher binding energy nucleons.

> **Fission:** A heavy nucleus (low binding energy per nucleon) is broken into two lower nucleus (higher binding energy per nucleon) with the release of energy. This process is known as fission.
> **Example:**
> $${}_{0}^{1}n + {}_{92}^{235}U \rightarrow {}_{92}^{236}U \rightarrow {}_{56}^{144}Ba + {}_{36}^{89}Kr + 3{}_{0}^{1}n + 200 \text{ MeV}$$

> **Fusion:** Two light nucleus (low binding energy per nucleon) are joined to form one nucleus of higher binding energy per nucleon and energy is released. This process is known as fusion.
> **Example:** ${}_{1}^{1}H + {}_{1}^{1}H \rightarrow {}_{1}^{2}H + e^{+} + \nu + 0.42 \text{ MeV}$

Radioactivity

- Radioactivity is the phenomenon in which nuclei of given species transform by giving out α or β or γ rays.
- α rays are helium nuclei; β rays are electrons; γ rays are electromagnetic radiation of wavelengths shorter than X-rays.

Nuclear Force

- The binding energy per nucleon is approximately 8 MeV, which is much larger than the binding energy in atoms.
- This high binding energy per Nucleon counters the repulsive force between protons and bind both protons and neutrons into the tiny nuclear volume.
- The nuclear force is much stronger than the Coulomb force acting between charges or the gravitational forces between masses but it's a short range force $\left(\propto \frac{1}{r^7}\right)$

MNEMONICS

Concept Name: Isotope, Isobar, Isotone

Mnemonics: ISO **T**ope **B**ar **T**one

Interpretation:

ISO—Tope	**P** i.e., number of PROTONs are same and number of NEUTRONs different In isotopes, number of protons are same, Number of neutrons are different.
ISO—Bar	No **P** No **N** i.e., both PROTONs and NEUTRONs differ in number (Total remains same.) In isobars, numbers of neutrons are different. Number of protons are also different. But the total nucleons remains same.
ISO—Tone	**N** i.e., numbers of NEUTRONs are same and number of PROTONs different. In isotones, number of neutrons are same. Number of protons are different.

NCERT CORNER

Exercise Questions

Q. 1. Obtain the binding energy (in MeV) of a nitrogen nucleus (${}_{7}^{14}N$), given m (${}_{7}^{14}N$) = 14.00307u

[NCERT Ex. Q. 13.1, Page 321]

Ans. Atomic mass of nitrogen ${}_{7}N^{14}$, m = 14.00307 u

A nucleus of ${}_{7}N^{14}$ nitrogen contains 7 neutrons and 7 protons.

So that, the mass defect of this nucleus,

$\Delta m = 7m_H + 7m_n - m$

Where,

Mass of proton, $m_P = 1.007825\ u$

Mass of neutron, $m_n = 1.008665\ u$

$\Delta m = 7 \times 1.007825 + 1.008665 - 14.00307$

$= 7.054775 + 7.06055 - 14.00307$

$= 0.11236\ u$

But $1\ u = 931.5\ \text{MeV}/c^2$

$\Delta m = 0.11236 \times 931.5\ \text{MeV}/c^2$

So that, the binding energy of the nucleus is:

$$E_b = \Delta mc^2$$

Where, c = Speed of light

$$E_b = 0.11236 \times 931.5\left(\frac{\text{MeV}}{c^2}\right) \times c^2$$

$= 104.6634$ MeV

So that, the binding energy of a nitrogen nucleus is 104.66334 MeV.

Q. 2. Obtain the binding energy of the nuclei ${}_{26}^{56}Fe$ and ${}_{83}^{200}Bi$ in units of MeV from the following data:

m (${}_{26}^{56}Fe$) = 55.934939 u

m (${}_{83}^{209}Bi$) = 208.980388 u

[NCERT Ex. Q. 13.2, Page 321]

Ans. Atomic mass of ${}_{26}^{56}Fe$, m_1 = 55.934939 u

${}_{26}^{56}Fe$ nucleus has 26 protons and (56 − 26) = 30 neutrons

So, the mass defect of the nucleus,

$\Delta m = 26 \times m_H + 30 \times m_n - m_1$

Where,
Mass of a proton, $m_H = 1.007825$ u
Mass of a neutron, $m_n = 1.008665$ u
Put the values,

$\Delta m = 26 \times 1.007825 + 30 \times 1.008665 - 55.93493$
$= 26.20345 + 30.25995 - 55.934939$
$= 0.528461$ u

But 1 u = 931.5 MeV/c^2
$\Delta m = 0.528461 \times 931.5$ MeV/c^2

The binding energy of this nucleus is:

$E_{b1} = \Delta mc^2$

Where, c = Speed of light

$$E_{b1} = 0.528461 \times 931.5\left(\frac{\text{MeV}}{c^2}\right) \times c^2$$

$= 492.26$ MeV

Average binding energy per nucleon

$$= \frac{492.26}{56} = 8.79 \text{ MeV}$$

Atomic mass of $^{209}_{83}$Bi, $m_2 = 208.980388$ u

$^{209}_{83}$Bi nucleus has 83 protons and (209 – 83) + 126 neutrons.

Hence, the mass defect of this nucleus is given as:

$\Delta m' = 83 \times m_H + 126 \times mn - m_2$

Where,
Mass of proton, $m_H = 1.007825$ u
Mass of neutron, $m_n = 1.008665$ u

$\Delta m' = 83 \times 1.007825 \times 126 \times 1.008665 - 208.980388$
$= 83.649475 + 127.091790 - 208.980388$
$= 1.760877$ u

But 1 u = 931.5 MeV/c^2

$\Delta m' = 1.760877 \times 931.5$ MeV/c^2

So that, the binding energy of this nucleus is given as:

$E_{b2} = \Delta m'c^2$

$$= 1.760877 \times 931.5\left(\frac{\text{MeV}}{c^2}\right) \times c^2$$

$= 1640.26$ MeV

Average binding energy per nucleon

$$= \frac{1640.26}{209}$$

$= 7.848$ MeV

Q. 3. A given coin has a mass of 3.0 g. Calculate the nuclear energy that would be required to separate all the neutrons and protons from each other. For simplicity assume that the coin is entirely made of atoms (of mass 62.92960 u). [NCERT Ex. Q. 13.3, Page 321]

Ans. Mass of a copper coin, $m' = 3$ g

Atomic mass of $_{29}Cu^{63}$ atoms, $m = 62.92960$ u

The total number of $_{29}Cu^{63}$ atoms in the coin,

$$N = \frac{N_A \times m'}{\text{Mass number}}$$

where,

N_A = Avogadro's number = 6.023×10^{23} atoms/g

Mass number = 63 g

$$\therefore \quad = \frac{6.023 \times 10^{23} \times 3}{63} = 2.868 \times 10^{22} \text{ atoms}$$

$_{29}Cu^{63}$ nucleus has 29 protons and (63 – 29) = 34 neutrons

$\therefore$ Mass defect of this nucleus, $\Delta m' = 29 \times m_H + 34 \times m_n - m$

Where,
Mass of a proton, $m_H = 1.007825$ u
Mass of a neutron, $m_n = 1.008665$ u
So,

$\Delta m' = 29 \times 1.007825 + 34 \times 1.008665 - 62.9296$
$= 0.591935$ u

Mass defect of all atoms present in the coin,

$\Delta m = 0.591935 \times 2.868 \times 10^{22}$
$= 1.69766958 \times 10^{22}$ u

But 1 u = 931.5 MeV/c^2

So, $\Delta m = 1.69766958 \times 10^{22} \times 931.5$ MeV/c^2

So that, the binding energy of the nuclei of the coin is given as:

$E_{b2} = \Delta m'c^2$

$$= 1.69766958 \times 10^{22} \times 931.5\left(\frac{\text{MeV}}{c^2}\right) \times c^2$$

$= 1.581 \times 10^{25}$ MeV

But 1 MeV = 1.6×10^{-13} J

$E_b = 1.581 \times 10^{25} \times 1.6 \times 10^{-13}$
$= 2.5296 \times 10^{12}$ J

This much energy is required to separate all the neutrons and protons from the given coin.

Q. 4. Obtain approximately the ratio of the nuclear radii of the gold isotope $^{197}_{79}$Au and the silver isotope $^{107}_{47}$Ag. [NCERT Q. 11.4, Page 321]

Ans. Given that,

Nuclear radius of the gold isotope $_{79}Au^{197} = R_{Au}$
Nuclear radius of the silver isotope $_{47}Ag^{107} = R_{Ag}$
Mass number of gold, $A_{Au} = 197$
Mass number of silver, $A_{Ag} = 107$

The ratio of the radii of the two nuclei is related with their mass numbers:

$$\frac{R_{Au}}{R_{Ag}} = \left(\frac{R_{Au}}{R_{Ag}}\right)^{\frac{1}{3}}$$

$$= \left(\frac{197}{107}\right)^{\frac{1}{3}}$$

$= 1.2256$

So, the ratio of the nuclear radii of the gold and silver isotopes is about 1.23.

Q. 5. The Q value of a nuclear reaction A + $b \to$ C + d is defined by Q = $[m_A + m_b - m_C - m_d]c^2$, where the masses refer to the respective nuclei, Determine from the given

data the Q-value of the following reactions and state whether the reactions are exothermic or endothermic.

(i) $^1_1H + ^3_1H \rightarrow ^2_1H + ^2_1H$

(ii) $^{12}_6C + ^{12}_6C \rightarrow ^{20}_{10}Ne + ^4_2He$

Atomic masses are given to be

$m(^2_1H) = 2.014102$ **u,**

$m(^3_1H) = 3.016049$ **u,**

$m(^{12}_6C) = 12.000000$ **u,**

$m(^{20}_{10}Ne) = 19.992439$**u** **[NCERT Q. 13.5, Page 321]**

Ans. (i) The given nuclear reaction is:

$^1_1H + ^3_1H \rightarrow ^2_1H + ^2_1H$

It is given that:

Atomic mass $m(^1_1H) = 1.007825$ u

Atomic mass $m(^3_1H) = 3.014049$ u

Atomic mass $m(^2_1H) = 2.014102$ u

According to the question, the Q-value of the reaction can be written as:

$$Q = [m(^1_1H) + m(^3_1H) - 2\,m(^2_1H)]\,c^2$$

$$= [1.007825 + 3.016049 - 2 \times 2.014102]\,c^2$$

$$Q = (-0.00433\,c^2)\text{ u}$$

But $1\text{ u} = 931.5\text{ MeV/c}^2$

$$Q = -0.00433 \times 931.5$$

$$= -4.0334\text{ MeV}$$

The negative Q-value of the reaction shows that the reaction is endothermic.

(ii) The given nuclear reaction is:

$^{12}_6C + ^{12}_6C \rightarrow ^{20}_{10}Ne + ^4_2He$

It is given that:

Atomic mass of $m(^{12}_6C) = 12.000000$ u

Atomic mass of $m(^{20}_{10}Ne) = 19.992439$ u

Atomic mass of $m(^4_2He) = 4.002603$ u

The Q-value of this reaction is given as:

$$Q = [m(^{12}_6C) - m(^{20}_{10}Ne) - m(^4_2He)$$

$$= 4.002603\text{ u]}\,c^2$$

$$= [2 \times 12.0 - 19.992439 - 4.002603]\,c^2$$

$$= [0.004958\,c^2]\text{ u}$$

$$= 0.004958 \times 931.5$$

$$= 4.618377\text{ MeV}$$

The positive Q-value of the reaction shows that the reaction is exothermic.

Q. 6. Suppose, we think of fission of a $^{56}_{26}Fe$ nucleus into two equal fragments, $^{28}_{13}Al$. Is the fission energetically possible ? Argue by working out Q of the process.

Given, $m(^{56}_{26}Fe) = 55.93494$ u

and $m(^{28}_{13}Al) = 27.98191$ u.

[NCERT Q. 13.6, Page 321]

Ans. The fission of $^{56}_{26}Fe$ is given as:

$^{56}_{26}Fe \rightarrow 2\,^{28}_{13}Al$

Given that:

Atomic mass of $m(^{56}_{26}Fe) = 55.93494$ u

Atomic mass of $m(^{28}_{13}Al) = 27.98191$ u

The Q-value of this nuclear reaction is:

$$Q = [m(^{56}_{26}Fe) - 2m(^{28}_{13}Al)]c^2$$

$$= [55.93494 - 2 \times 27.98191]c^2$$

$$= (-0.02888\,c^2)\text{ u}$$

But $1\text{ u} = 931.5\text{ MeV/c}^2$

$$Q = -0.02888 \times 931.5 = -26.902\text{ MeV}$$

The Q-value of the fission is negative. Therefore, the fission is not possible energetically.

For an energetically-possible fission reaction, the Q-value must be positive.

Q. 7. The fission properties of $^{239}_{94}Pu$ are very similar to those of $^{235}_{92}U$. The average energy released per fission is 180 MeV. How much energy, in MeV, is released if all the atoms in 1 kg of pure $^{239}_{94}Pu$ undergo fission ?

[NCERT Q. 3.7, Page 322]

Ans. Average energy released per fission of $^{239}_{94}Pu$, $E_m = 180$ MeV

Amount of pure $^{239}_{94}Pu$, $m = 1$ Kg $= 1{,}000$ g

N_A = Avogadro number $= 6.023 \times 10^{23}$

Mass number of $^{239}_{94}Pu = 239$ g

1 mole of $^{239}_{94}Pu$ contains N_A atoms.

So that, 1000 gm of

$^{239}_{94}Pu$ contains $\left(\dfrac{N_A}{\text{Mass Number}} \times m\right)$ atoms

$$\frac{6.023 \times 10^{23}}{239} \times 1000 = 2.52 \times 10^{24}\text{ atoms}$$

$\therefore$ Total energy released during the fission of 1 kg of $^{239}_{94}Pu$ is,

$$E = E_m = 2.52 \times 10^{24}$$

$$= 180 \times 2.52 \times 10^{24}$$

$$= 4.536 \times 10^{26}\text{ MeV}$$

Hence, 4.536×10^{26} MeV is released if all the atoms in 1 kg of pure $^{239}_{94}Pu$ undergo fission.

Q. 8. How long can an electric lamp of 100 W be kept glowing by fusion of 2.0 kg of deuterium?

Take the fusion reaction as

$^2_1H + ^2_1H \rightarrow ^3_1He + n + 3.27$ MeV

[NCERT Q. 13.8, Page 322]

Ans. Fusion reaction is:

$^2_1H + ^2_1H \rightarrow ^3_1He + n + 3.27$ MeV

Given that,

Amount of deuterium, $m = 2$ kg

So, 1 mole, i.e., 2 g of deuterium contains 6.023×10^{23} atoms.

2.0 kg of deuterium contains

$$= \frac{6.023 \times 10^{23}}{2} \times 2000$$

$$= 6.023 \times 10^{26}\text{ atoms}$$

It can be inferred from the given reaction that when two atoms of deuterium fuse, 3.27 MeV energy is released.

$\therefore$ Total energy per nucleus released in the fusion reaction:

$$E = \frac{[3.27 \times 6.023 \times 10^{26}]}{2}\text{ MeV}$$

$$E = \frac{3.27}{2} \times 6.023 \times 10^{26} \times 1.6 \times 10^{-19} \times 10^6$$

$$= 1.576 \times 10^{14}\text{ J}$$

Power of the electric lamp, P = 100 W = 100 J/s

Hence, the energy consumed by the lamp per second = 100 J

The total time for which the electric lamp will glow is calculated as:

$$= \frac{1.576\times10^{14}}{100} \text{ s}$$

$$= \frac{1.576\times10^{14}}{100\times60\times60\times24\times365}$$

$$\approx 4.9 \times 10^4 \text{ years}$$

Q. 9. Calculate the height of potential barrier for a head-on collision of two deuterons. The effective radius of deuteron can be taken to be 2fm. [NCERT Q. 13.9, Page 322]

Ans. As we know that,

When two deuterons collide head-on, the distance between their centres, d is given as:

Radius of first deuteron + Radius of second deuteron

Radius of a deuteron nucleus = 2 fm = 2×10^{-15} m

$d = 2 \times 10^{-15} + 2 \times 10^{-15} = 4 \times 10^{-15}$ m

Charge on a deuteron nucleus = Charge on an electron = $e = 1.6 \times 10^{-19}$ C

Potential energy of the two-deuteron system:

$$U = \frac{e^2}{4\pi\varepsilon_0 d}$$

Where,

ε_0 = Permittivity of free space

$$\frac{1}{4\pi\varepsilon_0} = 9 \times 10^9 \text{ Nm}^2\text{C}^{-2}$$

So that, $$U = \frac{9\times10^9\times(1.6\times10^{-19})^2}{4\times10^{-15}} \text{ J}$$

$$= \frac{9\times10^9\times(1.6\times10^{-19})^2}{4\times10^{-15}\times(1.6\times10^{-19})} \text{ eV}$$

$$= 360 \text{ keV}$$

So, the height of the potential barrier of the two-deuteron system is 360 keV.

Q. 10. From the relation $R = R_0A^{1/3}$, where R_0 is a constant and A is the mass number of a nucleus, show that the nuclear matter density is nearly constant (i.e., independent of A). [NCERT Q. 13.10, Page 322]

Ans. As we know the expression for nuclear radius as:

$R = R_0A^{1/3}$

where,

R_0 = Constant.

A = Mass number of the nucleus

Nuclear matter density,

ρ = Mass of the nucleus/Volume of the nucleus

Let m be the average mass of the nucleus.

So, the mass of the nucleus = mA

Therefore, $$\rho = \frac{mA}{\frac{4}{3}\pi R^3}$$

$$= \frac{3mA}{4\pi(R_0A^{\frac{1}{3}})^3}$$

$$= \frac{3mA}{4\pi R_0^3 A}$$

$$= \frac{3m}{4\pi R_0^3}$$

So that, the nuclear matter density is independent of A. It is nearly constant.

□□

SEMICONDUCTOR ELECTRONICS: MATERIALS, DEVICES AND SIMPLE CIRCUITS

CHAPTER 14

- **Energy bands:** According to Bohr atomic model, electrons can occupy only discrete energy levels around the nucleus. But when more than one atoms are placed nearby, due to mutual attraction between them, the discrete energy levels get transformed into energy band i.e., in place of discrete energy levels discrete energy band are found. These energy bands are composed of very closely spaced multiple energy levels.
- **Valence band:** The electrons which are present in the outermost shells of atom are called valence electrons. The valence electrons present in a series of energy levels form an energy band called valence band.
- **Conduction band:** Valence electrons are loosely attached to the nucleus. Even at room temperature few of them leave the band and become free. These free electrons conduct current in conductors and so called conduction electrons. The band which contains conduction electrons is called conduction band.

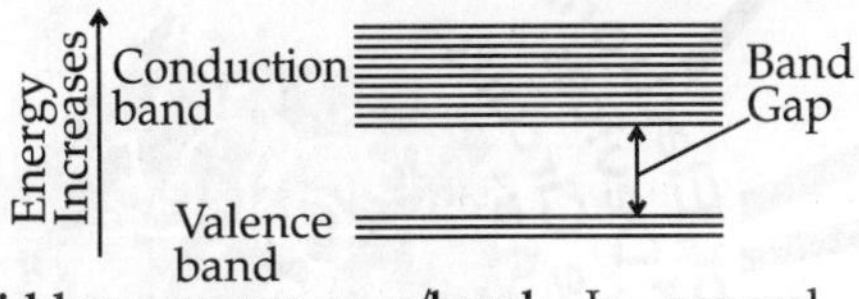

- **Forbidden energy gap/band:** In general, valence band is a band with lower energy in comparison to the conduction band and hence is found below the conduction band in band diagram. The gap between the highest energy level of valence band and the lowest energy of conduction band is known as forbidden energy gap / band.

Classification of conductor, semiconductor and insulator according to band structure

- **Insulator:** Insulator has large gap between the conduction band and valence band. No free electron is available. Large amount of energy is required to shift electrons from valence to conduc tion band. Sometimes it is impossible too. Generally forbidden band gap for insulators is more than 3 eV.

Scan to know more about this topic

Semiconductor Electronics

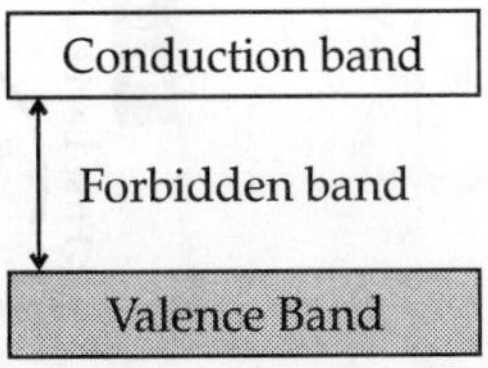

Scan to know more about this topic

Semiconductor

- **Semiconductor:** Semiconductor has slight gap between the conduction band and valence band. Little amount of energy is required to shift electrons from valence to conduction band. Such materials are insulators at 0K but starts acting as conductors when energy is supplied. For Germanium, forbidden band gap is 0.7 eV and for Silicon, forbidden band gap is 1.1 eV.

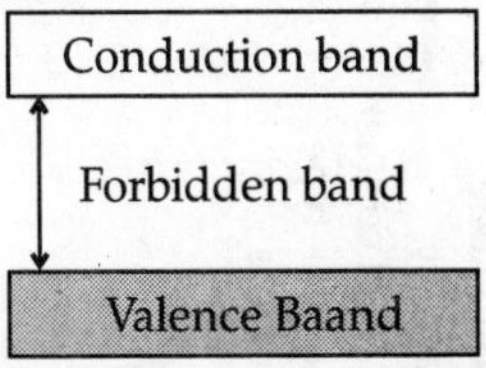

- **Conductor:** Conductor has overlapped conduction band and valence band. So, there is no forbidden band gap. Abundant free electrons are available.

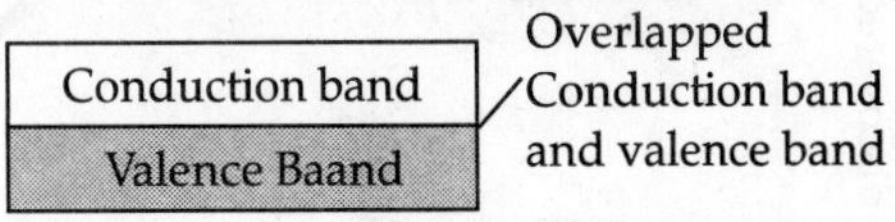

- **Semiconductor:** Group of crystalline solids having intermediate electrical conductivity between conductor and insulator.

Example: Group-IV elements like Silicon, Germanium.

These are pure semiconductors.

Example: Group-IV elements like Silicon, Germanium.

The outermost shell of Silicon has 4 electrons. They form 4 covalent bonds with 4 neighbouring atoms.

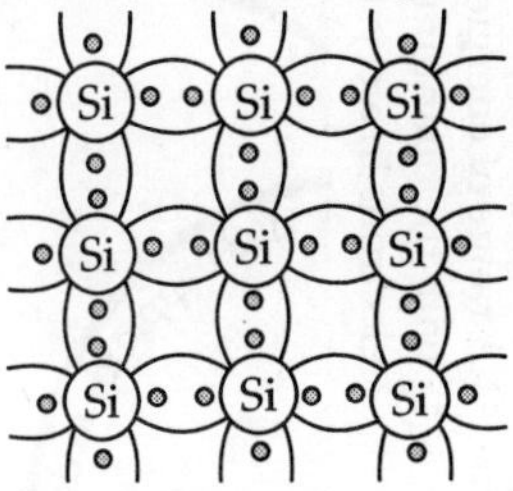

Germanium also has 4 electrons in the outermost shell. They form 4 covalent bonds with 4 neighbouring atoms.

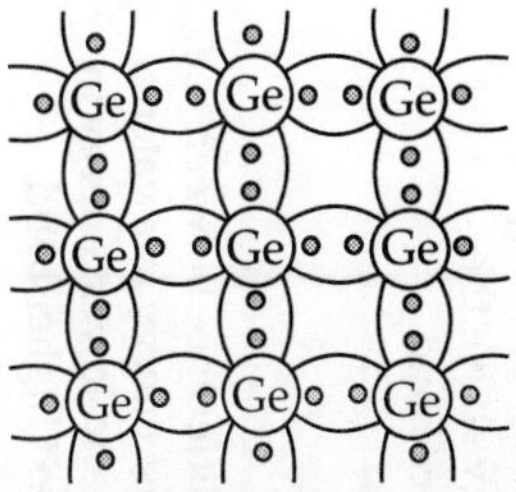

At 0K temperature, the conduction is empty. So, it behaves like an insulator. As temperature increases, the covalent bands gradually rupture.

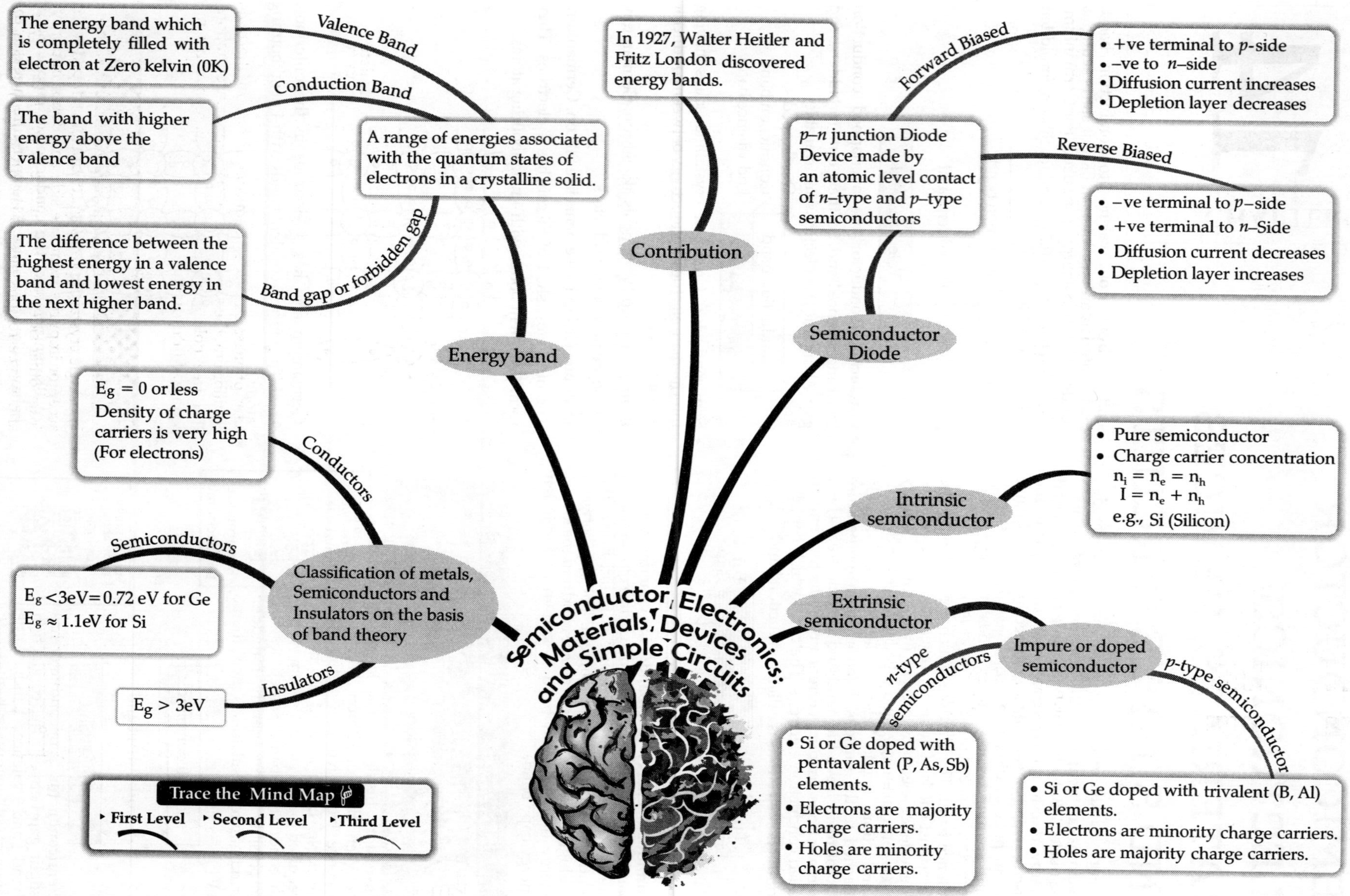
Semiconductor Electronics: Materials, Devices and Simple Circuits
Energy band
A range of energies associated with the quantum states of electrons in a crystalline solid.
Valence Band
The energy band which is completely filled with electron at Zero kelvin (0K)
Conduction Band
The band with higher energy above the valence band
Band gap or forbidden gap
The difference between the highest energy in a valence band and lowest energy in the next higher band.
Contribution
In 1927, Walter Heitler and Fritz London discovered energy bands.
Semiconductor Diode
p–n junction Diode Device made by an atomic level contact of n–type and p–type semiconductors
Forward Biased
• +ve terminal to p-side
• –ve to n–side
• Diffusion current increases
• Depletion layer decreases
Reverse Biased
• –ve terminal to p–side
• +ve terminal to n–Side
• Diffusion current decreases
• Depletion layer increases
Intrinsic semiconductor
• Pure semiconductor
• Charge carrier concentration
$n_i = n_e = n_h$
$I = n_e + n_h$
e.g., Si (Silicon)
Extrinsic semiconductor
Impure or doped semiconductor
n-type semiconductors
• Si or Ge doped with pentavalent (P, As, Sb) elements.
• Electrons are majority charge carriers.
• Holes are minority charge carriers.
p-type semiconductor
• Si or Ge doped with trivalent (B, Al) elements.
• Electrons are minority charge carriers.
• Holes are majority charge carriers.
Classification of metals, Semiconductors and Insulators on the basis of band theory
Conductors
E_g = 0 or less
Density of charge carriers is very high (For electrons)
Semiconductors
E_g <3eV=0.72 eV for Ge
$E_g \approx$ 1.1eV for Si
Insulators
E_g > 3eV
Trace the Mind Map
First Level
Second Level
Third Level

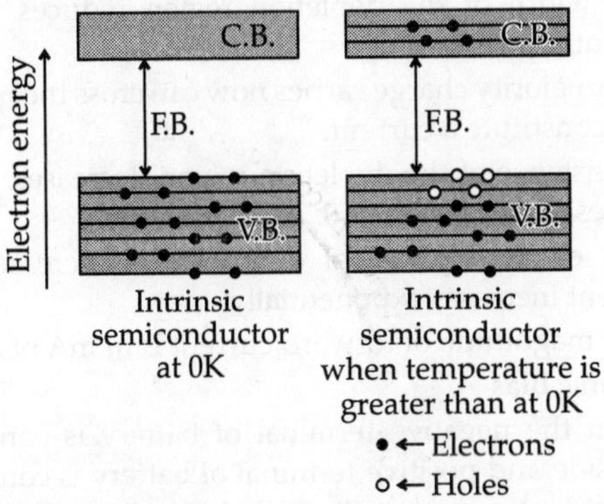

Due to rupture of a covalent bond two electrons are set free. As soon as an electron is freed an unoccupied state of (positively charged) is created. This unoccupied state is called hole.

Thus, free electrons and holes become available. Hence resistivity decreases and conductivity increases.

In pure semiconductor,

Free electron concentration (n_e)
= Free holes concentration (n_h)
= Intrinsic carrier concentration (n_i)

- **Fermi level:** The highest energy level an electron can occupy at 0 K is known as Fermi level.

  For intrinsic semiconductor it at the middle of the forbidden band gap.

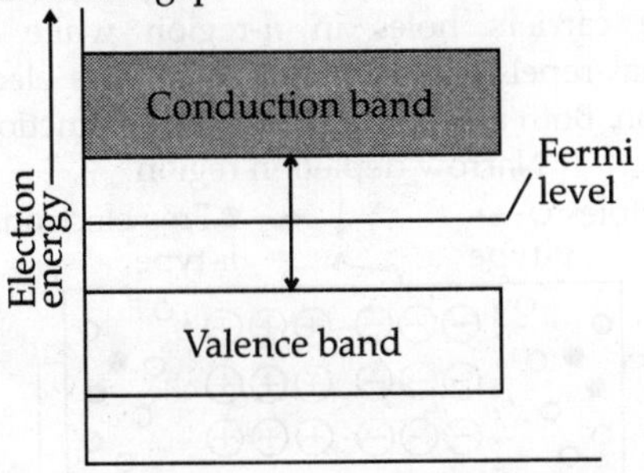

- **Extrinsic semiconductor:** When some impurity is added to pure semiconductor, extrinsic semiconductor is formed.

  Due to addition of impurity, the conductivity increases.

  The process is called doping.

  The impurity is called dopant.

  Types of extrinsic semiconductors:

- ***n*-type semiconductor:** When Group-V elements (such as P, As, Sb, etc.) are doped with pure semiconductor, then extra free electrons become available. Such extrinsic semiconductors are known as *n*-type extrinsic semiconductors.

  Such dopants are called donor.

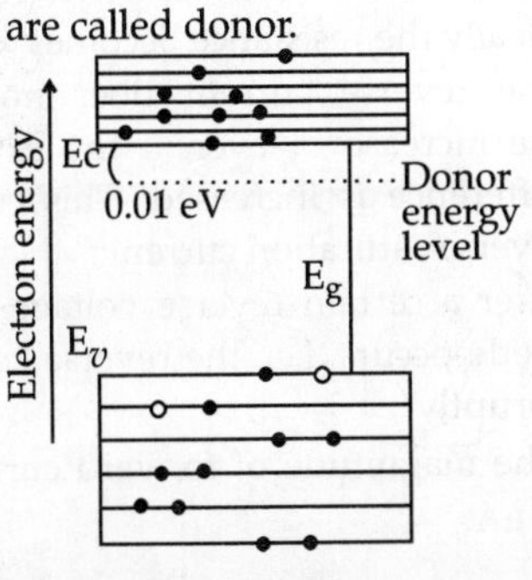

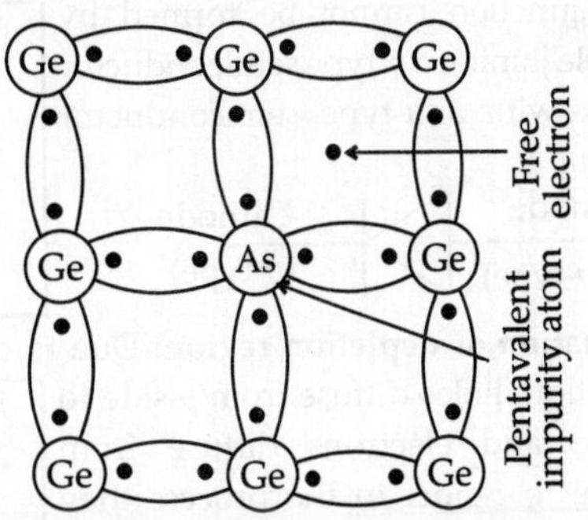

Free electron density > Free hole density.

Electrons are called majority charge carries. Holes are called minority charge carriers.

- ***p*-type semiconductor:** When Group-III elements (such as B, Al, In etc.) are doped with pure semiconductor, then deficit of free electrons occurs. So, extra holes are created. Such extrinsic semiconductors are known as *p*-type extrinsic semiconductors.

  Such dopants are called acceptors.

  Free hole density > Free electron density.

  Holes are called majority charge carries. Electrons are called minority charge carriers

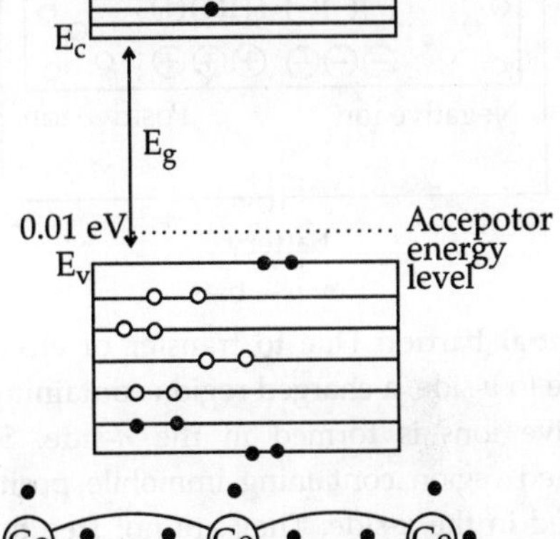

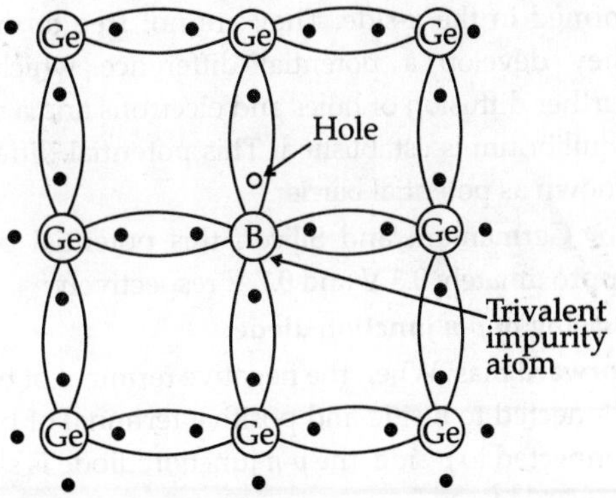

- **Law of mass action of semiconductors:** In thermal equilibrium, the product of free electron concentration and free hole concentration is equal to a constant square of intrinsic carrier concentration.

$$n_e \times n_h = n_i^2$$

p-n Junction

- If a single crystal of pure semiconductor is doped with acceptor impurity from one side and donor impurity from other side, then the surface at which the *p*-type and *n*-type regions meet is known as *p-n* junction or diode.

[*p-n* junction cannot be formed by simple joining a *p*-type semiconductor block with a *n*-type semiconductor block.]

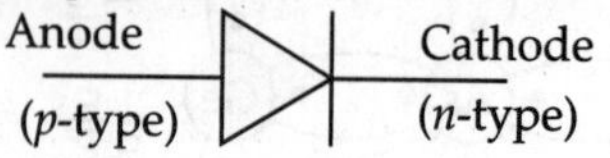

Scan to know more about this topic
Diode

➢ **Formation of depletion region:** Due to concentration variation, holes diffuse from *p*-side to *n*-side and electrons diffuse from *n*-side to *p*-side. In the process they recombine with each other and get neutralised which means there remains neither an electron nor a hole. Thus a region depleted of free charge carriers is formed on both sides of the *p-n* junction. Thus a depletion region is formed. This region is about 10^{-4} to 10^{-6} m wide.

Scan to know more about this topic
Formation of depletion region

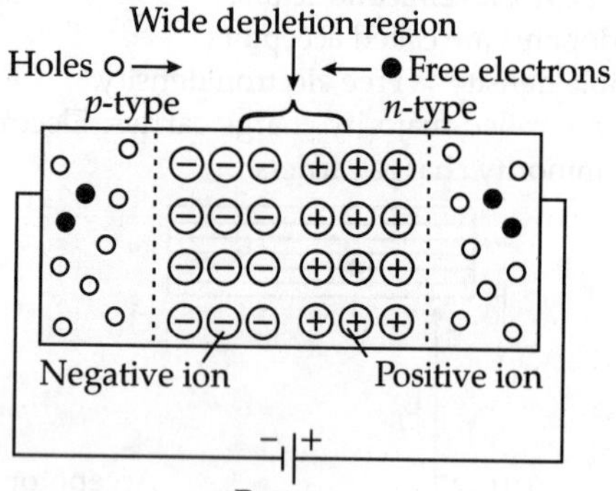

Reverse bias

➢ **Potential barrier:** Due to transfer of electrons, from *n*-side to *p*-side, a charged region containing immobile positive ions is formed in the *n*-side. Similarly, a charged region containing immobile positive ions is formed in the *n*-side. They are not free to move. So, they develop a potential difference which resists further diffusion of holes and electrons and a dynamic equilibrium is established. This potential difference is known as potential barrier.

For Germanium and Silicon this potential barrier is approximately 0.3 V and 0.7 V respectively.

➢ **Biasing of *p-n* junction diode:**

- **Forward bias:** When the negative terminal of battery is connected to *n*-side and positive terminal of battery is connected to *p*-side, the *p-n* junction diode is said to be forward biased.

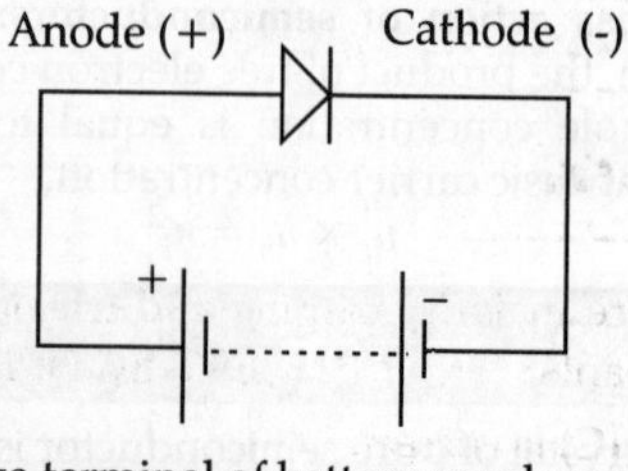

The positive terminal of battery repels majority charge carriers holes in *p*-region while negative terminal repels majority charge carriers electrons in *n*-region. Both are pushed towards the junction. So,

(i) the width of the depletion region reduces. Barrier potential decreases.

(ii) The majority charge carries now can cross the junction and constitute a current.

(iii) Resistance of the depletion region decreases. Ideally the resistance becomes 0.

(iv) As external potential difference is increased, the current increases exponentially.

(v) The magnitude of forward current is in mA of order.

- **Reverse bias**

When the negative terminal of battery is connected to *p*-side and positive terminal of battery is connected to *n*-side, the *p-n* junction diode is said to be reverse biased.

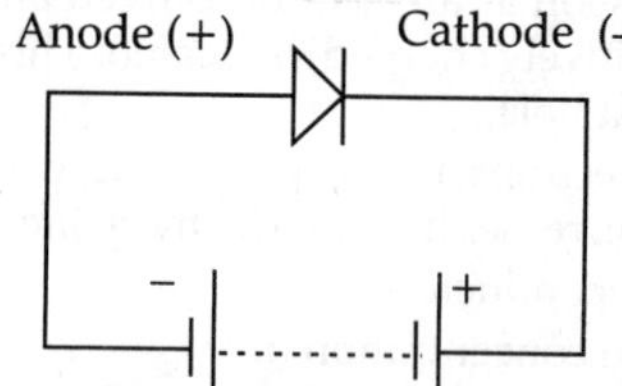

The positive terminal of battery attracts the majority charge carriers electrons in *n*-region while negative terminal attracts majority charge carriers holes in *p*-region. Both move away from the junction.

But the positive terminal of battery repels minority charge carriers holes in *n*-region while negative terminal repels minority charge carriers electrons in *p*-region. Both are pushed towards the junction. So,

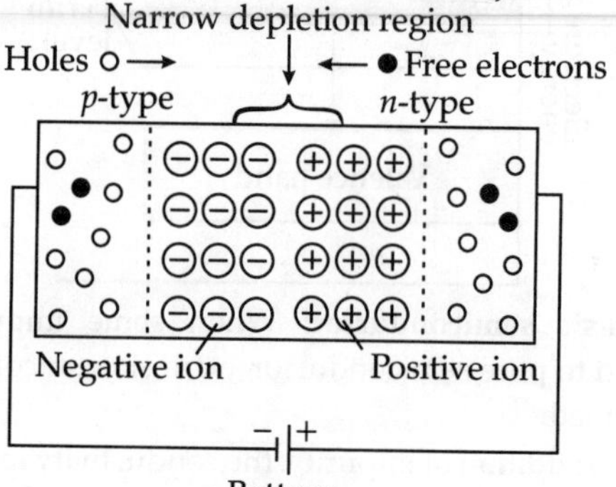

Forward bias

(i) the width of the depletion region increases. Barrier potential increases.

(ii) The majority charge carries now cannot cross the junction .

(iii) The minority charge carriers can now cross the junction. So a feeble reverse current flows.

(iv) Resistance of the depletion region increases. Ideally the resistance becomes ∞.

(v) The reverse current does not change with the increase of even if the external potential difference is increased. This current is called reverse saturation current.

(vi) After a certain reverse voltage break-down of diode occurs, i.e., the reverse current increases abruptly.

(vii) The magnitude of forward current is in order of μA.

V-I characteristics of p-n junction diode

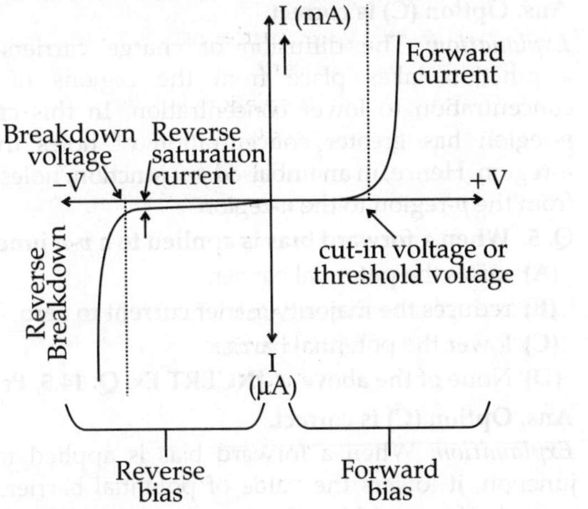

➢ Relation between V and I in a *p-n* junction diode:

$$I = Is\left[\exp\left(\frac{eV}{\eta KT}\right) - 1\right]$$

where I = current through the diode
V = applied voltage across the diode
I_S = reverse saturation current
e = charge of an electron
K = Boltzmann constant
T = Temperature in absolute scale
η = Material dependent constant (for Ge, $\eta = 1$ and for Si, $\eta = 2$)

Rectifier

- Rectifier is a device which converts AC to DC.

➢ **Diode as a rectifier:**

- **Half wave rectifier:**

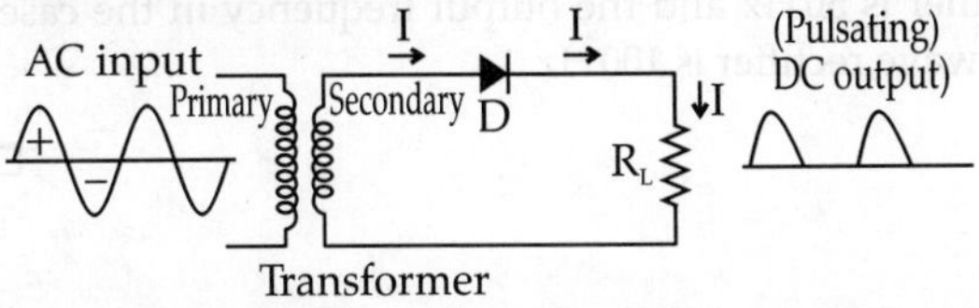

- The half-wave rectifier with single diode, allows current to flow in one direction.
- AC (V_{ac}) is connected to primary side of transformer while secondary terminals of transformer are connected to diode and load resistor in series.
- For positive half cycle of Vac the diode is forward biased the diode and conducts. A voltage appears across the load resistor.
- For negative half cycle of Vac, the diode is reverse biased and does not conduct.
- The output is not a pure DC. It is called pulsating DC.
- **Full wave rectifier:**

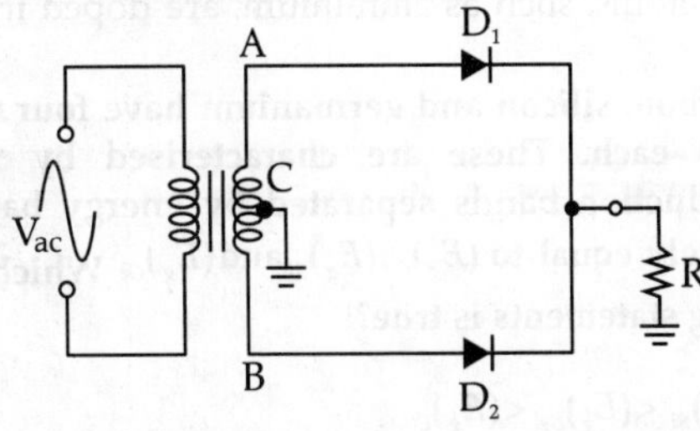

o A full wave rectifier uses centre tap transformers with two diodes.

o For positive half-cycle, A is at +ve potential, C is at 0 potential and B is at –ve potential.

So diode D_1 is forward bias and conducts D_2 is reversed biased and does not conduct.

o For negative half-cycle, A is at –ve potential, C is at 0 potential and B is at +ve potential.

So diode D_2 is forward bias and conducts. D_1 is reversed biased and does not conduct.

o Currents in both the cases through load resistor are available and unidirectional.

o **Output waveform:**

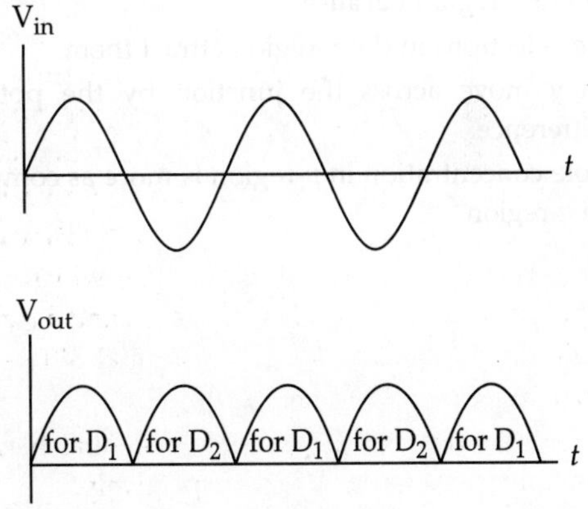

o The output is not a pure DC. It is called pulsating DC.

NCERT CORNER

Exercise Questions

Q. 1. In an *n*-type silicon, which of the following statement is true:

(A) Electrons are majority carriers and trivalent atoms are the dopants.

(B) Electrons are minority carriers and pentavalent atoms are the dopants.

(C) Holes are minority carriers and pentavalent atoms are the dopants.

(D) Holes are majority carriers and trivalent atoms are the dopants. **[NCERT Ex. Q. 14.1, Page 341]**

Ans. Option (C) is correct.

Explanation: In an *n*-type silicon the holes are the minority carriers. An *n*-type semiconductor is obtained when pentavalent atoms, such as phosphorus, are doped in silicon atoms.

Q. 2. Which of the statements given in Question 1 is true for *p*-type semiconductors?

[NCERT Ex. Q. 14.2, Page 341]

Ans. Option (D) is correct.

Explanation: In a *p*-type semiconductor, the holes are the majority carriers, while the electrons are the minority carriers. A *p*-type semiconductor is obtained when trivalent atoms, such as aluminium, are doped in silicon atoms.

Q. 3. Carbon, silicon and germanium have four valence electrons each. These are characterised by valence and conduction bands separated by energy band gap respectively equal to $(E_g)_C$, $(E_g)_{Si}$ and $(E_g)_{Ge}$ Which of the following statements is true?

(A) $(E_g)_{Si} < (E_g)_{Ge} < (E_g)_C$

(B) $(E_g)_C < (E_g)_{Ge} > (E_g)_{Si}$

(C) $(E_g)_C > (E_g)_{Si} > (E_g)_{Ge}$

(D) $(E_g)_C = (E_g)_{Si} = (E_g)_{Ge}$

[NCERT Ex. Q. 14.3, Page 341]

Ans. Option (C) is correct.

Explanation: Above mentioned three given elements, the energy band gap of carbon is the maximum and that of germanium is the least. The energy band gaps of these elements are related as :

$$(E_g)_C > (E_g)_{Si} > (E_g)_{Ge}$$

Q. 4. In an unbiased *p-n* junction, holes diffuse from the *p*-region to *n*-region because

(A) free electrons in the *n*-region attract them.

(B) they move across the junction by the potential difference.

(C) hole concentration in *p*-region is more as compared to *n*-region.

(D) All the above. **[NCERT Ex. Q. 14.4, Page 342]**

Ans. Option (C) is correct.

Explanation: The diffusion of charge carriers across a junction takes place from the regions of higher concentration to lower concentration. In this case, the *p*-region has greater concentration of holes than the *n*-region. Hence, in an unbiased *p-n* junction, holes diffuse from the *p*-region to the *n*-region.

Q. 5. When a forward bias is applied to a *p-n* junction, it

(A) raises the potential barrier.

(B) reduces the majority carrier current to zero.

(C) lower the potential barrier.

(D) None of the above **[NCERT Ex. Q. 14.5, Page 342]**

Ans. Option (C) is correct.

Explanation: When a forward bias is applied to a *p-n* junction, it lowers the value of potential barrier. In the case of a forward bias, the potential barrier opposes the applied voltage. Hence, the potential barrier across the junction gets reduced.

Q. 6. In half-wave rectification, what is the output frequency if the input frequency is 50 Hz. What is the output frequency of a full-wave rectifier for the same input frequency. [NCERT Ex. Q. 14.6, Page 342]

Ans. As per given that the input frequency is 50 Hz.

In case of half wave rectifier, the output frequency will be equal to input frequency.

The output frequency for half wave rectifier is, $= 50\,\text{Hz}$

In the case of full wave rectifier, the output frequency will be twice the input frequency.

So, the output frequency for full wave rectifier is $= 2 \times 50 = 100\,\text{Hz}$

So , the output frequency in the case of half wave rectifier is 50 Hz and the output frequency in the case of full wave rectifier is 100 Hz.

□□